CULTURAL EROTICS
IN CUBAN AMERICA

CULTURAL EROTICS
IN CUBAN AMERICA

Ricardo L. Ortíz

University of Minnesota Press
Minneapolis • London

Chapter 1 was previously published in *Borders, Exiles, Diasporas,* edited by Elazar Barkan and Marie-Denise Shelton (Stanford: Stanford University Press, 1998); copyright 1998 by the Board of Trustees of the Leland Stanford Jr. University; reprinted with permission from Stanford University Press, http://www.sup.org. Chapter 2 was previously published in *Annals of Scholarship* 12, no. 3/4; reprinted with permission from *Annals of Scholarship.* Chapter 3 previously appeared as "Revolution's Other Histories: The Sexual, Cultural, and Critical Legacies of Roberto Fernández Retamar's 'Caliban,'" *Social Text* 58, 17, no. 1 (Spring 1999): 33–58; reprinted with permission from Duke University Press. Chapter 4 previously appeared as "Hemispheric Vertigo: Cuba, Québec, and Other Provisional Reconfigurations of Our (New) America(s)," in *The Futures of American Studies,* edited by Donald Pease and Robyn Weigman (Durham, N.C.: Duke University Press, 2002): 327–40; reprinted with permission of Duke University Press. Chapter 5 previously appeared as "Café, Culpa, and Capital: Nostalgic Addictions of Cuban Exile," *Yale Journal of Criticism* 10, no. 1 (1997): 63–84; copyright Yale University and The Johns Hopkins University Press; reprinted with permission from The Johns Hopkins University Press. Chapter 6 previously appeared as "Fables of (Cuban) Exile: Special Periods and Queer Moments in Eduardo Machado's *Fabiola,*" *Modern Drama* 48, no. 1 (Spring 2005): 132–62; reprinted with permission from the University of Toronto Press, http://www.utpjournals.com; *Modern Drama* is a publication of the Graduate Centre for the Study of Drama at the University of Toronto.

Excerpts from the poems "Learning the Language," "In the Form," "Guantánamo," "Grandfather's Will," "The Things I Don't Remember," "Planning a Family," "Advice for the New World," "Honest," "My Father's View of Poetry," "Our Country of Origin," "He Interprets the Dream," "Poems in Jorge's Voice," "Political Poem," "Sonnet for Our Son," "The Cycle Begins Anew," "Adoption," "My Brother's Opinion," "Gay Parents Are Neither," "I Take Our Son to Cuba," "The Sonnet after This Must Wait," and "Technology and Medicine" are from Rafael Campo, *The Other Man Was Me: A Voyage to the New World* (Houston: Arte Público Press–University of Houston, 1993); copyright Arte Público Press; reprinted with permission of Arte Público Press.

Excerpts from "Before Safe Sex," "Rice and Beans," "Somewhere in Zambia," "The Choice Was Never Made," "Safe Sex," and "Safe Sex Revisited" are from Rafael Campo, *What the Body Told* (Durham, N.C.: Duke University Press, 1996); copyright 1996 Rafael Campo; all rights reserved; reprinted with permission from Duke University Press.

Copyright 2007 by the Regents of the University of Minnesota

Published by the University of Minnesota Press
111 Third Avenue South, Suite 290
Minneapolis, MN 55401-2520
http://www.upress.umn.edu

Library of Congress Cataloging-in-Publication Data
Ortíz, Ricardo L., 1961-
  Cultural erotics in Cuban America / Ricardo L. Ortíz.
    p. cm.
  Includes bibliographical references and index.
  ISBN-13: 978-0-8166-4795-8 (hc : alk. paper)
  ISBN-10: 0-8166-4795-X (hc : alk. paper)
  ISBN-13: 978-0-8166-4796-5 (pb : alk. paper)
  ISBN-10: 0-8166-4796-8 (pb : alk. paper)
  1. Cuban Americans – Intellectual life. 2. Exiles – United States – Intellectual life. 3. Cubans – Migrations. 4. Cuban Americans – Languages. 5. Spanish language – Influence on English. 6. Erotica – United States. 7. Eroticism in literature. 8. American literature – Cuban American authors – History and criticism. 9. Cuban Americans in literature. 10. Exiles in literature. I. Title.
  E184.C97O77 2006
  810.9'3259687291073—dc22   2006015038

Printed in the United States of America on acid-free paper

The University of Minnesota is an equal-opportunity educator and employer.

12 11 10 09 08 07 06   10 9 8 7 6 5 4 3 2 1

Contents

Preface

Cuban America in
Cuban English

Certain Soviet philosophers have told me in Moscow a
few years ago: the best translation of perestroika was
still "deconstruction."
—Jacques Derrida, *Specters of Marx*

Deconstruction seems to be . . . the Cuban way.
—Pico Iyer, *Cuba and the Night*[1]

Conventional wisdom has it that Cuban and, by extension, Cuban-
exile, Cuban American, and even Cuban-diasporic history is literary,
and therefore symbolic, and imagined, to its core.[2] From the nineteenth-
century exile poetry of the founder of Cuban democracy, José Martí,
to the ongoing, if increasingly vestigial, early twenty-first-century obsession with the symbolism attendant on a theme, exile and return,
especially off-island Cuban culture, across all its diasporic extensions,
has embraced an understanding of itself as mediated, especially if not
exclusively, by metaphor and music. But to say that Cuban-diasporic
history has a core is not to suggest it has anything like a center, and to
say that Cuban democracy has a symbolic founder in José Martí is in
turn not to suggest that the so-called Cuban nation, an entity that
neither the island nor any government installed on it could contain,
springs from any one definitive origin. This is perhaps why even a
national history of Cuba is, especially since the 1959 revolution, only

possible literarily, especially in the postmodern sense, as a complex function of dispersal, dissemination, and desire.

The exiled Cuban novelist Guillermo Cabrera Infante has argued (along these lines) that, with Martí, "Cuban literature was born in exile."[3] This may explain why, when Cabrera Infante opens his 1983 novel *Tres Tristes Tigres* (which he himself wrote and published while in exile in Europe) with an *advertencia,* or warning, to readers that "*El libro está en cubano*" (literally, that his novel *is* "in Cuban"[4]), the author implies that a specifically historical and cultural, rather than linguistic, modality is at work in his text. Cabrera Infante's pronouncement works simultaneously as both a warning and an invitation: *Tres Tristes Tigres,* written in a recognizably Cuban dialectal derivation from normative Spanish, also *enacts something Cuban* in its perverse play of vocalizations. Cabrera Infante goes on in the passage to describe this enactment as an attempt to "capture the human voice in flight," particularly the nocturnal jargon of those habaneros who in the 1950s haunted Havana's decadent underground.

But to insist, as Cabrera Infante does here, that one "writes in Cuban" or, better put, that one's text "is in Cuban" is not to insist that one's writing merely deviates from some normative concept of Spanish. It seems less, even, about the attempt to include all the possible Spanish dialects spoken in Havana in the time of which Cabrera Infante writes, so much as about the attempt to have his written language capture something of the spoken voice, of the spontaneous utterance, at once "underground, secretive," *and* "in flight."[5] Although contemporary rhetorical theory would question the presumption of spontaneity in any speech act given the preponderant weight of its performative dimensions, Cabrera Infante merely proposes here (I think) the possibility of writing "in Cuban" even if one does not literally write in Spanish or from Cuba. Cabrera Infante, who settled in Europe after years of disillusionment with Castro's revolution,[6] understands the historical and cultural importance of assigning, especially to texts written and read in exile and across an increasingly far-flung diaspora, the status or value of *cubanidad.* For this reason the following study owes a profound debt to his ingenious formulation: that a text "is Cuban" to the extent to which it manages to inscribe its own interstitial, fleeting quality, its own capacity for emergence, dispersion, *and* disappearance, its underground, secretive (non)being, its radical sense of exile from itself.

The perplexed, elusive grammar of Cuban-diasporic literary language translates directly, I would argue, into the perplexed temporality of postrevolutionary and especially post–Cold War Cuban-diasporic cultural and political history.[7] In his essay "DissemiNation: Time, Narrative and the Margins of the Modern Nation," Homi Bhabha formulates a radically alternative temporality for the narrative construction of the nation.[8] Bhabha's formulation will help me articulate the disjointed "temporality" of especially the post–Cold War Cuban scene, a scene initially termed by Fidel Castro as Cuba's "Special Period." But by now (that is, in 2006), it seems to have outlived, if not exactly survived, even that decade-old attempt to make not only chronological and historical but even narrative sense of the political impasse within whose logical *aporia* the Cuban nation (that exceeds and confounds any correspondence to the Cuban state) finds itself indefinitely, interminably caught.[9] According to Bhabha,

> the narrative and psychological force that nation-ness brings to bear on cultural production and political projection is the effect of the ambivalence of the "nation" as a narrative strategy. As an apparatus of symbolic power, it produces a continual slippage of categories, like sexuality, class affiliation, territorial paranoia or "cultural difference" in the act of writing the nation. What is displayed in this displacement and repetition of terms is the nation as the liminality of cultural modernity.[10]

It is precisely the stakes of thinking anything like, or anything past, a Cuban nationhood in this supposedly "post-Marxist, post-historical" moment that requires the kind of alternative critique of the symbolics of "nationness" one finds in Bhabha's work.

This proposition is certainly significantly tested in the writing of a number of emerging U.S.-based writers and performers of Cuban descent who, as the children of the great wave of Cuban immigration to the United States that followed Castro's revolution, write primarily if not exclusively in English, but with an ear for the polyvalent richness of language as such, a richness, however, made uniquely problematic for them by the complex positionings available to them in *their* language. In his introduction to *The Cuban Condition: Translation and Identity in Modern Cuban Literature,* Gustavo Pérez-Firmat sizes up the linguistic and cultural situation of this generation of Cuban American writers this way: "As a 'native' Cuban who has spent all of his adult life away from the island, the notion of a 'Cuban' voice is for me as alluring as it is problematic. A Cuban voice is what I wish I had, and what I may never have."[11] Other current writers, as disparate as the novelist Cristina García, the playwright Eduardo Machado, and the poet Rafael Campo, have posed much the same question for themselves, in similar if not identical terms. One quality their work shares, however, with that of many of their so-called post-Cuban compatriots is at least a thematic, if not more emphatically imbedded, fascination with the (inter)play of the erotic with(in) the otherwise conventional cultural and even political operations of an increasingly postnational, diasporic, yet still meaningfully "Cuban" imaginary.

Not surprisingly, sexuality heads the list of categories whose "slippage," Bhabha suggests, results from most attempts to (de)construct the "symbolic apparatus" of the nation. Certainly the question of a viable, reproducible *cubanidad,* or Cubanness, as posed for and by these writers in their (English) language, calls up the primal quasi-oedipal struggle between mother and father tongues, between a nostalgic longing for the lost *patria,* the feminine-gendered fatherland and the language in which they (only) remember or imagine *her,* and their grudgingly grateful capitulations to their adoptive patron-nation, and *his* generous but dispassionate language. The conventional and insistent gendering of these concepts immediately raises the question that will engage my study most directly, the question, that is, of the erotic dynamic (the *erotics,* if you will)[12] behind the ongoing formation and deformation of the experience of "the Cuban" outside of Cuba. This question, I would suggest, is best posed in a way that both invokes the conventionality of the oedipal struggle and the gendered categories it authorizes, and at the same time problematizes convention and category by keeping open the possibility that erotics is less a function of conventional gender positions and more often of variable yet simultaneous orientations toward desire and pleasure, orientations that, in their irresistible pull away from any (hetero)conventional correspondence between desiring subjects and the genders of bodies desired, very readily queer the complex general scene I have begun to describe here.

Erotics is also, in this case, simultaneously a productive and consumptive, consuming praxis, both culturally and politically; "desire," it might be said, is the third but silent term haunting the alliterative (il)logic of the two terms, "diaspora" and "disappearance," more substantively linked to the material in this book. Although I do not intend to devote much attention to reified categories of gender and sexual orientation in this study, it bears mentioning here that certainly issues of gender and sexual orientation have propelled much of the political and cultural debate, especially since, say, the 1980 Mariel boatlift around Cuba and Cuban America. In the course of this study I will have some opportunity to cite briefly examples of the Castro government's abuses of women, homosexuals, and of persons with HIV/AIDS, abuses that have earned Castro a great deal of criticism abroad and (more recently) at home. But certainly the Cuban American community centered in Miami shares equally in the guilt of homophobic and misogynous sentiment, even if it cannot enact its policies in as obviously programmatic a fashion. Sexual conduct and sexual status have played decisive roles in determining the fates of cultural figures as different as Reinaldo Arenas, Severo Sarduy, and Albita Rodríguez, all of whom lived as adults in Castro's Cuba before leaving. Sexual conduct and sexual status also figure prominently, however, as symbolically decisive elements in the literary work of such disparate figures as Cristina García, Rafael Campo, Eduardo Machado, and Achy Obejas, most of whom were born in Cuba but lived most of their lives from early childhood on in the United States. But these issues represent one limited aspect of a much larger and more complex system of erotic forces at play (and at work) in recent cultural productions by Cuban exiles, Cuban Americans, and, more generally, Cuban-diasporic figures based outside both Cuba and America.

This study also will make extensive use of important recent work on sexuality and erotics in Cuban American history and culture. Alongside Vera Kutzinski's historical work (in 1993's *Sugar's Secrets*) on the erotics of mixed-race iconographic representations of Cuban womanhood and Cuban national identity at large, for example, both Antonio Benítez-Rojo and Gustavo Pérez-Firmat have had occasion in their own best known work to chart the ongoing erotic dynamic in these cultural and national (de)formations. In *The Repeating Island*, Benítez-Rojo, drawing directly from Deleuze, Barthes, and Baudrillard, emphasizes the seductive quality of Caribbean texts' engagement of readers; for Benítez-Rojo "text and reader connect with each other like a machine of reciprocal seductions," in a "certain [Caribbean] kind of way" that will allow both text and reader to "transcend their statistical limits and . . . drift toward the decentered center of the paradoxical."[13] The problematic nature of erotics as cultural praxis certainly goes beyond the model of one reader's engagement with one text, however. In 1994's *Life on the Hyphen: The Cuban-American Way,* Gustavo Pérez-Firmat demonstrates the manner in which this "machine of reciprocal seductions" can cover a field of cultural experience available to, say, a generation of TV-viewing Cuban immigrants. Pérez-Firmat's loving analysis of Desi Arnaz/Ricky Ricardo as cultural signifier attempts to revolutionize the study of sexual politics in a cultural group, especially one with whom he identifies, *without* reducing his object of analysis to his own intrasubjective response to that signifier.[14] The tension generated by discrepancies among individual erotic positions and the larger erotic dispositions or sensibilities of the culture will receive a great deal of attention in this study; it certainly fuels much of the current debate concerning any possible political or cultural future for Cuban people as a coherent or viable group.

What I have been calling the "perplexed" erotics shaping Cuban American cultural articulations is further complicated by the general migratory dislocations of Cuban America. Historically, the experience of Cuban immigration to North America has been both internally and externally divisive. Externally, Cubans in the United States find themselves often the exception rather than the rule in discussions of the larger Latino immigrant experience in the United States. Internally, Cubans find themselves divided politically, culturally, and linguistically according to their generation and the relative degrees of direct experience they have had or are having with island culture, the unassimilated ghetto cultures in Miami and the Northeast, and the larger mainstream culture of the United States.[15] If there has been a Cuban diaspora within U.S. borders, it has taken (its) place(s) both geographically and generationally, along complex spatial and temporal coordinates simultaneously.

Such a dispersal, although it has had the advantage of freeing many Cuban Americans from what is perceived as the oppressive consensus of most of Cuban Miami, has had the corresponding disadvantage of isolating, silencing, indeed "disappearing," expressions of Cuban dissent in the United States, where Cubans living away from the community's centers must sacrifice the access to the cultural visibility that those centers so readily offer.[16] Bhabha articulates the temporal perplexity involved in much contemporary cultural production in the introductory essay of *The Location of Culture:*

> The borderline work of culture demands an encounter with "newness" that is not part of the continuum of past and present. It creates a sense of the new as an insurgent act of cultural translation. Such art does not merely recall the past as social cause or aesthetic precedent; it renews the past, refiguring it as a contingent "in-between" space, that innovates and interrupts the performance of the present. The "past-present" becomes a part of the necessity, not the nostalgia, of living.[17]

This displacement of nostalgia by necessity can be said to characterize the work of younger Cuban American writers and artists in contradistinction to the conserving work of the generation preceding them. It is largely on the borders between these divided spaces of experience that the emerging generation of Cuban American writers write, taking such paradoxical positions in their work that they often seem to build bridges between generations and ideologies and with the same gesture mark their divisions so powerfully as to suggest their irreconcilability. Writing in Cuban is "impossible" to the extent that it may never coalesce into one voice, one language, but for the writers and other cultural workers I will treat here, it is precisely this condition of impossibility that challenges, indeed *obligates,* them to write. As Cabrera Infante attempted to characterize a "Cuban" language that was simultaneously subterranean and airborne, I hope in the following pages to explore an alternative paradox, that writing "in Cuban" (and especially when that writing happens *not* "in Cuba") may indeed be simultaneously necessary *and* impossible.[18]

Any attempt to narrate the "history" of off-island, postrevolutionary and post–Cold War Cuban writing must thus begin with an examination of the phases of exile. This attempt immediately raises the question of the relation between historical continuity and discontinuity, a question that in its most profound sense brings us to the borders of an impasse, to the no-place of *aporia.* Cuban writing since the revolution, both from and from without the island, undergoes a tortuous and oftentimes bewildering set of historical and geographical displacements and superimpositions that defies easy thematic and formal classification. Profound differences in both aesthetic and political orientations can be observed among writers and other artists, as some effect of their histories in and out of exile. Those who stayed, and were either disaffected with Castro or not, cannot be easily classified together; a José Lezama Lima and a Nicolás Guillén, for example, ultimately formed such divergent relationships with the regime that it makes little sense to combine two such prominent poetic voices to find some coherent project in their work. Those who left as adults, as an immediate effect of the revolution, cannot be classed with those who, like Pérez-Firmat and the poet Ricardo Pau-Llosa, left as children with their families in the same historical moment. These last can also not be classed with those born or raised primarily in the United States (García, Machado, Campo, etc.) who bear additional differences, depending on whether they grew up in, say, Miami, New York, or the West Coast. Finally, there are those raised in and by the revolution, but who came to leave much later, say, in the Mariel boatlift of 1980, like Reinaldo Arenas and Pedro Zamora, or, even more recently, like Albita Rodríguez, after the dissolution of the Eastern bloc.

Mariel as a specific historical marker will serve as one, but not the only, point of chronological organization for my study; although the writers and other cultural figures I have selected to analyze represent most of the waves of Cuban immigration to the United States since the revolution of 1959, none of the work I analyze in the following chapters dates further back than 1980. In *City on the Edge: The Transformation of Miami,* Alejandro Portes and Alex Stepick argue that, as a result of the American backlash against the influx of new immigrants from Mariel, 1980 was a pivotal year in the formation of a specifically Cuban American identity in the exile community.[19] According to Portes and Stepick, even the term "Cuban American" was "seldom used before 1980," but became "the standard self-designation" of the community once it realized that it needed to respond in some coordinated way to the new backlash. The life histories of many of the people I discuss in these pages, as well as the stories they tell, bear out this observation eloquently: both Arenas and Zamora were themselves *marielitos;* Cristina García (in 1992's *Dreaming in Cuban*) and Eduardo Machado (in 1991's *The Floating Island Plays*) choose 1980 as the year in which to conclude their stories of exile; and most of the other artists I discuss here acknowledge the importance of the Mariel boatlift in ways that suggest its importance to their own understanding of the phases of exile. It bears remembering too that although the formation of a coalescent Cuban American identity occurred chiefly in response to a number of political events surrounding Mariel and the passing of an English-only initiative in Dade County in the same year, Portes and Stepick also observe that the migratory patterns of Cubans in the United States foreshadowed this renewed symbolic focus for at least fifteen years. Starting in 1965, "the U.S. government organized a large-scale initiative to resettle anti-Castro exiles away from Miami," but "by 1979, on the eve of Mariel, close to 80 percent of Cubans in the U.S. were living in Miami," making them "the most concentrated foreign-born minority in the country."[20]

A number of books appearing in the decade or so following Mariel tried in various ways to make sense of the Cuban-exile experience in part as a function of that event. Interestingly, the manner in which these largely cultural and sociological studies approach their analyses hinges on the turn of some potent metaphors; what is clear from the work of young Cuban writers emerging a decade later from the culture that these analysts study is that their writing attempts to both critique and transcend these metaphors, to give voice to fictions that shape, and make newly real, their history. In his sweeping 1992 study *Latinos*, for example, Earl Shorris observes that the Cuban experience of exile borrows directly, and mostly from tradition, the identification of exile and death. "The Greeks," Shorris argues, "understood exile as a form of capital punishment: not travel, relocation or emigration, but death. Nothing else radicalizes a person quite so thoroughly, nothing makes one quite so daring," he concludes ominously, "as to be already dead."[21] Although Shorris focuses as much on the generation of older Cubans who were then and, in fact, are still dying without realizing their wish of return to the homeland, he also suggests in his discussions of literary figures from succeeding generations, like Jorge Valls[22] and Roberto G. Fernández,[23] something of a posthumous quality in their writing. Much Cuban-exile writing, Shorris suggests, explores an almost de facto nostalgia that takes as its premise the absolute irretrievability of the past it still stubbornly desires.

David Rieff, in his 1993 book *The Exile: Cuba in the Heart of Miami*, makes frequent reference to what Cuban Americans term *el tema*, the theme, which Rieff tells us "describes for Cuban Miami everything from relating to the exile, to the possibility of change on the island, and to the role Cuban-Americans might play in it."[24] Between the uncompromising symbolic equation of exile and death, and the exhaustive operation of the catch-all *tema* that some argue dominates Cuban cultural life outside of Cuba, little space would seem to be left for viable literary expression. This is part of what I term the condition of impossibility for Cuban American writing.

And yet, it is in this impossible space that Cuban-exile, Cuban American, and Cuban-diasporic writing *happens*. In that space created, for example, by the mutual exclusion of ideas of exile and assimilation, which, as Rieff observes, "were ideas that did not mix" because "to assimilate was to accept that the exile was over, and, on a political level, that Fidel Castro had won,"[25] and by the simultaneously obsessive nostalgia for a past inscribed in Spanish and the lure of a successful present promised and delivered in and by American English, off-island Cuban writers *necessarily* write, and they write beyond the increasingly obsolete, and moribund, parameters of exile. Rieff, in a study bolstered by his own fine writing, comments at length on "the unquenchable fantasy of return" and its power to keep Cuban exiles from ever settling for or accepting one status or another, one side of this cultural and political endgame or the other:

> whatever distinctions it might have been rational to expect the Miami Cubans to draw among the wound, the wish and the reality, or for that matter, between what it was to be an exile and what it is to be an immigrant, drawing them came to seem the unlikeliest act of all for *el exilio* to perform. For to do so would have been, imaginatively at least, the grossest act of self-mutilation. The contradictions were infinitely preferable.[26]

These, I would argue, continue to be the stakes in current Cuban American and Cuban-diasporic writing.

Although it may seem that a good deal of important work on the Cuban American political and cultural scene has been written by non-Cubans, like Shorris and Rieff, for example, and by other prominent North American writers like Joan Didion and John Sayles, the specifically literary, symbolic, and imaginative exploration and articulation of the contradictions intrinsic to off-island writing *in Cuban* have also been taken up by a heterogeneous group of young U.S.-based writers with equally heterogeneous claims, and relationships, to the experiences and the qualities of *cubanidad*. These writers cover a varied landscape of thematic concerns: a landscape, however, in no way islandized or isolated by the overwhelming *tema* of exile and return. This study's primary focus on gender and sexuality will allow for an adequately full-bodied account of the socio- and psychodynamics fueling the larger exile-related thematics of nostalgia, and the often simultaneous desire for, and skepticism about, return. Both that desire, and that skepticism, have led, in turn, to an increasingly fertile and productive emphasis on the perseverance of something meaningfully and powerfully Cuban across an increasingly, and complexly diasporic geography. It is that geography that the following chapters attempt to map.

Acknowledgments

When I arrived at Georgetown University's English Department in August 1998, nearly half this book was already written, and I used to joke then that it was practically writing itself. Eight months later, in April 1999, a week after eulogizing the grandmother who raised me and as my father was undergoing chemotherapy for a cancer he would not survive, I found a lump on my left shoulder which turned out to be a cancerous lymph node, symptomatic of the non-Hodgkin's lymphoma with which I've lived (and which I've been surviving) ever since. When my father died in January 2000, I was in chemotherapy for the first time; when my mother also succumbed to cancer three years later, in May 2003, I was in the middle of a three-week stay at Georgetown University Hospital, undergoing the stem cell transplant that has kept me alive to this point. The book would have been dedicated to my grandmother and my parents in any case, but now it is dedicated to their memory.

And so much for the book writing itself. In the course of these exceedingly difficult years, I've been blessed with the love and support of more people than I could possibly name here, but all of whom share some responsibility for keeping me alive, and sane, and hopeful about a future (mine, this book's) that I knew not to take for granted.

At Georgetown these include a splendid, professional, caring team of doctors and nurses who literally kept me alive. As important, however, these include a long list of people who've transcended all the bounded categories of colleague, student, mentor, and even friend; they're family to me now, and while I don't name them all here, some absolutely deserve mention by name: Leona Fisher, Elizabeth Vélez, Joe Palacios, Patricia O'Connor, Penn Szittya, Verónica Salles-Reese, Ed Ingebretsen, Henry Schwarz, Angelyn Mitchell, Norma Tilden, Paul Betz, Joe Sitterson, and Karen Lautman. And (in loving memory) Jim Slevin and David Kadlec.

Beyond my Georgetown family, I also count the following people as beloved kin: José Muñoz, David Román, Randy Cole, Bob Kaner, Jocelyn Medawar, Michael Weiss, Framji Minwalla, Israel Reyes, Licia Fiol-Matta, Jennifer Doyle, and Diana York Blaine. In the period preceding my arrival at Georgetown, I could only indulge the impression that the book was writing itself because of the support and encouragement my work received from many colleagues, friends, and mentors at the institutions I'd previously called home, namely, Stanford, UCLA, San Jose State, and Dartmouth. From this period of my life I absolutely need to thank and/or honor the following: Mark Mancall, Daniel Calder, Jacques Derrida, Samuel Weber, Max Novak, Donald Pease, John Brenkman, and Jonathan Crewe. And finally, as the book was nearing completion, Tom Wortham and Rafael Pérez-Torres saved my life by welcoming me back to UCLA as a scholar-in-residence in the spring of 2004.

The book itself owes a debt of gratitude for its life to an army of mentors, editors, readers, and critics who helped me publish a number of its chapters as articles in various journals and anthologies, as well as to Richard Morrison and everyone else at the University of Minnesota Press who has had a hand in its evaluation, revision, and production.

As I write these remarks in early August 2006, and as international attention is mostly fixed on a serious crisis in the Middle East, news reports are claiming that Fidel Castro has for the first time in forty-seven years ceded significant power to his brother Raúl as he recovers from intestinal surgery. Between reports from the war zones in Iraq, Lebanon, and Israel, TV audiences in the United States and elsewhere have been regaled with images of crowds of Cuban exiles dancing in the streets of Miami's Little Havana, and making preposterous claims of political victory in the face of a fifty-year political stalemate.

This book is now, as ever, dedicated to my Cuban family in California, Florida, and Cuba, the dead certainly, but also the living: my sisters, my nephews, the rest of the Cubano/Güinero/Angeleno posse that keeps me close to the memory of my parents, and the Cubans in my family diasporically scattered in places like Hayward, California, Hialeah, Florida, and Güines, Cuba. Your inspiration, your perseverance, and your love made this book, and make my life, possible.

Introduction

Diaspora and Disappearance

Diasporic traversals question the rigidity of identity itself—religious, ethnic, gendered, national; yet this diasporic movement marks not a postmodern turn from history, but a nomadic turn in which the very parameters of specific historical moments are embodied and—as diaspora itself suggests—are scattered and regrouped into new points of becoming.

—Braziel and Mannur[1]

[For] Cuba's revolutionary children, . . . the body, and sex itself, have become the home-away-from-home, the resting point for so much homelessness, . . . this generation must [therefore] map the new world by reinventing gender and sexuality.

—Ruth Behar[2]

My favorite joking remark to make whenever anyone invokes the idea of a "Cuban diaspora" is to say that it's hard to have a diaspora when most of the parties scattered after and since the 1959 Castro revolution have recollected (themselves) in Miami. But I'm usually of two minds, actually, when I make this remark: in one I acknowledge to myself that even my own life history, as a Cuban-born, California-bred and -educated immigrant American with significant emotional and experiential ties to Los Angeles, the San Francisco Bay area, Paris,

1

New England, New York City, and Washington, D.C., belies my joking suspicion of the literally "diasporic" reach of off-island Cuban resettlement post-1959; but in the other I go along with my joke, if only to the extent that I've noticed how, especially in the past decade or so, the deployment, and even the nondeployment, of the term "diaspora" to refer to off-island Cuban experience since 1959 often seems more strategic than accurate, and in any case one instance among many others of a generally incoherent and nonrigorous use of the term in contemporary postcolonial and multicultural studies.

For this reason I appreciate the efforts of anthropologist James Clifford, in his 1997 book, *Routes: Travel and Translation in the Late Twentieth Century,*[3] to devote an entire chapter to a discussion of the concept of diaspora, both in terms of its historical (particularly Jewish) precedents, and in its contemporary manifestations, both practical and theoretical. In that study Clifford famously cites an article by William Safran that appeared in the first volume, published in 1990, of the journal *Diaspora;* in that article, Clifford tells us, Safran attempts a functional definition of diaspora, one that Clifford himself will both support and amend in the course of his subsequent remarks on the topic. For Safran, Clifford tells us, "the main features of diaspora" are as follows: "a history of dispersal, myths/memories of the homeland, alienation in the host (bad host?) country, desire for eventual return, ongoing support of the homeland, and a collective identity importantly defined by this relationship"; according to these criteria, Safran concludes, "we may legitimately speak of the Armenian, Maghrebi, Turkish, Palestinian, Cuban, Greek and perhaps Chinese diasporas at present and of the Polish diaspora of the past, although none of them fully conforms to the 'ideal type' of the Jewish diaspora" (Safran 84, quoted in Clifford, 247–48). Of course, much has changed in the world since the "present" of Safran's 1990 article, and even since the "present" of Clifford's 1997 book, and although those changes might in part enable the addition of other groups to Safran's list of examples, none of those changes, profound and even cataclysmic as some of them have been, have done anything to alter the status (or the diasporic quality, as it were, of experience) of any number of groups already included.

Of these, the one that will concern me here is the Cuban diaspora, which to me sounds an off note in Safran's list for any number of reasons, but perhaps the most important are (1) that it's the only group named whose nation of origin is in the Western Hemisphere, and (2) that with the possible exception of the Chinese it is also the only group named whose dispersal was primarily the product of the set of especially political conditions that, under the general title of the global Cold War, have largely disappeared since the writing and first publication of Safran's essay. It is with these important practical and historical modifications in mind that Clifford goes on to amend Safran's formula for determining diasporic status; first, he posits that beyond the generation of better, more accurate knowledge of authentically diasporic communities in the world, we also need to concern ourselves with a better understanding of the discourse of diaspora within which we might want to cast that knowledge; second, he acknowledges that chief among the weaknesses in Safran's formula might be its reliance on forms of tribalism and nationalism as factors in that determination, given the increasingly complex ways in which nation-states and national cultures do or do not line up in the face of increasingly mobile, increasingly fluid populations in the world. Clifford devotes significant attention to both the historical precedence of the Jewish diaspora and the contemporary deployment of diaspora discourse in the work of Paul Gilroy on the Black Atlantic to demonstrate how diasporic thinking might productively apply to situations with no definitive ties to either particular nation-states or national cultures, either as home- or host-lands.

I want to import some of Clifford's thinking here into my own work on Cuban American culture in part because of its problematization of precisely the nationalist/tribalist presumption that too often insinuates itself back into what I consider bad faith (or at least disingenuous) forms of diasporic thinking, forms that, if they were more honest with themselves, would have to recognize in their invocations of diaspora neither a critique of nor an alternative to nationalist discourse so much as a mask for it, and for the kinds of especially identitarian investments that it supports. When I mentioned earlier that the inclusion of Cuba in Safran's list sounded an off note to me, I didn't meant to suggest that it did so because of anything terribly exceptional about it among the other groups so much as because of its mere, but suggestive, difference from them. Exceptionalism has itself traditionally been a claim made in various contexts to support accompanying nationalist claims; so although I would resist making such claims for anything Cuban, and indeed I see a great deal of value in looking more closely at the ways in which especially recent Cuban experience across all its possible stages resembles non-Cuban experience across and among a wide variety of comparable groups, I do see some value here in maintaining some sense of a Cuban distinction, one that actually cuts right to, and at, the heart of nationalist thinking.

Indeed, what I want to turn to now is an examination of what diasporic thinking can and cannot do to help us determine what vestige of the national might still, or should, remain in play when we designate something, especially something off-island, as Cuban, Cuban American, or even Cuban-diasporic. It matters, of course, that Cuba still names an island as a mere geographic designation of a physical entity; things get tricky, however, past that point. Some Cubans would actually claim that the island and the nation literally parted ways with the 1959 revolution, that those remaining on the island and loyal to that revolution installed on the literal homeland a regime that betrayed rather than fulfilled what they took to be the nation's historical, destinal promise; hence Cuba the nation ceased to exist on Cuba the island after this political turn of events; no authentic Cuban, this thinking goes, could accept the Castro regime as anything but a perversion of that promise, and hence no authentic Cuban could freely choose to stay on the island under such conditions.

Revolutionary Cuba, of course, thinks about itself in exactly opposite terms. And although most conventional thinking since this moment of national bifurcation has generally conceded that Cuba is still Cuba, that those living there are still Cubans, and that those who left constitute something other than a nation (whether we call that something an "exile" or a "diaspora"), I would like, if only for the moment, to follow the journalist Ann Marie Bardach in calling these "the parallel universes of the Two Cubas: that of the largest island in the Caribbean . . . [the other one] in Miami, to which one and a half million exiles have fled," and I would also like to conclude, with Bardach, that "contrary to expectations, the most salient feature of the warring parties is not how different they are, but how similar"(Bardach, xvii–xviii).[4] I'll return to Bardach before closing off this discussion, but for now it bears noting that her remark implicitly compares Cuba not to the scattered diasporic groups in Safran's list, but to those nations that underwent, like Cuba, simultaneous geographic and ideological splitting in the course of the Cold War. The two Cubas, according to this thinking, line up alongside the (formerly) two Germanies, the (formerly) two Vietnams, and the still-split Koreas; one could also in this context make a case I suppose for at least two Chinas, maybe more; and although current conditions for these countries have resolved or failed to resolve their divisions in ways as various as the conditions that produced them, Cuba still comes off as different from any of them in important ways.

The first, most obvious difference is geographic: Cuba didn't split into two warring zones, although one sometimes imagines some chunk of the island, roughly a tenth of its landmass, breaking off and floating north just far enough to beach itself where the Everglades meet the Florida Keys. The other differences are subtler and more salient; off-island Cubans claim loyalty to the same flag that still represents the Cuban nation and the Cuban state, remaining on-island; off-island Cubans claim the same source of national patrimony in the legacy of José Martí, whom they see as a champion of a liberal, democratic free enterprise, whereas on-island Cubans hail him as the model of an anticapitalist, anticolonial resistance and critique fulfilled in and by the revolution. Bardach also notices on both sides "the Cuban predilection, spanning centuries, for *caudillos*—political bosses," a predilection leading, she argues, to "two parallel tragedies: the hijacking of the Cuban Revolution by Fidel Castro, and a similar phenomenon, albeit modified, in Miami—as exiles seeking freedom have been shunted into silence by hard-liners bent on revenge, retribution, and power"(Bardach, xviii). Bardach makes these observations in the preface of her 2002 book, *Cuba Confidential: Love and Vengeance in Miami and Havana,* which primarily collects a decade's worth of her journalistic pieces on post-Cuba's warring capitals and situates them

all in the frame of the Elián González affair, which held the national
(and international) media's attention through much of the early
months of 2000, and on which she reported for a number of major
U.S. magazines and newspapers.

Of the many things about postrevolutionary Cuban history that
l'affaire Elián highlighted, Bardach argues, perhaps the most important has been how that history has played itself out like "a huge family
feud," one "infused . . . with an emotionality that is the stuff of Greek
drama, with plotlines borrowed from Shakespeare and the afternoon
telenovelas"(Bardach, xvii). This recourse to the rhetoric of family on
Bardach's part points directly to the other factor complicating the
Cuban/American/diasporic scene, namely that authentic Cubanness
is also very much a function of familial belonging; so while many
off-island Cubans will posit either an abstract enemy, the ubiquitous
Cuban-communist traitor to the nation or concentrate all their en-
mity on the less abstract but still iconic figure of Fidel Castro, they
will in the same conversation never question the authentic Cubanness
of whoever in their own family remains on the island, and for whatever reason.

Beyond the neatness of the two-Cuba split, however, lie far messier
modes of designating degrees of authentic and inauthentic Cubanness. Most of these, of course, occur off-island, among those whom the
literary scholar Isabel Alvarez-Borland has called "extra-territorial"
Cubans[5]; off-island Cubans can be found, literally, everywhere, and although certainly one overwhelmingly large, and loud, concentration
remains in South Florida, even there its influence has spread well beyond the confines, and the politics, of Calle Ocho and Hialeah. The
other significant geographic concentration of Cubans in the United
States remains in and around Union City, New Jersey, but Cubans can
be found not only all over the tristate area around New York City, but
also in Washington, D.C.; San Juan, Puerto Rico; Los Angeles, California; and increasingly in parts of the American Midwest (Chicago in-
cluded) and the rest of the American South (especially perhaps but not
exclusively in New Orleans). These Cubans are in part therefore actively participating in the larger Latin Americanization of North
American cultural and political life, and if one can speak diasporically
of a black Atlantic world, we can also speak increasingly diasporically

of a Latinized American world that no longer corresponds neatly to any geographic designations of region, state, or nation.

But for all this, claims to nationalist authenticity persist, even in these increasingly hybridized, extraterritorial contexts; Miami Cubans can, in part quite legitimately, claim a closer connection to Cuba's traditions, hence to Cuba itself, less because of their geographic proximity to the island and more because of their success in having transplanted so much of the culture to their adopted extraterritorial home. To that extent, non-Miamian off-island Cubans are often very quick first to concede that success, and only then, depending on their own dispositions, to express either gratitude or regret concerning their own comparative success at maintaining ties to their cultural roots in usually far less hospitable (if not more hostile, often at least more indifferent) environments. The addition of chronological to the already complicated geographical conditions I've been outlining only complicates things further; Cubans have been leaving Cuba in succeeding and continuous waves of emigration since the 1959 revolution, and depending on how old they were when they left, how far along in the course of the by now nearly half-century-old revolution they left, and how much time (if any) they chose to stay in the Miami area, they will develop very different levels and qualities of loyalty and adherence to whatever they value about their own Cubanness. Add even to this heady mix the ingredient of succeeding generations, of the off-island-born children, grandchildren, and even great-grandchildren of these Cuban émigrés, and inevitably that potent degree of "immanent" Cubanness will dilute, if not exactly weaken, or disappear entirely, into the wider, more generally differential field of cultural otherness currently resolving and dissolving itself not only in the United States, but in most large and relatively "open" societies in the world today.[6]

In the following sections of this discussion I introduce and briefly analyze some representative instances of social, cultural, and political practice across a variety of mostly U.S.-based but nevertheless diasporic Cuban positions and locations. I describe and comment on these fairly concrete, and discrete, manifestations of Cuban-diasporic work in order to privilege local praxis over general theoretical conceptualization as the preferable, because most commensurate, way of approaching, and understanding, the most salient properties of contemporary diasporic praxes as such. I also want in the following sections to begin the work of situating these praxes in relation to a compelling anxieties about what I call varying forms of "disappearance" as diasporic communities confront both the demands of assimilation and accommodation into surrounding host cultures, as well as the irresistible demands of a future that increasingly diminishes hope for the kind of redemptive return to the homeland that in part constitutes such communities as "diasporic" in the first place. In addition, I focus on the manner in which this anxiety in turn compels an almost obsessive insistence on reproduction, always simultaneously social, cultural, and sexual, as the most effective means for self-perpetuation, and therefore nondisappearance, into that future. Finally, I want to begin tracing here how that obsession with self-reproduction reinforces often already existing patriarchal, heterosexist presumptions, and a corollary set of often persistent regulations, about especially sexual practices (both literal and symbolic) that either do or do not comply directly with these reproductive demands. In the Cuban/American/diasporic case, the sexual wars accompanying the political and cultural wars raging at least since 1959 have often taken rather distinctive, certainly spectacular form; "erotics," sexuality, passion, kinship, and other often body-based manifestations of nonrational forms of human (individual and collective) connection and interaction tend to inform profoundly if not dominate much of the best and certainly most influential scholarly work emanating from the North American academy on the general Cuban/American/diasporic situation.[7] The present discussion thus offers itself as a modest, if strategic, contribution to, and correction of, that ongoing project, in ways and for reasons that will become clearer as the present discussion unfolds.

It Takes La Villa *to Raise a Diasporic Consciousness*

Since 1968, a club, or *círculo*, of expatriate Cubans, all hailing from the same rural town of Güines and settling in Los Angeles, has produced a quarterly newsletter entitled *La Villa*. In the more than thirty-five years since its initial publication, *La Villa* has managed not only to remain in constant, active circulation, but also to consolidate and maintain ties among an otherwise fairly widely dispersed population of subscribing readers and their families, friends, and other associates. Members of this population continue to this day to consider themselves active, present citizens of a "municipality-in-exile" with no other location than the one they in part remember, in part imagine sharing, especially when any two or more of them gather in the name of their common history in, and their common, ongoing devotion to, that place. *La Villa*'s function as chief organ of communication has been crucial for this Güinero/Cubano/Angeleno community, in part because Cubans who settled in Southern California never concentrated themselves in any single neighborhood, as other Cubans famously did in South Florida and even, perhaps less famously, in northern New Jersey.

To this extent, *La Villa* has also served as limited but effective compensation for two missing, absent "villas": one the actual municipality of Güines itself, which, lying 20-some kilometers from Havana, receded from any literal relation to space, and to time, as it increasingly emerged in the pages of *La Villa* in grainy black-and-white photographic reproductions collected in every issue under the heading of "Güines de Ayer"; the other, the adopted "villa" of the Los Angeles metropolis, a city whose vast dimensions and complex demographics proved, even in the mid-1960s, too daunting a challenge to the relatively small group of displaced Cubanos, to say nothing of the smaller subgroup of displaced Güineros, in their earliest attempts to establish anything like a visible cultural presence there. Images explicitly representing Los Angeles rarely appear in *La Villa*'s pages, however; images do abound of gatherings, either in meeting halls, restaurant banquet rooms, or even private Güinero homes, all presumably located in Southern California, but to the extent that they serve as Güinero/Cubano spaces in those instances, they much more readily denote the diasporic traces of Güines, and perhaps of Cuba more generally, than they denote, or even connote, anything about LA.[8]

To the extent that Los Angeles does appear in explicit form in the pages of *La Villa*, it does so in its most official, practical, logistical features; that is, as named on the official seal of the Círculo Güinero, which always appears on the front page, and in the other identificatory titular spaces of the newsletter (on the front page, in the editorial information, and the postal address). It appears as well on some, but not all, of the commercial advertisements interspersed in *La Villa*'s pages; mostly these advertisements take the form of enlarged versions of business cards for modest local enterprises (a restaurant called Little Havana in Manhattan Beach, a cement and concrete layer in LA proper), although for each LA-based ad there is at least another for a business based in Miami (an optician in Coral Gables, a retirement home in Kendall). This suggests that although the newsletter identifies itself primarily with its California-based readership, it concedes that this readership remains perhaps constitutively mobile, especially in its consistently ongoing, hence at least temporally stable, connection not only to its place(s) of literal origin but also to those other spaces in (scattered) conjunction with which it constitutes itself as authentically diasporic.

It bears mentioning here that the Círculo Güinero de Los Ángeles sees itself as mostly independent from, and only categorically subordinate to, a larger national exile group, the Municipio de Güines en Exilio, which produces its own newsletter, *Ecos del Mayabeque,* which in its title honors the Mayabeque River that runs through Güines, and from which Güineros also derive the alternative self-appellation of Mayabequinos. *Ecos del Mayabeque,* founded two years before *La Villa* and therefore (by 2004) approaching nearly forty years of publication, boasts only Miami-based ads, and more of them in total number than *La Villa,* including a number for businesses named after the town itself, like Güines Landscaping in Hialeah and Güines Air Conditioning in Southwest Miami. This last point suggests another crucial difference between the Cuban communities in LA and Miami; in the latter, being Cuban cannot offer much in the way of a marker of distinction. In Miami it matters mightily if you're from Güines, or from Cienfuegos, or from Camagüey, although in LA it's enough to be Cuban in order to mark yourself as distinct (for better or worse) from the majority of other Latinos around you.

Although in another project I hope to look more closely at the LA club's newsletter across the many years of its publication to trace in greater detail how it both participated in as well as recorded the re-

consolidation and maintenance of a precariously desituated, culturally (if not otherwise) vulnerable community, here I only want to
draw attention to some recurring features of the newsletter to establish something of its preferred strategy for going about the work of an
explicitly diasporic form of cultural perpetuation in, as, and through
varying forms of (self-)reproduction. In addition to galleries entitled
Güines de Ayer and, on occasion, Güines de Hoy (respectively, Güines
of "yesterday" and "today"), *La Villa* also regularly features galleries
of snapshots submitted by readers and other contributors under the
headings "Galería Infantíl" and "Crónica Gráfica," which together
offer an enormous pictorial archive of the births, baptisms, first com-
munions, *quinceañeras,* progress through the various stages of public
and private education, participation in collegiate and other athletics,
confirmations, graduations, weddings, festive gatherings across all
degrees of attendance and formality, deaths and funerals of persons
either themselves born in or somehow descended from or related to
persons born in the town of Güines, and therefore official citizens of
its diasporic double, the Angeleno "villa Güinera" itself. Although
most death notices take verbal form in a printed section entitled
"Notas de Dolor," death, especially as the simultaneous passing into
both mortality and obsolescence of the generation that first established the Círculo and its *Villa,* haunts all aspects of the newsletter
and its primary readership, and this has been especially true since the
early 1990s.[9]

As early as 1985, the Círculo had closed the doors of its long-
established meeting hall on Alvarado Street just west of downtown
Los Angeles because members no longer needed it as a practical resource; many had in the twenty years since the club's founding become themselves both socially and economically established enough
in their new home to do without the weekly social gatherings at the
space. In addition, the generation who established the club was beginning to give way to the generation of its certainly more "Americanized" if not fully assimilated children, many of whom not only did
not marry other Güineros, but did not marry other Cubans, and were
therefore accelerating what I call in what follows the phenomenon of
Cuban/exile/diasporic "disappearance" into the larger demographic

and cultural fabric of late twentieth-century polycultural Los Angeles, and by extension into the larger North American society to which LA might be said to stand in some sort of idiosyncratic, but telling, synecdochal relief. This phenomenon perhaps begs for statistical study, but in powerfully anecdotal ways it is documented in both the "Galería Infantíl" and the "Crónica Gráfica" sections of La Villa, where, for example, what remains of a newborn's cubanidad might come down to just one of two of his or her transculturally, translinguistically hyphenated surnames.

Generally speaking, however, the U.S.-based Cuban-exile generation (to which La Villa's founders belong) encountered most powerfully the ghost of its increasing, especially political, obsolescence with the end of the Cold War; when Cuba's revolutionary regime failed to fall with its counterparts in Eastern Europe and in the Soviet confederation, many exile-generation U.S. Cubans began to brace themselves for what had before seemed historically unthinkable: that Castro's revolution would, indeed, outlast them, and they'd die without having realized their dream of return. Nowadays the picture galleries of both La Villa and Ecos del Mayabeque are increasingly filled with large sections dedicated to birthday celebrations for surviving exile Güineros who are entering their seventies and eighties, as well as to elaborate obituaries, in words and images, to those who are passing away in increasing numbers. Even the editorial sections of volumes of both newsletters, appearing as recently as the last issues of 2005 and the first of 2006, have marked in increasingly passionate terms the growing political and cultural divide across and among generations of off-island Cubans and also the looming possibility that such a divide threatens the very existence not only of both the newsletters and the clubs that produce them but also of the very people who have historically constituted, and been constituted by, both of these diasporic cultural organs.

The chief irony imbedded in this outcome, of course, is that all of these cultural organs may indeed be suffering partly, if not primarily, as a result of their own success. If indeed what a newsletter like La Villa was designed to do was to maintain a sense of communality in perpetuity through not only its own production, reproduction, and

circulation but also through what it could both document and promote as the parallel production, reproduction, and circulation of
Güinero subjects and bodies in and through the cultural and other
spaces of its adopted host city and nation, what it could not quite
manage was the maintenance of direct, identificatory, affective ties to
Güines (or even more generally to Cuba) for anyone (like, for example,
first-generation children of exile Güineros) who either had never
been there or were unlikely to marry, and have children with, anyone
else connected in any way to their "home" town, their "home" nation,
or even to their spectral, absented *"villas en exilio."* For a queer reader
who has spent most of his queer life fending off the homophobic and
heterosexist interpellations and admonitions (of quite varying degrees of intensity and hostility) of many members of *La Villa*'s lifelong readers (including my parents, my more distant relatives, and an
army of either concerned or suspicious *socios* of theirs), I cannot help
but read in all its most regular features a ferociously heterosexual
presumption about the best, indeed only conceivable, way to manage
cultural perpetuation and reproduction, that is, of course, through
heterosexual biological reproduction as buttressed in and by almost
all the social and cultural rituals celebrated in those features.

But as a subscriber to *La Villa* since my father's death in 2000 and
as someone who appreciated the honor the newsletter accorded my
mother in her very moving obituary in 2003, I want to offer my own
ongoing subscription to *La Villa* (as well as my writing about it here)
as one sign of what might eventually function as an alternative (perhaps even a queer) form of continuation and contiguation toward
any (future) community that might want to see *La Villa* survive beyond the imminent (and potentially catastrophic) generational turn
that all these many deaths already occasion. Not that this receding
generation has been completely helpless, or flailing, in its attempts
to confront the more irresistible force(s) of historical and cultural
change. For all that it has maintained an unwavering devotion to the
same exile ideology that, along with the equally unwavering devotion
to a revolutionary ideology on the island, has ensured, in fact, that
little continues to change for Cubans everywhere on the political
front, leaders like *La Villa*'s editors and the annually elected "Junta

Directiva" governing the Círculo have accommodated themselves quite readily to changing conditions over which they have little comparable control. My research into the history of *La Villa* and the Círculo has been greatly assisted, for example, by the establishment of a website, http://www.circuloguinero.org, where interested readers can turn to see for themselves how the organization continues to define itself in terms of its own explicitly termed "diasporic" status, and how it has managed to take productive advantage of emerging technologies to further strengthen its efforts to maintain its ties to its core constituency while reaching out to a larger audience beyond that constituency. And although *La Villa* continues well into the twenty-first century to publish exclusively in Spanish, the website features versions in Spanish and in English; at some point the newsletter, if it insists on surviving in print, and in hard copy, may also have to concede to the changing linguistic orientation of its changing readership.

Such a linguistic shift, for just such a cultural organ as *La Villa*, has already been imagined, in the fictional form of "*The Southern Pearl*, The Voice of the Municipality of One Hundred Fires in Exile," by Roberto G. Fernández in his 1988 novel *Raining Backward*.[10] Early in his mottled, satirical narrative, a paragon of the low postmodern style, Fernández imbeds his loving but nevertheless biting parody of a *Villa*-style community newsletter, this one based in early-1970s Miami and dedicated to exiles from the Cuban city of Cienfuegos. Fernández's most audacious fictional invention in the scene may consist of his imagining such a newsletter publishing an "English Supplement" at all, given especially its potentially negative political repercussions in the Miami of those still-early, exile-dominant years; and although Fernández's decision to compose this novel more or less completely in English (he had previously published two novels and a story collection in Spanish) in part required him to present *The Southern Pearl*'s text in English, it did not require the explicit fictional apparatus of the "English Supplement." But Fernández does not hold himself exclusively or even primarily to the demands of a realist verisimilitude in the composition of his novel; he's just as interested in the other textual and linguistic effects that the nonrepresentational registers of language and print allow him to produce, and to exploit, in ways that still manage to accentuate the message he goes about conveying. Although Fernández may not be the only writer to have made metaphorical hay out of the English translation of Cienfuegos (see the poet Richard Blanco's fine collection of lyrics, *City of One Hundred Fires*), he may be the first to make meta-metaphorical hay out of it. Proper names, whether of persons or places, usually don't "translate," at least according to the accepted protocols of both formal and even informal translation. "Cienfuegos" refers to a city in Cuba and does so without any modification of its spelling, in both Spanish and English; "One Hundred Fires" literally does not, therefore, translate from Cienfuegos and thus marks a failure of translation, and perhaps as well a failure of anything like a neat or congruent supplementation, or even substitution, of one language by another.

Like *La Villa*, *The Southern Pearl* busies itself with all manner of documentation of its own (as well as its community's) perpetuation and reproducibility: it starts out with an announcement of the "golden" fifteenth birthday (and hence entry into sexual maturity and availability) of Caridad "Connie" Rodríguez, one of the novel's chief characters and an embodiment of almost everything that can go wrong in the process of acculturating from a mostly Cuban to a mostly (North) American sensibility; it also announces a wedding, a crowning of a six-year-old beauty queen, the various infirmities of various aging readers (including one suffering from "a waterfall in her left eye, which is causing her difficulty with her vision" [34]), and even news of the successful (and impressively diasporic) resettlement of another family of readers to Urbana, Illinois. Fernández closes the text of the newsletter with, predictably, parodies of the kinds of commercial announcements regularly featured in *La Villa;* the last of these, for a restaurant called Friends of the Sea, includes the following menu of its mistranslated (because literally translated) "specialties of the House: SHRIMP at the little garlic/SAW at the oven/CHERN at the iron/FLOUR with Moorish crabs/SEAFOOD sprinkle/PULP in its own ink" (35). The last of these items brings the text back to perhaps the most acute awareness of its own textual status; "PULP" actually means to translate from *pulpo*, Spanish for "octopus," but instead translates out of the discourse of seafood altogether to the discourse of genre, and especially of a literary genre to whose sexual, emotional, and narrative excesses Fernández's own text very flamboyantly aspires. For all the references to fluids like rain and seawater in which his narrative and its discourse mostly find themselves awash, Fernández's text mostly swims in what some might find to be the murky obfuscation of its own self-referential "ink," although I for one find genuine insight, and bracing clarity, in the games his language plays with itself and with its readers. Fernández's narrative may sport, and sprout, more "legs" (and extensions) even than the octopus to which it compares itself, but with every discharge of its ink it takes flight and manages surprising movements that only the most sympathetic, and *simpático*, reader can hope to follow.

If Fernández's narrative enjoys some stability from the fixity of its geographic setting in Miami, it invites powerfully congruent forms of instability in the ways it plays with both time and the alternative "spaces" of language and textuality, as I have already begun to suggest earlier. Indeed, chronology and language work in the most destabilizing way in his novel when Fernández treats the issue of language politics most directly; the novel, published in the late 1980s, satirizes quite brilliantly the mentality of especially English-only movements in the United States as attempts to control the transcultural effects of large foreign migrations like the one that has been filling South Florida with Cubans. Many studies treating the Cuban and post-Cuban histories of Miami will, for example, make large claims for the importance of just such a movement, coinciding in the early 1980s with the influx of Cuban *marielitos* to Florida's shores, as a watershed moment in the Miami-Cuban community's progress toward greater entrenchment as a more-or-less permanent factor in the political landscape of the city and county.[11] In *Raining Backwards* Fernández dramatizes a similar clash, but he sets it almost a decade before the moment of its actual historical occurrence. A later chapter (153–58) in the novel transcribes the discourse of WMIA, the local television station's "Six O'Clock News," which leads with the following story:

> In a five to four decision, the United States Supreme Court has declared that it is unconstitutional to prohibit the use of lan-

guages in the United States and that persecution of Spanish-speakers by the Tongue Brigade is equivalent to violation of the civil rights of the handicapped. The case, which has attracted the attention of the whole nation, is particularly important in the Miami area because it is the headquarters of the Tongue Brigade. "Speaking in any other tongue, and especially in Spanish, is a form of disglosia, a degenerative disease centered in the brain," wrote Chief Justice Kurt Kempis. The Chief Justice added that those suffering from the handicap ". . . should be given help and special therapy." The case requires the federal government to set up treatment centers where ". . . education will lead to prevention and help to curb the spread of the disease."[12]

Fernández's healthy skepticism about all forms of cultural and political sanctimony more than reinforces the tonal and conceptual complexity of this passage. Just as his own deployments of not only bilingual but really polyglot resources resist any easy categorization (they signal neither gestures to simple verisimilitude nor to an equally simple, predictable reverence for linguistic or cultural authenticity as such), so his generally allegorical treatment of the dynamic of U.S. language politics in this passage resists any easy correspondence to the major players and positions shaping that dynamic. Opposing the outlandishly comical reasoning leading to the Supreme Court's decision to the too-familiar, militant ideology of the Tongue Brigade whose efforts it thwarts, Fernández refuses to allow his dramatization of the conflict to line up in any conventional, recognizable way with any corresponding groups or movements in reality. Instead, the episode, and the passage narrating it, point out the absurdity and the wrongheaded premises of the entire debate precisely by refusing to replay its game in either thinly or elaborately disguised fictional form.

"Disglosia," we know, just as accurately describes the actual (and productive) operations of language, and of languages, in Fernández's text as it satirically renames either any dysfunctional non-Anglophone linguistic orientation or any variation on the state of Anglo-Hispanic bilingualism to which Fernández, or Chief Justice Kempis, might want to accord exceptional status. And although recourse either to the

planned "treatment centers where '... education will lead to prevention ... of the disease" or to the "Division of Communicable Dis-
eases" at the "Health and Rehabilitation Department" in Fernández's
imagined U.S. federal government might actually lead to an equally
imagined "special therapy," I would posit here that Fernández's favored form of linguistic "therapy" complies much more closely, if
paradoxically, with the "disglosic" pathology that his text both embraces and performs. And to this extent Fernández's text "corresponds"
to some reality less through anything like the logic of analogous, conceptual correspondence, and more through a kind of pantomime, or
mimicry, as it tries not merely to comment or report on the qualities
of being Cuban/exile/American in the world he observes and partly
makes (up) in his writing, but in the ways it tries to behave, or misbe-
have, like, or in some type of performative congruence with, that reality. The satirical mimicry in *Raining Backwards* of the discourses of
both a *Villa*-style newsletter and a local television news report, and
the insistence in both passages on couching that mimicry in the complex double-knot of translation (between, say, the languages of
Spanish and English on one level and on the languages of history and
fiction on another), of its simultaneous necessity and impossibility,
allows the novel to invoke, perhaps even critically activate, the diasporic conditions of which it is itself in part a function, without
merely passively reproducing or representing those conditions.

Just as Fernández recognizes the anxiety about especially cultural
self-perpetuation in his diasporic community's need not only to publish something like *The Southern Pearl* but also to fill its pages with
visual and verbal reminders of both the past that continues to determine the chief elements of its identity and of its success in surviving
into a foreign and at times deeply inhospitable present, and future, he
also recognizes the corresponding (although never equivalent) anxiety in the host community's response to an increasing, and increasingly powerful, "foreign" presence on its home turf. What *La Villa*,
especially in its insistence on maintaining its publication almost entirely in Spanish, and *The Southern Pearl*, in its highly unlikely concession to a highly unimaginable English-reading constituency, do
together is mark to some extent both the scale and the scope of dias-

poric ambivalence, diasporic anxiety, and diasporic vulnerability, even in the case of a community that, comparatively speaking, has enjoyed an unusual degree of both stability and acceptance in and by its host culture.

Angels of (Post-)History: Albita's Una Mujer . . . and Obejas's Days of Awe

Having paired *La Villa*'s more conventional (re)productive, recuperative diasporic work with its critical, fictional counter in the form of Fernández's invented *Southern Pearl,* I would like now to both extend and reinforce the cultural studies methodology of that discussion with another illustrative coupling, this time of two perhaps better known U.S.-based, Cuban-diasporic cultural workers, the Cuban-born and -bred Miami-based musician Albita Rodríguez and the Cuban-born, Chicago-bred and -based journalist and fiction writer, Achy Obejas. Given that both Albita (as she is known professionally) and Obejas are fairly out about their own lesbian sexual orientation(s), my turn to their work will also hopefully deepen what has up to this point remained the mostly implicitly queer dimension of the general analysis and critique of the work of diasporic cultural reproduction that I hope to offer here. What I most hope to offer in my brief discussions of the operations of queer diasporic reproduction in their work is a model of the critical methodology characterizing all the chapters that follow and ultimately comprise the larger argument about the work of both cultural and political "erotics" on the part of a much wider variety of U.S. Cuban and other off-island cultural workers as they negotiate in that work the conflicting and often uncompromising demands of both their ongoing diasporic situation(s) and the ever-encroaching threat of a "disappearance" into a future that offers no apparently hospitable home for them.

No image, I would argue, better exemplifies the assertion about the centrality or eloquence of the body (as articulated in the epigraph from Ruth Behar opening this introduction) in the Cuban postrevolutionary imagination than the one to be found on the surface of singer Albita Rodríguez's 1997 compact disc, *Una Mujer Como Yo* (*A Woman*

Like Me). Albita, who also figures prominently in chapter 5, spent all of her early life in Cuba and had already enjoyed success as an entertainer there before defecting to the United States in 1993; in a very short time she both established herself in Miami's "Latin" music scene, thanks especially to the sponsorship of Emilio and Gloria Estefan, and began to build a growing, enthusiastic following as a live performer. At first fairly cagey, if in fairly obvious ways, about her sexuality, she produced in very rapid succession three studio albums, all playing to significant degrees euphemistically with her unconventional appearance (1995's *No Se Parece a Nada*, or *Unlike Anything Else*), as well as with rumors about her sexuality (1996's *Dicen Que...*, or *They're Saying That...*), and even with her very status, at least as a sexual person(a) (1997's *Una Mujer Como Yo*).[13] Always unapologetically "out" about her intense Cuban nationalism, as well as about her critical views of the Castro government's legacies of personal and other forms of repression, and about her devotion to some of the most traditional forms of Cuban musical expression in both composition and performance, Albita nevertheless posed a serious problem for promoters of hers wishing to sell her as a very charismatic performer with potential "cross-over" appeal across populations of consumers including not only Cuban exiles, and non-Cuban U.S. Latinos but also an even wider "mainstream" audience of non-Latino U.S. fans of what was then a still-nascent "Latin" pop-musical boom.

Although all three of her early U.S.-produced albums bear the symptoms of the complex pressures under which Albita was forced to both maximize her appeal and profitability while at the same time minimizing the degree to which those pressures required from her artistic, political, and even more personal forms of compromise, the accumulating wear on her creativity is detectable across the three, and that wear translated unambiguously into an unfortunate wear on her sales and in turn on her relationships with her initial sponsors and promoters. *Una Mujer Como Yo* therefore figures as the culmination of this unfortunate trend; although the pictorial apparatus of the CD's packaging attempts to market Albita by feminizing her image and by posing her in mostly conventionally glamorous and festive situations either alone or with the mostly male members of her band, none of the songs on the disc approach either the catchy, anthemic verve of the great up-tempo songs on *No Se Parece a Nada* (see my discussion of "Que Manera de Quererte" and "¿Que Culpa Tengo Yo?" in chapter 5) or the exquisite abjection of that disc's extraordinary "Bolero Para Nostalgiar" (also discussed in chapter 5).

The image that graces the actual surface of the *Una Mujer* disc does, however, represent Albita's most explicit attempt to comment on the themes that both enlivened and elevated so much of the musical work on especially the first disc. In the stark contrast of black-and-white photography, the cropped image shows Albita from behind, and only from the waist up, in profile and full makeup, eyes closed, her hair bleached as starkly white as her body, hands spread, either in surrender or support, against an indeterminately black background, and with a map of the middle region of the Western Hemisphere, prominently featuring both the Florida peninsula and the island of Cuba, printed with marker or tattooed down the exact middle of her back. We cannot know from the image whether she is standing (hence being photographed from behind) or lying down on her stomach (and being photographed from above). Although the image itself is "upright" with respect to the other graphics on the disc, that's not how it appears when the disc is in motion, when Albita appears to fly in circles, getting and going nowhere, even as her music plays. Finally, although the image suggests that Albita is mostly nude, she does at least wear a ring on what in the orientation of the picture would be the ring finger of her right hand. I thus include Albita in the discussion I develop here for reasons that go beyond the perhaps immediately apparent ways that she might be said to practice a political and cultural erotics in response to her own off-island Cuban experience. Of all the creative figures I discuss in this introduction, she is the only one who is actually based in Miami; Roberto Fernández may have left at least his heart in Miami, but he has for many years resided in Tallahassee, where he teaches at Florida State University. But Albita, because of her relatively late arrival (in the course of both her life story and the history of her especially Cuban-exile experience) in Cuban America, cannot be said to represent any of the most stereotypical of experiences and attitudes either defining or attributed to Cuban Miami and its still-dominant "exile" generation.

This fact may not be enough to qualify her as literally "diasporically" positioned, but to the extent that any study of the diasporic experience among off-island Cubans must fully measure the complexity and scope of that experience, it should include some (especially so nonexemplary a) representative of some other "Cuban" Miami than the one that has mostly claimed that title for the past fifty years. Albita's provocative image on the 1997 CD thus functions in this respect for any number of reasons. First, the image could be read as the visual correlative of the sentiments expressed in her earlier "Bolero para Nostalgiar"; the Cuba figured at the exact center of her back renders in visual terms the Cuba that exiles can no longer see, the one they left behind, the one that can only appear to them in fantasy, either as conscious nostalgia or unconscious dream. Her bolero, by turns erotic and elegiac, and often both at once, certainly suggests some possible equation for the physical gratification of sexual union and the emotional gratification of return to and reunion with a beloved homeland; at the same time, the song leaves the singer/lover in the suspended state of anticipation, suggesting perhaps some degree of hopelessness, or at least indefinite interminability, to a desire fueled too exclusively by fantasy ever to enjoy realization. The 1997 CD image that so powerfully allegorizes exilic memory, exilic nostalgia, and perhaps exilic melancholy, pushes even further at this hopelessness; unless she trains herself in some pretty demanding forms of contortion, the pictured subject will never directly see the image of the island, given its location. The image, in fact, visualizes this impossibility directly through its performance or embodiment of what can only be termed the subject's blindness; it renders in spectacular visual form a kind of disappearance, or nonappearance, that might arguably be said to mark constitutively the chief condition that both enables and disables both diasporic and exilic subjectivity. The irony, and the paradox, of this logically untenable position, of course, is only reinforced by the fact that this most elusive, and inaccessible, of desired objects is rendered so by its very immanence, by its unerasable inscription into and upon the desiring, and mourning, subject's flesh.[14]

The simultaneity of the erotic and the elegiac plays into the complex significations of Albita's image in a number of additional ways. Stripped of the glamorous and festive trappings that adorn her in the rest of the images featured in the CD's packaging, here, on the body of the disc itself, as it were, Albita can certainly be said to offer herself erotically, in at least a fairly literal sense, to the gaze to which her image makes itself available, but beyond that, and more imaginatively, to any set of sexual scenarios that most literal offering might trigger and occasion. Very few such consequent sexual scenarios would lead, presumably, to anything like biological reproduction, and in fact, given the quality of mourning that also haunts the image, one can't help but trace the set of sexual associations raised by the image to the point of imagining even a necrophilic outcome to some such encounter with it. But although Albita's visual comment on her diasporic orientation can certainly be termed in part abject, and in part elegiac, I would not characterize it, even on this, the darkest of her three early U.S. CDs, as exclusively or even primarily despairing. The very willingness she exhibits to lay bear, in the most starkly visual way, the deep structural impasses to anything like a "logic" to diasporic thinking, or diasporic sentiment, reveals in turn a practical, cautious optimism regarding what she can imagine and posit of a future that is not only available but rendered more eminently possible by her ongoing (and in equal parts reverential and perverse) embrace of her diasporic *cubanidad* and her equally diasporic queerness.

In contrast to the image that seems so bent on what lies relentlessly behind the singer, two songs on *Una Mujer* turn their upbeat and uptempo attention to what potentially lies before her with all (and only) the seductive power of a promise. Both songs, Albita's own "Tócame Con Un Beso" and "Año Nuevo, Vida Nueva" by Julia Sierra and Rafael Mariño, move the disc in its later tracks toward a new year's celebration, which always occasions, especially among Cuban exiles, their version of the traditional (and traditionally diasporic) Jewish toast of "Next year," although for Cubans not in Jerusalem of course but in the "Havana" that mostly houses the temple of their memory and their desire. By referring at all to the new year, Albita certainly means to raise these associations among her listeners in that (to her) most familiar of audiences, but rather than raise a toast to Havana and to the past they house there, Albita's character in "Tócame . . . " embarks on a rather different voyage and toward a very different form of fulfillment. "Tócame . . ." is, in fact, an act of playful if telling seduction as the lyrics themselves make clear: they pretty straightforwardly request "one more kiss" (*un beso más*) from the object of the singer's desire at the same time they reassure the object that the kiss, although harmless (*no hace daño*), will go unnoticed by the rest of the crowd celebrating the new year. So even although it's harmless, the kiss will pack the extra titillation of being *contrabando*.[15] And although there might be all manner of reason for the lovers keeping the kiss hidden, none is given; in addition, the (male) gender of the beloved is so barely suggested (an impressive feat, given the relentless gendering of nouns, pronouns, and adjectives in Spanish) on just two verbal occasions as to render the conventional hetero-presumptive sexuality of the scene highly questionable. Even the gender of the singer remains a mystery until the very last line when the singer finally, and very dramatically, declares, "Quiero que sepa to' el mundo/Que tu boca tiene dueña" (very roughly translated, "I want everyone to know/That your mouth has an owner"). Revealing the female gender of the singer who so insistently (and in classic top/butch/masculine style) pursues her otherwise passive, demure object adequately queers the sexual dynamic of the song, even (I would argue) if that "object" turns out to be, however improbably, male.

Beyond that, the dramatic situation that the song stages and choreographs very effectively displaces the conventional, even archetypal, ritualization of exilic nostalgia that anyone might expect from an off-island Cuban new year's celebration and supplants it with the planting of one queer kiss, a kiss signaling not only a different kind of desire, as well as a different, desiring temporal orientation toward some future, any future, rather than a once (and only one allowable, if impossible) past, but also the possibility of a different, and commensurably queer, set of (re)productive effects to that desire and its eminently more possible fulfillment. The suspension of time in an intensely potentialized present, which the new year's celebration perhaps most powerfully ritualizes and embodies, immediately in the diasporic context raises a specter from at least one more ancient cultural register, and that is the figure of Janus from classical mythology. In their introduction to 2003's *Theorizing Diaspora* (entitled "Nation,

Migration, Globalization: Points of Contention in Diaspora Studies"), Jana Evans Braziel and Anita Mannur describe the two-faced
allegorical embodiment of the chronological impasse as one among
other "prevailing metaphors applied to the diasporic individual or
diasporic communities [which, they argue] must be rigorously interrogated"(9). "Janus," they tell us, "the figure drawn from the Greek
pantheon whose gaze is simultaneously directed both forward and
backward," and for this reason the traditional source for the name of
month of January, therefore both "suggests a certain temporality" as
it "looks to the future and the past" but also remains for good reason
inadequate to the task of explicating the contemporary diasporic
experience. "[W]hat," for example, they ask, "happens when one does
not want to look back for political and economic reasons?" Such a
question, these writers conclude, articulates one of the chief challenges to the current critical and discursive practices defining "diaspora studies" most generally; the field, they go on to suggest, "need[s]
to move beyond theorizing how diasporic identities are constructed
and consolidated and . . . [to] ask, how are these diasporic identities
practiced, lived and experienced?"

The contraband kiss that Albita requests of her beloved in
"Tócame . . ." might offer one queer response to the question that
Braziel and Mannur pose to "diaspora studies" and to the business as
usual of its prevailing critical constructions of both time and place.
One has, of course, to imagine the impossible if one wants to follow
Albita down this path; one might have to imagine, in other words, the
kiss as the one Janus might manage if his (or her) two faces were able
to see one another rather than figure, as s(he) traditionally does, the
impossibility of "facing" the past and the future simultaneously (and
therefore ensuring each one's constitutive blindness to the other). If
the image of Albita that I've already read in these pages suggests both
a blindness produced by a too-obsessive turn toward the past, the fact
that it only features one profile reinforces the sense of limitation (as
blindness, unconsciousness, death) to that particular kind of (exilic,
nostalgic, melancholic) temporal and historical orientation, then
perhaps the image that graces the cover of the same disc offers some
vision of an escape from, or resolution to, this untenable position.

Although much more can be made of this image beyond what I can say concerning it here, the response that the double image of Albita's face (as she both confronts herself in a mirror and, in a moment of liberating self-deprecation, smiles at herself and looks away) poses to the question left open by the more conventional, Janus-style confrontation of past and future in either the diasporic or the exilic imagination is striking. Her closed eyes here reject the more-than-latent narcissism that might be read into the use of the mirror to double the exposure of the face, although the enigmatic smile on the subject's face suggests some form of enjoyment, fulfillment, perhaps even reconciliation, of an otherwise split, alienated, or fragmented subject with, and to, itself. The secret knowledge she appears to share with herself, like the queer, contraband kiss shared in a moment of full, frontal, pleasuring contact, can both be said to reveal the possibility of some alternative, deviant future, some queerly more productive set of possibilities than any imagined yet by the exilic, diasporic audience to which Albita's work, across all levels and registers of representation, most directly speaks and sings.[16]

I'd like to couple these remarks concerning Albita's work with a complementary analysis of the diasporic creative practices of another queer off-island Cubana, this time the fiction writer Achy Obejas, who has since 1994 released three significant and consistently well-reviewed volumes, beginning with 1994's story collection *We Came All the Way from Cuba So You Could Dress Like This?* and continuing through two novels, 1996's *Memory Mambo* and 2001's *Days of Awe*. Obejas was born in Cuba in 1956, a few years before the revolution, which she and her family fled by boat in 1962; they settled rather improbably in the midwestern United States, landing eventually in Chicago, where Obejas mostly grew up and where much of her fiction is set. Obejas has for good reason earned a great deal of critical praise and scholarly attention; she rose to prominence a bit too late to earn explicit, sustained discussion in Maria Cristina García's discussion of Cuban-diasporic writers in *Havana USA* (1996), but her work figures quite prominently in two more recent and equally important studies by Isabel Alvarez-Borland and Pamela Maria Smorkaloff. These two critics in turn figure prominently in my more general discussion of Cuban/American/diasporic studies (see the next section of this introduction), but both of their studies appeared well before the publication of Obejas's *Days of Awe*, which is the text I want to address most directly here.

Even more than Albita's glancing references to the Cuban/Jewish analogy that establishes in part the "diasporic" quality of the postrevolutionary, off-island Cuban experience, Obejas in her second novel makes the Cuban/Jewish association work more productively and on both metaphoric and even metonymic levels. Indeed, the narrative is primarily devoted to narrator/protagonist Alejandra San José's discovery of her own family's hidden Jewish patrimony. But even before she has "Ale," as she's called, arrive at the full realization of that legacy, Obejas has her make a number of foreshadowing observations about the historical and conceptual logic of the initially mostly metaphorical correspondence. "Other Latin Americans and some Americans who've had contact with Cubans," Obejas has Ale inform her readers, "call us the Jews of the Caribbean . . . a phrase," she goes on, that "has a familiar currency in exile"(104). Although Ale explains that the comparison can operate by turns as praise and as criticism, she offers as part of her analysis something like a vernacular version of the criteria that James Clifford (quoting William Safran) offered in *Routes* for determining the diasporic status of any group in question.

The complex play of the general and the local, of the universal and the particular, in Ale's extended meditation of the question of diaspora merits the following long quotation:

> When we are called the Jews of the Caribbean, it's almost an accident that, like Jews, we are a people in diaspora and that, like Jews, we are a people concerned with questions and answers and the temperament of a god that could make us suffer, like Job, so inexplicably and capriciously. . . . Growing up in Rogers Park, where a great many doors sprouted mezuzahs and the local Jewish community center kept up a steady stream of activities, I found other commonalities: Cubans and Jews both had families in which people had peculiar accents, both cooked funny foods, both were obsessed with a country in the Third

World, both lived lives in the subjunctive, and both, quite frankly, thought they were the chosen people. In Rogers Park—in spite of the pockets of Asians, recently arrived Africans, and miscellaneous refugees from Central America and Eastern Europe—I was so surrounded by Jewish culture and life that I grew to believe Thanksgiving was the fall equivalent of Pesaj.

Of course, the other process that Obejas narrates here is the deepening and maturing of Ale's own diasporic consciousness; although she may begin by observing in rather childish terms similarities in "peculiar accents" and "funny foods," by the end of even just this passage she starts to awaken to a more fully-informed "Third World" consciousness that at least promises finally to see, even in the local cultural contours of her childhood home, the qualities of a new world (dis)order defined more by the heterogeneous confluence and contact among multiple diasporas than by any single and simple national or identitarian categorical term.

The most evocative logical tension in Ale's formulation of what some might call the "Jew-ban" analogy, however, hangs suspended between, on the one hand, the profoundly unstable conditionality of the diasporic experience (of what she calls "lives lived in the subjunctive") and the certainty that presumably comes with the conviction of being "the chosen people." That logical tension extends rather readily beyond logic to the oftentimes equally demanding protocols of grammar (the subjunctive being, for example, a far weaker and more rarely used verb tense in English than in Spanish) and of narrative (and especially of a diasporic narrative that, like Obejas's, knows itself to offer some comment on, if not compensation for, the disruption if not utter failure of some national-historical narrative to maintain its promised, and presumed, claims to unity and to coherence.) If, as scholars as various as Louie Pérez Jr., Emilio Bejel, and Doris Sommer have established, the effort to forge a Cuban national identity has since the nineteenth century acquired some part of its power and its efficacy from its allegorical inscription in some very influential narratives of fulfilled and redemptive heterosexual union, which Sommer has famously called "foundational fictions," then I would like, especially with Obejas's help here, to argue that these practices extend into the spaces and phases of even twenty-first century Cuban-diasporic and (as part of that) Cuban American experience, in the form of confoundational fictions like *Days of Awe*.

The confounding of the Cuban national narrative, in the hands of a writer as supple and dextrous as Obejas, can take many simultaneous and related forms, but here I will take her cue and emphasize at once the historical (not so much in the sense that the 1959 revolution and consequent initial exodus confounded expectations of a more coherent national narrative, but in the sense that the equally unexpected *longue durée* of the exile and diasporic experiences has compelled the imagining of post- and transnational narratives as potentially more viable and durable into a future that, as time passes, shows little sign of waning); the cultural (as, for example, two figures as different yet complementary as Albita and Obejas demonstrate, in the work I discuss here, about what doing cultural work in some diasporic-subjunctive "tense" might mean, especially for whatever trace of post-national *cubanidad* might hope not only to remain, or survive, but actually to thrive beyond any given present moment); and the sexual (especially with respect to how not only women but queer women artists imagine contributing, both imaginatively and practically, to that future). In her 1992 novel, *Dreaming in Cuban*, Cristina García, Obejas's sister-novelist and fellow chronicler of Cuban-diasporic experience, has her protagonist Pilar Puente observe that, because of all the lies told to bolster either side of the exile/revolutionary divide since 1959, "There is only [her] imagination where [Cuba's] history should be"(138). This is certainly one of the most quoted lines, not only in García's work but also in Cuban American literature more generally; and although García attributes it to a young woman painter coming to terms with her own Cuban American identity in the 1970s (García's narrative culminates with the events leading up to the 1980 Mariel boatlift), it has an equally powerful resonance in the period of, and following, the novel's publication. Its appearance in 1992 arguably positions García's work as the first major piece of Cuban American literature to appear, and to begin to define, the post–Cold War off-island, Cuban-diasporic, and Cuban American experience;

it also, and just as powerfully, poses the most important challenge to off-island Cuban cultural work (and to those who produce it) to appear after it, thus including the work of Albita, Obejas, and most of the other writers and artists who concern me here.

Obejas, I would argue, responds most directly to that challenge in just as evocative a passage from *Days of Awe;* in it, Ale suspends her ongoing narrative of her accelerating discovery of the extent of her family's Jewish roots to relate an exchange between herself and her parents concerning a dream her father has around the time he learns that his mother, who remained in Cuba, has died. As Ale tells it, the significant features of the dream are as follows:

> At about this time, my father began to have dreams about a wounded angel . . . [which first appears to him] in Havana . . . as a black shadow [that] dropped from the sky . . . [and which he first] thought was a bomb of some sort, except that . . . it left a residue of sensation, like a rush of feathers fanning his face. When he looked over the balcony, however, it was . . . a badly battered angel that lay on the ground . . . [and that,] neither male nor female by his estimation, had bloodlessly torn a wing, its clean white bones protruding from its shoulders . . . In my father's dream, the Havana street kids . . . stuffed the bone in and patched the wing by tearing pieces of their own clothing. When the angel finally came to, cradled in the arms of the urchins, its face was as dirty and innocent as theirs . . . In his dream, my father threw the angel a rope down from our balcony, but when the creature finally reached our apartment and tried to fly from there, its wings sputtered and it fell into the panicky crowds. The angel then picked itself back up, wiped its face with an arm that now sported a wristwatch, and disappeared into the tumult, where the cops were swatting people with billy clubs, and the kids went back to playing ball (213–14).

There is certainly no shortage of feathered androgynes appearing across twentieth-century writing in moments, and passages, of powerful historical resonance, from Yeats and Benjamin to Tony Kushner, and although Obejas is clearly drawing deeply and widely from this very rich cultural and critical vein, I'm less interested in what we might call the "constative" (although they're indisputably relevant) and more with the "performative" dimensions of the scene she dramatizes around the iterations, reiterations, and interpretations of this dream. "My father," Ale goes on to tell us, "did not have this dream once but many times," and together her parents "pondered" over it "for weeks and weeks, each consulting their own gods . . . until they finally determined that the dream was a sign of approbation," primarily for having left Cuba (214). " 'The angel is us,'" Ale's mother declares, "irreparably wounded because we left our country,'" and, her father joins in, "it disappears into the unruly crowd—which is the United States . . . the way that we are also becoming a part of the fabric here, in spite of our injuries.'" Ale, however, insists on disrupting this scene of relatively easy collaboration and consensus-building between her parents, asking, "But doesn't the angel disappear into Cuba, into a Cuban crowd?" which provokes in turn the following paternal admonition: "Well, yes . . . but it is important, Alejandra, not to translate things too literally" (214).

Several things bear noting at once about this scene: first, although Obejas stages it in part to pit opposing anxieties about historical "disappearance" on the part of Ale and her parents, in neither case can that anxiety be reduced to the mere conventions of immigrant anxiety over assimilation into the dominant, in their case overwhelming, host culture. Rather, her parents evince a fear of an even more profound surrender of their exilic hopes of return ("it can't be that the crowd is Cuban," her mother insists to close out the scene, "because, though we are Cuban, we can't return, even if we wanted to" [214]) occasioning a more traumatizing experience of historical "disappearance" while Ale herself, swept up as she becomes in her own fascinated obsession with what she uncovers of her family's buried history, risks losing herself completely to the pull of a past that threatens to shake just as profoundly her existing, and fundamental, sense of her own identity. Second, it matters that this moment of family crisis occurs not just through what Ale half-jokingly calls "one of my first and last excursions into the realms of prophecy" but as a scene of conflicting translations and interpretations of a confoundedly enigmatic dream text; as part of the larger allegorical operation

of Obejas's text, it is important to note here too that while Ale's father
pursues a career in the United States as a literary translator, his
daughter half follows him by working once she grows up as an inter-
preter for diplomatic and commercial delegations to Cuba and the
rest of Latin America.

Finally, I want to argue that if this anecdote about Ale's father's
dream also functions as a pause in the larger unfolding of her narrative, it is a powerfully pregnant pause, and pregnant, specifically, with
all the potential and the paradoxical promise of exilic, diasporic desire, and hope. In this scene Ale collaborates with, even as she deviates
from, her parents' efforts to imagine themselves into some possible
future; "all adolescence" still in the moment in her life when the inci-
dent occurs, Ale still has a hand in helping her parents imagine together some perpetuation of themselves into some meaningful
future. To this extent, what ultimately matters more than their Cuban
or American identity is the fact that the crowd into which they see
themselves disappearing consists primarily of children:

> "The angel comes from the crowd and then disappears into it,"
> said my mother.
> "No, it falls from the sky," I said, all adolescence.
> "Yes, yes, but then it's with the children, who are part of the
> crowd, and it returns to the crowd," my mother insisted, an-
> noyed with me.

This annoyance reflects in part Ale's relatively closer identification
with her father, but it does not at any point develop beyond fairly
modest forms of alienation in her general relationship with her
mother; indeed, generally speaking, Ale enjoys a genuine and positive
bond with both her parents, one that survives the many and sometimes serious points of contention between them. And it is in this
bond that Obejas grounds not only her own inspiration but also her
optimism for what that "angel" might mean to a community of readers that, beyond Ale, her family, and even Obejas herself, might have
to come to some alternative hermeneutics than the one(s) that have
conventionally and traditionally dominated narratives (fictional and
otherwise, allegorical and otherwise) with designs on either the for-

mation or reformation of national identity or national history as such. Indeed, what Obejas's evocative micro-narrative-as-dream-text seems to signal instead is the need among all such readers to fashion alternative critical approaches, especially ones willing not just to tolerate but to embrace the possibility that what will remain of the national in much literary, and perhaps especially novelistic, utterance to come (and especially from writers representing diasporic and otherwise extraterritorial communities) will be traces, ruins at best, embodied in the scene just explicated by the injured, grounded, disappearing angel who promises everything and guarantees nothing, about what it can or should mean, and to whom, if the questions posed to it, and of it, persist in privileging, to the cost of everything else, identitarian anxieties, whether about nation, culture, language, gender, or sexuality.

Diasporizing Cuban America (n Studies)

I begin this final section with the following rather telling passage from *Havana USA,* historian Maria Cristina García's 1996 study, because of the alternative rationale it offers me for reading off-island Cuban experience diasporically. "A discussion of Cuban exile and Cuban American writers," García tells us:

> requires looking beyond south Florida. While some authors live among their compatriots in Miami, others have chosen to live elsewhere—some to avoid the petty intrigue and squabbling of exile politics, others because they have academic appointments in colleges and universities around the country. Still others prefer to live in vital cultural centers like New York, Los Angeles, Paris, Rome, Madrid or London, where networks of artists and writers offer support and inspiration . . . Miami [nevertheless] serves [them] as both a mirror and a lightning-rod: reflecting the best and the worst of Cuban culture, it both attracts and repels them.[17]

As the subtitle of her book makes clear, and as I have already observed once in an earlier footnote to this discussion, the idea of describing off-island, even if just U.S.-based, Cuban experience as "diasporic" never seems to occur to García. And yet she finds herself obligated in the last full chapter of her book to cast a rather widely dispersed glance, well beyond the geographic limits defining the rest of her study, to say anything at all about the intellectual and expressive accomplishments of off-island Cubans, especially of their critical and creative contributions to our greater understanding of that experience. She primarily attributes this phenomenon to a series of "choices," which she in turn attributes to this population, and although most of the factors she lists as influencing these choices have some validity, none really presents itself as so compelling as to do adequate justice to such a striking, and important, historical fact.

The problem begins, of course, with García's rather diplomatic representation of South Florida "exile politics" as merely "petty," given to "intrigue" and "squabbling," as though she were indeed only talking about the plot of a *telenovela,* or the latest episode in some ongoing narrative of family discord. But given García's own discussions of the intense hostility, even violence, with which some in the exile community can and do respond to cultural work that suggests any openness to any political position with regard to Cuba other than their own, it's not surprising that so alarmingly high a proportion of writers, artists, and other off-island intellectuals of Cuban descent know that they take their careers, in some cases even their lives, in their own hands if they dare to produce and to circulate their work directly to that audience. Beyond all the issues regarding availability of "academic appointments" and resources in relatively more "vital cultural centers," why would any self-respecting and self-protective artist or writer want to subject himself or herself to the kind of treatment that community inflicted on the playwright Dolores Prida in 1986, on Nelson Mandela in 1990, or that still, as García tells us in her conclusion, promotes a "climate of censorship" where all who "support Fidel Castro . . . or who favor tolerance and dialogue are branded *comunistas* and suffer discrimination, and sometimes even verbal and physical abuse"?[18] Ann Marie Bardach's *Cuba Confidential,* published six years after García's study, not only confirms that little actually changed, well into the first decade of the new century, in the attitudes of this still-influential element in the exile community, but also makes clear just how serious especially the threats of "physical abuse" on the part of representative exiles must be taken. This turn to the diasporic, whether explicitly named as such or not, in García's otherwise laudable attempt to include some coverage of the cultural dimensions of off-island Cuban experience in her study, does seem to signal an important critical and discursive shift in what Cuban American cultural studies work emerges in North America after 1996. As I suggested a bit earlier in this introduction, part of this shift can be explained by the effect that the so-called end of the Cold War has had on the way off-island Cuban experience has been available to reconstrual outside the Cold War–inflected rubric of "Revolution" and (mostly if not exclusively Miamian) "Exile." In addition, the simultaneously geographical and generational dispersal of writers and artists that García maps in the passage opening this section has only been reinforced, and further complicated, in and by the generation of writers and artists emerging since the publication of *Havana USA*. Of the writers who chiefly concern me in this study, only the novelist Cristina García (no relation to the historian) receives any mention in García's *Havana USA,* and that is a brief acknowledgment of the impressive critical success of the latter García's 1992 novel, *Dreaming in Cuban*. In addition to the New York–bred, LA-based García (who since 1992 has published among other titles two additional major novels, 1996's *The Agüero Sisters* and 2003's *Monkey Hunting*), I will devote significant attention in this book to the poet Rafael Campo (New Jersey–bred, Boston-based, and author since the mid-1990s of four major collections of poetry as well as an equally important memoir) and to the playwright Eduardo Machado (LA-bred, New York–based, already known by the early 1990s for his impressive, ambitious four-part cycle, *The Floating Island Plays*, and author of a growing list of theatrical titles, most recently 2003's *The Cook* and 2005's *Kissing Fidel*). The more-or-less simultaneous emergence of at least this trio of writers, each of whom has enjoyed considerable critical and even commercial success, thus compels the current study to look beyond not only the discourse of exile, but even some still-active, proto-national discourse of hyphenated Cuban American hybridity, and to interrogate further what the still-emerging

discourse of diaspora might offer us in our attempts to more fully
and more adequately understand what we take to be the ongoing
trajectory of off-island, mostly U.S.-based experience on the part of
persons and populations still willing to claim for themselves some
meaningful relationship to Cuba and to *cubanidad*.

What, I want to ask here, should be the fate of Cuban-diasporic
thinking and the Cuban-diasporic study it might produce, in this be-
wilderingly accelerating historical trajectory away from and against
the originating national term according to which it persists in naming itself? This seems to me as good a time (and a place?) as any to ask
this question, if only because 2004 marked a decade since the 1994
publication of Gustavo Pérez-Firmat's very influential and somewhat
controversial study, *Life on the Hyphen: The Cuban-American Way*.[19]
A collection of ingenious cultural studies dissections of various
modes of Cuban American cultural production, Pérez-Firmat's argument in that book went quite directly against the political grain of
much of U.S. Latino studies at the time (and perhaps still today) by
actively and explicitly celebrating what he calls Cuban American culture's "'appositional' rather than oppositional" relation to mainstream U.S. culture, a relation, in his terms, "defined more by
contiguity than conflict" and therefore more accurately representative of "the Cuban experience in this country, lives lived in collusion
rather than collision"(Pérez-Firmat, 6). Although Pérez-Firmat's argument couldn't strictly speaking be called assimilationist, it lent
itself easily to such a reading; beyond that, it was unabashedly
Miami-centric, and just as fixated on the cultural work of what we
now generally call the one-and-a-half generation of Cubans, Gloria
Estefan being perhaps the most famous of them, who were born in
Cuba but mostly raised in the United States, "too young," therefore,
"to be Cuban and too old to be American" (Pérez-Firmat, 6).

Perhaps the most troubling aspect of *Life on the Hyphen*, however,
was its claim not only to define, but also to restrict to only one legitimate mode, what Pérez-Firmat wanted to call the Cuban American
"way," as though that larger (arguably Cuban-diasporic) community
could have all of its experiences, and especially its positive cultural
achievements, subsumed into those of just one generation, no matter

how influential, situated in just one community, no matter how siz-able, and how loud. Pérez-Firmat's work also set the stage for at least one other important trend in what I can only ambivalently call the still-emerging field of Cuban American studies, and that is its being characteristically located in, and practiced by specialists in, Latin American or even romance language studies rather than in depart-ments of English or American studies. Especially in the various fields of literary studies, what books have appeared in the ten years since *Life on the Hyphen* that treat Anglophone Cuban American literature and culture with any degree of seriousness and depth have mostly come from Latin Americanists or scholars housed in departments of Spanish or romance languages.

Two such prominent studies are Pamela Maria Smorkaloff's *Cuban Writers On and Off the Island* and Isabel Alvarez-Borland's *Cuban-American Literature of Exile*. Both these scholars treat literary production by U.S.-based Anglophone writers of Cuban descent as primarily if not exclusively derived from a literary tradition emanat-ing from Cuba and from Cuban Spanish; this is in part understand-able, given that both teach in Spanish departments, but their works nevertheless do tend at least to take for granted, if not in fact to natu-ralize, a literary and cultural genealogy for writers like Achy Obejas and her fellow novelist Elías Miguel Muñoz that mostly sees their work as meaningful as a function of their relationships to, say, canon-ical Hispanophone Cuban novelists like Alejo Carpentier or José Lezama Lima, or to the larger Cuban national and political histories within which Smorkaloff and Alvarez-Borland would like to feel in-cluded, even as Cuban exiles, themselves. In some ways I see the work I am embarking on here as in part a completion or supplementation rather than a correction of the work done by scholars preceding me in the field; but I don't expect or want simply to "Americanize" more fully the contexts in which any of the Cuban American writers I study are read. In other words, I'm not interested in merely showing that a novelist like Cristina García owes as much to, say, Toni Morrison or Wallace Stevens as she does to Reinaldo Arenas or Alejo Carpentier, or that a poet like Rafael Campo may owe more to Thom Gunn or to William Carlos Williams than to José Martí.

Significantly, both Smorkaloff and Alvarez-Borland take recourse to the rhetoric of diaspora as they develop their analyses. For Smorkaloff, the term helps her name the group of texts by off-island Cuban writers that she wants to include in what she mostly calls a strictly "Cuban" literary tradition. To this extent "diaspora" allows her to name something other than exile and therefore to include a writer like Obejas who, although Cuban born, grew up stateside (in Chicago), and who appears to identify against her parents' "exile-generation" politics and values and with something closer to the Cuban American identity of the permanent immigrant. It also allows her to include non-U.S.-based writers like the novelist Zoé Valdés, who defected from Cuba in the 1990s and who has based herself in Paris ever since. Curiously, Smorkaloff opposes "diaspora" not to "exile" but to the more conventional literary-critical term "canon," arguing mostly implicitly that "canonicity" is something one only bestows on texts in the course of building a national, and a nationalist, literary tradition. Diasporic writers are therefore not only physically excluded but actually logically constituted as the outside of the operations of national cultural "canonical" formation. But in Smorkaloff's hands this opposition cannot logically hold; "canon" and "diaspora" ultimately join rather than disjoin the links in the chain of a Cuban-national literary lineage that acknowledges but does not surrender to the break occasioned by the departure not only of so many Cubans (and therefore so much of Cuba) from the island but also of so much "Cuban" writing to languages other than Spanish.

Alvarez-Borland's recourse to the rhetoric of diaspora is no less limiting; she often refers to what she calls "the 1959 diaspora," apparently as a way to give the off-island consequences of the events of that year some equal status to what we usually invoke as "the 1959 revolution." The phrase also helps her name the general extraterritorial post-1959 Cuban experience as something other than "the exile," which would perhaps raise too many distracting political specters to allow her to do the critical work she wants to do. Although Alvarez-Borland, as the title of her book suggests, keeps her sights trained on exclusively U.S.-based Cuban explorations of the theme of exile, she, like Smorkaloff, insists on broadening her focus to include non-

Miami-based writers. Unlike Smorkaloff, however, the term "diaspora" doesn't appear to operate much beyond its general, historically descriptive function for her; thus although both writers deploy the rhetoric of diaspora in their work, with some important differences it mostly contributes to what I would call a mostly compensatory, quasi-nationalist, rather than critical postnationalist, transnationalist, or certainly genuinely "diasporic" project.

Rather than attempt either to police, correct, or discredit the valuable work done by Pérez-Firmat, Smorkaloff, Alvarez-Borland, and others to trace something of a continuation of a Cuban literary and cultural tradition to various of its postrevolutionary, off-island extensions, I hope instead merely to note the limitations and gaps in their work in order to both supplement and complement it. Although I acknowledge that critical supplementation of this sort often also aspires to a supplanting of the work it criticizes, I do not offer my work in these pages as an improved and obviating substitute for it so much as an attempt to augment the knowledge it's begun to produce. Without doing so in any kind of overweaning, programmatic way, what I actually hope to do here is mark the trajectory from "diaspora," the first word in the title of this introduction, to "America," the chief organizing term in the book's title. I hope in turn that the readings I offer here (of work by mostly postrevolutionary, off-island, U.S.-based, and Anglophone writers and artists of Cuban descent) will work not as another compensatory exercise in national(ist) canon building for a tradition rendered necessarily manqué by the 1959 revolution and its many scattered consequences, and instead as an example of how work that consciously situates itself in a time of bewildering and accelerating political, economic, and cultural change might still want to think about the vestiges of the national and the vestiges of the cultural (especially the literary) as they haunt what remains of a "Cuban" situation in (North) America.

To this extent, I do not, as a practitioner in the disciplines of literary and cultural studies with primary ties to the fields of contemporary Anglophone literatures, as well as American and U.S. Latino studies, offer my work as better suited but as equally legitimately suited as my predecessors' in Spanish and Latin American Studies departments to

study the topics in which we all share an intense, sincere, and hopefully *critical* interest. And by no means do I suggest, in staking a disciplinary claim to this material, that I am substituting either English
for Spanish, or America for Cuba, as the more salient categories
under whose aegis such a study should be conducted. Indeed, I don't
even read the national terms as conceptual equivalents to the extent
that "Cuba," all recent critical work that invokes the term notwithstanding, still mostly conjures the specter of a coherence and even
coterminousness among national, cultural, and historical registers of
whatever one wants to qualify as "Cuban." "America," especially as invoked by many currently practicing Americanists across and within a
variety of disciplines, is often made to name exactly the opposite, that
is, the set of conditions that mostly disables any and all such invocations of nationalist coherence on the part of not only traditional na-
tivist (North) Americans, but also of all other *othered* "Americans,"
whether or not they try to assimilate into a coherent America, the
(past and future) impossibility of which their very presence constitutes the most eloquent and compelling testimony.

PART I

BODIES OF,
BODIES IN EVIDENCE

Chapter 1

Pleasure's Exile: Reinaldo Arenas's Last Writing

*In one of my first statements after leaving Cuba I had
declared that "the difference between the communist
and capitalist systems is that, although both give you a
kick in the ass, in the communist system you have to
applaud, while in the capitalist system you can scream.
And I came here to scream.*

—Reinaldo Arenas

Outside prevailing constructions of nationality organized around the
native and the immigrant, there is the exile. To the extent that Cuban
American and Cuban-exile writing of the last generation can be said
to have fashioned a voice for itself in the larger contexts of main-
stream- and immigrant-American literature, it has nevertheless retained in its own internalized dialectic a profoundly imbedded
tendency toward self-marginalization and self-alienation. This is
nowhere more apparent than in the body of work produced by
Reinaldo Arenas in the decade of exile he spent in the United States
between his expulsion from Cuba in the 1980 Mariel boatlift and his
1990 suicide during the last stages of his bout with AIDS. Arenas's
work, more than that of any other Cuban writer in America, defines
the role of a literary production caught in the pre-"Special Period,"
that moment of historical and cultural suspension between the so-
called end of the Cold War in most of the world and the tenacious

grip of Castro's vestigial, if not quite spectral, Marxism on Cuba's and Cuban America's political life, a grip that persists even into the twenty-first century.

Particularly in his autobiography, 1992's *Antes que Anochezca* (translated by Dolores Koch and published in 1993 as *Before Night Falls*, which also served as the basis for director Julian Schnabel's very well-received 2000 film) and his less successful "first" American novel, 1989's *El Portero* (also translated by Koch and published as *The Doorman* in 1991),[1] Arenas's writing grapples with the simultaneous transition from one cultural and economic environment to another, from one prevailing conception of production and consumption, of labor and pleasure, to its arguably radical opposite. This chapter charts this transition, with special attention to its "erotics" because these practices transpire in and through that most difficult space of intersection between constructions of simultaneously sexual and political subjects, an intersection that marks in the space of the Cuban-exile imagination an aporetic point in its negotiation of especially male Cuban identity as at once masculine, virile, and rigidly anti-Marxist with the stark reality of Arenas's heroic, defiant, and fluid effeminacy.

There is always a temptation of reading a culture whose prevailing mythologies have so profoundly an oedipal cast primarily through Freudian and post-Freudian psychoanalytic categories.[2] That approach will be unavoidable here as well. Although this chapter will give privileged focus to the more "material" effects of Arenas's encounter with the doubled, split history of his people(s), there will be some occasion to analyze the symbolic construction of Cuban political reality as a function of a quasi-oedipal struggle between the hysterically, murderously hated Fidel, *el hombre, él,* and *Cuba bella, la patria,* the feminine-gendered fatherland to whom Cuban exiles consecrate their deepest loyalty, their most profound fidelity. This will, however, serve as one approach among others in my analysis of Arenas's explicitly literary interrogation of the political stakes involved in the emergence of a definitive literary voice for the Cuban/exile nation(s), especially as it reached a certain level of establishment and consolidation, at least in 1980s Miami. Putting it another way, I hope that asking the question of textual pleasure, as a function of both masculine and feminine, normative and queer sexual/textual praxes, in both semiotic and other terms, will lead us back to more direct political questions of what kind of labor (and by whom) produces politically efficacious forms of pleasure (and for whom).

The Doorman, *the Exile, and Threshold Experiences*

Arenas completed *The Doorman* just as he was falling ill but before his diagnosis, and in this sense the novel stands as a curious "last" text, Arenas's last major work of fiction before his imagination takes on the intense purgatorial pitch, the queerly undead tonality of his writing under the unequivocal sentence of death. Ironically, however, *The Doorman* shares with the later chapters of the autobiography, which were written after the diagnosis and well into the "progress" of his illness, Arenas's hyperbolic vision of freedom, a vision that never lost its appreciation for both abandon and abundance. In general Arenas's excesses have always seemed to me closer to Jonathan Swift's than to Gabriel García Márquez's, to whom he might be said to bear a more obvious resemblance.[3] He "screams," and laughs, from a position whose complexity, one might say whose impossibility, requires the kind of textual self-immolation one finds in Swift at his most perverse. The figure of Juan, the doorman himself, recalls the figure of the exiled writer for which Swift has traditionally served as a chief paradigm. Stationed at/on a threshold or border, Juan ministers to travelers, ferrying them from one point to another in a journey in which he plays an exclusively instrumental role. The travelers in this case, however, are only symbolically migratory; they are the New York apartment dwellers living in Juan's building, making their routine daily journeys between work and home, between the public world and the private fantasy spaces of their respective cubicles. The travelers are therefore symbolically island dwellers, ensconced in their isolated cells, but daily called to the mainland of collective experience; they recall the army of solipsistic projectors in Swift's Academy of Lagado on (perhaps not coincidentally) Gulliver's floating island of Laputa.

To this extent the door itself functions symbolically as a conduit or channel, connoting in at least the Cuban imagination *el charco*, the watery passage or "puddle" between Cuba and Florida. In Spanish *la puerta* will always echo *el puerto*, the port, the space of both hopeful departure and safe arrival at the beginning and end of the journey. The doorman is in turn defined according (we might say *reduced*) to the object with/on which he labors, at the same time that that object has only the most tenuous relationship to objecthood. The door is also the eye, the paradigmatic "door" of perception. Thus to have one's protagonist work as a doorman also allows him to work as the paradigmatic subject in a narrative structure, to stand for the subject who works on/processes objects, and others, through its Kantian categories. The door is thus both the doorman's thing and a no-thing, at once solid and empty, an obstruction and a space of passage. As such it *is* text, if it is possible to say this; perhaps it is more apt to say the door performs textuality, or, more simply, *texts*, transitively and not. In either or both cases a symbol of promiscuity to be sure, the door allegorizes the promiscuity of the sign, of any symbol, that is, in the hands of a fertile artistic imagination.

Like a doorman keeping vigilant watch on a threshold, in the constant state of having threshold experiences, Arenas thus writes both in and out of the experience of exile. His name suggests that even symbolically, as well as in more literal ways, he was cursed (implicitly by his mother, who named him) with having to anchor his experience to a shifting surface of sand, between the border-space of the shore, between earth and sea, but also in the arena, the *arenal*, the centralized, localized space of spectacle and performance. It is (t)here that Reinaldo enjoys his uneasy, precarious rein; it is (t)here that "she" is most *la reina*, the queen, of both the arena and the shore. This play with the unmappable space of the border or threshold extends to the anachronistic structure and frame of the two texts that concern us here.

Later in this discussion I will have occasion to analyze the last chapters of the autobiography, where Arenas inscribes the dissolution of his last years in the dissolution of reason and sense, a surrender to the forces beyond order that had always governed his life. These include "madness," "witchcraft," and "dreams," terms that serve as titles to some of the later chapters. The embodiment of madness is his lifelong friend Lázaro Gómez, who also served as the inspiration for the

title character of *The Doorman*. Lázaro served as the sole witness to
Arenas's own past; as such, his occasional bouts with mental instability and his limited education reinforced the quality of childlike innocence necessary to establish a link with childhood itself.[4] The sense of
brotherly tenderness that Arenas felt for his friend recalls the love of
the young narrator of *Celestino antes del alba*, Arenas's first novel, for
his visionary, poetic cousin. And in the later novel, Juan the doorman, described as "a young man who was dying of grief," suffers from
the doubled disenchantment of having been forced to leave his own
childhood behind in emigrating to the United States, and in having to
confront a culture profoundly alienated from its own innocence, its
own authentic past or history.[5]

The "million" narrators of *The Doorman*, the Cuban-exile community speaking, stereotypically perhaps, with one voice, sum up
Juan's predicament this way:

> Ten years ago Juan had fled his native Cuba in a boat, and set-
> tled in the United States. He was seventeen then, and his entire
> past life had been left behind: humiliations and warm beaches,
> fierce enemies and loving friends whom the very persecutions
> had made even more special. Left behind was slavery, but the
> complicity of night as well, and cities made to the measure of
> his restlessness; unbounded horror, but also a human quality, a
> state of mind, a sense of brotherhood in the face of terror—all
> things that, just like his own way of being, were alien here.[6]

Although the choice of an (ironically) univocal communal voice raises
its own aesthetic and philosophical questions of subjectivity and the
force of ideological group-think, in Arenas's hands these questions are
always directed back toward the individual and the limits of the collective to "make something" of him. This is clear, for example, in the
limited sympathy with which the narrative bloc treats its subject:

> But we, too (and there are a million of us), left all that behind;
> and yet we are not dying of grief . . . so hopelessly as this young
> man. . . . He arrived in the United States an unskilled laborer,

like most of us, just one more person escaping from Cuba. He
needed to learn, just as we did, the value of things, the high
price one must pay for a stable life: a well-paying job, an apartment, a car, vacations, and finally one's own house, preferably
near the ocean.[7]

The narrative chorus's summation of Juan as "just one more" of the
million they comprise must, I think, be read doubly; the assessment
absorbs him into the sum at the same time that it singles him out,
makes of him the remnant or remaining one "more" in excess of that
comfortable, completed sum. More than an exemplary narrative of
immigrant success through hard work and the acquisition of real
property, Arenas's impersonation of this community (and the ironic
take on its values suggested in this passage) also undermines the distinction it would place on its own accounting of "value," "price," and
"cost." He leaves open the question of whether the inventory of ac-
quisitions signifies either the material comforts of "a stable life" or
the "high [spiritual] price" one must pay for that life.

What Remains: The Ghost, the Decadent, and the Death of Desire

Like the alienated, ascetic Juan, never far from his threshold, Arenas
himself occupied a perplexed position in the various "economies" into
which he found himself inserted. Both in communist Cuba and late-
capitalist North America, Arenas, as a gay man especially, found himself in excess, existing as the remnant of a corrupt past constructed in
the former case as a holdover of bourgeois decadence, in the latter as a
holdover of aristocratic decadence. In his study *Gays Under the Cuban
Revolution*, Allen Young makes the often-observed point that Cuban
communism simply borrowed from Soviet policy the conviction that
homosexuality (and the decadent sensibility it nurtured) were "'the
product of the decadence of bourgeois society and fascist corruption"
in order to uphold a policy of homosexual persecution that for equally
cynical reasons the homophobic Batista government did not pursue
as comprehensively.[8] The figure of decadent sensibility plays a similarly vestigial role in the classical bourgeois imagination.

Such a figure does make an appearance on *The Doorman*'s stage, but in curiously redoubled form: although Juan himself remains sexually ambiguous, Arenas saves much of his critical commentary on urban gay America for his treatment of the one gay couple in Juan's building, the "Oscar Timeses."[9] The pair has changed their individual names for the one name they share, and in their years together have come "to resemble each other so closely, both in body and in temperament, that they really appear to be the same person." They are, in fact, only distinguished numerically, going as "Oscar Times One and Oscar Times Two." In this and other respects, they inhabit the extremes of assimilation and conformity in *The Doorman*. Their homosexuality, their erotic orientation toward the same, literally reinforces this, and the fact that one of the Oscars hails from Cuba and the other is a Scottish American who ironically has taken his assimilationist cues from his lover casts an even more complex irony over the entire situation. Arenas's attack of North American gay conformity is scathing and organized chiefly around an obsessive pursuit of pleasure, which, in its narcissism and material luxuriance, seemed to the philosophically eroticist Arenas as particularly alienated and debased.[10] As he remarks of their frequently failed sex hunts in Manhattan, the Oscars would often "out of boredom, frustration, habit, or just as a last resort . . . end up sleeping together, but at the moment of reaching climax, instead of pleasure they experienced the frustration of possessing or being possessed by repulsive mirror images of themselves."[11]

This refusal to identify with the already overly identificatory structure of the 1980s-era gay male society he found in the United States exacerbated Arenas's general state of exile; he discovered his chief refuge, understandably enough, in his writing, which for him was always intimately linked with his sexual dispositions. In the autobiography, Arenas makes this connection clear. In Cuban Miami especially, he observes, artists and in particular writers were considered with an odd kind of suspicion: "The sad fact," Arenas tells us, "is that Cuban exiles were not so interested in literature; a writer was looked upon as a strange, abnormal figure."[12] It is impossible not to hear in the Spanish term *anormal* its conventional concomitant, *maricón*, or faggot. What strikes the conventional *machista* Cuban sensibility as culturally suspect immediately also strikes it as sexually suspect. Miami

culture seemed to Arenas a distillation of some of the worst features
of the Cuban character, especially in terms of its sexual politics: "The
typical Cuban machismo has attained alarming proportions in
Miami. I did not want to stay too long in that place, which was like a
caricature of Cuba, the worst of Cuba."[13] It is not surprising, therefore, that Arenas's investments in his writing and in his sexuality so
strongly paralleled each other. Cuba, both at home and in exile,
treated its writers as badly as it treated its queers; indeed, it seemed
not to distinguish the one from the other.[14] Eloquently, emphatically,
Arenas responds to this imposed disappearance with his own form of
transgression through ostentation and excess: he wrote, and fucked,
prolifically, promiscuously, with an abandon that looked, and felt, to
him like freedom.

It is, I think, plausible to characterize the limited aesthetic success
of *The Doorman* as a symptom of what Arenas seemed to feel was the
suffocatingly commodity-obsessed pursuit of happiness (that is,
maximization of pleasure) among all culturally and economically assimilated "Americans," Cuban or not, queer or not. As I have already
noted, each of the hyperinsulated apartment dwellers in *The Doorman*'s Habitrail universe constructs a "private Idaho" for him or herself, each an extension of some idiosyncratic pathology fostered and
buttressed by some elaborately commodified fetish system of both
possessions and beliefs. Anyone familiar with Arenas's pre-exile work
will recognize in *The Doorman* the allegorized struggle of a literary
imagination to break free of the ponderous clutter of simulacra (both
material and conceptual), in order to reaccess the less alienated, mediated relationship with "nature" or "reality" that characterizes the
creative sensibility, and faith, fueling the earlier fiction.

Eco-criture

That the narrative of *The Doorman* should also include a culmination
in the reaccessing of the infinite (here in the exemplary guise of the
sea) also belies the logic of "getting there" via the finite, the particular,
the material. Juan's ultimate success in realizing his vision of liberation comes through a rejection of the social, of the human, and the

reinvention of language in a discourse with animals, with a renatural-
ized, reconstituted nature. Arenas's investment in the power of the
natural is one of the signature elements of all his work. The biographical sources of this relationship are documented in the early chapters of *Before Night Falls*. In his review of the translation, Roberto
González Echevarría sums this up nicely: "To say that Arenas grew up
close to nature," Echevarría observes, "may sound like a cliché, but in
this case the phrase could not be more literal. Among his favorite
childhood pastimes were eating dirt, from which he got a big belly
full of worms, having sex with various animals and playing with mud
in the falling rain."[15] That even his reviewers should take recourse to
clichés and literality to naturalize the language with which they describe Arenas's intense familiarity with the natural speaks to the force
of this bond. There is in all Arenas's writing, then, a radical naturalism that, I would argue, earns that writing the curious status of an
eco-criture.

Juan discovers a method of communicating with the tame domesticated pets of his tenants, and with them he plots a strategy of liberation that ultimately reintegrates him, and them, into a "past" even
more distant than that of lost childhood or cultural history. In this
sense he is a combination of Doctor Doolittle, Gulliver among the
Houyhnhnms, and Noah effecting a new creation, a new nature out
of the ruins of that murdered by decadent, materialist culture. This
culminating vision in *The Doorman* is suggestively apocalyptic in
scope; Juan heads with the animals on a transcontinental and eventually global procession, swelling the ranks of his natural army with all
imaginable creatures and inanimate objects. Arenas leaves Juan at the
conclusion of *The Doorman* on a significant threshold; as they reach
"the equator," the "thunderous stampede" of animals "is deafening."[16]

Ironically, although *The Doorman* should conclude with the silence into which the deafening roar of nature's rebellion relegates us,
it doesn't. The last words of the text are given to two competing sets
of exiles: one the set of a million narrators, who threaten to use the
imminent catastrophe in revenge for their suffering, and the other
the doorman himself, whose vision of nature at play, liberated from
all structure, from all order except for the promiscuous symbolism of

the door, necessarily, perhaps tragically, excludes the very figure of the doorman, whose fate it is to wait, in permanent exile, for no fate at all:

> At the end there would be a door for the dove to enter into her land of dreams . . . A huge door of green branches and creeping vines in perpetual bloom would await the parrot, the squirrel, the cat and the orangutan, so they could play forever. . . . Yes, doors of sunshine, doors of water, doors of earth, doors of flowering vines, doors of ice, . . . tiny doors or immeasurable ones, deeper than the air, more luminous than the sky, would be awaiting the animals to take them to a place where nobody could spy on them through telescopes, or send undercover agents after us. . . . And through these doors everyone, finally, will eagerly rush in.
>
> That is, all except me, the doorman, who on the outside will watch them disappear forever.

The informing wish of Arenas's text returns us to the doorlike space of the metaphor, of language as transfiguration, where the writer, the exile, the excluded attendant upon doors awaits, at once witnessing and enacting the rite of liberation for others.

The last chapters of the autobiography extend the apocalypticism of *The Doorman* even further into super-, one might say hypernaturalism. Lázaro's madness, which became the type for Juan's in the novel, quickly translates into increasingly poetic and powerful images driven by an eroticized feminine principle. Madness and queerness are semantically linked by the correct Spanish usage, and the idiomatic Spanish deviation, of the term *locura;* Arenas had had occasion in the Cuban sections of the autobiography to inventory the four classes of *locas,* of "queens" he had known in Havana. In the New York section, he turns his attention to the relationship between that other archetype of deviant femininity, the witch, and the erotic principle organizing his life. "The world," Arenas insists, "is really full of witches" of various types, whose *reino,* or reign, extends beyond fantasy to reality. Arenas's world is indeed saturated by witchcraft; he not only includes most of the prominent women in his life in this category, but also his mother herself, in whose hyperbolic symbolism the list culminates: "the noble witch, the suffering witch, the witch full of longing and sadness, the most beloved witch in the world: my mother . . . with her broom, always sweeping as if nothing mattered but the symbolic meaning of the act."[17] Arenas writes with the same appreciation of the purely symbolic value of the act; the witch extends even beyond the figure of the mother to contain the gender-transcendent figure of the queen, *la loca* ("Sometimes witches would assume a half-masculine form, which would make them even more sinister"). Although he never explicitly identifies himself as such, the momentum of the passage leads us compellingly to Arenas himself, writing as his mother sweeps, the pen replacing the broom as the material locus of a labor whose production is symbolic, magical, but for that reason no less material.

Before Night Falls: *AIDS and the Possibility of a Pro-Life Suicide*

The autobiography would be incomplete without the suicide note (literally Arenas's "last" writing) to which it so inexorably leads, but most of it was written not only well before his death, but also before the completion of his fictional work. It is preceded by an introduction entitled *El fin* ("The End"), which also came "last" in the chronology of its composition, a text that most directly addresses the issue of the disease that finally destroyed him. "Last words" thus come first, and last, in Arenas's recounting of his life. Time and history work different shifts in both the life and the fiction; in the former Arenas marks the transformation of his literary output by the day of his diagnosis. All his subsequent work operates in the odd, protracted time space, the chronotope, one might say, of the anticipation of the end; this is most pointedly suggested in the title of the autobiography. It is here, in this inverted, paradoxical space, that we can return as well to the question raised by Arenas's attempt, at the end of his life, in the intimate threshold of his own fatal moment, to understand AIDS not metaphorically, but literally. AIDS stood for Arenas emphatically *outside* the register of the natural, as an unnaturally systematic, all-too-humanly perfect death machine whose only plausible source or origin was for him the closet space of state secrecy, of public conspiracy, of obscene activity perpetrated openly by silent "majorities."

Susan Sontag observes in *AIDS and Its Metaphors* the rarity with which "political metaphors" are used "to talk about the body"; "likening the body to a society, liberal or not," Sontag goes on to explain, "is less common than comparisons to other complex, integrated systems, such as a machine or an economic system."[18] Arenas not only provides one such extended comparison in the introduction to the autobiography, he also employs it in the manner that, as Sontag observes later in her essay, reflects AIDS's readily available capacity to "serve as an ideal projection for First World political paranoia," especially in the way that it can stand not only as "the quintessential invader from the Third World," but more so as "any mythological menace."[19] Arenas's own feelings about AIDS, as expressed in the autobiography, suggest something of this paranoia and of the mythological extremes to which it can be carried. At the same time, they remind us of the already mythological cast of the imaginative, ideological, and cultural work done on AIDS by "First World" reactionary liberalism.

To quote Arenas at length:

> the actual nature of AIDS seems to be a state secret . . . as a disease it is different from all others. Diseases are natural phenomena, and everything natural is imperfect and can somehow be fought and overcome. But AIDS is a perfect illness because it is so alien to human nature and has as its function to destroy life in the most cruel and systematic way. Never before has such a formidable calamity affected mankind. Such diabolic perfection makes one ponder the possibility that human beings may have had a hand in its creation.[20]

The suggestion that somehow AIDS began as an orchestrated political conspiracy against marginalized communities is certainly not exclusive to Arenas, but in his hands it takes on a particular eloquence, especially given the context of the triple exile into which AIDS throws him.

Sontag herself observes near the end of *AIDS and Its Metaphors* the connection between late-capitalist hyperconsumerism and a prevailing construction of pleasure that at least superficially informs some of the sexual and cultural practices of the gay male communities of urban America discussed earlier. "One set of messages of the society we live in," Sontag argues, "is: Consume. Grow. Amuse yourselves. The working of this economic system," she continues,

> which has bestowed these unprecedented liberties, most cherished in the form of physical mobility and material prosperity, depends on encouraging people to defy limits. Appetite is *supposed* to be immoderate. The ideology of capitalism makes us all connoisseurs of liberty—of the infinite expansion of possibility. . . . Hardly an invention of the male homosexual subculture, recreational, risk-free sexuality is an inevitable reinvention of the culture of capitalism.[21]

For Arenas, however, "liberty" predicated on either side of the term "connoisseurship," as either a function of the accumulation or collection of goods or of the hyperrefinement of taste, was perhaps descriptive of a "free," but always of a closed, economy on some level of circulation, but it failed to guarantee pleasure as the effect of a necessarily *open* economy. What "liberty" a closed liberal economy could promise its agents rang of liberal dogmatism to Arenas, to which he would persistently oppose the promise of a liberation from all dogmatism.

This is most clearly reflected in several passages critical specifically of totalitarian dogmatism in communist Cuba. These passages, in effect constituting brief asides within the course of his narrating the events of his life in Cuba, resonate through his subsequent experiences in exile. "All dictatorships," he observes at one point, "are sexually repressive and anti-life. All affirmations of life are diametrically opposed to dogmatic regimes";[22] the simultaneously oppressive and repressive practices of a system as orthodoxly homophobic as Castro's translate fairly directly into the practices of all systems of power predicated on exclusion and closure. As Arenas goes on to observe about AIDS in the context of global politics, "all the rulers of the

world, that reactionary class always in power, and the powerful
within any system, must feel grateful to AIDS because a good part of
the marginal population, whose only aspiration is to live and therefore oppose all dogma and political hypocrisy, will be wiped out."[23]
All system, therefore, all dogma takes on in Arenas's thought the
function of *thanatos,* manifests the death drive even as it promises its
"free" but limited menu of pleasures to the world. All such economies
operate under the principle of scarcity, regardless of the wealth they
generate; all such economies restrict, repress, and exclude practices
and pleasures based on the anti-principle, the unthinkable idea of life
as limitlessness, as pure abundance.

Arenas thus recognizes the profound distinction between a chok-
ing totalitarianism (the aggressive intellectual impulse toward totali-
ties) and the infinite, abundant playfulness of language (the fluid,
oceanic fullness of life). His condemnation of all repressive power as
life destroying receives particularly eloquent expression in the nearly
symmetrical treatment Arenas's text gives to the opposed repressions
of the right and the left. Arenas observes, for example, the manner in
which all tyranny murders laughter in his analysis of the Castro
regime's most tragic effect on the once-vital Cuban character:

One of the most nefarious characteristics of tyrannies is that
they take everything too seriously and destroy all sense of
humor. Historically, Cubans have found escape from reality
through satire and mockery, but with the coming of Fidel
Castro the sense of humor gradually disappeared until it became illegal. With it the Cuban people lost one of its few means
of survival; by taking away their laughter, the Revolution took
away from them their deepest sense of the nature of things. Yes,
dictatorships are prudish, pompous, and utterly dreary.[24]

Arenas's own profound, proto-Bakhtinian sense of the philosophical
dimensions of laughter, its ability to inform our sense of "things," extends equally to his critical evaluation the more subtle, but similarly
life-killing, thing-obsessed materialism of Miami Cubans. "In Miami,"
he observes, "the obsession with making things work and being prac-

tical, with making lots of money, sometimes out of the fear of starving, has replaced a sense of life and, above all, of pleasure, adventure,
and irreverence."[25] This disillusionment with the bourgeoisie did not
prevent Arenas from feeling an equally strong alienation from the liberal intellectual left, especially in the academies of North America.[26]

No Conclusions: Pleasure, Politics, and the Art of the Impossible

Arenas's simultaneous and reciprocal condemnation, of both conventional left and right positions, positions *him* more strategically
than ambivalently in the space of politically driven literary and critical discourses, posing against each an alternative critique more accurately representative of Arenas's own politics. Judging from her 1993
essay on Cuban politics and art institutions, "Aesthetics and Foreign
Policy," Laura Kipnis would argue against Arenas's collapsing of all
restrictive cultural regimes. "If culture is seen as central to social reproduction," Kipnis argues, "it seems to follow that . . . in a society
that reproduces itself, in the first instance, politically, as Cuba, artists
are subjected to the terrors and rigors of current political policies"
and thus "in Cuba, where art institutions are by definition political
and politicized, the political meanings of works emerge unmediated,
with more genuine potential to be subversive to reproduction."[27]

Later in the article Kipnis will have occasion to turn to a much earlier essay on Cuban culture by Susan Sontag.[28] Kipnis's response to
what she feels is Sontag's overaestheticized judgment on the failures
of Cuban culture might transfer fairly directly into a response to
Arenas's similar views. Kipnis dismisses Sontag's claim for a "triumph
of 'erotics' over 'hermeneutics,'" arguing that it merely fulfills "the desire for the self: certainty of a subjectivity outside history, a desire for
the immediacy of the unmediated relation, not only to the work of
art, but to all the rest of political and social life, as well."[29] Implicit in
Kipnis's critique of Sontag is a critique of what she terms the subject
of Enlightenment, particularly "the eighteenth-century aesthetic subject"[30] whose intolerance of any critical dialectic had already been
marked by Adorno and Horkheimer.[31] The idea that Sontag's or

Arenas's eroticist critical strategies present little more than the re-
trenchment of the one-note aesthetic subject of the Enlightenment
seems dangerously reductive to me, certainly restricted to the limited
space of an outdated, and never fully efficacious, ideological polarity.

It is *precisely* the fate of art subversive to the revolution that
Arenas's autobiography charts and that his pre-exile work underwent. Although Kipnis concludes that, in a cultural environment as
radically politicized as Cuba's, "the concept of counter-revolutionary
culture . . . does have a reality . . . , whereas the possibility of a truly
political art or a counter-hegemonic art is to a large degree absorbed
by art markets and institutions here," Arenas would counter that
Cuba's cultural bureaucracy only ironically ensured the political
power (especially of art subversive of the revolution) not by absorb-
ing it, that is, at once co-opting it and fostering its life, but by repress-
ing it, indirectly expelling it out of the domestic sphere of cultural
exchange. Arenas was an artist in exile long before his physical expulsion from Cuba. As the history of the composition of his masterwork,
the novel *Otra Vez el Mar,*[32] makes clear, the ideology that cultivates
the political construction of all art also guarantees the disappearance,
via confiscation and destruction, of art construed as politically dangerous, unless it is secreted out of the country like contraband. What
"genuine potential to be subversive to reproduction" such art might
be said to have, at least in theory, in a system where "the political
meanings of works emerge unmediated," seems then profoundly
compromised by the system's own paranoid perception of precisely
that subversive potential.

A more viable analysis of the political function of art, and of the
concomitant experience of a subversive, irreverent, laughing pleasure, can be found in the early 1990s work of Slavoj Žižek. Žižek's
work seems to me to offer the most opportune articulation of precisely this impossible experience of pleasure; in a section of 1991's
Enjoy Your Symptom!: Lacan in Hollywood and Out entitled "The
Subject of Enlightenment,"[33] Žižek explains the persistence of the
monstrous in bourgeois cultural artifacts by declaring, "You cannot
have both meaning and enjoyment." The monstrous, as one embodiment of the limit of meaning or sense, stands then as empty, plastic,
promiscuous form, the "'objective correlative" for Žižek of "the pure

'subject of the Enlightenment,'" which can no longer be "contained" or "bound" by "the texture of symbolic tradition," and that therefore "is a monster which gives body to the surplus that escapes the vicious circle of the mirror relationship." Žižek likens it to both the monstrous and the phantasmatic: "The Phantom," in the Opera or out, "embodies the excess aristocracy has to renounce in order to become integrated into bourgeois society." As such it is "a kind of 'fossil' created by the Enlightenment itself as a distorted index of its inherent antagonism: what was," Žižek goes on to explain, "a sovereign expenditure, a glitter of those in power, an inherent moment of their symbolic status, . . . falls out from the social space whose contours are defined by utilitarian ideology, and is perceived as decadent debauchery epitomized in the bourgeois myth of a corrupted demonic aristocrat."[34] This association is rendered more profoundly ironic by the knowledge that Arenas himself was of the poorest social background, his entry into "decadent," cosmopolitan culture coming at the hands of the very revolution that would consequently persecute him for having taken to it so readily.

In *For They Know Not What They Do*, Žižek provides the theoretical basis for the cultural analysis he presents in *Enjoy Your Symptom!* In this text, also from 1991, Žižek tries to locate the excessive place of Lacanian *jouissance* or Barthean "bliss" in the political imagination, in the political dimensions of the construction of a "subject of Enlightenment." "Where one doesn't (want to) know," Žižek argues, "in the blanks of one's symbolic universe, one enjoys, . . . enjoyment [thereby being] the 'surplus' that comes from our knowledge that our pleasure involves the thrill of entering a forbidden domain—that is to say, that our pleasure involves a certain displeasure"; as such, this inverted construction of the subject's pleasure occasions an extended train of deconstructive moves. Totalitarian social order, Žižek argues, reexternalizes, "outs" one might say, the superego; it occupies, as "the discourse of Stalinist bureaucracy" did, a position which, because it stands for "neutral, 'objective knowledge, . . . a knowledge not subjectivized by means of the intervention . . . of some Master Signifier—is in itself mischievous, enjoying the subject's failure to live up to impossible demands, impregnated by obscenity—in short: super-egotistical."

Thinking in terms of a discourse that, like Castro's, totalizes the

possible by declaring that "The Revolution" defines its practical and
conceptual limits ("Within the Revolution, everything; outside the
Revolution, nothing") one can appreciate the fate of the subject confronted with this looming epi-psychical image; it inflicts on itself what
Žižek calls a "self-torture provoked by the obscene super-egotistical
'law of conscience.'" It is precisely this "super-egotistical imposition
of enjoyment which threatens to overflow our daily life" by thinking
for the subject, and giving the subject no choice but to obey the injunction, "*Carpe diem,* enjoy the day, consume the surplus-enjoyment
procured by your daily suffering," an injunction that in turn becomes
for Žižek "the condensed formula of 'totalitarianism.'" Žižek's theory
thus casts in high relief Arenas's more immediate observations,
quoted earlier, about the "chaste," "anti-vital" character of all "dogmatic
regimes" that force-feed the masses "the surplus-enjoyment procured
by [their] daily suffering" in precisely the inverted, ironic form of a
boredom that saturates everything imaginable.

It is against the murderous boredom of repressive, totalizing systems that Arenas laughs and screams.[35] From the allegory of the
doorman and his door to the witch and her broom, from the metaphoric values that cluster opportunistically around the images of the
madman, *la loca* and the queen, we find ourselves having to conclude
that the limitless expanse of Arenas's imaginative geography is also
always and only the "one" fluid space (more nomadic than monadic)
of the metaphor, of the gesture of translation, of all metamorphosis
in process. This place remains, however, unmappable; it remains the
no-place, the aporetic point, where all opposition dissolves into mere
difference. Aporia does not, however, necessarily translate into atopia
or utopia; what position metaphor and transformational narrative
may be said to occupy in the cultural imagination of a ruiNation as
self-alienated and dispersed as Cuba may be more difficult to map
than to situate. It may stand, for example, for the gaps that currently
exist geographically, politically, and culturally between Cubas and
Cubans and that continue to widen and proliferate, especially as the
once-"Special" period of post–Cold War Cuban American history at-
tenuates itself further into endless indefinition and nonresolution.
It certainly can no longer, however, be adequately positioned on, or

as, the transitional and translational hyphen on which, as Gustavo Pérez-Firmat argued in 1994, Cuban Americans could then be said to most fully live their own conflicted, individual and collective cultural dualities.[36]

Although the narrative of Arenas's life begins with a chapter entitled "Las piedras" (The Stones), in which he recalls his earliest experience, at two, of eating the dirt off the ground of his grandparents' farm, in his final chapter "Los sueños" (The Dreams), he will say that his earliest memory is of a dream in which he is about to be devoured by "an enormous mouth" ("*una boca inconmensurable*" in the Spanish).[37] The consuming incommensurability of these two competing origins, of these two "first" original memories articulates the general indeterminacy of Arenas's life as textualized, of his text as he lived it, but they also speak to competing histories his people have embraced as the incommensurate, originating narratives of his nation. Even at the point of his death, Arenas seems to have known that the darkness into which he was peering was that of the familiar "confusion" between life and what is not life that had always both cursed and blessed both him and his compatriots. Arenas concludes his suicide note, his "last" writing and the last piece of the text that we call his autobiography, in the temporal mode of an impossible "already." Having laid responsibility for his death at the feet of Fidel Castro, and having encouraged Cubans both in and out of exile to continue their struggles for liberty, Arenas cast his suicide in terms of an impossible optimism, in a future certainty only a liberating understanding of the nonrelation of life to death can provide. "Cuba will be free; I already am."[38]

Chapter 2

Docile Bodies, Volatile Texts: Cuban-Exile Prison Writing

> *In Communist countries you have, as Milosz once said,*
> *the captive mind. But what about the captive body? Let*
> *me speak now of sadder, wiser men . . . poets in prison,*
> *captive minds in captive bodies.*
> —Guillermo Cabrera Infante[1]

Empresses of Ice Cream in the Post-Empire

In the oddly twisted dynamics of U.S.–Cuban cultural and political debate(s), especially those arising in the post–Cold War Special Period in Cuba, alternative sexualities and the cultural practices connoted by them came to displace more direct political discussions about the future of the diasporic dissemiNation,[2] also (and still today) called Cuba, but increasingly without any easy correspondence to any one place, or nation, or state. Perhaps the most prominent example of this decade-old debate accompanied the wide distribution and success (in 1994–95 and in the United States) of Cuban director Tomás Gutiérrez Alea's *Strawberry and Chocolate* (1993), a film based on writer Senel Paz's 1991 novella, *El lobo, el bosque, y el hombre nuevo* (*The Wolf, the Forest, and the New Man*).[3] Although the open discussions of the value of homosexual citizens to the revolution in both the film and the story reflected a relaxation of policies and attitudes toward homosexuals in Cuba, the discourse of the "New" Revolutionary "Man" or citizen is actually as old as the 1959 revolution itself, when it cropped up (as I briefly observed in chapter 1), already indebted to an even older Stalinist ideal. Unfortunately, neither Paz's book nor Gutiérrez's film suggested that the concept of the "New Man" was any closer (even a half century later!) to abandoning the values of hypermasculine stoicism and toughness celebrated in the Soviet Union in the 1940s.

The debate to which *Strawberry and Chocolate* nevertheless made such an unprecedented contribution raged on both sides of the Florida Straits, for at least the two decades preceding its release, as a secondary feature of the larger quarrel about Cuban revolutionary politics and their fallout on and off the island. It rose to prominence over those preceding years, beginning with the wide distribution of the 1984 documentary film *Improper Conduct* produced by Spanish cinematographer Nestor Almendros and Orlando Jimenez-Leal,[4] and it has only intensified. With the end of the Cold War, Cuba came to rely increasingly on tourism from Western European states and Canada, whose citizens were then and still are more likely to care about Cuba's treatment of its queer citizens than perhaps official and unofficial representatives of its old communist trading partners did. There, were, of course, also more likely to be potential tourists in these nations who were themselves openly queer and concerned about spending their vacation dollars at Cuban resorts. To this extent, the release of *Strawberry and Chocolate* in the West functioned somewhat as a commercial gesture of goodwill to Cuba's new trading partners; official homophobic policy on the island served as an issue that could see, and show, progress more readily than other complicated political problems Cuba faced, such as maintaining its political and economic autonomy, especially as severe hardships brought on by both Special Period policies and the U.S.-led embargo ensued, and in the face of increasing trade with these overwhelmingly more powerful and wealthy partners.

Indeed, even a decade following its release, *Strawberry and Chocolate* still works as both an attractive tour of the treasures of old Havana and a meditation on the internally, intrinsically related issues of sexual

freedom and freedom of public artistic expression. Its two brief moments of pained self-castigation, the scene in which the artist Germán
destroys his sculptures to protect his control of their exhibition and
the brief mention of the UMAP labor camps for queers, barely
scratch the surface of the deep, complex history of political, cultural,
and individual repression to which they allude. All of this was, of
course, meant to appeal directly, perhaps exclusively, to a metropoli-
tan sensibility in the developed world, an idea confirmed by the film's
more limited exposure, and impact, in the country of its production.

To the extent that *Strawberry and Chocolate* still represents a welcome relaxation of revolutionary Cuba's cultural and sexual policies,
it is matched by the U.S.-based Cuban-exile community's simultaneous embrace of certain openly queer Cuban cultural figures, often
(unfortunately) for similarly politically expedient reasons. The appearance of Almendros's *Improper Conduct* in 1984, for example, arguably did less to challenge the homophobia that the exile community
still shared with its revolutionary sibling than it did to provide a convenient, unambiguous cause to indict Castro on an issue that would
matter to more liberal elements in the United States and the West.
But by the time the generation of *marielitos* came of age in the early
1990s, the exile community found itself directly challenged by the
increasingly visible presence of defiant, uncompromisingly queer
Cubans in their midst. Two prominent examples, both gay men who
died very public deaths from complications directly or indirectly due
to AIDS, were Reinaldo Arenas (the main subject of chapter 1) and
the AIDS activist and media figure Pedro Zamora. Prominent queer
Cubanas like Achy Obejas and Albita (both of whom I discuss at
length in the Introduction) were also just beginning to make their
mark on exile culture at the time.[5] As the continuing visibility of such
figures, both living and deceased, suggests, cultural and political conditions continue to evolve both on the island and in the exile community, and with that evolution, one can argue, Cubans everywhere
find themselves relatively more free to exercise more of their rights as
sexual and cultural (if not as political) citizens.[6] What follows here is
an analysis of how these varying but interimplicated registers of meaningful belonging to supplementary forms of collectivity continue to

inform, and to deform, Cuban experience and anything like the prospect of a viable Cuban future, across any and all spaces that persist in claiming for themselves some meaningful relationship to Cuba.

The Public House of Prison Writing, or New Freedoms for New Citizens

In the course of the 1990s, a number of people, many of them writers by vocation, have published memoirs of their experiences in the political prisons and detention centers of Castro's Cuba. These include Reinaldo Arenas, Heberto Padilla, Armando Valladares, and Ana Rodríguez.[7] Although the primary motive for writing such a memoir is likely to contribute to a historical record of political abuse, on the part of at least Arenas and Padilla, the motive seems to be equally about making a case for the political consequences of art. Indeed, both Padilla's *Self-Portrait of the Other* (1989) and Arenas's *Before Night Falls* (1991) are generically hybrid texts, literary autobiographies primarily, but insistent in their attempts to record political injustices suffered. These memoirs act as well as borderline texts to the extent that they have contributed in part to a transition across literary generations in the exile community that I discussed in detail in the Introduction. Although an entire generation of "immigrant" or "ethnic" Cuban Americans was born and matured to adulthood in the United States since the early 1960s, relatively later arrivals, like Arenas and Padilla, have brought with them a store of memories, which having transpired in a more exclusively Cuban (and revolutionary) space seemed to the more "established" but younger generation of Cuban Americans to be located in the past that their parents hoped to escape by emigrating. Padilla, for example, was detained and forced to declare his "self-criticism" in 1971; Arenas was imprisoned in Havana's Morro Castle in the early 1970s and spent the rest of the decade fleeing state surveillance. Both men left Cuba in 1980 and wrote their memoirs in the course of the next decade. These texts illustrate how, in the temporal matrix of especially Cuban-exile history, political abuses in Cuba belong to a past that always precedes, and necessarily explains, the "present" of exile and immigration.

Although exile has been said to feel like captivity to those who refuse to accept its finality, that is, the inevitability of its conversion into immigration, exile has also certainly been preferable to imprisonment for those who have suffered the latter. Necessarily a choice of nightmares, exile and detention together present a challenge to the subject that may indeed bear in it the traces of undecidability. No one (the conventional argument goes) freely, willingly "chooses" either. One almost always, however (and according to the aesthetic corollary to this "liberal" political ideology), chooses to write. And to write, especially in the literary mode, *is* (again, according to this conventional logic) to write freely. This would not be the case, however, for texts of confessions (like Padilla's) written under threat of violence or torture; it is, indeed, contingent on the presumption they wrote freely that we hold literary writers to so unique a standard of responsibility and accountability. It is precisely the question of the open exercise of rights that might accrue to sexual and cultural citizens I want to address in detail in this discussion. In this more generally post–Cold War, postcolonial, and even (diasporically) postnational historical moment, in which local and national governments in many parts of the world are radically rethinking their policies toward immigrants and thereby radically transforming their conception of the citizen, I would like to contribute the following analysis of what happens to persons who find themselves caught between the competing nightmares of repression at home and rejection abroad. I want to locate this analysis in the bounded but articulate space of a certain kind of writing, the prison memoir and its fictional variants, to which certain exiles have turned in order to testify, outside of political court but within a space of political judgment, to the inextricable relationship between "freedoms" we conceptually separate into categories such as sexual, political, and artistic.

Writers of prison memoirs choose public rather than private models of democratic citizenship. Their response to totalitarian repression specifically is not to turn to the radical, and radically private, individualism of the "liberal" far right but to an alternative, public communalism always already implicit in their correspondingly public defiance during incarceration and in their decision to compose

and to publish their testimonies once freed. Memoirs by former political prisoners expelled from the countries that imprisoned them
thus pose precisely the challenge of writing freely of unfreedom and
of reading freely of unfreedom in a manner that immediately raises
the stakes of writing, and reading, both politically and responsibly.
They trigger an economy of signification that is free but not open.
These actions of reading and writing bear the burden of political
consequence as heavily as compliance and resistance, as negotiation
and disobedience do. And perhaps for this reason, the responsibility
that readers in relatively free states (and in relatively open societies)
must bear in reading the testimonies of former prisoners in relatively
more repressive states (and more closed societies) can instruct us
more clearly on the larger but congruent responsibilities we take on,
embrace even, as willing citizens of the nations and other collectives
we meaningfully claim.

Poetry as a House of Correction

It is in the suspended "present" time of exile that we find a different
kind of writer, like Ricardo Pau-Llosa, a Cuban American poet who
emigrated with his family as a young child in the early 1960s, who
grew up in Cuban Miami, and who has fashioned a formidable poetic
voice for himself in (Cuban) English. Pau-Llosa has produced a number of collections of mostly lyrical verse, prominently among them
one entitled *Cuba,* published by Carnegie-Mellon in 1993. In that
collection, Pau-Llosa has included a poem he calls "Conscience,"[8]
which enacts a kind of redoubled indictment of political abuse and
hypocrisy on the part of Fidel Castro and a significant supporter of
his, Nelson Mandela. What we might call the "text" of "Conscience"
uses a fairly controlled free-verse structure to report the testimony of
an unidentified former political prisoner recently freed from Cuba. It
moves in careful stages across three verse paragraphs, from the introduction of the voice of the former prisoner to his description of the
common occurrence of the detention, torture, and eventual rape of
"adolescent boys who get caught/writing anti-government graffiti."
"Conscience" uses a shrewd strategy of historical, geographic, and

subjective displacements to make its indictments; a strategy which, however shrewd, is also at least disingenuous if not outright unconscionable in its cynical exploitation of male rape as a form of dehumanization, and its troubling invocation of Mandela as Castro's partner in the heinous crime that Pau-Llosa restages.

"Conscience" troubles itself, however, by destabilizing its own textual singularity or integrity. The text of "Conscience" just described contains no explicit mention of Mandela, which occurs in an epigraph placed between the title and the text of the poem. "Conscience" has also been placed strategically to face, perhaps to confront, another poem, an elegy in villanelle form addressed to and entitled, "Reinaldo Arenas." "Conscience" thereby opens up and reaches beyond its putative textual boundaries. Beyond even the real history to which it claims to testify, "Conscience" also reaches out to its companion poem, "Reinaldo Arenas," and to the work of the writer to whom it is dedicated, perhaps to the genre of writings of which Arenas's autobiography partly exemplifies (and which Pau-Llosa himself could never legitimately write), and thereby to Padilla, perhaps, but also to Mandela, himself the prototype of the political prisoner in the late twentieth century.

Although Pau-Llosa might argue that he has been responsible in merely quoting Mandela, allowing the epigraph to "speak for itself," that already suggests a certain disingenuousness about the structure of responsibility behind any act of quotation. Nowadays we mostly hear such pathetic excuses from right-wing commentators who claim to be not merely misquoted but quoted specifically "out of context" when declarations they've made are used against them. However, Mandela's praise of "Castro's Cuba" for "its love of human rights and liberty" certainly deserves some better contextualization from Pau-Llosa than that it be surrounded by the title and the text of his "Conscience." Beyond the ironic but superficial counterpoint of Mandela's nearly thirty years in political detention, any more detailed study of Mandela's own life, of his radically different relationship than Castro's to his own nation's Communist Party, of his radically different relationship than Castro's to his own nation's racial politics, and of his radically different philosophical relationship than Castro's to the value of violent and nonviolent resistance to oppression, would, one would think, work against the political and moral efficacy of a gesture that includes Mandela on the stage of Castro's political theatre of cruelty.[9] Especially in the face of Cuba and Cuban America's own very complicated racial history, the attack on Mandela, however indirect, seems deeply ill considered.

"Conscience" fares no better in the context of sexual politics. Here, perhaps, the odd estrangement of body and voice in the poem takes on its most suggestive meaning. Voice in "Conscience" is rendered passive and disembodied in the same gesture: a "flight" brings some "former political prisoners" to the United States, "One" of whom "is being interviewed on the radio." The poem's speaker, presumably in the listening audience, hears what is now merely "the voice" of the interviewed prisoner narrate the common experience of hearing the screams of the tortured boys emanating from another cell. The poem's speaker, hidden in his passivity as audience, models the invisibility of the interviewed prisoner's radio voice as the prisoner plays passive audience to the screams of the invisible boys. All either can do is listen, read, and remember: "the voice" describes how it would listen to the screams, chiefly to discern age, youth being presumably a marker of innocence and a measure of (limited) agency. Eerily like a reader of poetry, the voice isolates "details that reveal the victim's age,/like the pitch of the screams and the number of sobs," an almost musical interpretation of "pitch" and "number" that serves only to satisfy the voice's interpretive skills: "The voice was always able to confirm/the accuracy of his evaluation in the morning/when the guards bring the boys out." The voice's fascination with the success of its evaluation seems to have little to do with "value" as an ethical measure, though, and more to do with the purely quantitative "accuracy" of guessing the boy's age and perhaps thereby the degree of his putative innocence. Given that the voice has already established some odd qualitative features in the experience ("When a boy is being beaten, the voice says,/the screams are different than when a man/or a woman is being tortured" and that if "the boy" manages to "call out for his mother" it "removes all the mystery"), its avowed fascination with the boy's age seems only to contribute further to a marked prurience on the voice's part.

The purpose behind this suggestion of prurience is finally made explicit "when the guards bring the boys out," and the last of the three verse paragraphs of "Conscience" can devote itself to the description of the gang rape of the boy by the "common prisoners" and occasionally the guards, although "Mostly they just watch." In a poem of oddly disembodied voices, the materialization of the body, especially the sacrificial body of the boy/victim given up to rape, cannot help but signify. The "beatings" the poem describes recur more regularly than the beats in its lines but in doing so implicate the poem in precisely the act of horror they rehearse. No one gets off lightly in Pau-Llosa's "Conscience," perhaps not even the passive "listening" voice of the poet/speaker himself. But whatever complicity in the failure to stop these abuses (for, like most of us, "mostly just watch[ing]") that the poet may accept for himself, he leaves open certain other questions of poetic and political responsibility: chiefly, can he use a scene of same-sex rape in a Cuban political prison without at least implicitly exploiting the homophobia of his intended audience, and can he indict an otherwise admirable black political leader for his allegiance to Castro without exploiting the racism of that same audience? These problems are further complicated, of course, by the fact that Pau-Llosa himself has never been a political prisoner, unless he constructs his own sense of exile as such.

Mandela, of course, has had such an experience, and thus for Pau-Llosa to challenge him by including such an incendiary quotation as an epigraph to his "Conscience" takes on an even more complicated set of risks. Poetry, traditionally, at least, the most public of discourses, necessarily takes on a public set of responsibilities. A public poem that openly challenges a public figure thus implicitly acknowledges itself as a political statement open to equally political evaluations. To the extent, for example, that "Conscience" was intended to "correct" the view of Cuba put forth in Mandela's statement, it becomes a correctional instrument, empowered by whatever surviving cultural institutions that still empower poetry, used against Mandela. In a sense it throws Mandela back into a correctional institution, if only to straighten him out about a historical fact or two. That it does so through the staging of same-sex rape throws the whole economy of straightness and correctness into an entirely different register, however. The ferocity of the act "Conscience" builds up to describe suggests a parallel hostility toward the object of the poem's "corrective" will. If the poem catches Mandela in the act of praising someone that the poet takes to be an amoral tyrant, does it not throw him into its own house of correction, forcing him to witness if not to undergo the kind of thing that goes on there? To what extent does the poem, beyond its own limited, passive sense of complicity in political crimes, reenact precisely the "criminal act" it condemns in others?

Curiously, what it condemns in others becomes a different proposition when that place of the other is occupied by the writer commemorated on the page "Conscience" faces. It is difficult to guess what Reinaldo Arenas would have thought of "Reinaldo Arenas,"[10] but certainly the problem of sexual symbolism as a public and political instrument might provide a key to such a puzzle and, alongside an intertextual analysis of some of Arenas's writing in comparison with Pau-Llosa's, will serve to open the following discussion of political erotics in the actual genre of prison writing more fully.

Adonais in Exile

Although "Conscience" exhibits a profound appreciation for poetic control in the handling of its putatively free-verse form, "Reinaldo Arenas" manifests that appreciation explicitly as an expertly handled villanelle. Pau-Llosa's elegy to Arenas does not, however, mimic the exuberant exhibitionism of its subject's own writing: it is, indeed, too modest and cloying for its own good. Not only does it make no explicit mention of Arenas's sexual disposition or of his illness, it situates Arenas's heroic suicide in ambivalent terms, both politically and poetically. References to Arenas alternate between appreciative acknowledgment of his "whole spirit" that "stands" against tyranny even when the body begins to fail and the suggestion of spiritual failure in Arenas's final act. "Exile is a voyage," the poem begins, one "we are hoping always will end,/but not like yours, with a fistful of pills." It is unclear whether the collective we, presumably the "we" of the Cuban-exile community, can include Arenas, given his unacceptable choice of conclusion to his voyage. Arenas, of course, left final responsibility for his death ambiguous: his suicide note, which punctuates but does not close the text of his autobiography, declares that AIDS will not "kill" him anywhere nearly as significantly as Fidel Castro has through his historical responsibility for Arenas's persecution and exile. Pau-Llosa, in never explicitly mentioning Arenas's condition, opens up the possibility of reading his suicide as a pure act of capitulation to despair: "Exile is a voyage we know will end," he concludes, "even if the spirit breaks like a glass in a clenched hand." It is difficult to accept Arenas as a "broken" spirit, even in his last days. As I argued in chapter 1, both his autobiography and his suicide note establish that Arenas died as a result of his uncompromising sense of his own dignity and of the need to defy the overwhelming forces, biological and historical, intent on destroying that dignity.

The elegy's silence on the subject of Arenas's sexuality is made even more apparent given its juxtaposition with the very explicit scene of same-sex rape in "Conscience." If "Conscience" is meant to chastise Mandela for his support of Castro, it seems that the weapon for that castigation, the shocking scene of male rape, inverts itself into the odd verbal "chastity" of "Reinaldo Arenas," which in its silences perhaps chastens its subject for weaknesses that go beyond the failure the poet sees as implicit in suicide. In his essay "Reinaldo Arenas, or Destruction by Sex," Guillermo Cabrera Infante also suggests that Arenas's exuberant sexual passivity would eventually have destroyed him, with or without AIDS or Fidel. In Pau-Llosa's poem, Arenas's body in particular seems earmarked for its failure to "stand" phallically against oppression and injustice. In this way it parallels the play of disembodiment in "Conscience"; there the testimonial voice of the political prisoner gives way only to the image of the boy-prisoner's body given up to violation, whereas in the elegy, Arenas's individual body and spirit both "fall" and "break," although presumably without damage to the collective, nationalist spirit of the exiled "we." Later in this chapter I have an opportunity to discuss how Pau-Llosa, Cabrera Infante, and Heberto Padilla operate as heterosexual commentators on their homosexual literary counterparts. Each in his own way seems bent on contributing, however awkwardly, to the ongoing struggle in patriarchal Cuban culture with the homophobia for which both the exiled Cuban bourgeoisie and its communist enemies on the island must be indicted. Although Pau-Llosa's elegy uses Arenas's death as an occasion to condemn the Castro government's policy of sending homosexuals to "labor camps which like islands/in that sea called *patria* bloom to kill/every hope," it is certainly true the homophobia that led to the detention of Cuba's gay men and women extended to the entire *patria,* the Cuban "nation" as an admittedly discontinuous, diasporically scattered "whole" rather than merely or exclusively the government in place on the island.

Whatever motivated Pau-Llosa, therefore, to elegize Arenas as he does in a space contingent to that in which he chastises Mandela as he does, may tell us more about Pau-Llosa's own role in Cuban America's struggle to free itself of all its repressive historical and cultural legacies than it does about either Mandela or Arenas. Indeed, Pau-Llosa's conservatism, the love of order and discipline that drives his politics *and* his poetics, may tell us more about the defining parameters of the future of so-called mainstream Cuban America than the political aesthetics of any other Cuban-exile or Cuban-diasporic writer I treat here. What is it that Pau-Llosa seeks to resolve in the simultaneous treatment of sexuality and politics we encounter in these two and other of his poems? Pau-Llosa himself may have given us the best direct answer in an interview published in *Poet's Market '93,* with the publication of the *Cuba* collection in which "Conscience" and "Reinaldo Arenas" both appear.[11] There Pau-Llosa told Deborah Cinnamon that "his poetry is not specifically political, but an ethical and moral challenge." Pau-Llosa goes on, in a direct quotation, to declare, "I do not belong to any group; I have been no one's protégé. In ethnic and political terms and the expectation attached to them in the contemporary scene, I am the quintessential alien: a Cuban exile writing in English and a liberal who is also an anti-communist." Certainly such a bold declaration would seem to settle any doubt about the ironic distance Pau-Llosa, who stresses his nonmembership in "any group" must then be understood to take from the "we" who voice their profound ambivalence toward Arenas in the elegy. Certainly the declaration reflects some concern with the status of "alien" or outsider, although it is odd that it presumes the conceptual possibility of a "quintessential alien" based even more oddly on the conditions of his writing in his acquired "second" language, and his being an anti-communist "liberal."

There is little room here to pursue further the fine theoretical point of the compatibility of quintessence and alienness; more so-phisticated theorists of alterity than I am would very likely take issue with the proposition that such authoritative (let alone essentializing) paradigms of cultural or political difference can hold, logically at least. More salient here is the question of the political and ethical sta-tus of Pau-Llosa's work. Clearly the poetry is inevitably more political than the poet cares to admit, and especially perhaps in ways he re-fuses (disingenuously, strategically) to recognize; and certainly this politics is intimately tied in with the question of ethics. Although Pau-Llosa's work clearly targets the moral abuses of Castro's govern-ment, those abuses cannot be said to pose difficult challenges to judg-ment. Conversely, the poems I have been discussing certainly do pose an ethical problem, especially relating to standards of respect and re-sponsibility, in their treatment of two historical figures, Mandela and Arenas, whose political lives may not fit into the easy moral con-structs of the Cuban-exile community, the "we" Pau-Llosa simultane-ously claims and disclaims.

The Myth of Self-Rectifying Homophobia

Along with declaring his adherence to a challenging ethical standard, Pau-Llosa goes on in the *Poet's Market* interview to declare an adher-ence to a high standard of aesthetic rigor: "I am interested in philoso-phy, art and history and not at all interested in gratuitously parading feelings, flashing neuroses, or poeticizing the banalities of everyday life. Among other subjects, I am concerned with the desperate history of my native country, Cuba, but I am not interested in catchy, sim-plistic, and marketable ethnic themes. I don't mambo."[12] Certainly Pau-Llosa's formal restraint and his choice of large themes, evident in the two poems at issue here, confirm the sincerity of these remarks. And, given his choice of Cuban cultural practices to reject, he cer-tainly seems disdainful of the success of Oscar Hijuelos, whose large unwieldy novels celebrate much that is "gratuitous," "neurotic," and "banal" in the Cuban temperament. But there seems to be more than a mere, and uncharacteristically Cuban, stoicism to Pau-Llosa's temperament: his refusal to mambo, his curious performative analogue to the discursive sins of "parading," "flashing," and "poeticizing," suggests that, beyond his distaste for rhythms of the body there is a more profound distaste for the kind of excess and spectacle associated with certain profoundly sexualized forms of cultural performance.

Without simply claiming that behind Pau-Llosa's refusal to mambo we might find an element of repressed homophobia or misogyny, it certainly bears observing that his diction here suggests a distaste for subversive exhibitionism of a playful, sexual sort. Exhibitionism, of varying sorts, has certainly traditionally characterized some queer elements in both Cuban and American literature and culture, and in both content as well as in style. Diego, the gay character in *Strawberry and Chocolate,* certainly "mambos"; that is, he "parades" and "flashes" and "poeticizes" his way through the story and the film in ways that would make conventional Cuban men, new and old, wince. In the course of his dance, however, Diego manages to invoke the legacy of major homosexual figures in Cuban cultural history, chief among them the poet and novelist José Lezama Lima, an aesthete and hyperbaroque stylist whose work does more than merely mambo. Lezama Lima, a "universal Cuban" according to Diego, provides a formidable counterpoint to the anemic image of the new Cuban man proposed by either the revolution or its tough-minded enemies abroad.

I must clarify at this point that my problems with Pau-Llosa's work have little to do with my appreciation of his talent, and certainly it would be absurd to lay responsibility for the homophobia of Cuban culture at his door. His work is in this way symptomatic of a much larger, deeper pathology than I can hope to map completely in this study. But it is certainly easy enough to find analogues to his refusal to mambo in other Cuban heterosexual male writers: Heberto Padilla, for example, whose detention and forced confession in 1971 for alleged counterrevolutionary activities became an international cause célèbre, writes in his memoir, *Self-Portrait of the Other,* of the split in the Cuban literary sensibility between those who followed José Martí's legacy of stoicism and those who emulated the Spanish tendency toward baroque excess, a tendency both Padilla and Cabrera Infante term "Góngorism." "Martí," Padilla tells us, "was a grave man, distant and untypical of a Cuban . . . humorless," showing "no interest in satire and even less in parody."[13] Of Lezama, Padilla counters that "every time I approached his poetics, I found myself violently dispatched to the realm of pure language, his one and only kingdom,"[14] and that this "violent dispatch" produced an equally violent, negative reaction in himself: "To me," Padilla confesses, "it was clear that his work embraced the worst vices of literature . . . [in its] baroque style . . . [and] impressive extravagance." Padilla thus shares with Cabrera Infante and to some extent with Pau-Llosa a tendency to link such aesthetic excesses with sexuality. In the case of Lezama, Padilla tells us, the link was officially sanctioned by the Cuban state: "Sexual conduct was a determinant factor" in cultural policing in Cuba, and "the commissars of Cuban culture" publicly termed Lezama's long surrealist novel *Paradiso* (1966) a "monument to the fag."[15]

Imbedded in Padilla's memoir is the narrative of Raúl Castro's personal war against Cuba's queers and against her artists. "Raúl," Padilla remembers, "had been fascinated with the Chinese Cultural Revolution. He wanted to put the ideological direction of the country in the hands of the armed forces . . . because he thought the best way to impede the unruly liberalism of certain militants was through the general militarization of culture,"[16] and for Padilla this cultural move complemented Raúl's political move of instituting work camps for homosexuals. In the course of his detention, Padilla is told by the officer in charge of his case, a Lieutenant Alvarez, that the state wanted "to put an end to the problem of intellectuals in Cuba" following Ché Guevara's own dictate that "all writers are in a state of Original Sin,"[17] but Padilla surmises that the true engineer behind the increasingly repressive policy against intellectuals was Raúl, who "was at last realizing his long-standing ambition to purge the cultural sector, applying the same methods he had used before to elevate the morals of the country by creating the infamous UMAP camps."[18] Padilla's suspicions were confirmed, he tells us, by *Pravda*'s Vitali Boroski, who tells him that Raúl is indeed "Enemy number one of all of you" writers, given that "One of his biggest phobias is culture."[19] The seriousness of the stakes behind Raúl Castro's war against Cuba's writers is underscored by Cabrera Infante in his long essay "Bites from the Bearded Crocodile," chronicling the same campaign: "a Communist country," Cabrera Infante writes, "lives and dies by the book" and will therefore consider "a war of words . . . warfare by other means." In such a place, he goes on, "Silence is the last refuge of the class enemy, and skepticism a dangerous deviation to the Right."[20] It should not come as a surprise ten years after the era of the "culture wars" in the United States that conservative politics of either the right or the left should link sexual phobia with a phobia toward art; indeed, we should learn a decisive lesson from the odd scene of, say, Jesse Helms or Lynne Cheney, finding themselves in bed with Fidel's brother Raúl Castro on the issue of public arts funding.

Arenas Unbound

Without abandoning these straighter exile writers altogether, I again turn to the work of Reinaldo Arenas himself, who, as a protégé of Lezama Lima, came in some way to manifest the political and aesthetic promise of his mentor better and more significantly than anyone might have predicted while Arenas was still alive. Arenas's work will serve me here to respond in more specific ways as well to the strategic problems, political, ethical, and aesthetic, of Pau-Llosa's employment of Cuban political prisons and same-sex rape as tools in his campaign to discredit Castro and his supporters. Initially a darling of the revolution, by the late 1960s Arenas found himself immersed in the profoundly paranoid, phobic, and repressive environment created by Raúl Castro. Whereas Padilla, an openly practicing heterosexual man, may have provoked only one of Raúl Castro's phobias, the flamboyant, and flamboyantly talented, Arenas provoked all of them. Oddly enough, in many significant ways Arenas embodied many of the qualities of the revolution projection of the "New Man." Cabrera Infante calls him "the only Cuban novelist who could be called a child of the Revolution; . . . being a peasant," Cabrera Infante adds, Arenas "was adopted by the Writers' Union as the great red hope of the revolutionary novel."[21] This projection, based on Arenas's very earliest work, was soon enough disappointed; under the tutelage of Lezama, Arenas quickly discovered a manner in which to exhibit his sexual and aesthetic dispositions as openly and defiantly in his work as he did in his person. He was, in Cabrera Infante's words, "a Havana *loca,* a mad girl . . . [who] didn't do anything to suppress or to hide it."[22] His work, too, became increasingly explicit in its references to same-sex desire and pleasure, and his developing literary style increasingly more complex and elusive, especially in its critical references to political life in Cuba. By the early 1970s, Arenas was actively pursued by State Security, an aunt with whom he lived in Havana had turned state informant, and Arenas literally could not begin any piece of writing without fear of its eventual confiscation and destruction. As I discussed in chapter 1, Arenas chronicled this period of his life in great detail in his autobiography, but these passages are less relevant to the topic of the present chapter than the writing he produced as a direct result of his inevitable incarceration for sexual corruption of a minor in the early 1970s.

To the extent that passages in *Before Night Falls* qualify as a prison memoir, they contribute a profoundly different analysis of the sexual politics of prison life in Cuba than we are likely to find in the more conventional memoirs of former political prisoners who are heterosexual. More importantly, *Before Night Falls* offers readers of Cuban political and cultural history an alternative analysis of the Castro government's human rights abuses than we find in the politically charged exile poems of Pau-Llosa discussed earlier. Arenas's time in prison taught him more, it seems, about the function of public invasions into private life, about the very unstable border presumably dividing the two realms to begin with, than we find in Pau-Llosa's very public poetic statements. Ironically, Arenas's period of incarceration in Havana's infamous Morro Castle isolated him from the two symbolic embodiments of freedom that dominate his imaginary: the sea and celebratory same-sex intercourse. "In prison," Arenas recounts, "sexual intercourse became something sordid, an act of submission and subjugation, of blackmail and violence, even of murder in many instances."[23] Consensual sex on the part of perfectly free agents becomes a conceptual and practical impossibility in prison, therefore, by virtue of the very fact of incarceration. Although some may take issue with Arenas's sentimental (and liberal) view of "free" subjective agency and its spiritual value, I would like to focus this analysis more exclusively on Arenas's observations about the impossibility of privacy and private action in such public institutions.

For Arenas, the "beauty of the sexual relationship lies in the spontaneity of the conquest *and in its secrecy*,"[24] a secrecy impossible to achieve in a space of social intercourse completely informed by state power. It is no longer a question of who literally observes the act, but that the actors cannot escape the necessarily coercive context in which they perform it. "In jail," Arenas goes on, "everything is obvious and miserable; jail itself makes a prisoner feel like an animal, and any form of sex is humiliating." All conventional dichotomies that shape social life are thus suspended once the dichotomy of public/private breaks down, as Arenas observes it doing in prison. Outside of prison, even sex conducted in public spaces, like parks and fields, can maintain its secrecy, its element of the private. Sex in prison can be spur of the moment yet not spontaneous because the overwhelming regimentation of prison life and the always-supervised distribution of bodies suspend all contingency, all "real" spontaneity, in the rigid matrix of their orderliness. Prison time happens outside the register of open-ended history and chronology; sexual prisoners in Arenas's Cuba had no narrative of rehabilitation or reform open to them, and political prisoners were only extended the opportunity to confess and declaim their alleged counterrevolutionary sentiments and actions.

Although Arenas was rarely held in isolation or confinement, it is clear from his account of life in the gay wards of the Morro that interaction with others in such an environment did little to produce a sense of time passing in any meaningful narrative modality. "Homosexuals," he recalls, "were confined to the two worst wards of El Morro: these wards were below ground at the lowest level, and water seeped into the cells at high tide," marking time as an interminable repetition, and making these wards reminiscent of "the last circle of hell" for Arenas.[25] Other authoritative aspects of social reality were similarly suspended in El Morro: the guards, Arenas observes, were as imprisoned in their commission to that place as the prisoners, and for all that the queer prisoners were there for homosexual activity, in prison they were ironically free to perform their queerness openly. Perhaps because "they never had anything to lose" once confined, Arenas surmises, gay prisoners "could afford the luxury of being true to their nature, to act queer, to make jokes, and even to express admiration to a soldier." That prison should afford a space of possibility for open queer expression may not seem so paradoxical to some: the paradoxes of identity formation and expression in prison do not stop so short. In such a prison, where the only possible sexual interaction is same sex and where the potential that sex will become an instrument of even murderous violence is so great, the contexts in which identities are claimed and performed become ever more elaborate and ambiguous.

Discussing Arenas's novella, "Arturo, the Brightest Star" in *Gay and Lesbian Themes in Latin American Writing* (1991), David William Foster echoes Arenas's observation that sexual prisons and labor camps opened up a space of sexual possibility for some prisoners.[26] The *locas* in Arenas's story, Foster observes, were "not only left to recreate, mostly undisturbed by the authorities, their micro-society in the camps—to dress and make themselves up as they please, to have the social interaction they please—but they are also allowed to be readily available objects of exploitation for the camp guards ... [who] may use them for sex as they wish, as long as they are not public about it."[27] But Arenas is careful to distinguish among degrees of free, coerced, and violently forced sex in the prisons and camps: in *Before Night Falls*, for example, he provides an anecdote from his experiences in prison that oddly parallels the situation related in Pau-Llosa's "Conscience" of the rape of a young male prisoner. "At the baths," Arenas tells us, "I once saw all the ward chiefs fucking an adolescent who was not even gay," and the anecdote immediately becomes generalized into a history of repeated, almost ritual practice. The boy, Arenas goes on, "had to keep on making his ass available, against his will, to all those people." From the anonymity of the one boy he saw raped once in the anecdote, to the generalized description of his repeated rapes, Arenas extends his observations even further:

many "boys who were not homosexual but were raped repeatedly by the men," Arenas tells us, "would eventually declare themselves queer so that they would be transferred to the queer ward, where at least the fairies would not rape them."[28] The inversions here are numerous and complex; presumably heterosexual young men are only susceptible to sexual violation to the extent that the presumption of their heterosexuality can be sustained, and once they declare themselves queer, which in Cuba would mean passive and effeminate, they are transferred into the oddly less threatening custody of the "real" queers. There, the chain of presumptions might conclude, they would ironically have access to fellow inmates with whom they might exercise their own active heterosexual disposition. And although Arenas might still insist that sex in its full human dignity remains impossible in prison, at least in this last case it might not fully be an act of coercion, either as punishment, torture, or rape.

Enlightenment and Unfreedom: An Inevitable Foucauldian Turn

In many such observations, scattered throughout his fiction and his memoirs, Arenas seems fully if intuitively to understand crucial aspects of Michel Foucault's analysis, in 1977's *Discipline and Punish*, of the modern prison. As an implementation of a certain technology of power, the detention of sexual minorities in Cuba's prisons did not inhibit the performance of alternative sexual practice in those prisons; in fact, in some ways it positively enabled such performance. "Power," as Foucault famously asserted, undoubtedly "produces, it produces reality; it produces domains of objects and rituals of truth";[29] and Arenas provides many clear examples of this operation in his prison writings. In the story "Arturo, the Brightest Star," Arenas describes the queer prisoners in a labor camp in terms that at least parallel Foucault's: the queens in Arturo's ward bore a "docility in the face of persecution, [a] take-whatever-comes-along meekness," that made them "do anything, suffer any terror, turn the other cheek to any insult, and immediately include it in their traditions, make it indigenous, incorporate it into the folklore, the daily calamities," thus exhibiting their "gift for transforming terror into familiar ritual."[30] Nothing could more literally demonstrate Foucault's analysis of the making-instrumental of the body through discipline than the practice of "farming" sexual prisoners out to labor camps known as "Military Units for the Aid of Production" (UMAP, as noted earlier, is the Spanish acronym). As the queens in the camps spend their days laboring under coercion in sugarcane fields, at night they learn a more complex form of self-discipline ironically through the self-deprecating camp rituals Arenas describes. "Discipline," Foucault tells us, "produces subjected and practiced bodies . . . [it] increases the forces of the body" in terms of economic utility and "diminishes these same forces" in terms of political docility.[31] Sexuality, as Arenas observes, is farmed out doubly to the UMAPs: the enlistment of alternative sexual subjects to do literal farmwork is complemented by the localizing and confining of gay men to places accessible to guards and soldiers.

As we have already observed, for Arenas prisoners' actions are always compromised as free, private acts by the generalized state of surveillance under which they live, and although for him the mechanisms of power that create these conditions in Cuba might be more visible than in more liberal political systems, they nevertheless fall within the purview of the Foucauldian critique of power and invisibility. "Disciplinary power," Foucault tells us, is typically "exercised through its invisibility; at the same time it imposes on those whom it subjects a principle of compulsory visibility. In discipline, it is the subjects who have to be seen, . . . It is the fact of being constantly seen, of being always able to be seen, that maintains the disciplined individual in his subjection."[32] Indeed, Foucault's analysis, coupled with Arenas's literary rehearsal of the Castro state's disciplinary policies, suggests just how much a totalitarian system like Cuba's has stood to learn from the early penal reforms of the enlightened West. It should not be surprising, therefore, that in Self-Portrait of the Other, Padilla should offer several observations about Fidel Castro's sense of identification with a figure like Robespierre.[33] Certainly with the rise of secular bourgeois orders, certain shifts were required in the metaphysical and royalist bases of penal practice that may have been further extended or distorted by the radical politicization of crime under communism. Foucault is particularly adept at articulating the shift in the symbolic status of the criminal in the classical *epistème*: "the criminal designated as the enemy of all . . . falls outside the pact, disqualifies himself as a citizen and emerges, bearing within him . . . a wild fragment of nature; he appears as a villain, a monster, a mad-man, perhaps, a sick and, before long, 'abnormal' individual."[34] Such an analysis of the figure of the criminal clearly anticipates the later analysis of other socially deviant types, primarily the homosexual, and in a society whose phobias are as cultural as they are sexual, the artist. In such a society, the artist and the queer eventually will, as Foucault says of the criminal, "belong to a scientific objectification and to the treatment that will be correlative to it."[35]

In Castro's Cuba, the diagnostic equation of intellectual, homo-sexual, and criminal with pathology was all too clear from the inception of the UMAPs in 1967 on. Cabrera Infante calls Cuba's homophobia itself "an infamous collective illness," an "obsession with queers, queens and kinks" that led directly to the institution of "concentration camps for homosexuals, especially those with a cul-tural bent." He cites Ché Guevara's specific conviction that "homo-sexuals [were] sick people who must give way to the politically healthy 'new man' made by communist Cuba."[36] Heberto Padilla makes a similar observation in his autobiography: "The homosex-ual," he tells us, "was not a problem for the new society. Quite the contrary, it was a leftover of the *ancien régime* which undermined the Revolution."[37] Homosexuals, whether remnants of an obsolete na-ture or a perversely decadent bourgeois order, could thus be "cured" through sequestration and often violent Pavlovian conditioning, or the "problem" of homosexuality could be obviated technically by simple incarceration. In either case, the eradication of homosexuality and the technological construction of the "new man" were to go hand in hand in the new Cuba. It is thus perhaps that Cuba discovered a way to modernize itself by following some perverse version of a pro-gram devised, according to Foucault, by eighteenth-century French ideology. This program, "a general recipe for the exercise of power over man," exploits, according to Foucault, "the 'mind' as a surface for the inscription for power, with semiology as its tool; the submission of bodies through control of ideas; the analysis of representations as a principle in a politics of bodies that was much more effective than the ritual anatomy of torture and execution."[38]

It is perhaps this analysis of Foucault's that best explains his more provocative argument in *Discipline and Punish* about the paradoxical relation between the body and the vestige of soul allowed by secular liberal ideology. The rehabilitated criminal, the institutionally reformed subject, is in some ways the paradigm of the always already "free" but chastened subject of liberal ideology. "The man . . . we are invited to free," Foucault argues, "is already in himself the effect of a subjection much more profound than himself." Indeed, a "'soul' inhabits him . . . which is itself a factor in the mastery that power exercises over the body," and to that extent "the soul is the prison of the body."[39] Such an argument would, I think, have posed more of a semantic than a practical problem for a writer who, like Arenas, takes recourse to a more conventional form of soul/body dialectic in order to describe his experiences in prison. Arenas recounts, "my body could not understand that it had to remain for months or years in a bunk full of fleas and in that sweltering heat." Against the body's failure to understand its own suffering, Arenas initially poses the resilient optimism of the soul: "the body," he argues, "suffers more than the soul, because the soul can always find something to hang on to, a memory, a hope." Ultimately, however, even the rigid conventionality of the soul/body dialectic collapses in the grip of absolute captivity. The "poor body" feels the impoverishment of its own contingent abject physicality precisely when it "understands" that even "the soul could do nothing for it under those circumstances."[40]

In Arenas's work, it may perhaps be the moment in which he observes straight prisoners declaring themselves gay to escape further violence that he begins to understand the threat such power exercises over anything like an authentically free subjectivity. As he observes these young men pass through a series of coerced and public sexual performances and declarations for the sake of mere survival, their actions mark for him the extreme limit of subjection to the apparently pervasive mechanism of power in which they (and, under not altogether different circumstances, we) are all caught. At such a point, the cumulative effect of the punishment they have experienced would have no apparent conceptual relationship to their putative crimes. "Horror," as Foucault puts it, is no longer "opposed to horror in a joust of power; it is no longer the symmetry of vengeance, but the transparency of the sign to that which it signifies; what is required is to establish, in the theatre of punishments, a relation that is immediately intelligible to the senses and on which a simple calculation may be based; a sort of reasonable aesthetic of punishment."[41] In the absence of a political context in which any authentic spontaneity might be possible, all that is left for the prisoners in the UMAPs and the gay wards of the Morro is the injunction to perform interminably, repetitively their queerness, sincere or not, as a constitutively self-violating act.

Between Corpus and Corpse: Sade, Sarduy, and the "Bodies" of Prison Writing

Without straying too far from the topic at hand (and in all its persistent, relentless topicality, haunted even some years into the new century by images of bodies in detention, from those held in the U.S. naval base in Guatánamo, Cuba, to those photographed in Baghdad's Abu Ghraib prison), it bears mentioning here that my move to Foucault is not merely a convenient or contingent move toward theory. Imbedded in much of the discourse of exile as it bears on questions of justice, freedom, power, and their abuses are questions that contemporary theory, especially in its critique of the legacies of enlightenment, continues to address directly and productively.

Another queer and diasporic Cuban writer, Severo Sarduy, who settled in Paris after the revolution and who also died in the 1990s of AIDS complications, observes in his own theoretical work the relevance of poststructural critical strategies to articulations of the Cuban political situation. Just beneath Foucault's turn to the idea of a "reasonable aesthetic of punishment" in his analysis of early modern French prisons lurks perhaps the most complex early modern French prisoner, the Marquis de Sade, whose work fascinated Sarduy. In a series of short theoretical essays first composed in 1969 and much later (in 1989) translated and published under the title *Written on a Body,*

Sarduy devotes significant attention to Sade.[42] In those essays, Sarduy employs a politically charged semiotic analysis, indebted in equal parts to Bataille and Barthes, to understand the political and public dimensions of actions performed in institutional confinement. Sade provides Sarduy with an embodiment of the public exhibitionistic prisoner who transforms his confinement in obscurity into performance. With Sade, Sarduy argues, "writing fulfilled its essential mission of dis-alienation, since that type of theatre, breach and spectacle was created . . . from solitude and confinement," thus turning "prison" into its "opposite: theatre;" and "cell [into] stage."[43]

What is "written on a body" for Sarduy seems emphatically written as, or on, Sade's body, and as the "body" or corpus of his work, as the perverse remnant of a past order, the bodily order of aristocracy, and the corpse of any obsolete, dead, *ancien*(t) regime. As Sade's persistence mocks the viability of the new regime, so perversity persists in its cruel mockery of the semiotic basis of any new order, until that order learns to absorb and rehearse that cruelty in its own operations. Once "the machinery of belief and the authority of God (or the King, who is his metaphor) have been toppled," Sarduy argues, "the master/slave dialectic can be established"; but although conventionally this transition is read as moving toward symbolic order and away from arbitrary, corporal power, Sarduy sees a greater reciprocity in it. "The servant," Sarduy argues, "no longer obeys in the *name* of something," the undeniably symbolic power of the divine or monarchical authority, but "in the name of the law of the strongest" in the person of the agent representing the ruling class, party or other interest.[44] Thus the persistence of the body in any political order that covers or buries it with symbolic value requires that any act of transgression against the order generating that value retain something of the perverse. Resistance, an "erotic act" like "blasphemy, . . . devotes each scene" in which it can be performed "to mocking invisible power (God) in order to permit the fall of visible power (the King); it claims each act in the name of atheism and revolution."[45] Out of this conflation of religious, political, and erotic transgressions, Sarduy is able to generalize a theory of transgression that can also account for the vicious nature of putatively revolutionary but actually authoritarian regimes bent on directing interminable rehearsals of this authority.

As a pervert choreographs the scene of the fulfillment of his desire, so both authoritarian master and resistant slave confront each other on a representative stage of conflicting powers and desires, each bent on taking control of the scene. On this stage, however, clearly marked dialectical relations of power necessarily dissolve into the ambiguities of the perverse. This space of an impossible representation dissolves for Sarduy into the "Vertigo of [an] unreachable instant," where "perversion is the repetition of the gesture confident of reaching it. And in hopes of reaching the unattainable, of joining reality and desire, of coinciding with his own ghost, the pervert breaks every law."[46] And as master and slave bleed into each other in this scenario, so do subject and object: "Sade's hero," Sarduy tells us, "renounces subjectivity in order to attain his goal" and thereby signals the primacy of the object, of our buried status as objective bodies, in all analyses of sadomasochism and voyeurism/exhibitionism. "At the center of sadism," Sarduy concludes, "there is no subject; sadism is the object's unadulterated search."[47]

Sarduy's fascination with sadeian performance must be understood, I think, in the context of Castro's own publicly avowed identification with Robespierre, as observed by Heberto Padilla. Even in his last interview with Castro before leaving Cuba in 1980, Padilla reports that Castro seemed no closer to a resolution about what to do with dissident artists in his Cuba. As long as "intellectuals" in Castro's view remained less "interested in the social aspect of revolution" and more "interested in their freedoms," then there would be no choice for him but to rehearse Robespierre's painful historical lesson: "We must be hard, inflexible, severe; sin by excess, not by default."[48] This difficult lesson is, of course, demonstrated in Robespierre's own time in and by Sade; the prisoner and the tyrant clash in the moment and the space in which each will attempt to establish ideal conditions for the fulfillment of his own fantasy. In this sense it is Sade (as much as Robespierre, and perhaps because of his ingenious response to the socio-symbolic order embodied in Robespierre) who supplies Castro with the rules for the disciplining of his country's unruly artists and perverts. Castro's houses of correction are theaters for the enactment of a far more grotesque perversity than any Reinaldo Arenas could have imagined.

As Sarduy concludes, all "sadistic systems" are reduced to "repetition," to "the precise, inflexible code of positions and gestures prescribed" by the sadist in his search for "the object, lost forever but forever present in its deception."[49] Authoritarian discipline, reliant as it is on unswerving repetition, on the kind of interminable return of the same observed by Arenas in the rituals of the prison wards he knew and imagined, betrays in this manner its own basis in the perverse. For Sarduy, "repetition is the support of all perversion, . . . of all ritual"; it is always a sacrificial ritual that murders one body, the living body, in the hopes of resurrecting the lost body, the dead body politic, perhaps, choked by the grip of a totalizing control. Totalitarianism, in the context of Sarduy's analysis, becomes a "prescription for optimum conditions in order that a presence . . . might appear and validate the participation of objects, . . . might become incarnate and bestow the quality of being on what was previously only thing"; it insists on the hope that out of such ritual a revitalized body politic might spring, an "erotic phantom" coinciding "with the physical fact of bodies" that might "justify with its presence the display of forces and blasphemies."[50]

Putting Freedom through Its Paces or, Is There Art without Discipline?

The play and display of bodies and forces in this sadeian disciplinary scene may seem distant from some of the more strictly cultural scenes with which this discussion began, namely Gutiérrez Alea's film and the literary works of Paz, Pau-Llosa, and Arenas. But the theoretical and historical links among artists responding to the worst cultural crimes of Castro's revolution and their historical forebears, the cultural criminals of the French Revolution, are not just conceptually, but also culturally and historically, insistent. The 1959 revolution did not entirely liberate Cuba from its patriarchal tradition and all its concomitant sexual orthodoxies. The revolution's ideological call to (and for) a "new" man or citizen remains fraught with a kind of utopian idealism that will always require the kinds of excessive politicized modes of cultural discipline instituted by the French Revolution and unmasked for their equivocal basis in perversity by Sade. Arenas's testimonial to the treatment of artists and queers in Cuba, especially when contextualized in the generally Cuban-diasporic constellation of texts by writers like Padilla, Cabrera Infante, and Sarduy, understandably refuses to engage in a countersadism to make its point. In both *Before Night Falls* and "Arturo, the Brightest Star," Arenas resists the temptation to which Pau-Llosa succumbs so readily; he does not exploit the undeniable crimes he witnesses merely for the sake of political correction. Arenas's enraged textual *grito* is always generally or anonymously directed, except when he directs it at Fidel Castro. Although they remain a generation apart in their experiences of exile and assimilative immigration (if not quite in age), however, both Arenas and Pau-Llosa have both chosen to participate as cultural citizens in a public debate about the public nature of certain sexualized political practices. In doing so, they both contribute to an evolving and ever more complicated scene in which various forms of postnational, and genuinely diasporic, Cuban "citizenship" can for the first time be enacted. For all its limitations and equivocations, the post–Cold War relaxation of policies against gay and lesbian Cubans on the island certainly seems to be matched by the emergence of audible gay and lesbian voices in U.S.-based, off-island Cuban culture, a parallel if not entirely coincidental development. Out of this development, unimaginable as it was for so long, perhaps other equally unimaginable developments will issue.

Radical change in the Cuban political situation, however indefinitely deferred, remains inevitable; one question that remains outside the scope of prediction, however, is the extent to which such a change will involve violence. It should be our hope that Cubans from all parts of the diaspora, including the island itself, will take our cues from Arenas and direct our rage generally at history, perhaps equitably at ourselves, but without any rehearsals of the kinds of sadistic scenes that Arenas witnessed and condemned. As Foucault has observed, there is no symmetry to vengeance, no truly "reasonable aesthetic of punishment" that can somehow correct the past the way Pau-Llosa, for example, sought to "correct" Nelson Mandela. Prison writing (at least as I hope to have treated it here) does not seek to punish the punishers, even if it does indict and condemn them; it seeks instead to demonstrate the (meaningful, if limited) freedom of the writer, free as much from a sadeian compulsion to vengeance as from the sadistic grip of his or her former captors, and to challenge the reader to read with a deeper appreciation for the duties and responsibilities to which our own (limited, but meaningful) freedom calls us.

Chapter 3

Revolution's Other Histories: Legacies of Roberto Fernández Retamar's "Caliban"

The underlying assumption is here a relatively old one, found again and again in the conflation of literary and literal decadence, in the wild corruption of the letter and the body alike. For the revolutionary imagination, the pleasure of the text, given to dissipation and wasteful dissemination, reflects and expands the pleasure of the flesh, expands it, somewhat paradoxically, as the threat of a generalized sexual narcissism: after all, one cannot focus on the play of the signifier without being in some way withdrawn from the work of society. . . . The narcissistic, sexually driven subject has, it appears, an art of its own.

—Brad Epps[1]

Brad Epps's epigraph concludes a passage of his exhaustive study of Cuban revolutionary sexual politics, a passage that specifically analyses statements issued by the Cuban government in the course of the revolution's first decade on the topic of the so-called proper role of artists, writers, and intellectuals in a revolutionary culture. Those statements range chronologically from Fidel Castro's "Words to Intellectuals," issued in 1961, to the Declaration issued after Cuba's

First National Congress on Education and Culture in 1971. In both statements, Epps argues, one can read a creeping but nonetheless virulent homophobia in the symptomatic rhetorical conflation of the homosexual and the intellectual, a conflation that functions to varying degrees of explicitness in this series of public statements. In the later "Declaration," for example, "homosexuality" appears explicitly "on the rhetorical heels of prostitution, . . . described as a 'deviation' and as a form of 'social pathology.'" The Declaration uses this formulation in order to base its refusal to permit that, "by means of 'artistic quality,' recognized homosexuals win influence and have an effect on the education of our youth," a proscription that puts into unambiguous and specific application Castro's more general condemnation, in his speech closing that conference, of "'privileged minorities' who have 'monopolized the title of intellectual' and whose writings are useless, mere expressions of decadence." Castro, Epps is careful to observe, "does not refer directly to homosexuality" in his own speech, "but he shadows it forth in his depictions of the 'unproductive parasite' and 'intellectual rat' for whom aesthetic value is found in anything that entertains, diverts or helps to wile away boredom."

Recent and ongoing scholarly work, in which Epps's article is an exemplary moment, and to which I hope my preceding two chapters have also contributed, has already established convincingly the fact of the Cuban revolutionary government's early abuses of its queer and dissident artists and writers.[2] It will not be my intention here to repeat that work, but to use its discoveries to interrogate further one of the more significant intellectual legacies of that particular moment in Cuban political and cultural history for recent critical political and cultural discourse in the United States. Months following the April 1971 Congress, Roberto Fernández Retamar's essay "Caliban" appeared in the *Casa de las Américas Review*. In its conclusion, Retamar has occasion to quote Castro's closing remarks to the Congress, citing specifically his most general statement on the practical and ethical functions of revolutionary art and revolutionary criticism: "We, a revolutionary people," Castro told the Congress, "value cultural and artistic creations in proportion to what they offer mankind. . . . Our evaluation is political. There can be no aesthetic value in opposition to man. Aesthetic value cannot exist in opposition to justice, in opposition to the welfare and in opposition to the happiness of man. It cannot exist!" The statement sounds almost theoretical, as though Castro were making some argument about art's intrinsic function, as though by virtue of its defining characteristics the aesthetic could not be conceived in opposition to justice, welfare, or happiness. But the statement was not made in so felicitous a performative context; Castro's is more a statement of policy rather than theory, one in which the final, declamatory "It cannot exist" functionally translates into the prescriptive "It must not exist" and, indeed, into the imperative "It will not exist."[3]

Indeed, in the same month as the Congress, Cuban authorities arrested and detained the poet Heberto Padilla (whose work figured prominently in my chapter 2) for "counterrevolutionary" activity consisting of preferring the work of already-exiled novelist Guillermo Cabrera Infante over that of Lisandro Otero, a writer more sympathetic to the revolution, in a 1967 review, and for writing a novel, *Heroes Are Grazing in My Garden,* which, in the writer's own words, "is not a denunciation or an allegation, not even testimony which might aspire to verisimilitude. Rather, it is a text through which certain conflicts and certain beings pass like shadows."[4] Padilla's curiously indeterminate description of his novel, in a memoir written after his release from Cuba ten years after his detention, speaks rather eloquently to the subtle but lasting effects of such violent censorship. His accounts of conversations during his detention with a Lieutenant Alvarez, the officer in charge of his detention, suggest some cause for Padilla's lingering anxiety. When Padilla refuses to sign the confession written for him by Cuban authorities, declaring, "I never plotted against the powers of the state," Alvarez fires back about the international reaction to his detention: "That is what you expect. Intellectuals are untouchable. That is what you hope for. Your friends will begin to mobilize—if they did that kind of work for the state, we would have more consumer goods that anyone else in the world." And later, as the police pressure on Padilla to sign his "confession" intensifies and turns literally violent, Alvarez threatens, "We can destroy you even though we have no legal justification for doing so; . . . right now you represent a dangerous tendency in the nation and we have to eradicate it."[5] Cabrera Infante himself reports on the "international uproar" sparked by Padilla's detention and eventual forced public confession: "The mail carried . . . an open letter . . . to Fidel Castro himself . . . signed, surprisingly enough, by such leftist writers and sponsors of the Revolution as Jean-Paul Sartre and Simone de Beauvoir, Italo Calvino, Marguerite Duras, etc." and "After [Padilla's] Soviet-style confession . . . there was an even more vehement and indignant letter to Castro, signed by yet more writers on the Left like Nathalie Sarraute and Susan Sontag. The undersigned were ashamed (and angry) at the outrage of a poet confessing to imaginary political crimes."[6]

The Padilla case, combined with the 1971 Congress, is the informing context of Retamar's self-declared polemic "Caliban." Retamar himself admits this in his 1986 follow-up to that essay, "Caliban Revisited." The Padilla case and its consequent firestorm of letters of accusation, denunciation, and condemnation are, Retamar writes, "the spark that fired the writing of 'Caliban' . . . my piece was not born in a vacuum but rather at a particular time that was marked by passion, and—on our part—indignation at the paternalism, the rash accusation against Cuba, and even the grotesque 'shame' and 'anger' of those who, comfortably situated in the 'West' with their fears, their guilt and their prejudices decided to proclaim themselves judges of the revolution."[7] Retamar's indignation, still palpable in the later essay, certainly energizes the earlier piece: it certainly overwhelms the "spark" provided for it by the Padilla case itself, which makes a brief, occluded appearance in the first paragraph of "Caliban" as "the recent polemic regarding Cuba that ended by confronting, on the one hand, certain bourgeois European intellectuals (or aspirants to that state) with a visible colonialist nostalgia; and, on the other, that body of Latin-American writers and artists who reject open or veiled forms of cultural and political colonialism" and later, when Retamar takes on Carlos Fuentes as one of a number of Mexican intellectuals critical of Padilla's treatment, the case reappears as "the wild vociferation occasioned by a Cuban writer's month in jail."[8] Although I am not exactly certain what risks I take as an openly gay, politically progressive North American academic critic from a working-class Cuban-exile background in plying this ground, I certainly acknowledge that this is tricky, risky ground to ply. Retamar's essay has enjoyed considerable esteem in the United States, especially on the part of progressive Latino and Latina and other academics of color, as well as by theorists of postcolonialism more generally, and has, especially since its publication in English in the late 1980s, spawned a genealogy of critical and scholarly texts as rich and complex as the one it itself fashions in its own pages.[9] I do feel, however, that that very fashioning of a "Calibanic" genealogy demands further scrutiny, and that what new insights that scrutiny produces might in turn recast, especially but not exclusively in political terms, some of the work done subsequently in the United States and abroad in the name of "Caliban."

What "Caliban" Schooled

My chief aim in explicating certain passages of Retamar's Calibanic manifesto closely is to highlight the otherwise imbedded homophobia of his rhetoric, especially in those moments when he does the direct taxonomic work of classifying who does and who does not belong in the "school" of Caliban, who does and does not speak for, or from, an "America" he opposes to that lying to the north but emanating from the west by terming it, following Martí, "Ours." Indeed, the repeated and insistent recourse to the first-person plural pronoun, in possessive form or otherwise, begins already to mark the larger classificatory rhetorical function of the essay. On the bright side, the evocation of the grammatically plural person in turn evokes the sense of community and solidarity among persons and groups of persons to which perhaps most of us strive; on the other, darker side, it inevitably effects that happy inclusion by some necessary exclusion, perhaps more than one, and certainly not only that of the northern imperialist against whom "our America" opposes itself. Epps devotes strategic attention to this grammatical bind, and its sexual- and political-positional analogues, in his essay on Arenas, an essay that, for all of its interest in the events surrounding the 1971 Congress, devotes no significant attention to Retamar or his essay. In "Proper Conduct," Epps initially pursues this pronomial play for its sexual

corollaries: "while the Cuban revolution seeks a surrender of the individual to the collective," he argues, "a sacrifice of the ego to the (ego)
ideal, it refuses what it sees as a surrender, in the flesh as in the mind,
of one man to another. While the former 'surrender' is understood in
terms of empowerment (I surrender the I to be stronger in and as the
We), the latter is understood in terms of disempowerment, degrada-
tion and abjection (I surrender to another, stronger I)."[10] This is certainly the manner in which the game of us and them plays itself out in
Retamar's essay, which in one respect can be boiled down to a process
of inventorying, of listing and categorizing, selecting the anticolonial-
ist sheep from the presumably procolonialist goats (or vice versa, as
the insistent gender privileging in Retamar's essay would demand).

The primary operation of "Caliban" has been termed genealogical;
Retamar devotes most of the essay to naming his forebears in the line
of Caliban, from at least Martí at the turn of the last century on. At
the same time, and because he wants his essay to function dialecti-
cally, Retamar sets up a parallel but opposing line, typified by although not beginning with Uruguayan José Enrique Rodó's 1900
pamphlet "Ariel." The most consistent pattern to be detected in
Retamar's treatment of those figures he rejects is, for better or worse,
the femininization or hysterization of these otherwise male writers.
The "Ariel" figure itself, rejected ostensibly for its traditional association with a willing servitude to the master, is often figured as well as
the "airy," obsequious, feminine counterpart to the roughly recalcitrant (and potentially rapacious) Caliban.[11] This insistently gendered
set of associations haunts the larger Latin American intellectual
legacy of Rodó's essay, well beyond Retamar's use of it.[12] In fact,
Retamar keeps a certain sympathy for Rodó in play, if only because
Rodó retained a deep suspicion about the United States; Retamar
takes greater issue with an analysis of Rodó by the Latin American
critic Emir Rodríguez Monegal, who, from his base in París, had been
instrumental in promoting the new Latin American fiction as it
emerged in the late 1960s. Rodríguez Monegal, in emphasizing Rodó's
own aestheticist, modernist tendencies over his political analyses effectively, in Retamar's terms, "emasculates Rodó's work" and betrays
the extent to which he (Rodríguez Monegal) himself was "a servant

of imperialism . . . afflicted with 'Nordo-mania.'" Rodó's stance against, again in Retamar's terms, "North American penetration" was at its most "gallant" in its "exalt[ation of] democracy, moral values and emulation," and in "defense of our values."[13] A fate similar to Rodríguez Monegal's befalls the nineteenth-century Argentine writer Domingo Faustino Sarmiento, whose famed *Facundo: Civilization and Barbarism* of 1845 is tainted for Retamar by its open admiration of North American culture. According to Retamar, Sarmiento's "travels in that country produced in him a genuine bedazzlement, a never-ending historical orgasm."[14] The assignment of sexualized pathologies to two such disparate writers as Sarmiento and Rodríguez Monegal at least establishes that, without serious regard for the legitimate political problems one might encounter in their work, Retamar himself is not above damning them in large part through the rhetorical use of the sexual innuendo. And why not? This was very much in keeping, as I began to show in chapter 2, with the spirit of the times in late 1960s/early 1970s revolutionary Cuba, where the slightest suggestion of a rumor of ideological or sexual deviance, or preferably both, could prove permanently damning.[15]

Retamar treads more lightly around two other literary figures of indisputably more formidable stature, Jorge Luis Borges and Carlos Fuentes. But both of them are open to a certain displaced form of sexualized suspicion; Retamar pauses in the course of his literary housecleaning to mention, for example, "The extraordinary vogue enjoyed by linguistics in recent years," a vogue he associates with "the attempt at ahistoricization peculiar to a dying class: a class that initiated its trajectory with daring utopias in order to chase away time and that endeavors now, in the face of adversity, to arrest that trajectory via impossible uchronics." Literary postmodernism suffers for Retamar from its status as symptom of bourgeois decadence, and both Borges and Fuentes, in turn, are contaminated by the same decadence to a pathological degree. Borges, "a typical colonial writer" for Retamar, is "a man of diabolical intelligence" for whom "the act of writing . . . is more like the act of reading," and this perverse, "diabolical" inversion of scriptural convention qualifies Borges to "exemplify Martí's idea that intelligence is one—and not necessarily the best—part of a man."[16] Fuentes's guilt comes chiefly by association; in addition to his inexcusable turn from social realist to more semiotically playful novelistic forms and his collaboration with the "Mexican literary Mafia" that broke with Cuba over the Padilla affair, Fuentes also "elaborates a vision of our literature, our culture," which, according to Retamar, "coincides with that of writers like Emir Rodríguez Monegal and Severo Sarduy."[17] We already know at this point in "Caliban" what Retamar thinks of Rodríguez Monegal; from that we might surmise that Sarduy shares more with him than that they both lived as Latin American expatriates in France or that they both had a hand in helping promote groundbreaking Latin American fiction from there.

Sarduy broke with the revolution early and in the late 1960s became Latin American editor for Editions du Seuil as well as a close associate of the *Tel Quel* group organized around Roland Barthes. His only other mention in Retamar's "Caliban" is a curt dismissal of his literary and critical work as "neo Barthean flutterings," a phrase that is no less painful in Spanish: *mariposeo neobarthesiano*.[18] Anyone familiar with Sarduy's work (which I briefly discuss in chapter 2), or even Barthes's will understand just how inadequate, if not inappropriate, "fluttering" may be said to describe the quality, either intellectual or stylistic, of that work; anyone familiar with either man's sexual proclivities, and with idiomatic Spanish, will certainly understand exactly how "fluttering's" translation back into *mariposeo* is to be taken. This is perhaps not the place to defend Sarduy's work against the charge of "Arielesque" flightiness or of its curiously concomitant sin of proimperialist collaboration. This is the place, however, to establish that, for Retamar, the figure Caliban cuts through the tradition he wants to fashion from Martí on does little to dismantle at least one form of mastery, that of the patriarchal institution that privileges a rigid, masculine toughness, that institution which, in its uncompromisingly oppositional, resistant stance will brook no "penetration" and one for whom all signs of openness, even the most vigilant of critical engagements, translate immediately into passive, effeminate weakness. Gender positions and their symbolic counterparts thus serve Retamar here as more than effective rhetorical turns; they do much of the cultural police work required by his project, a project not only determined to condemn "the frivolous way in which some intellectuals . . . call themselves leftists," but also determined to ensure that truly organic intellectuals in this proto-Gramscian, Calibanic mold will be precisely not "frivolous," not "fluttery."

In addition to Martí and Castro, Retamar also mentions Ché Guevara's contribution to the cultural police work necessary for the cultivation of a correct revolutionary sensibility; Ché's "Man and Socialism in Cuba," Retamar tells us, includes an important "censure of decadent art under modern capitalism and its continuation in our society" and is remarkable for "the astonishing clarity with which he foresaw certain problems in our artistic life."[19] In a chapter from his book *Tropics of Desire* (2000), José Quiroga has made strategic use of an anecdote from Ché's life as an international emissary of the revolution to clarify further the nature of Ché's insight into these "certain problems": in Algiers in 1964, Ché "saw a volume of Virgilio Piñera's *Teatro completo* in the Cuban embassy" and "hurled it against a wall," shouting, "How dare you have in our embassy a book by that foul faggot?"[20] Quiroga uses the anecdote to occasion his exploration of Piñera's own textual self-closeting, one necessitated at least in practical measure by a Cuban revolutionary program, cited in both of my chapters 1 and 2, which called for the cultivation of a "New [Socialist] Man" generally along unmistakably Stalinist lines. According to "El Ché," Quiroga observes, "the space of the faggot is diametrically opposed to the hygiene of the revolution." Epps expands on this particular aspect of the psychosexual positions imbedded in this new socialist rhetoric; he cites a discussion of the new man's salient qualities in Roger Lancaster's *Life Is Hard: Machismo, Danger, and the Intimacy of Power in Nicaragua*. "The 'New Man' and the 'New Society,'" Lancaster argues, "are envisioned as hardworking, diligent, and studious, pure and without corruption. The aspect of machismo that the New Man embodies is the ascetic side, not the hedonistic one. The cult of the New Man, then, produced a cultural atmosphere in which homosexual practice . . . was at least publicly regarded as more suspect than before, tainted with the image of indulgence or corruption."[21] "New Man" ideology thus walks that very fine line between overt homosexual behavior and the kind of generalized homosocial but desperately antisexual male bonding dependent on the intense repression of that overt behavior. Should any grouping, national, communal, or otherwise, of such "new men" occur, Epps concludes, "it must be clear that one of them retains, even as he puts it problematically into practice, an ideal of masculinity: assertive, insertive, invasive. . . . In fact, the de-sexualization of love between men, the sublimation of homosexuality *en masse*, appears to be part of the selflessness and self-sacrifice that the Cuban leader[ship] deems necessary to social solidarity."[22]

The jump, then, from "New Man" rhetoric to the instrumental but no less tropic invocation of Caliban by Retamar is a short one. Simultaneously in the peculiar sexual tenor of Retamar's attack of those who lose in the *¿Quien es más macho?* game he plays in his essay and in the insistent recourse to plural pronominal play, the "Caliban" essay performs precisely the exclusions and censures it praises in more practical arenas. Indeed, it may well be that in the very act of invoking the ideal of Caliban, the essay does the necessary work of keeping his presumptive "other" in interpellative play. Beyond its insidious deployment of polarized gender qualities, Retamar's argument does nothing to dismantle other conventional dichotomies opposing, say, reality to representation, history to fiction, struggle to pleasure. Cultural laborers bear a unique and anxious burden in the Manichean system preserved by Retamar's essay, one that immediately disqualifies them the minute they dare to privilege signs over referents or even to combine them in any inventive way. They especially suffer if they indulge at all in the pursuit of pleasure, as though that were somehow automatically incompatible with the new socialist aesthetic. Pleasure especially becomes the purview, it seems, of those recalcitrant individualists who fail to withstand its seductions, who give themselves up to temptations that stronger men, men with collective values uppermost in mind, easily resist. It is easy to see how the cultural laborer thus opens himself up so readily to sexual and other suspicions; he is always already, like the homosexual, "interpellated by the revolutionary regime as problematical and peripheral," to quote Epps, confronting "the limits of society" and recognizing "the exclusionary shape of the 'we' by recognizing the 'I' as excluded."[23] This interpellation, kept in play if not created by the rhetoric in which the culture worker is simultaneously called and condemned, in turn calls attention to what remains undecidable in Retamar's essay: precisely what inhabits that tortured border space between the historical and the representational, between the material and the discursive.

Although for the most part Retamar preserves the division and implicit hierarchy privileging the historical over the linguistic, there is also at least one passage when, in a moment of disarming candor, he admits that oftentimes hard historical lessons are learned, not in the places where history is conventionally understood to unfold (the trenches, say, or the streets) but "in the flesh." This brief but telling passage suggests that Retamar at least implicitly understands the complexity of his own sexualizing of the history he is in the process of helping shape discursively. Bodies, flesh, we know, matter and signify; and in the way that the former effect relies on the function of the latter, "bodies" simultaneously comprise as they occupy one site in which they may be said to transpire both materially, as affect, and discursively, as significance.

Reschooling "Caliban"

In "The School of Caliban," the concluding section of *The Dialectics of Our America* (1991), his important historical and genealogical study of the literature of "all" the Americas, José David Saldívar has occasion to quote a familiar argument of Fredric Jameson's: "'History,' said Fredric Jameson, 'is what hurts, it is what refuses desire and sets inexorable limits to individuals as well as to collective praxis.'"[24] To this extent, history functions fairly analogously to the Lacanian "Real" that refuses desire by always stubbornly returning to its place; Saldívar uses this concept in his own attempt to "queer" Caliban by reading Chicana poet Cherríe Moraga's hybrid text *Loving in the War Years* as commensurate with Retamar's revision of the Calibanic tradition. Saldívar's choice of Moraga is strategic in more ways than one, however; by enrolling her rather than, say, a gay male writer in the "school" whose student body he gathers in this essay, Saldívar can either subsume questions of sexuality and sexual identity quite generally under questions of gender or sidestep the question of male homosexuality and its most material practices altogether. His separate chapter on Arturo Islas's frustrations in generating interest for his first novel among mainstream publishers in the United States barely mentions Islas's modest explorations of Chicano homosexuality at all, and in the concluding essay the only writer called on, for all the familiar reasons, for rejection to the school is Richard Rodríguez. Moraga's *Loving* qualifies her for admission, however, "because she wants to deal with gender empowerment, sensuous culture, and the libidinal economy, not relations of meaning" and thus her "linguistic reality's paradigm" is, according to Saldívar, "*The Tempest*: Survival, for her, demands that Chicanas resist the master's language; after all," he concludes, because "Prospero's conquest of the Americas is a male conquest, written from the male perspective."[25] Although Saldívar is careful to mention that Moraga's specifically lesbian feminism takes as a chief target homophobia in Chicano culture, most of the material in *Loving* that he addresses directly performs this critique on the most general level of an inverted family romance: Moraga's romance of her Chicana mother in rivalrous opposition to her white father. If "history" indeed is "what hurts," what is left unaccounted for in Saldívar's otherwise sensitive account of Moraga's work is precisely the work, and play, of the bodies on whom that "hurt," that pain, is most directly inscribed; and also, not surprisingly, the "pleasure" inscribed there as well, at least when "desire" can have its say, can effect a liberating resignification that subverts the "Real's" moribund auto-repetition. This is especially evident in Moraga's extraordinary lesbian-erotic verse, none of which finds its way into Saldívar's analysis.

Saldívar's anxiety with the specifically sexual aspects of Moraga's work appears symptomatic of the larger "Calibanic" tradition's relation to what remains of patriarchy after a too-limited postcolonial critique has done at least the theoretical work of dismantling the nationalist and racist vectors of empire.[26] What "discipline" one learns in the "school" of "Caliban" founded by Retamar and promoted by Saldívar might in the long run prove too ascetic, too resistant to forms of critical practice that perform their subversions in specifically sexual, and especially homosexual, spaces and modalities. In general,

Saldívar's strong appeal to Retamar in *The Dialectics of Our America* could use closer scrutiny, if only to put into greater relief the sexual politics contextualizing the situational specificity of "Caliban"'s composition. This will not be the place to undertake such a task; it will have to suffice here merely to suggest that if, according to Saldívar, Retamar's vision of "Caliban" negates "the master-slave relationship,"[27] it may only do so as an inversion rather than a subversion of these positions, an inversion that merely allows an exchange of places in the hierarchy rather than a dismantling of the structure of imbalance. In addition, it may well be that if "Caliban" only allows "desires either to participate in the historical process of hegemony or to resist its domination," that we, as cultural critics whose task in part is to articulate historical conditions enabling the productions of both cultural artifacts and pleasurable effects, may do well to request a fuller menu of options. If, as Saldívar argues, "Third World American intellectuals and writers in a postcolonial world . . . have a choice to make; either they can side with Prospero . . . and help fortify ruling culture and hegemony or they can side with Caliban, 'our symbol,' and help resist, limit and alter domination in the Americas"; and if, as he argues elsewhere, we can find "Caliban's revolutionary overturning of Prospero's disciplinary techniques of mind control, repression and anxiety" in the events issuing from "January 1959—namely in the Cuban Revolution,"[28] then it may be well to "decide" for a vigilant, critical undecidability rather than accept a limited choice of nightmares.

Sex Education

In "Nationalizing Sissies," a provocative essay that claims to offer an alternative to the residual master–slave structure characteristically imbedded in postcolonial discourses like Retamar's, José Piedra argues that sexualizing that structure by translating it into terms of a "bully–sissy" relation might provide us "with a libidinally tainted counterpoint to the colonialist takeover," one that provides especially for the colonized "sissy an avenue of anti-colonialist subversion and for both sissy and bully a form of postcolonial compromise."[29] This model of the power struggle may indeed improve on the standard

master–slave model to the extent that it allows for a greater articulation of gender difference, as well as for a certain greater psychic complexity by virtue of the greater degree of intimacy characterizing the
sissy–bully dynamic. In no way, however, should Piedra's elaboration
of this alternative power dynamic be taken merely to substitute one
rigid dialectic with another, on either Piedra's part or mine in using
him. Piedra's model succeeds where others fail precisely because of
his insistence that nothing is so stably "oppositional" about the
sissy–bully exchange; it borrows especially from theories of sadomasochism an appreciation for the deep structural ambiguities of
such relationships.[30] "In the sissy–bully exchange," Piedra argues, "it
is difficult to tell who was whom, in what way, and to what extent.
Whether symbolically or actually, passively or provocatively, anally,
orally, or any other way, for a challenging or passionate instant or forever, the sissy bullies the bully. This type of reversible behavior relates
to the theory and practice of sadomasochism, viewed as a willful alternative to the will-crushing colonial pact."

Piedra's "sissy" manifesto exemplifies a larger movement not to reject notions like Retamar's "Caliban" but to relax and expand the possibilities for critical and practical subversions of mastery in *all*
colonizing exchanges beyond the restrictive parameters of the "bully"
confrontation with "bully" suggested by "Caliban." Piedra describes
his as a project to "upgrad(e) the notion of the receptive cultural
agent of colonialism, presumably passive females and males, into a
subversive force capable of transforming libidinal traps into political
trenches with a touch of nationalism."[31] Piedra is careful, however,
not to relax his model so much that it collapses back into "instances
in which the sissy action smacks of being merely a powerless reaction,
[or] even a cynical accommodation, to invasive bully techniques";[32]
instead, Piedra envisions new communal configurations, emergent
antinationalist proto-nations comprised of "desperate and disparate
nationals who breach singly or together through traditionally subjugated, critically secondhand and/or second-class identities built from
within, against and beyond the borders of dominant nations and national paradigms."[33]

In some ways, Piedra's work constitutes a complicating deviation, a
salutary ambiguation against the conventionally polarized models of

subaltern political behavior as either exclusively resistant (if it's 'active') or reactive (if it's 'passive'). His may, in fact, constitute one productive attempt to develop further what Judith Butler has in other contexts described as the albeit difficult, limited possibility of an "agency without mastery."[34] In one respect, Piedra offers a necessary corrective to Gustavo Pérez-Firmat's assertion, in 1994's *Life on the Hyphen,* that the general Cuban American example of immigration and cultural assimilation somehow speaks in favor of models of cultural and political engagement he describes as receptive, accommodating "bi-culturation," operating more in the spirit of "apposition" than "opposition," of "collusion" rather than "collision," of "contiguity" rather than "conflict."[35] Pérez-Firmat should, I think, be congratulated for "sissifying" his own critical demeanor enough to position himself on a bicultural-libidinal "Desi" chain that conjoins him bisexually to both Desi Arnaz and the North American Lucy he loves. In general, however, *Life on the Hyphen* tends too readily to embrace not so much hegemonic U.S. culture, even as embodied in Desi's embrace of Lucy,[36] but the pleasures of a deviance that precisely and strategically deviates (and distracts) from the complex scenarios of pain in which not only the Cuban, but all, histories of displacement, dislocation, and dispersal transpire.

Piedra's insistence on the sadomasochistic complexity of the sissy–bully engagement demands the active and critical remembering of historical "pain." To this extent, Heberto Padilla's memoir *Self-Portrait of the Other* may be said to perform this engagement more fully, because more ambivalently, than Pérez-Firmat's admittedly provocative sexual performance in *Life on the Hyphen.* Curiously spare in style, Padilla's memoir nevertheless explores (as I observed already in chapter 2) in considerably intimate detail the complex psychological dynamics of the tyrant–subject relationship. After a passage describing an interrogation culminating with a beating that put him in a hospital, Padilla tells us:

> While I was in the Military Hospital, Fidel Castro came to see me. I remember the clanging of iron doors and the panache of the escort making way for him in a place where even inanimate objects would have dropped to their knees to let him pass. I remember . . . he waved a dossier, pacing back and forth with

giant steps, and never looking me in the eye. "We two are the
only ones who have to be here. Today I have the time to talk to
you; and we have a lot to talk about." . . . Yes, we had time to
talk—time for him to talk his head off, to heap scorn on the literature of the world, because "getting revolutionaries to fight
isn't the same as getting literary men to fight. In this country,
they have never done anything for the people, neither in the last
century nor in this one. They are always latecomers jumping on
the bandwagon of history. . . . "He must have seen himself as an
impressive leader standing majestically before a no less impressive adversary dressed in a faded uniform, scar still fresh on his
forehead, his body still aching from the kicks of history.[37]

Padilla, who was not gay, exhibits in this passage a striking willingness to observe and record Castro's person and demeanor more intimately than their actual closeness in the scene would compel. To this
extent, he shares with Reinaldo Arenas, in whose own memoir the
record of persecution at the hands of the same authority is more explicitly homosexualized, a tendency to be, as Epps puts it, "so shadowed by political reality, by all kinds of plots and misalliances, that
the work that bears his name is the work, figuratively speaking, of
others as well. It is in this sense, that the more he [Arenas, but also,
I'm suggesting, Padilla] is against Castro's Cuba, the more he is in it,
even in exile . . . one might even say," Epps concludes, "that Arenas' is
an extreme case of the revolutionary infidel and in-Fidel."[38] Padilla
would hardly have blinked at the suggestion that he bears a similar
homoerotically ambivalent fascination with Castro as Epps argues
for Arenas; he might, however, have bristled at the terminology of the
characterization of his relation to Castro as one of sissy to bully, but
in his memoir he certainly exhibits an admirable openness to the sexuality (if not to the aesthetics) of his queer comrades in letters, such
as Piñera, Sarduy, and Lezama Lima, as well as a clear understanding
of his own abjected position vis-à-vis Fidel.

   In addition, from reading either of their memoirs, no one could
confuse either Padilla or Arenas's "deviations from correct revolutionary opinion," in either their work or behavior, as in any way
symptomatic of bourgeois decadence or collusive with the interests

of North American cultural or political hegemony. Indeed, as exiles in the United States, both writers have had opportunities to testify, in work they could only have published in the West, against the worst excesses of expanding Western capitalism, Western bourgeois liberalism, and even the very cultural and commercial decadence that the revolution itself decries. Often their testimonies ring with the same indignation one hears not only in Retamar, but in Martí before him, who, unlike his revolutionary disciple, indeed lived in the belly of the same beast to which Padilla and Arenas exiled themselves.[39]

In addition to Piedra's essay, we can also turn an equally provocative study by Van Gosse of the early revolutionaries' function as homosocial fantasy projection, this time not for Cuban society itself, but for middle-class North America's restless male adolescents in the mid-1950s. Entitled *Where the Boys Are: Cuba, Cold War America and the New Left* (1993), Gosse's book argues that, at the time Castro's troops were organizing in the Sierra Madre and became the subject of a famous 1957 CBS news special, the ensuing "Yankee *fidelismo* was [grounded in] the extra-political world of spontaneous action for its own sake," and that "Fidel became [liberal, intellectual] America's Rebel With a Cause on a grand scale, but his popularity in the U.S., especially among young men, exceeded expectations. In this context," Gosse goes on, "the collapse and reinvention of traditional boyhood and manhood provided the raw material for behavior that was not subversive or oppositional in any sense, but simply nonconformist."[40]

Gosse's study, therefore, exemplifies in yet another respect the complex interrelation between the historical and what might yet be called the discursive if not aesthetic; the televisual projection into North America of glamorized, bearded rebels in the Cuban mountains marks "the beginnings of a cult of Fidel [in] desire in its rawest forms, both in its politics and its lack of politics." According to Gosse, "The [Cuban] bad boys, with their millions of admirers and imitators, portrayed variants on an outlaw sensibility keyed only to the recovery of pleasure, and a rejection of the fierce will to repression with which American men in the postwar period had become identified." The space dividing the U.S.-bred cult of Fidel from the nearly simultaneously emerging postcolonial critical-discursive "school" of Caliban (that which, Retamar tells us, begins with the publications of Octave

Mannoni's *Psychologie de la colonisation* in 1950 and Frantz Fanon's *Black Skin, White Masks* in 1952)[41] might in fact not be so great; if, as Gosse argues, "the recovery of desire" in the U.S. instance "through pleasure and the body, whether the kind of teenage sexuality dormant since the heyday of the young Frank Sinatra, or that which had always been unseen, like Ginsberg's homosexuality, was crucial to the watershed of the mid-1950's," then perhaps as crucial on the postcolonial scene, but perhaps for historical reasons not explicitly articulated, we can detect the beginnings of a male homosocial fascination, one Retamar would probably disavow, with the unquestionably homo- and gynophobic figuration of "Caliban."

Conversely, Retamar actually indulges in the "Caliban Revisited" essay in a little boys'-club fantasy work of his own, constructing a scene of odd historical reconciliation and redemption that not only suggests marked homosociality but that indeed crosses the line between the historical and the literary with a curious but unmistakable "flutter":

> There is just one world, [Retamar intones] in which the oppressor and the oppressed struggle, one world in which, rather sooner than later, the oppressed will be victorious. . . . The tempest has not subsided. But *The Tempest*'s shipwrecked sailors, Crusoe and Gulliver, can be seen, rising out of the waters, from terra firma. There, not only Prospero, Ariel and Caliban, Don Quixote, Friday and Faust, await them, but Sofía and Oliveira, and Colonel Aureliano Buendía as well, and—halfway between history and dream—Marx and Lenin, Bolívar and Martí, Sandino and Che Guevara.[42]

Quite a party, to be sure; this is an oddly utopian moment for the rigidly anti-idealist Retamar, one that exposes in the nonspace "halfway between history and dream" a figure of undecidability analogous to the one "in the flesh" Retamar lets slip by, even as the place where the hardest historical lessons are learned, in the earlier essay.

If I've clearly not come to praise Retamar in his analysis, neither, I should clarify, have I come to bury him. I'd like to understand my position in relation to him and other key members, like José David

Saldívar, of at least one school of Caliban as analogous to the one
Edward Said assumes toward them in his chapter in *Culture and
Imperialism* entitled "Theories of Resistance Culture."[43] There I think
Said actually gets wrong something of the spirit of especially
Retamar's invocation of Shakespeare if not his character when he
terms it an "affectionate contention . . . for the right to represent the
Caribbean . . ." though it is indeed motivated by "an impulse to con-
tend [that is] part of a grander effort to discover the bases of an integral identity different from the formerly dependent, derivative
one."[44] Said acknowledges, I think rightly, that "Retamar's choice of
Caliban over Ariel signals a profoundly important ideological debate
at the heart of the cultural effort to decolonize, an effort at the restora-
tion of community and repossession of culture that goes on long
after the political establishment of nation-states."[45] But even Said tem-
pers this praise with a corrective, one that strategically employs Fanon
to caution that, while becoming "aware of one's self as belonging to
a subject people is the founding insight of anti-imperialist nationalism," that ensuing "nationalist consciousness can very easily lead to
frozen rigidity."[46]

It is perhaps the strong impression I have of this "rigidity" in
Retamar's essay that makes me question its viability, if overly revered
and then left unrevised, as an instrument in the larger contemporary
project of genuinely politically liberating critical and cultural practices, a project I understand contemporary "Americas" Studies to
claim for itself. I'll end this section of my argument with a final citation of Said, who warns us, and, perhaps more gently than I've done,
cautions Retamar, that "the dangers of chauvinism and xenophobia
remain very real," even in movements of anti-imperial resistance and
liberation driven by nationalist configurations and that it may well be
"best when Caliban sees his own history as an aspect of the history of
all subjugated men and women, and comprehends the complex truth
of his own social and historical situation."[47]

Affirmative Action

The question I hope to have put to Retamar (and his disciples) at least
implicitly in the preceding discussion is the role of the writer and

critic in revolutionary and postcolonial projects larger and more complex than those taking place on his island, or in any one national space, whose response is commensurate to that scope and to that complexity. In the rest of this chapter, I hope to suggest briefly how the "Caliban" model of subversive creation and intellection might be manipulated and opened enough to include, for example, openly queer and queer-identified U.S. Latino writers like the novelist Arturo Islas and the poet Rafael Campo, both of whom combine questions of ethnic and sexual alterity in their work in trenchant subversion of that which passes for normal on both counts but who also perform much of that subversion through a playful and even solicitous engagement of canonical forms and canonical writers, not the least of among whom is Caliban's creator, William Shakespeare.

Such an analysis not only challenges the limits of Retamar's vision but interrogates more fully the myopia of a "revolutionary imagination," which, returning to the epigraph by Brad Epps with which this chapter began, too easily assumes that "the pleasure of the text, given to dissipation and wasteful dissemination, reflects and expands the pleasure of the flesh, expands it, somewhat paradoxically, as the threat of a generalized sexual narcissism" since "one cannot focus on the play of the signifier without being in some way withdrawn from the work of society."[48] This last assertion seems to me not only conceptually lazy but strategically conceived to police cultural and critical work, and workers, in the manner I have been outlining here. I hope at this point to relax considerably as well my own policing correction of Retamar, his "Caliban," and their school; there are other scenes of instruction to enter here, spaces in which alternative disciplines may produce alternatives to discipleship and in which some more serious and open attention to aesthetics may in turn generate a more responsibly historicized and politicized understanding of the experiences of pleasure.

To this end, Ramón Saldívar's argument concluding his own influential study of *Chicano Narrative* rearticulates the relation of historical discursivity to the "realness" of events in a manner that lends itself well to the analysis at hand. There Saldívar defines "the 'Real' [as] an outer limit that the subject approaches in the anxiety of moments of truth—moments of personal crisis, of the loss of identity, or of the agonizing polarizations of revolutionary situations such as those experienced by the subjects of contemporary Chicano narrative. The make-up of 'history,'" he goes on to conclude, "is not so much the empirical events of the world as the self-inscription and symbolization in texts of those events and in our thinking about them."[49] Saldívar's terms, I think, can bear some slight modification and translation: the "outer limit" of the "Real" against which discursively constituted subjects collide and collapse can be read as a rim, a site of discontinuity to be sure, but one where the intense experience of an extremity that cannot be reduced to an opposition of irremediably polarized terms nevertheless holds the possibility if not the promise of some "give" to that limit, of some beyond to that border; and to this extent certainly the quality of this confrontation is not at all exclusively characteristic of Chicano narrative or even of Latino discourses most broadly conceived. If anything, I'd like to mime Saldívar's analytical moves in this passage, a critical point in a chapter he entitles the "Reconstruction of American Literary History," to demonstrate their susceptibility to a collusive critical queering, one might say a sissification, which may in turn not only allow for a more representative enrollment policy for an alternative school of Caliban but will also significantly reconfigure whose "America" and whose "literary history" such a school would reconstitute in its study.

Briefly, then, let me turn to important literary texts by two openly gay Latino writers in order to begin the process of revising the policy of enrollment in such a school. The first, Arturo Islas's novel, *La Mollie and the King of Tears,* was completed but unfinished at the time of his death from AIDS complications in 1991, but it was published for its interest to scholars and students of Islas in 1996; it concludes with a chapter entitled "Just Like Romeo and Juliet," a chapter that simultaneously resolves the novel's narrative conflicts and dissolves its textual and linguistic elements.[50] By any aesthetic standard *La Mollie* is deeply imperfect; the author saw his story line through to its end, but much of the local work of developing character, constructing anecdote and scene, and polishing language, remained to be done. Nevertheless, *La Mollie*'s ambitions are as much about its own status as a work of art and as a linguistic construct because they are about the cautionary tale it tells about cross-cultural and cross-sexual communication and can therefore be legitimately analyzed accordingly. *La Mollie* plays aggressively with its Anglo and non-Anglo genealogies and, in frequent sparkling moments, manages impressive effects. Islas's novel consists of a first-person narrative performed as an impromptu monologue by Louie Mendoza, a Texan Chicano who comes to San Francisco and finds love with a wealthy Anglo woman named Molly. Louie is interviewed in a hospital waiting room by a silent interlocutor, a student collecting human interest stories, as Molly lies in a coma after taking a serious fall. Louie's story covers his entire life and culminates in the extraordinary set of events that keep him from getting home to Molly before her accident.

Louie's language represents an impressively sustained exercise on Islas's part in working-class Chicano street language, or *caló*, a dialect he rarely dared reproduce in his earlier novels. The risk pays off more than occasionally for Islas, as in this crucial digression in the last chapter on the untranslatable names of Mexican *pan dulces*, literally "sweet breads":

> I wish I could tell you the names of them sweet breads in Spanish, man, cause changing em to English makes em lose their flavor. Don't get me wrong, neither. I think everybody needs to know English to get by in this country—the real English, not that liar's language the businessmen, lawyers and politicians use. Don't even get me started on those dollar-bill words and sentences we're supposed to learn 'cause it ain't English. . . . I even like Shakespeare's language better than that gobbledygook. . . . I don't want everybody to speak like me—that would be boring—but I don't want nobody telling me I can't talk this way neither. And all this caca about which is the real mother tongue—our language is accents, man.[51]

This last declaration, in a Chicano novel that makes frequent loving nods to the British literary tradition, from Shakespeare through the line of ribald novels featuring lustful Molls and Mollys, counters almost directly the use of the first-person plural in the discourse of "our" America championed by Retamar. Who, for Islas, is the "we" who can claim that "our language is accents"? Few readers would accuse Islas of anything like an unreflective or cloying anglophilia after reading *La Mollie*, but neither would one find in his text a simple nationalist or even identitarian solution to the Chicano community's political and cultural trials in the United States.

Islas's relationship to queer culture is just as complex and ambivalent; one of the transformative scenes in the last chapter of *La Mollie* takes place in a gay South-of-Market leather bar called the Mind Shaft, where the injured and desperate Louie has gone in search of his gay brother Tomás. Louie's descriptions of what he observes there betray both the author's intimate knowledge of, and deep ambivalence toward, such scenes:

> the guy that's standing next to me['s] . . . all naked except for a pair of boots, a cowboy hat, and about a dozen clothespins clamped onto different parts of his body, even down there, where I never dreamed I would see one. . . . We used to have some pretty crude initiation ceremonies in our gang, man, but nothing like this. We only pretended we were gonna hurt guys where it hurt the most—but we never actually did it. This dude made me thinka them stories about Indian tribes and the kindsa rituals they put young bucks through before they'd make it into manhood. He made me forget all about my own pain just thinking about what it must feel like to be pinched in the you-know-what. . . . I'm telling you, man, what them sissies can take is more than any straight guy I ever know could take or would want to. I gotta hand it to them fruits—they can handle pain better than me.[52]

The Mind Shaft, a wildly alternative scene of discipline than the "school" of Caliban imagined by Retamar, certainly still has its lessons to teach us about the relationship between power, the practices we term either erotic or aesthetic, and the complex of sensations they produce, a complex that bears no simple conceptualization into the binaries of pleasure and pain. Islas, certainly an expert handler of "literary" English, could not from these or any other passages in *La Mollie* be said to have been "learned in the master's language" but to "curse" him in turn; instead, Islas's language, his "language of accents," provides him with an opportunity to forgo the whole dynamic of mastery without ignoring the historical legacies of power. If anything, I think, he can be said to engage in a practice that is equally his as it is Shakespeare's: the practice of a comic, and comically subversive, discourse, one not without precedents but always in the process of transformation, one that never loses sight of pleasure even as it puts itself through the rigors, not to say the pains, of its chosen rituals, the disciplining rehearsals of form and convention.

In the four collections of poems he has thus far published, Cuban American poet Rafael Campo makes what are both simultaneously more and less explicit nods to Shakespeare and his various legacies than those by Arturo Islas I've just discussed. The earliest collection, 1994's *The Other Man Was Me: A Voyage to the New World,* begins with a section entitled "Learning the Language," signaling rather readily Campo's willingness to invoke certain Calibanic (and other Shakespearean) echoes.[53] These "first" of his collected works comprise even as they explicitly perform a kind of literary apprenticeship on Campo's part. By undertaking this poetic voyage to a "new world," Campo means in turn to undergo a process of education that neither rejects nor surrenders to the precedents of Western literary tradition; indeed, Campo's new world invites the retention of old forms by breathing new life into them via a radical process of what can only be called (and here I mean to echo Judith Butler) strategic resignification. "Learning the Language" begins with a poem, "Camino Real," which signals ironically that the "royal way" in which these poems are directed lead to no resuscitated golden land (or age) but to ever sharper and more refined forms of verbal expression at once literary and critical. "I speak by cutting ruts in air," the poets declares, "cutting" at once to rupture and route a line and a lineage, combining in a single verbal gesture the violently institutionalizing inscription of a whole colonizing history *and* the legacy of critical cultural reactions to it. This poet's inheritance bears all the complications of its doubleness, from its inherent dialectal bilingualism to its intrinsic dialectical materiality. "The Spanish that I never knew at all," he confesses, "My heritage and punishment, the walls/At once too sharp and weak to lean upon," nevertheless generate(s) quite a productive tension with the English out of which these lines are spun, a tension productive enough to land the poet, "In the Form" (literally, of the sonnet) by the end of this first section.

These notions recur in a number of the poems comprising the body of "Learning the Language"; often Campo personalizes the larger literary, cultural, and political histories into which these poems fit by translating them into the terms of his own filial relations. Spanish is both his father's language and the language of a particularly Hispanic patriarchy; it is the language that, having been learned literally from the father, becomes the instrument of both the son's indenture to and liberation from paternal and patriarchal authority. "I write to you in English, Father," the poet-son explains in "San Fernando," "Because I am evolving. I'm freer/Than I was before. My hairy chest/Contains a thumping drum, some resolving/Process, a demand to be loved." One can almost imagine these as softened sentiments from, but certainly still potentially assignable to, a Caliban learning in his own way to demand his freedom from Prospero, and certainly the insistence of island images in Campo's explicitly Cubanized work reinforces this association.[54]

In "San Fernando" the poet goes on to accuse, "When you/Fooled me, it was like I'd been to Cuba" and in so doing confesses to an illicit fantasy that combines his own projection of his exiled father's perhaps misplaced desire to revisit or even return to his home with his own quasi-oedipal desire *for* his father. "Cuba" for the poet takes the place of the passive objectified woman in the conventional homosocial triangle, but in this case she is explicitly identified with masculine elements that conventionally go repressed in such a scenario: "The dark men. The inaccessible island,/Like the parts of you I couldn't see/Beneath your towel." The poet's strategic perversion of his father's otherwise conventional exile desire for return develops further in the following poem, "Belonging," which elaborates the fantasy of return, this time on the son's part, but never without some attention to the displaced desire of (and for) his father: "I went to Cuba on a raft I made," he tells us, "It felt so sleek and dangerous, like sharks/Or porno magazines or even thirst." Although he discovers there "nothing but the same damn sun,/Indifferent but oddly angry, the face/My father wore at dinnertime," still the poet feels a compulsion to stay, so he "stripped," he tells us, "And sat there naked in an effort to attract some cannibals, but no one came." What positive or negative fantasies the poet held, and the extent to which they were borrowed from his father's own store of fantasies, give way at poem's end to a desire for "a book/That told the history of my lost people." Although a conventional reading of such a wishful declaration might reinforce a conventional understanding of history's privilege over fantasy, that is, over fiction, and over literature and art in general, such a reading would disrespect the unconventional poetic imagination from which this declaration issues.

Indeed, Campo's decision to answer the wish in "Belonging" and to conclude "Learning the Language," with a Shakespearean sonnet as fastidious and playful (at once) as "In the Form," articulates as it performs precisely the complex, ambivalent relationship to genealogy, tradition, and even heritage that perhaps only a queer Caliban could assume. The key to the text may be held in the observation that the sonnet, and perhaps all formal verse, derives its energy from negatives and absences ("Tension. Words withheld. A rhyme/Where memory has left its watermark."), but if the poem is an answer to the wish in "Belonging" for "a book/That told the history of my lost people," the keys to "In the Form" are multiple and various. Campo can claim various configurations of a "lost people" to whom he might belong, not least among whom are those who know intimately that no discussion of genealogy can take genealogy for granted as the neutral, not to say natural, result of any particular kind of sexual, textual, or cultural reproduction. This sonnet's critical turn is a parenthesis about parenting occupying lines 4, 5, 6, and most of 7, a grammatical disturbance of the coherence of the first and second quatrains, and a celebration of the phonetic and syntactic perversions imbedded in the failure of "stork" to rhyme with "work," and of the stork's work to correspond in any simple way with Shakespeare's. "(My parents," the poet remembers once "arguing about the stork,/And whether it appears in Shakespeare's work:/'Let not the marriage of true minds—'/ 'That's enough, dear!')" The aborted quotation of *one* Shakespearean sonnet does nothing in this instance to prevent the successful iteration of *the* Shakespearean sonnet, however; instead, it demonstrates rather convincingly what remains possible beyond the limitations of any restrictive opposition of the historical and the aesthetic.

What Campo's meticulously Shakespearean sonnet performs is indeed the rediscovery of a "history," that of a people "lost" not *from,* but *in* the Shakespearean sonnet, at least as it has been traditionally received and officially reproduced; "In the Form" reclaims a history in literary texts for homoerotic desire without choosing to sacrifice either history or literature, and it is perhaps this refusal to choose between them that marks most eloquently the depth of the poem's political insight and commitment. In this respect it also performs most explicitly the work of a revolutionary artist who knows better than to sacrifice either of the drives implicated in that complex term; history may indeed be "what hurts," but pleasures have their histories too, and there is nothing either politically irresponsible or simply narcissistically self-indulgent about a well-crafted sonnet that acknowledges its origins in "A passion gone berserk" and likens its work to that of "A whetstone where the ax of language grinds/Until precision is its point, until/The carving out of one's own heart is fine/And painless as a summer's breeze."

That both Campo and Islas solicit Shakespeare openly, perhaps defiantly, says as much about their desire to announce their own queerness as it does to challenge the restrictive anglophobia (often masking an insidious homophobia) of what often passes for U.S. Latino critical discourse in the wake of Retamar's "Caliban"; Spanish, we know, is no less the colonialist's language than English and no more the mother tongue of historically marginalized communities than English. Writers like Campo and Islas thus provide us with both a challenge and an opportunity, to put more fully into practice critical procedures that acknowledge the transnational movements and multilingual forces shaping cultural production in spaces increasingly loosely termed "American." The challenge to practitioners in both "American" and "Americas" Studies may indeed be to return one of Retamar's own cherished sources, José Martí, who devotes strategic attention in his oft-cited 1891 essay "Our America" to the role of the "American" versus the "European" university, and to ask ourselves anew, much more than a century since the publication of that essay, and at a moment when the possibilities for cultural and intellectual exchange between Cuba and *all* her "American" neighbors appear likely to expand, what the cultural critic's role should be in the ongoing process of shaping truly representative "American" Studies in truly representative "American" institutions.

PART II

FROM EXILE
TO DIASPORA

Chapter 4

Hemispheric Vertigo: Cuba, Québec, and Our (New) America

In the same way that . . . transnationalism can be mobilized by the state in the interest of properly nationalist ends, so too can the psychic imaginary—in even its most individuated and privatized instantiations—negotiate the terms of transnationalism so as to solidify the identification of the individual "citizen" with the national entity whose hegemony transnationalism itself has been understood to challenge. . . . The exact character of the relation between the two, though, is anything but predictable or definitively fixed.

—Phillip Brian Harper[1]

Going Up to Go Down, Going North to Go South

"Pleasure" would almost always be my response to the question, "And what is your purpose in visiting Montréal?" posed to me by Canadian border guards whenever I crossed into Québec from Vermont, at the checkpoint where U.S. Interstate 89 became the much smaller Canadian rural highway 133. Having left the San Francisco Bay Area in 1996 to take a teaching job at Dartmouth College in New Hampshire,

I spent the following two years rather unsuccessfully trying to adjust to life in a remote New England town; part of that process entailed frequent visits to more cosmopolitan nearby settings, especially Montréal, which, although an hour further away from Dartmouth than Boston, offered an infinitely more seductive, and satisfying, set of cultural and recreational opportunities to me. Although both Boston and Montréal boast thriving gay communities, and both certainly exhibit the growing influence of the Latin American diaspora through the very visible, and audible, presence of Spanish speakers on their streets and in their neighborhoods, Montréal clearly offers a more fascinating and in many ways even intellectually challenging intersection of these sexual and transnational cultures, an intersection further complicated by the presence of Québecois cultural and Canadian national elements in the same scene.

Crossing the border into Québec was always informed for me by two associations I could never quite divorce from the act: one was always occasioned by a road sign appearing just below the checkpoint, which, rather than informing travelers they are just about to enter Canada, announces instead that they are just crossing the latitudinal line marking the halfway point between the Equator and the North Pole; the other, less tangible but by no means less bewildering, had to do with my own set of memories of past border crossings at an analogous geographical site, the U.S.–México border at Calexico/Mexicali where, in the course of the 1970s, my family found themselves as they traveled back and forth from suburban Los Angeles, where we lived, to San Felipe, a fishing village and beach town on the Gulf Coast of Baja California. Both associations triggered intense cognitive dislocations, one spatial and the other temporal, but both were also necessarily and significantly informed by geographical and historical contexts overlaying, and overwhelming, the presumably more neutral vectors of space and time. Knowing, for example, that the Canadian border marked some halfway point between Ecuador and the Arctic, that as many latitudinal zones crossed Canada as crossed not only the United States and México but also crossed all of Central and a good portion of South America, not only sparked (thanks to my admitted ignorance of geography) a new respect for the dimensions of the Canadian land mass but also demanded some serious reconsideration of the presumably descriptive functions of such geographical categories as hemispheres, continents, and regions, especially as they underwrite, in terms of their fictive correspondence to, such political, cultural, and other symbolically, imaginatively constituted "spaces" as nations, states, and even communities.

But if my frequent confrontation of this road sign left me feeling unmapped or remapped in primarily spatial ways, by making me think, as I traveled literally "up" the map, of all that lay to the South (or "below"), my equally frequent, mostly cursory, encounters with border guards plunged me back into my own personal and political past, raising familiar but distant ghosts I never expected to revisit in a place so putatively far from home. My family left Cuba in 1966, when I was five years old, and settled in a working-class neighborhood of Los Angeles County. Like many Cuban exiles of their generation, my parents took their time about securing permanent resident status, and certainly citizenship, for us, primarily to indulge the fantasy of returning home to Cuba once Fidel Castro was deposed and his revolution discredited. But by the mid-1970s, it became clear that exile would be a longer-term condition than they'd hoped; they gave up the ghost of imminent return, and we became resident aliens. Green cards in hand, my family immediately began driving to México on every possible occasion, as many Cubans in Southern California did, both to enjoy the familiarity of México's Latino culture and to enjoy the beaches of the Gulf of California, whose waters, unlike the Pacific's, were warm and reminded them of the Caribbean. But even with proper documentation, border crossings were never easy for us, thanks primarily to our coloring, our surname, and my parents' very audible Spanish accents; so crossing into México was one thing, but crossing back over to the United States always left us with a feeling of profound illegitimacy. Guests in both the country we lived in and the country we visited, getting back over from the latter to the former always left us feeling at best provisionally situated, not quite at home in either place, perhaps least, and most, at home at the border itself. U.S. border guards in particular never failed to be suspicious of the documentation we so readily presented to them and rarely failed to have us pull over for more thorough searches of our car and more thorough investigations of our history and our motives for travel.

Crossing into and out of Canada in the period that I lived in New England visited these feelings of illegitimacy back on me in surprising ways; a U.S. citizen since 1983 and a frequent traveler to Europe in the course of my well-financed graduate school days, I thought myself rather worldly and, well, accustomed to the ritual of customs. My sense of unease at this particular border, however, had less to do with my (certainly by now more stabilized) political status and more to do with my sexual status; oftentimes my primary if not exclusive purpose in traveling to Montréal was to immerse myself in the familiarity of the queer urban cultural environment of the city's Village district, a neighborhood that although very uniquely Québecois in many of its qualities certainly bears many of the qualities of North American queer, and especially male, culture generally and quite visibly. My response to the Canadian border guards seemed, to me, the appropriate one: "Pleasure" was for me in part a coded but for that reason no less directly truthful way of saying "Because I'm queer." But the pleasures available to me in Montréal were never simply, or even exclusively, defined by its sexual cultures; whatever unease I felt about disclosing myself, even indirectly, as a sexually motivated tourist to these representatives of Canadian state authority was always counteracted by my equally strong, and in some ways more legitimate feeling: a desire to immerse myself in a Latin(o) culture, one not simply defined by the Francophonic elements of Québecois culture but also by the obvious presence of Hispanophone "Latin" Americans in significant numbers, hailing from a variety of nations, on the same streets.

I begin this chapter of loosely collected observations with the juxtaposition of the epigraph quoting Phillip Harper's extraordinary conclusion to his most thoughtful essay with my own selection of highly personal anecdotes to underscore the tension Harper so usefully elaborates in that passage. Much of Harper's own argument in *Private Affairs* disorients itself around the affective quality produced so often, especially for those of us Harper describes as "nonnormative citizens," marked in a variety of visible if not interchangeable ways by disadvantageous social and other differences, by the new opportunities for border-crossing mobility enabled in part by the "new" transnationalism Harper mostly takes to task in that essay.[2] I hope in the following sections of this discussion to refine the edge of productive critical tension that Harper began to hone in *Private Affairs* by offering a series of events, of varying levels of public notoriety, each of which offers in turn an example of what I take to be the challenge that the new and highly paradoxical transnationalism poses for North American culture critics, especially for those committed in their work to a liberating politics, one that tends largely to assume that some (although not just any) transcendence of the authority and power of the nation-state is not only desirable but necessary to the fulfillment of their project. As I juxtapose here localized and often quite ephemeral occurrences with the more generalized analytic they occasion, I remain aware of the necessarily uneasy passage from the local to the general (which is not identical to the trip some take far too easily from the local to the global) that trails such moves, regardless of the clarity or precision of their mapping. That unease I here rename the malaise produced by the vertiginous counterflows against which contemporary diasporic transnational subjects (whether Cuban, American, or otherwise) must navigate to get, virtually (and certainly actually!) anywhere.[3]

Global Gloria

In *The Myth of Continents,* the critical geographers Martin Lewis and Kären Wigen make the following observation about the traditional dependence of geographical knowledge on colonial and imperial politics:

> "Latin America" is one of the earliest of the world regional designations, dating back to the middle of the 19th century . . . originally defined by military strategists, and our conceptualization of it still bears the taint of imperial thinking. . . . Latin America was deliberately coined by French scholars in the middle of the 19th century as a way to refer simultaneously to the Spanish-, Portuguese-, and French-speaking portions of the Americas. At the time, the French government under Napoleon

III was plotting to carve out a new empire in the region, and the notion of a "Latin" essence linking French with Spanish- and Portuguese-speaking American countries had a great appeal as a way to naturalize such a project. . . . [B]y disinterested criteriae this "Latin" region of the French imperial imagination never made sense; certainly Haitians have less in common with residents of Argentina than with neighboring Jamaicans, . . . strictly speaking, a linguistic definition would mean that Québec, too, ought to be considered part of Latin America.[4]

If any one event could serve as the paradigm for my encounter with this alternative conceptualization of Latin America, and therefore of Latin Americans, it would have to be the evening of September 4, 1996, when I saw Gloria Estefan in concert at Montréal's Molson Center. Part of her *Evolution* world tour, the concert was designed to promote *Destiny*, which was at the time Estefan's first English-language album of original compositions in five years and released in conjunction with her recording of "Reach," one of the two official anthems of the 1996 Atlanta Olympic Games. It bears mentioning here that the other official anthemic diva of those games was Céline Dion. One can only second-guess the strategy that went into choosing these two singers to represent this particular Olympic moment: although both sing primarily in English now, English is neither one's first language, and although together Estefan and Dion can be said to embody something of a larger "American" inter- or even transnationalism, they only achieve this status by downplaying their specific national, cultural, and linguistic origins, origins that in both their cases situate them in contexts (Cuban, Québecois) where "nationalism" itself remains not simply contested but radically, constitutively, undecidable. It also bears mentioning here that Estefan's two Spanish-language albums preceding *Destiny*, *Mi Tierra* and *Abriendo Puertas* (*My Land* and *Opening Doors*, respectively), performed a characteristically Latin American double gesture for these post–Cold War, postcolonial times. The first celebrates Estefan's specifically Cuban national roots in both the lyrical content and musical forms of most of the songs, and the second opens out to include forms indigenous across the rest of Latin America and the Caribbean and celebrates in its lyrics a pan-Latinism on the basis of language and culture meant to counteract divisions among nations based on geography, politics, and economics. Both of these Spanish-language albums enjoyed considerably more crossover appeal than Estefan and the Miami Sound Machine's earliest recordings in Spanish because they followed the extraordinary success of her English-language recordings from the mid-1980s on.[5]

So when Estefan invaded Dion's home turf in the late summer of 1996, she came armed with a more varied repertoire than she might have been able to perform at any other time in her career. This in part explains why, for an audience whose members spoke primarily French and/or English, Estefan felt comfortable singing more Spanish-language songs but also why she gave that audience the choice of having her conduct her banter with them either in Spanish or in English. The audience very volubly, and perhaps predictably, chose Spanish. In the liner notes to *Destiny*, Estefan explicitly describes the project under way in her most recent albums as a "bicultural" endeavor; but given that certainly more than two languages and more than two cultures were at play at the Molson Center that evening, the decision to contextualize the music and to connect directly with her audience in Spanish did more than reinforce anything like a simple "biculturalism" in Estefan's work. Although certainly a significant number of Canadian Latinos were in attendance that evening, one must presume the majority of people in that audience had requested the performer communicate to them in a language they did not understand. Although this gesture could be read as an affirmation (or perhaps even fetishization) of the performer's Cuban and Hispanophone roots, it could also be read as a refusal, one that she actively invited, of her equally strong, although perhaps not equally authenticating, North American and Anglophone orientation.

As such, the gesture can also be read doubly as an affirmation and refusal of the various forms of nationalism and national identity circulating in this complex performative space; the cultural and linguistic collusion between performer and audience here produces in effect the deconstruction and reconstruction of the national simultaneously by sacrificing in part an Anglophonia that represents not only the presence of the United States and its increasingly global cultural and economic reach but also the dominance of English as Canada's majority language. By asking Estefan, admittedly at her own behest, to address them in Spanish, this Québecois audience agreed, in effect, to collaborate with her in an elaborate fiction, one predicated on an active, willful denial or forgetting of the actual national configuration defining the moment in favor of an imagined, desired "Latin" transnation where Francophones and Hispanophones could, impossibly, communicate with one another without or beyond translation. The collective psychic dynamic operating in this gesture might locate for us the place where, for better or worse, resistance meets repression, where what we take as ideology meets what we suspect to be unconscious in a complex interaction whose effects are not always predictable, legible, or coherent. One has only to consider the effect on an audience member of hearing nonetheless in a Spanish he or she literally does not understand a message, an articulation, of a desire for some alternative "world" order that is at once political, cultural, and linguistic.

To render this analysis in more practical, tangible terms, one has only to isolate two gestures in Estefan's performance most directly symptomatic of the paradoxical (il)logics of the inter-, trans-, and even just national forces at work, and at play, at the Molson Center that evening. Perhaps the most dramatic, *theatrical* moment in the concert came when, near the end of the show, Estefan stepped into a spherical cage, studded with mirrored tiles, a kind of hollowed-out disco ball, and glided over her audience with the help of wires and pulleys—a gutsy move, to be sure, for a performer who'd famously suffered a serious back injury some years before. But also a punning, and cunning, elaboration of the promises and pitfalls of the too-fragile pleasures of a transcendent globalism: as go-go girl Gloria did the cha-cha over her rapt audience, the globe serving as her stage alternately remained transparent, exposing the performer's body within, or blinded that audience at moments when the lights hit the mirrored bars at strategic angles. The literally visual interplay of blindness and insight during this number (the song was the up-tempo "Higher") enjoyed its conceptual analogue in the performance of Estefan's most recognizable Spanish-language anthem, "Mi Tierra," which, for all its explicitly and exclusively Cuban lyrical references, can easily serve as a kind of gestalt of the nation, seemingly anyone's nation, in the opportunity it offers to any audience to celebrate their devotion to their homeland simultaneously with Estefan's celebration of hers. With the "Mi Tierra" number, Montréal's Molson Center exploded into its giddiest moment of mass *jouissance* that night. Audience members waved the flags of various Latin American nations, representing in part Montréal's own various Latino communities, and in general it was impossible not to take into account how a song like "Mi Tierra" not only would, but must, play in Québec, whose recent history could be measured by the string of failed plebiscites on the question of national autonomy.

Thus Estefan's performance, on that night and in that place, and presumably on other nights and in other places scattered around the world, reflected, perhaps even asserted, the proposition that a certain transcendent cultural globalism (set to a seductive "world" music to which so many of us would like to dance) can, for all practical consideration, barely disguise its predication on the very conventional, traditional political and economic nationalisms it so explicitly and evocatively desires either to sublate or to overcome. At best, one can only temporarily and unsuccessfully repress the other, a point most eloquently made in and by the name of the venue where Estefan's intoxicatingly (and intoxicatedly) transnational, translational jamboree situated itself. Montréal's Molson Center names precisely the event's underwriting by an ever-expanding multinational corporation whose prominence in one of a growing number of transnational industries and international markets reflects as precisely the complex infrastructural forces that only cynically and opportunistically invoke the same nationalism so sentimentally serenaded by Estefan and celebrated by her fans.

Nuestramerica.com: A Historical Aside and a Note on Martí

In the Fall/Winter 1998 issue of its newsletter, *Cuban Affairs*, the liberal, pro-dialogue Washington- and Miami-based Cuban Committee for Democracy reported that "Ambassador Peter Boehm, Canada's representative to the Organization of American States, delivered the keynote address" at the CCD's annual banquet, where his "message of engaging Cuba in contrast to U.S. policy of isolating the island was well received by . . . the audience."[6] Boehm, reportedly "the first Canadian official ever to speak to Cuban Americans in Miami," symbolized in his very presence before such an audience in this particular city the bewildering rate at which changes in the complexity of the political, economic, and even cultural vectors on the North American scene continue to accelerate, oftentimes more quickly than one might imagine, given their failure to register meaningfully on either the popular consciousness in the United States, to say nothing of official U.S. policy toward Cuba. Canada has come to provide, in its remarkably open attitude toward economic and political engagement with Cuba's revolutionary government, a viable alternative model for the imagination of a progressive reconfiguration of "North American" systems of not only political and economic but also cultural exchange that orients itself along admittedly incongruous axes defined by not only Ottawa and Havana, but also Montréal and Miami. These axes not only sidestep Washington altogether, but in including Miami and Montréal, themselves important stages of "American" cultural operations, also reflect the significant generational shift in attitudes toward U.S.–Cuba relations among Cuban Americans in the core exile community. This shift in part explains the vocally anti-Castro Estefan's willingness to play in a nation with such open ties to Castro's government.

At the same time that the CCD newsletter reported on Ambassador Boehm's talk, *Hemisphere* magazine, published by Florida International University's Latin American and Caribbean Studies Center, reported on Canada's evolving role in determining economic policy across the Americas. In his article, "Canada's Southern Exposure," Canadian political scientist Peter McKenna devoted considerable space in what was primarily a report on Canada's "active role at the April 1998 Summit of the Americas in Santiago, Chile" to Canada's critical relation to Cuba.[7] Canada, McKenna reports, has "become Cuba's largest trading partner and greatest source of foreign investment," and Canadians, he adds, "also rank first in terms of hard-currency carrying tourists to the country." That some, admittedly more progressive, Cuban American institutions should begin turning to Canada for a different perspective on, perhaps a different paradigm for, Cuban American relations bodes well perhaps for a broadly perceived Cuban American future, if only in that it offers some alternative to the choke hold that the U.S.-led trade embargo and Fidel Castro's intransigence in the face of it have had on imagining anything positive in store for a more exclusively U.S.–Cuban future. Commenting on then-Canadian prime minister Chrétien's controversial visit to Cuba in the same month as the Santiago summit, McKenna observes that although "the visit allowed Canada to reaffirm its economic relationship with Cuba before the U.S. embargo is rescinded," it also allowed Cuba to "underscore the antiquated and absurd nature of US policy toward the island."

Canada's recent emergence on the Latin American, specifically Cuban American, scene also begins to correct a certain geographical and geopolitical myopia, emanating from the south and perhaps originating in part on an analysis of hemispheric relations dating back as far as, but also as recently influential as, José Martí's famed essay of 1891, "Nuestra América."[8] In the course of his argument in "Our America," Martí develops both a historical analysis and a future vision involving what he considered the two great partners in Western Hemispheric relations: Latin America, the "Our" America Martí saw emerging from the night of Spanish and Portuguese colonial rule to take its place as a conglomeration of politically autonomous states but profoundly interrelated cultures on the political stage alongside, and on an equal footing with, something he calls "North America," the other term completing what Martí calls "the two halves of the continent." But all the qualities that Martí ascribes to this "North America" more than suggest that he means exclusively the United States. His North America is populated, he tells us, by "an enterprising and vigorous people, who scorn and ignore Our America," a people he later terms "vindictive and sordid masses" favoring only their nation's "tradition of [presumably both political and economic] expansion." Martí concludes this passage by admonishing that "its good name as a Republic in the eyes of the world's perceptive nations puts upon North America a restraint that cannot be taken away by childish discords among our American nations."

Martí's own perception here perhaps leaves something to be desired; the willful absenting of Canada from the geopolitical scene as constituted in and by Martí's rhetoric must certainly be pressed beyond its semantic and geographical inaccuracies in order to underscore a dangerous and willful self-blinding.[9]

Rhetorically, at least, Martí's conflation of the United States with North America may reflect nothing more than his desire, a desire shared by many of us still, to correct and critique the U.S. willful (and ongoing) identification of itself as, simply, "America." But this is, of course, as easily accomplished by referring to the United States as, well, the United States. Of course, in 1891, conflating the United States and North America may only have reflected something of Canada's actual relative irrelevance to the scene of hemispheric politics, at least as it was perceived by Martí. In either case, such a proposition certainly can no longer hold, and, in turn, neither should the inaccurate, if still strategic, rhetorical uses to which the term "North America" is put when it only, however critically, renames the United States. Finally, I do not mean to call here for any redeployment of "North America" as an umbrella term collapsing into itself the United States and Canada or even the three nations making up the "North America" of the infamous so-called free trade agreement. I only mean here to point out the partial responsibility of one eminent Latin American writer in the conventional absenting of Canada from certain powerfully imagined, and powerfully strategic, configurations of continental and hemispheric space, and of the political exchanges possible within them, through the course of the twentieth century.

It may bemuse us to discover that we still need to work to imagine Canada "in" North America, let alone to imagine, meaningfully, a Canada "in" Latin America. But more than either of these crucial realities of the early twenty-first century, it might have bemused Martí even more to discover that, of all the emerging Latino communities in the major cosmopolitan cities of this newly reconfigured "North" America, the one that honors him with a major website is Montréal's. *Nuestramerica.com,* a primarily Spanish-language clearinghouse of information about resources available and cultural events of interest to Montréal's growing Latino population, offers me the opportunity to assert the following truth about movement through at least cultural and virtual spaces in this new *América*: especially from outside Canada, anyone navigating through the Web to reach *nuestramerica* will have to go, at least by typing the ".ca" abbreviation in its URL, significantly, symbolically, "through" Canada.

Postscript

In October 1999, when then-U.S. president Bill Clinton visited Canada to dedicate the new U.S. Embassy in Ottawa, more reminders emerged of Canada's actual "place" in all or any of the "Americas" at play in this discussion. Addressing specifically the question of Québec's sovereignty at an international conference on federalism held at a resort in the province, President Clinton had these thoughts to share with his audience: "The suggestion that people of a given ethnic group or tribe or religion can only have a meaningful existence if they have their own independent nation is a questionable assertion. . . . The momentum of history," he added, "is toward political integration, not disintegration."[10] Although on its face President Clinton's statement may hint at something of a salutary transculturalism at least in his vision of the relation between cultural and political entities, one must hear in such statements the hum of the globalizing economic machine that is in a sense not only still underwriting, but compelling, this expanding integration. As in the scene I described of Gloria Estefan's concert, one can argue ad infinitum ad nauseam if it was a "good" night for Cubans, or for Québecois, or even for Canadians or "Americans," but it was undeniably a good night for Molson and for Sony (Estefan's label). Also, and in closing, one has only to imagine President Clinton, or his current successor, making the same seemingly benign, but ultimately deeply patronizing, speech in Chiapas, or in Peru, or in Puerto Rico, to understand just how emphatically "in" Latin America Martí's "North" American/U.S. popular imaginary actually still supposes Québec, and indeed all of Canada, to be.

Chapter 5

Café, Culpa, and Capital: Nostalgic Addictions of Cuban Exile

Prologue: An Anecdote over Coffee

David Rieff opens *The Exile*, his 1993 study of "Cuba in the Heart of Miami," with a chapter that combines an archetypal formulation of the expectation of a general return with anecdotal details of specific recent voyages back to Cuba on the part of various Cuban exiles.[1] In many ways Rieff's work in *The Exile* demands this precarious balance between archetypal and anecdotal treatments; the archetypal especially asserts itself in the qualities Cuban exiles share with traditional patterns of exile inscribed, for example, in the historical books of the Old Testament. To the extent that Cubans in exile persist in toasting (as I mentioned in my discussion of Albita in the Introduction) to a "next year in Havana" that never comes, the culture clearly marks itself within, and according to, the contours of a historical paradigm that both promises return and staves it off by virtue of its structural reliance on the indefinite deferral of that return. In this sense the toast exhibits the double edge of any performance of the historical via a precedent model: it may assert a historicity in that performance, but it also marks the assertion of historicity as performance and as performative. Return is certainly not guaranteed by the invocation of any historical or traditional archetype of exile or (as the logic would follow) of diaspora. To wait for such a return to realize itself only holds one (individually, collectively) at bay, at the mercy of whatever

134

palliative, and mostly psychological, effects are held in, and by, such a redemptive and impossible promise.[2]

It is, of course, at the level of the archetypal that the Cuban-exile imaginary has traditionally found itself held in captivity, in a hopelessly idealized addiction to the redemptive promise of return. On this level, Rieff tells us, by the early 1990s, even the "people who ate, slept and breathed exile politics" realized the faith in the promise was becoming increasingly embarrassing, something to hide but certainly not to abandon; the topic of return, referred to by that community as the theme, *el tema*, "only came up haltingly" in public conversation or it "had to be precipitated, like a chemical reaction, by a long boozy evening."[3] The persistent, abstracted *tema*, perhaps the most eloquent symptom of the larger archetypal malaise, appears then (as a desublimated chemical precipitate) only in combination with other addictive substances. In the context of this anecdote, the substance is alcohol; but Cuban-exile culture is if anything eminently susceptible to the seductive call of other material substances, as well as other abstracted substantives.

As with the veiled anecdote of the boozy evening, Rieff oftentimes regales us with a touch of the dramatic. Another, perhaps more tellingly general anecdote, dramatizes an encounter between a Cuban-exile mother and the son who has just returned from a brief trip to Cuba:

> Later, over coffee . . . the traveler is more than likely to be reproached. "When you left, I thought I would die, and while you were gone, I died a little each day," a Cuban mother of a friend of mine told him the day after his return. . . . [H]er remark was the kind of reproach indulged in by Cuban mothers, who in Miami are often indistinguishable in terms of stereotypes from the Jewish matrons of Miami Beach. It was posing, and performance, of course, but only trivially. Cuban Miami . . . is a place where the dead are never far from people's minds, and in which the past and the present are constantly elided.[4]

The Cuban mother guilts her son, on one level, for the betrayal his return poses to the larger archetypal idea of Return; to this extent the rhetorical distance between stereotype (her resemblance in behavior to the "Jewish matrons of Miami Beach") and archetype (her faith in the archetypal structure of exile drawn from Jewish tradition) is suggestively short and certainly "performative" to the extent that it invokes the authority of certain preexisting discursive models. As short indeed is the psychic distance between motherly guilt(ing) for personal abandonment, its accompanying anxiety (the worry over what might befall her son in Cuba), and the larger guilt built into the structure of exile, the guilt of abandoning the motherland, of having succumbed to historical, political, and certainly economic pressures that outweigh one's patriotism, one's fidelity to one's *patria*. Beyond these elisions lurks the even larger problem of exile nostalgia, the projection into the past of the lost, mourned, and necessarily idealized object of desire. Nostalgia, as a form of mourning, is necessarily ambivalent, a psychic labor haunted by the guilt one bears for that loss, the sneaking suspicion of complicity and culpability in the loss that weighs the mourner down.

Rieff's staging of the anecdote thus belies its own anecdotal function by confirming, again, what is archetypal about the encounter. Even the likely marker of its specificity, the telling detail of the coffee "over" which the conversation takes place, functions more symptomatically than idiosyncratically. The Cuban cultural body, both off- and on-island, is nothing if not caffeinated, caffeine driven, and addicted. More than the booze that "precipitates" confessions of adherence to the *tema*, coffee is the drug that fuels that mania. More sobering than intoxicating, coffee may indeed still be rising to true prominence as the nectar inspiring a responsible Cuban historical vision, even as it has in past times driven both Cuban ambition and Cuban corruption, in *all* cultural spaces self-defined as "Cuban." It may indeed be coffee more than any other substance, or substantive, that can best register the ongoing, relentless Cuban political and historical impasse. Rieff himself observes that among Cubans still faithful to the delusion of an archetypally constructed return, it would be troubling to confront the fact that "the Cuba [they] treasured no longer existed in Cuba itself, up to and including *café cubano,* which . . . was all but unobtainable on the island."[5] In other ways, contemporary Cuban-exile, Cuban American, and Cuban-diasporic writers and artists discover in coffee as rich a metaphorical resource for their articulations of especially the post–Cold War, postnational Cuban situation as producers find it a rich material resource and consumers a potent chemical stimulant. Such symbolic circulations of coffee through limited but not closed textual economies will take up the following sections of this chapter, the first dealing primarily with Eduardo Machado's *Floating Island Plays* (1991), the second with Albita Rodríguez's earliest U.S.-produced musical recording, 1995's *No Se Parece a Nada,* and the last with a constellation of mostly non-literary analytical texts on both U.S. Cuban culture and the general post–Cold War moment. Broader considerations of the metaphorical and material operations of addiction in these pieces of literature, music, and theory will in turn serve to comment on the "official," disingenuous mythologizing of Cuban history by the still-prevailing political voices in the Cuban-exile community, especially as these voices continue to define and delimit the possible discursive constructions and practical applications not only of Cuban exile but of off-island Cuban experience more broadly construed.

Café

In *The Modern Ladies of Guanabacoa,* the first of the four *Floating Island Plays,* Eduardo Machado has one brother in a 1920s bourgeois Havana family ask another, and in a deceptively offhand way, "What would we do without *café?*"[6] Perhaps it is because Cuba was known more for the quality and quantity of the coffee it consumed than the coffee it produced that anthropologist Fernando Ortiz organized *Cuban Counterpoint,* his late-1930s study of Cuba's economic and cultural history, around its two more famous export products, tobacco and sugar.[7] Perhaps in 1940 tobacco and sugar offered themselves more readily to the gaze of external global capital as the chief signifiers in Cuba's larger economic portfolio; coffee, in contrast, figured primarily as the domesticated and domesticating fuel of Cuba's still-developing national identity. As Ortiz himself observed, the consumers of Cuban tobacco, especially cigar smokers, were too select in status and number, and the consumers of sugar too universal. The Cubanness of the tobacco might suggest something of the class standing of the smoker, but certainly it would not Cubanize him. Sugar could certainly not be said to affect in any way the cultural orientation of its consumers, precisely because of its universal utility and appeal. Coffee, however, performed a kind of nationally defining cultural work in Cuba, unrivaled by any other cultural production except perhaps for music: the capacity to enjoy a thick, too-sweet *tasita de café cubano* marked your *cubanidad* like no other capacity for pleasure could.[8]

Machado's ambitious "cycle" of four plays, *Floating Islands* (all composed in New York in the late 1980s and published together as a finished work in 1991), bears eloquent witness to this concentration of symbolic and culture-building force around coffee. Its inaugural piece, *The Modern Ladies of Guanabacoa,* runs on the energy generated by the constant preparation, service, and enjoyment of *café cubano. Modern Ladies,* set in Havana just before and after the stock market crash of 1929, is by itself an ambitious work, one that sets the groundwork for Machado's subsequent dramatization of economic and political developments in Cuba in the mid-twentieth century through the experiences of a large, ambitious middle-class Havana family, the Ripolls. *Modern Ladies* also concerns itself very seriously with gender, and the sexual divisions of labor in the Ripoll household frame a great deal of the action, down to the symbolic and practical circulation of *café.* Act 1 of *Modern Ladies* plays out in part through the courtship of the Ripolls' daughter Manuela by Oscar Hernandez, a taxi driver with more than a little entrepreneurial spirit. The Ripolls are merchants, and Oscar is as interested in selling them on his plans for a city bus company in Havana as he is in selling himself as a potential son-in-law. He therefore sets out to seduce all the Ripolls but primarily Manuela's father and brothers, who gather during his first visit to hear him extol not the virtues of their girl but the charms of Cuban coffee. As the men wait for the women to serve them, brother Mario asks, "What would we do without *café*?" which compels Oscar to embark on a cultural history of coffee that in many ways echoes Ortiz's work in *Cuban Counterpoint.*

Both Ortiz and Machado seek to demonstrate that, if you push this cultural history far enough, you come to realize the dangers of underestimating the historical power of our most quotidian cultural practices. Weaving Machado's narrative (through Oscar) and Ortiz's, we can reconstruct a fuller history than each gives individually but a history that in both cases travels from obscure roots in traditional ritual practice to the most basic of the secular, liberal West's ideological values. "Yes, *café*," Oscar intones, "It used to be a religious drink. . . . The name derives from the Arabic, 'Kahwah.' "[9] Ortiz, relying on an earlier study by Heinrich Jacob (Berlin, 1934), supports this proposition, reporting that "coffee, . . . Abyssinian negro by birth, became popular in Mecca between 1470 and 1500, and spread from there throughout Arabia to the world of Islam, as far as Constantinople."[10] Oscar's more comical account identifies a particular "thirteenth-century . . . preaching Arabian mulatto [who] observed how the cows after they ate the fruits of some trees became animated," and who, from this observation, was inspired to concoct a brew from these "fruits" that when he fed it to his followers enabled them "to stay awake throughout [his] religious services." This awakening, in Ortiz's hands, leads directly to the larger putative "awakening" of early modern enlightenment: "reason," Ortiz tells us, "starved and numbed by theology, to revive and free itself, needed the help of some harmless stimulant that should not intoxicate it with enthusiasm and then stupefy it with illusions and bestiality."[11] Ortiz extends his inventory of "harmless stimulants" to include tea, chocolate, and, of course, his real focus of study, tobacco. "All," Ortiz concludes, "had the common properties of stimulating sensual appetites. All had religious connotations. . . . And all finally won a swift and sweeping victory" in the West "because of their early alliance with capitalism, which made them the stamp of fashion, of rank and wealth, and a rich source of profit for the individual and the state."[12]

This early alliance goes well beyond coffee's purely economic properties. To the extent that coffee simultaneously stimulates reason and the "sensual appetites," it would seem to comply with the contradictory ideological demands of liberal enlightenment. Its distracting seductions as a commodity would find some resistance in its stimulating properties as a substance. For all its susceptibility for inclusion in Ortiz's inventory of "status" objects, coffee's own status as "exotic" object has been lessened considerably, by its own capacity as "a stimulant of thought." According to Ortiz, "when around 1554 the public coffee houses were opened in Stambul, they were called by the people . . . 'schools of the learned,' and coffee was given the name of 'the milk which nourishes thinkers.'"[13] Anyone familiar with the work of Jürgen Habermas and Terry Eagleton[14] will know how the public consumption of coffee in early modern Europe, especially in the eighteenth century, played into the generation of "rational, public discourse," and Avital Ronell finds occasion to acknowledge the caffeine addictions (Voltaire's, Balzac's) at the heart of the French enlightenment.[15] Machado has Oscar pick up the narrative of this intellectual tradition at the point where it establishes itself in "Europe as well as America . . . where students seated around a table . . . discussed very passionately, politics, literature, poetics and art."[16] And if coffee stimulates impassioned thought and speech, it eventually stimulates action, even historical action in the most conventional sense: "Some of these establishments," Oscar recounts to his rapt audience, "like . . . Merchants' Coffee House, have become a part of history. . . . It was there in . . . 1774 [that] a 'Committee of Correspondence,' started by New Yorkian patriots, sent a letter to a group of Bostonians proposing the union of the American colonies."[17]

The invocation of the union of North American states prompts two divergent results in Machado's text. The immediate and superficial response on the part of Oscar's audience is to turn the anecdote into an occasion for commenting on the cultural differences between Cuba and the United States as encoded in their forms of coffee consumption. Ernesto, another Ripoll brother, declares, "They drink such weak coffee," to which Mario Ripoll adds, "Like dirty water," and finally Miguel Ripoll chimes in with "I could never drink it." The disdain in which these Cubans hold *café americano* borders on the stereotypical; it is also hypocritical, given the extent to which bourgeois Cubans and (both before and since 1959) bourgeois Cuba have taken intense political and economic stimulation from U.S. sources. Indeed, the Ripolls look not only to a U.S. model in their attempts to fashion their entrepreneurial scheme to update public transportation in Havana, but they depend at least in part on the patronage of tourists from the United States. Machado's text eventually synthesizes economic and chemical stimulation from "outside" through the metaphoric function of *café*. Later in *Modern Ladies,* when Oscar begins to plot his takeover of the bus company from his father-in-law and brothers-in-law (whom he plans to put on salary), he explains himself to Manuela through the following analogy:

> OSCAR: In business you must blend meticulously all the ingredients. Number one, the boss equals the owners; number two, then there are the workers; if you have these things clearly defined, it'll work one hundred percent of the time. In any type of business . . . It's the way they blend *café* . . .
> MANUELA: Kahwah. (She laughs)
> OSCAR: The right beans together make black gold, for white gods.[18]

Although I do not mean to ignore the complex racial alchemy that has run through the cultural history related in tandem by Machado and Ortiz, my concern with coffee's symbolic operations necessarily favors class and nationality because those are the categories of analysis that Ortíz and Machado have favored. Much as Ortiz's history documents the westernization (and eventual Cubanization) of coffee and as Machado's play embellishes that history and stages its cultural effects directly, Machado at least does little more than suggest the repercussions for Cuba of the racial history ground into both the symbolic repercussions and practical demands of producing and consuming not only coffee but most other distinctly Cuban commodities, from sugar and tobacco to the conga and the mambo.[19]

Rather than follow that history further in any kind of linear fashion, it is time to break from the line of thought concerning coffee in its most literal manifestations and go on with it, perhaps, as it disseminates itself symbolically into the text of Cuban-exile culture since the moment Cuba itself broke from the lines of its own previous histories in 1959. Machado's text performs this kind of dissemination both in and after *Modern Ladies*. That play exploits the symbolic resources of tobacco, especially in the form of women smoking cigarettes to establish greater parameters of personal freedom, as well as the more literal Cuban-bourgeois mania with business and profit, to establish the larger structural susceptibility to addiction in what might be termed a certain Cuban cultural *mentalité.* The pieces following *Modern Ladies* in the *Floating Islands* cycle perform this dissemination even more elaborately. By the time *Broken Eggs,* the last of the *Floating Island Plays,* brings surviving members of the original Ripoll clan to late-1970s Woodland Hills, California, *café cubano* loses much of its prominence as defining cultural substance; in the course of dramatizing the events surrounding Manuela and Oscar's granddaughter Lizette's wedding to her Jewish fiancé, Machado figures his characters' assimilation to U.S. culture through consumptions of various drugs of choice, licit and otherwise. *Broken Eggs* opens with Mimi Márquez, the bride's sister, drinking a Tab;[20] her Aunt Miriam unapologetically extols the powers of Valium at every opportunity;[21] Oscar, Mimi's brother, repeatedly snorts cocaine;[22] and occasional references to alcoholism and to voodoo "powders" occur. Without exception, however, these individual pathologies, even to the extent that they individuate and mark characters, all point to the general structure of a pathology most accurately defined as nostalgic, melancholic, and certainly collective. Miriam's Valium pills, for example, her "little pieces of magic," fulfill the archetypal exilic promise of return by transporting her, she tells us, to "Varadero, the Gulf of México, Santa María del Mar." After the disastrous wedding and reception for Mimi's sister Lizette, Miriam offers to take her sister-in-law Sonia, Lizette and Mimi's mother, on such a return, but Sonia refuses. Miriam insists, "A Valium—that's the only certain thing. It reassures you. It lets you look at the truth," and by play's end Sonia and the other characters leave Miriam in the haze of her Valium's "truth": "I'm already there [in Varadero]," Miriam declares as she lies supine on the dance floor of the Woodland Hills Country Club, "miles and miles into the beach and the water is up to my knees . . . I float . . . I'm in, I'm in the place where I'm supposed to be."

Sonia's refusal to follow Miriam to her Valium Varadero signals Machado's own refusal to immerse himself in the same delusory medium: Sonia, the central character in *Broken Eggs,* learns some hard lessons about the dangers of such delusions, and collective addictions to them, lessons that Machado clearly hopes will reach his own community. Early in *Broken Eggs,* Sonia still harbors the fantasy of return, both for her estranged marriage (she and Lizette and Mimi's father, Osvaldo, are divorced and he's remarried) and for her estranged nation. She initially believes her mother Manuela's "promise" that "someday [Cuba] will be a reality again," but by the end of the play she warns her own just-married daughter that "Promises are something nobody keeps."[23] If Machado has learned any additional cultural lessons from Fernando Ortiz, one might be the structural felicity of the counterpoint. *Broken Eggs* effectively ends, one might argue, in a contrapuntal pose between two dances on the floor of the country club, one Miriam's stuporific wriggling on it, the other Sonia and Mimi's tango over it. Machado's counterpoint also has direct echoes to older dialectics than Ortiz's, however; in some ways Miriam's narcosis corresponds to that of a particular kind of "lotus eater," one who succumbs to the attractions not only of the chemical, but of the ambience it generates around those who ingest it in concert.[24] Miriam insists on the collective nature (and therefore comfort) of the various Cuban-exile pathologies she embodies: "We were all alcoholics . . . all perverted," she declares to her family, a family in which, she insists, "Everyone['s] . . . got a drug."[25] Against a collectivity defined by common consumption, Machado counterposes Sonia's rehabilitated individuality, one that retains the quality of irreducible isolation in exilic experience. When Mimi warns her mother that they have outstayed their welcome at the country club, Sonia makes her final statement: "That's all right, Mimi. I've been kicked out of better places."[26]

Machado's symbolic dissemination of other fluid substances besides and in addition to coffee thus works in the context of exile to fuel as impossibly complex a process of national construction and deconstruction as that currently under way in all cultural spaces, which, like those he stages in and as *Floating Islands,* continue, even into the twenty-first century, to call themselves "Cuban." Breaking with the continuity and homogeneity of the historical line as deftly as his characters break eggs (and promises), Machado allows his readers

to analyze certain insistent repetitions, as well as certain failures to repeat, in the larger, and irreversibly diasporic, Cuban historical scene.[27]
In the next section of this chapter, the rhythms and patterns of consumption as staged by Machado will superimpose on those in Albita
Rodriguez's earliest "diasporically situated" lyrical expressions, and
these in turn will readily inform the more general nostalgizing practices persisting still in Cuban-exile literature and culture. It bears repeating here that, in and out of exile, Cubans are caught in a kind of
chronic and aporetic addiction to an idea, and this conceptual addiction manifests itself phenomenally in all manner of substantial addictions. These in turn trouble if not foreclose precisely the fantasy of
linear time that feeds their congruent fantasies of return, reunification, and restitution, fantasies to which they're hooked and of which
they take emotional, imaginative, and other psycho-symbolic "hits,"
almost as often as they drink coffee.

Culpa

"Cuba," the exiled novelist Guillermo Cabrera Infante once declared,
"is, of course, *mea maxima culpa* . . . guilt . . . is not a feeling foreign
to exile."[28] The relationship between exile and guilt is perhaps more
direct than Cabrera Infante's quasi–double negative suggests. Certainly Cabrera Infante exploits the quasi-echo, the fractal rhyme of
"Cuba" and "culpa" to signal more than the failure of these markers to
achieve either conceptual or even phonetic similarity or foreignness
from each other. That one's *cubanidad* should become the marker of
one's guilt, the incontrovertible sign of one's culpability, results precisely from the necessity of bearing that mark, of confessing to one's
cubanidad, outside Cuba. Few Cuban-exile artists have confronted
this relationship more directly than Albita Rodríguez, the cabaret
singer and composer. I have already had occasion to discuss Albita's
life, and her work, in the introduction to this book, but I remind the
reader of some salient facts about her in order to frame the present
discussion here. Albita and her band members walked across the
U.S.–México border at El Paso in 1993 when they were supposed to
be in Colombia on an extended visa to record material and rehearse

their act. In remarkably short time, Albita became the darling of
Miami's exile and entertainment communities, performing to enthusiastic crowds at the Centro Vasco, signing with Emilio Estefan's
record company, and befriending Madonna and her style gurus,
Ingrid Casares and Gianni Versace. Albita's first U.S. recording, *No Se
Parece a Nada,* appeared in the summer of 1995 and immediately
commanded the attention of the national press.[29]

As the title of the collection immediately suggests, *No Se Parece a
Nada* (roughly translated, "Unlike Anything Else") concerns itself simultaneously with Albita's literal experience with foreignness, both
her adopted nation's to her and her own within that nation, but also
with the broader scope of the uncanny, the "unhomely" experience
that accompanies the various other ways she resembles nothing else.
In a *Los Angeles Times* article, Mike Clary called Albita "the reincarna-
tion of a 1930's European chanteuse, a Berlin Cabaret singer trans-
fused with Latin blood,"[30] and in an accompanying review of her disc,
Enrique Lopetegui called her "a female Cuban singer with the voice of
a male tango singer from Argentina."[31] That the popular press should
so immediately remark on Albita's embodiment of various hybrid
states, in terms of both culture and gender, bears strong witness to
her almost irreducible uniqueness at least among practitioners of her
craft. Clary's reference to the transfusion of "Latin blood" into the
person of a Weimar-style transvestite performer misstates the true
process of transformation here; Albita began with *latinidad,* or more
specifically *cubanidad,* and the morphing into that happy stylistic
wedding of Chavela Vargas–style Latina folk singer and Marlene
Dietrich in a tuxedo came later, as a kind of sartorial comment on the
more radical cultural reversals that Albita's music performs. These reversals, even before the assistance of costuming, were erotic and political at once because Albita's music bears explicit witness to her
lesbianism as the central, informing component of her curiously patriotic *cubanidad.*

This is no better articulated than in the third song on her disc, a
cut Clary describes as "a sentimental Miami anthem" presumably because it asks a question that can never be taken as simply rhetorical or
as exclusively either personal or political: "¿Qué culpa tengo yo,"

Albita asks, "de haber nacido en Cuba?" "What fault is it of mine to have been born in Cuba?" asks the question in a grammatically apt way, if one wanted to understate the role of the responsible subject; another way, perhaps more clumsily, to put it would be, "How culpable am I that I was born in Cuba?" if instead one wanted to underscore the active participation of the "I" in the posing of the question and in the interrogation of one's accountability to, or for, one's nationality. The song is admittedly both sentimental and anthemic: it begins in the ballad style of the *bolero,* a style given to sentimental turns of nostalgia often bordering on hopelessness (*boleros* being "abjection's songs" according to Arnaldo Cruz-Malavé).[32] But the song promptly ignites into the up-tempo mode that more often characterizes at least the musical dimension of Cuban-exile culture's musical self-articulations. The song's insistent repetition of both the refrain and the name of "Cuba" contributes to its power, a power that goes beyond the mere "catchy" quality of any good musical or rhythmic hook, to something more infectious, if not indeed addictive. For these reasons among others "¿Qué culpa tengo yo?" soars beyond the point of self-torturing guilt; this is neither the apologetic nor confessional mode of the exile caught gazing at the fact of her abandonment of home, family, and nation. Instead, the tone of the song is pure defiance: to be Cuban is, according to Albita, in part to love freedom, to bear adversity with optimism. It is also to bear in oneself a kind of "blood" that pulses and rises, that both captures one and sustains one at a level of passionate corporal intensity equal to the demands and challenges of having been "born" Cuban in this apparently interminable historical moment.

These demands and challenges certainly have their analogue for Albita in her having been "born" queer in the same historical moment.[33] Albita announces the specifically eroticized dimension of her politics in the first cut of the disc, a song composed for her by Luís Ríos called "Que Manera de Quererte." Ostensibly the celebration of obsessive love, an "authentic madness" that begins by "caressing" the singer's will and ends by "possessing" it, the song interrogates directly the relationship between will and desire, and it concludes with a kind of reversal of the conventional relationship between freedom and captivity in mind and body. "Where could I live if not in your sex," the singer asks, "a febrile delirium, a pulse or waving of a desire that frees my body from its spell."[34] There is little question what manner of "sex" the beloved in this case should have, and therefore what gender she should be, if it can accommodate the lover wishing to find habitation in it. Again, Albita's questions belie any mere rhetoricity; what "guilt" she should feel for the tenacity of her erotic desires is assigned a similar response as the question of her "guilt" for having been born in a nation whose historical situation requires some of its most patriotic citizens to exile themselves from it. The constant address of political and personal destiny characterizes much of the lyrical material on *No Se Parece a Nada*: the love songs all ponder the quality of what is *not* chosen about desire, and the more general songs of national and cultural affirmation assert the ironically joyful helplessness of "being-Cuban," its undeniable pleasures even in the face of painful political and historical conditions.[35]

Because I cannot claim the expertise to study these songs musically, I would direct the reader's attention to ongoing work by cultural critics on the significance of music and dance to the formation and performance of sexual, cultural, and national identities, especially in Latin American and U.S. Latino/a cultures.[36] Certainly much is to be made from these analyses about the way that Cuban tempos keep a certain kind of Cuban "time" and yet fail to synchronize a coherent history because of the profound disjunctions between time and history in what we might call the contemporary Cuban "moment," the post–Special Period, post–post–Cold War "moment," which increasingly bears no more defining a quality than its apparent inability to end. But even in lyrical content, Cuban-exile music has at least tried to "keep time," if not kill it, even in the face of temporal and historical impasse, if not impossibility. "At its best," Gustavo Pérez-Firmat argues in 1994's *Life on the Hyphen*, "this music was reiterative, helping to promote the continuance of Cuban culture outside Cuba"[37] and to this extent, he concludes, it could tolerate the conflict implicit in a project of cultural preservation that, even in its most emphatically nostalgic turns, was in fact innovating a new and unprecedented culture in exile.

Albita Rodríguez's work in the mid-1990s represents perhaps the most significant twist in the work of Cuban-exile musical self-representation as analyzed by Pérez-Firmat. Although she herself did not participate in the evolution of the "Miami Sound" in the first three decades of the exile, she arrived just in time to take up, exploit, and critique (in part by queering) its most salient features. Albita's music, like that of her exile cohorts, "feasts on contradictions"; to borrow Pérez-Firmat's terminology, "it flaunts its roots only to consume them," retaining "a conflicted, cacophonous strain" even as it has focused increasingly on the analogues between personal and political forms of abjection and alienation. Pérez-Firmat observes, for example, that the popular "Miami Sound" always exploited "the language of love . . . to convey . . . but also control . . . political frustrations," and therefore that in most "Cuban-American love songs the lost lover is always a stand-in for the lost island."[38] Speaking specifically of Gloria Estefan and her husband Emilio, who produces and composes much of her music, Pérez-Firmat's comments certainly also apply to the Estefans' former protégée. In the liner notes to *No Se Parece a Nada,* Albita dedicates the disc both to José Martí (for, among other things, having once written that "the best way to speak, is to act") and to Emilio Estefan, her producer then, for following the letter of Martí's dictum both personally and professionally. As I have already observed, Albita conflates speaking and doing, expression and action, as directly as she conflates personal and political passions. This conflation, perhaps the most potent gesture in her general repertoire as a performer, fuels her unique *erotics* by rendering them most effectively, and productively, performative.

This uncanny synthesis is perhaps best exemplified in the least typical (in terms of tempo) cut on the disc, her stunning "Bolero para Nostalgiar." Recognizing that she speaks to a culture for whom "nostalgia" operates grammatically less as a substantive and more as an infinitive verbal form, Albita offers up a kind of tonic, if not antidote for Cuban America's most profound psychic addiction.[39] As with desire in songs like "Qué Culpa Tengo Yo," nostalgia "arrives" suddenly, surprising the subject/singer in an unguarded moment. Nothing about its arrival is willed by the singer, who confesses to surrendering to the overwhelming power of the emotion. The lyric again poses questions that belie their rhetoricity; ostensibly and conventionally about "nostalgia" for a lost beloved, the singer never specifies much about the relationship except that she is "lost" and "thirsty" for the memory of "having been two." The "thirst" is significant because the particular nostalgia she feels is not the dreamy desire for an ideal past but the sober awakening to loss: it is the "nostalgia of dawn" that renders "memories" as "sips of coffee." Most of the verse stanzas, however, pose unanswerable questions: "How can one conceive of so much inequity/In aggrandizing life beyond the limits of hope? . . . How can one conceive of so much liberty/If we lack the air to sustain the wings of . . . ?" Literally the questions not only go unanswered but remain grammatically incomplete. They ring with the familiar quality of Cuban-exile experience to the extent that they describe the inconceivability to many recent arrivals from Cuba of North American affluence and the kinds of freedom it buys. Even sexual freedom, itself arguably a function of a certain level of material well-being, is interrogated here; the newly liberated sexual subject questions the unprecedented freedom to "love and love," presumably to excess, in that such freedom "agitates the body in order for the calm" to remain inaccessible, at least incomplete in the formation of thought.[40]

Albita's music thus bears out Pérez-Firmat's general observation about Cuban American culture in at least one other significant way. If, as Pérez-Firmat argues, "Cuban Miami" remains "[t]o this day . . . by turns nostalgic, estranged and foundational" but is nowhere near as nostalgic now as it used to be,[41] then perhaps it is in a song like Albita's *bolero* that we hear the shift in tone of that nostalgia not as a diminution but as a modulation. After more than forty years of a general but no less compulsive mourning, Cuban nostalgia is no longer so intoxicating, and much more likely than not quite sobering. For as recently exiled a person as Albita, this may make some sense, if only in that the Cuba she mourns in some respects still exists; Albita cannot, like those Cubans exiled since 1959, mourn yesterday's Cuba, "*la Cuba de ayer*," which has become an increasingly abstract concept, the methadone for a community of addicts who have yet to realize they've kicked their habit, if only because their supply of the "real" drug has long been

exhausted. Albita's nostalgia may typify instead the still-nascent relationship of a more diasporically oriented population of Cuban
Americans to a Cuba they may actually reach someday (if they haven't
been there already), not to return to, but to visit for the first time.
Having (as I suggested in the Introduction) "confounded" rather than
founded a hyphenated, hybridized polyculture for themselves outside
of Cuba, these Cubans, and I count myself among them, can never return to a nation they have never been to.[42] And indeed, any Cuba to
which we may be allowed to go en masse will by historical necessity be
a Cuba that never existed before. There is no Cuba "after Castro" yet,
but it is in the imagining of this Cuba that nostalgics, even of the sober
kind, give way to futurics, to the active projection of a once-and-
future *cultura Cubana*, perhaps an impossible project historically but
certainly as dangerously addictive a product of psychic and cultural
labor as those fueled by *café* and *culpa*.

Capital

Perhaps Albita's appeal to a stylistic Germanicism in her dress can
serve as a warning against a fairly odd Cuban dependence on German
historical and philosophical precedents. To the extent that her music
redefines the relationship between the "misty old Cuba before Fidel"
with which marketers of nostalgia might still be in love and "the post-
socialism Cuba the bankers and realtors are waiting for,"[43] certainly
her U.S. Cuban audience, of all generations, can take heed of the difficulty lurking in the incommensurability of these two projections.
And if any example of the difficulties of reunification can currently
offer itself to the Cuban imagination in this post–Special Period period, it is certainly the German example. Rieff acknowledged the danger of this eventuality near the end of his book. "In the end," Rieff
argues, "Cuban Miami's strongest hope lay not in its nostalgia, however profound, for the Havana of yesterday, but in its mercantile expectations of restoring the Cuba of tomorrow";[44] "love of Cuba,"
based in memory, fuses for Rieff with that other Cuban passion, "love
[of] . . . business," fueling in turn the "oscillat[ion] from reminis-
cence to business plan, from a narrative of loss to the prospect of psy-

chic closure"[45] in the U.S. Cuban imaginary of the early 1990s. However it is that we might distinguish between reunification and re-conquest as available historical paradigms for either imagining or analyzing Cuba's future, it is just as important to balance one's attention between the material and, for lack of a better word, the spiritual properties of this eventuality.

Before (and perhaps beyond) even the obvious historical and political debt Cuba owes to a Germanic Marxism and even a French "post-Marxism,"[46] Cuba had been mainlining certain other strains of German philosophy in its attempts to make sense of its historical destiny. According to Heberto Padilla, Cuban intellectual life in the 1950s almost prepared the way for Fidel and the revolution through its enthusiasm (without reservations and without reserve) for Hegelianism. For Padilla, the challenge to Cuban artists and intellectuals in the 1950s was to capture in image and concept "the fleeting, inexplicable and multifarious thing that was Cuban reality—a mixture of intractable history and geography" that Padilla himself "could neither decode nor reflect" in his work.[47] "Cuban literary life in the fifties," Padilla recounts, "was utterly impoverished"; trapped in a symbolic economy of such scarcity, figures like the novelist José Lezama Lima were provoked into declaring that "the essence of a Cuban sense of things was only the spirit at the margins of history," thus betraying the "indispensability" of Hegel as an "authority for Cuban intellectuals . . . at the beginning of the second half of this century."[48] Perhaps in part because of this disposition toward a Hegelian idealism, which Cuban exiles may have smuggled with them into the United States in the late 1950s, the trajectory of Cuban-exile history since then can only be traced through its dependency on the foreign substance of a (relentlessly seductive, relentlessly deferred) Hegelian teleology.

Joan Didion's *Miami* (1987) suggests this in some provocative ways. Didion's characteristically ingenious formulations of the history she analyzes redeem the limits of her cultural sympathy for Miami's exile-generation Cubans.[49] Indeed, the chief criticism leveled at Didion's book has been that she almost xenophobically treats Miami's "Latinized" political influence on U.S. politics as a kind of toxic shock from which Washington has failed to recover in thirty years; one can read in the seedier elements of Ann Louise Bardach's *Cuba Confidential* (2002) both a continuation and an amplification of Didion's earlier argument. Didion observes how, at a 1985 mass commemorating the anniversary of the Bay of Pigs invasion, "paper thimbles of Cuban coffee distributed" afterward "had the aspect of a secular communion, the body and blood of *patria, machismo, la lucha,* sentimental trinity";[50] "*la lucha,*" however, the Cuban "struggle" consecrated ritually here becomes in Didion's analysis a profaning influence, a toxin in the bloodstream of U.S. political history, "a matter of assassinations and bombings on the streets of American cities, of plots and counterplots and covert dealings involving American citizens and American institutions, of attitudes and actions which had shadowed the abrupt termination of two American presidencies and would eventually shadow the immobilization of a third." This toxic economy, however, flows both ways in Didion's larger analysis; for all that some "foreign" presence in the U.S. body politic seems to have exhibited itself in the symptomatology of political crises, from the JFK assassination and Watergate to Iran-contra, the United States certainly shares responsibility for the situation by having made the kinds of impossible promises to Cuban exiles that have kept them narcotically attached to Washington.

"Miami," Didion admonishes, "remains our most graphic lesson in consequences,"[51] a lesson Didion organizes around the "sequence" of historical and teleological promises made to Cuban exiles by American presidents:

> "I can assure you that this flag will be returned to this brigade in a free Havana," John F. Kennedy said at the Orange Bowl in 1962 (the "supposed promise," the "promise not in the script," the promise "made in the emotion of the day"), meaning it as an abstraction, the rhetorical expression of a collective wish; a kind of poetry, which of course makes nothing happen.... [I]n 1983 ... Ronald Reagan ... added this: "Someday, Cuba itself will be free ... "just more poetry, another rhetorical expression of a collective wish, but Ronald Reagan ... was speaking here to

people whose historical experience has not been that poetry makes nothing happen.[52]

This history of a promise repeatedly offered and indefinitely deferred, a promise always reinvoked in the act of mourning the losses in human life and historical time since the moment of a revolution (and an exile) whose consequences refuse to cease, and to go away, marks the Cuban exile as a chief but not exceptional "specter" of both Marx and Hegel.

What Didion describes and only partially formulates in *Miami* is perhaps best articulated theoretically in Jacques Derrida's analysis of the "messianic promise" that persists beyond Judaism in the secular historical philosophies continuing to work through late capitalism. Cuban exiles' penchant for toasting that impossible "next year in Havana" certainly supports Derrida's observation, in 1994's *Specters of Marx,* that the "war for the 'appropriation of Jerusalem' is today the world war. It is happening everywhere, it is the world, it is today the singular figure of its being 'out of joint.'"[53] Like the general "regime of reunification" invoked by Ronell in her analysis of Heidegger and "German destiny" in *Crack Wars,* the general nostalgia for "anyone's Zion" poses for Derrida the chief challenge to the thinking of anything like a future. Indeed, "what remains" for Derrida "irreducible to any deconstruction . . . is, perhaps, a certain experience of the emancipatory promise; it is perhaps even the formality of structural messianism, a messianism without religion, even a messianic without messianism, an idea of justice . . . and an idea of democracy—which we distinguish from its current concept and from its predicate today."[54] What "Cuba" there is to come is certainly implicated in the larger elements of the "justice" and "democracy" to come, those promised but that remain to be thought. The vestigial Hegelianism in Cuban-exile ideology and the spectralized Marxism persisting on the island may each remain constitutionally intolerant of the kind of promise that perhaps only a certain deconstruction can articulate, but it may be the only drug left to them in the world-historical black market.

That future "Cuba" remains poised in "the gap between an infinite promise, . . . and the determined necessary . . . [t]hat has to be measured against this promise," between "the effectivity and actuality of the democratic promise" and "the communist promise," both of which must "always keep within [them] . . . this absolutely undetermined messianic hope at [their] heart, this eschatological relation to the to-come of an event *and* of a singularity, of an alterity that cannot be anticipated"[55] for all that it *can* be awaited. In this sense, perhaps, the unnameably post–Special Period of our fractured, disjointed present may be all we have of a home, or nation, one into which we must be willing to invite the "foreign" visitor from that radically other place, the future. That visitor, always approaching if not yet arriving, can, like Elijah in the Seder, be prepared for; making him coffee, perhaps, even Cubans (on and off the island, in a general diaspora in which we all find ourselves commonly, if not equally or identically, situated) may await him actively, exercising what Derrida calls a "hospitality without reserve, welcoming salutation accorded in advance to the absolute surprise of the *arrivant* from whom or from which one will not ask anything in return, and who or which will not be asked to commit to the domestic contracts of any welcoming power (family, state, nation, territory, native soil or blood, language, culture in general, even humanity)."[56] The coffee thus offered and the door thus opened, in such a gesture of generosity and hospitality, define the space available only to the most responsible and responsive historical imagination; it is the "just opening which renounces any right to property, any right in general," if only because such expectations belie the presumption that what we await "cannot be awaited as such, or recognized in advance."[57]

And to those exiles still among us who persist in arguing that suspending our expectations of a redress of rights, especially property rights, would be the most intolerable of capitulations, one might well argue that it is precisely in such a refusal that we participate in the ever-indefinite delay of the eventual, which will come, but on no one's exclusive terms. "[S]uch a hospitality without reserve . . . is," for Derrida, "the condition of the event and thus of history," and despite its intolerability for those among us who have struggled and waited so long for a justice based on vindication and a freedom based on victory, it may well be that "without this experience of the impossible," of the intolerable, "one might as well give up on both justice and the event," as well as on "whatever good conscience one still claims to preserve. One might as well," to have done with Derrida's words, "confess the economic calculation and declare all the checkpoints that ethics, hospitality or the various messianisms would install at the borders of the event in order to screen the *arrivant.*"[58] If Cubans, especially those remaining in literal exile, persist in thus guarding their borders against the future, in thus preserving this restrictive geography for their national destinal space, the eventuality they (in their stubborn, compulsive refusal to surrender their claim to lost property and lost capital) may persist in delaying, if not preventing, is precisely that of their own still-possible return home.

Chapter 6

Beyond All Cuban Counterpoints: Eduardo Machado's Floating Island Plays

There are several times of the specter . . . no one can be sure if by returning it testifies to a living past or a living future. . . . Once again, untimeliness and disadjustment of the contemporary . . . communism has always been and will remain spectral: it is always still to come and is distinguished, like democracy itself, from every living present.

—Derrida, *Specters of Marx*[1]

The more we try to animate books, the more they reveal to us their resemblance to the dead.

—Geoffrey Hartman[2]

Although Eduardo Machado's four-play cycle of Cuban and Cuban-exile histories, *Floating Islands,* was published by the Theatre Communications Group in 1991, it did not receive its first major West Coast production, at the Mark Taper Forum in Los Angeles, until three years later; and in the course of those years both Machado's plays and the national and diasporic histories they evoke underwent major revision.[3] Of the four plays, the one that bore the most revision was the third, *Fabiola*. The four pieces together recount the story of three connected, extended, and eventually dispersed bourgeois Havana families, the Ripolls, the Hernández, and the Marquezes, beginning with the first family's rise to economic and social prominence in 1920s Havana, through the marriages that connect them in subsequent generations to the other two families in the decades preceding the 1959 revolution, to the revolution and its aftermaths in Cuba (which is, importantly, *Fabiola*'s time), and finally, in the last installment, to the ambivalent moment of the family's exile "success" in 1980s suburban Woodland Hills, California. The first and last installments of the saga already received some attention in chapter 5.

The differences between the earlier published and later performed versions of *Fabiola* are considerable and significant. In the following, the first of four sections to this discussion, I mostly do the expository work of summarizing the plots of the two versions, focusing on the earlier, then the later, in turn, while scattering some points of local analysis along the way. Subsequent sections take up, in order, aspects of *Fabiola* and of the *Islands* cycle generally that situate Machado's work in such salient contexts as the vexed ideologies still (mis)directing Cuban familial, (trans)national, and diasporic histories, the theory and history of theater, drama and performance as they inform the plays, and the legacies of spirit, that is, of ritual and religion, still haunting practices staged in the many theaters relevant to Machado's Cuban American work, from the literally theatrical to the cultural, political, and even economic.

Historical Countertimes

In the earlier *Fabiola*, the eponymous character dies in childbirth in 1954, but the action of the play picks up from 1955 as the Marquezes, chief among them Fabiola's widower Pedro, continue to reel emotionally from her unexpected death and the odd disappearance of her body from the family's mausoleum. Performing by turns Catholic masses and Santeria rites, the Marquezes seem primarily concerned with freeing Fabiola from the purgatory in which she must undoubtedly still be caught, as well as freeing themselves from the anxiety that she may in fact be haunting them in their own house. This *Fabiola*'s first act also establishes that Pedro is desperately in love with his own brother, Osvaldo, and the two have been having an on-again-off-again affair since their adolescence, continuing even during their marriages to their respective wives, Fabiola and Sonia. Although Machado strategically foregrounds these domestic scandals, they stand not so much in dramatic privilege as in narrative counterpoint to the events that punctuate the story he needs *Fabiola,* in both of its versions, to tell. Indeed, the element of fraternal homosexual incest in Machado's play functions quite centrally as one of the chief forms of the play's perversions of prevailing historical, familial, and even theatrical conventions and institutions; it is a central contention of this discussion, as in all the chapters of this book, that *Fabiola*'s "queer" moments, in both versions (as well as in the four-play cycle generally), simultaneously "queer" the "momentousness" presumptive in official readings of the historical event, the family crisis, and the theatrical performance.

In turn, I argue here that Machado's revision of *Fabiola*'s narrative itself figures a kind of historical marking that might best be understood as operating within the negatively productive (il)logic of what I want to call the play of Cuban-historical "countertimes." My use of the term "counter" in the course of this discussion clearly echoes the famous contrapuntal conceit of Cuban anthropologist Fernando Ortiz's classic anthropological work, *Cuban Counterpoint: Tobacco and Sugar,* which I have already had occasion to mention previously, most significantly in chapter 5.[4] But whereas Ortiz in that volume emphasized the positive, productive felicity of the contrapuntal, allegorical dance between Cuba's two chief economic products in tracing Cuba's cultural history, my emphasis on the "counter" here aligns itself more closely with Derrida's reading, in a short piece on Shakespeare's *Romeo and Juliet* entitled "Aphorism/Countertime," of the negatively productive dynamic of the contretemps, that is, of any missed narrative and/or historical opportunity. Following Derrida's analysis of the contretemps that dooms the star-crossed lovers of Shakespeare's play, I would argue that Machado's play analogously performs the tragic fallout of a missed historical rendezvous between the two chief forces, revolution and exile, marking Cuban time, and making (impossible) Cuban history, since 1959.[5] I want to look here at how Cuban-national, Cuban-exile, and Cuban-diasporic histories have, at least since the 1959 revolution, obeyed the (il)logic of that contretemps, first through these larger framing countertimes of revolution and exile but also in the variously called "posthistorical," and even "Special," period(s) following the end of the Cold War, when all parties involved contributed to the absenting of Cuba from the general if not global historical processes that have at least since 1989 determined most other nations' fates.

The rest of the earlier *Fabiola* follows the Marquez family through the events of the revolution from the vantage point of the home in which all the play's action is set: Fabiola's body, it turns out, is discovered in another family's vault, but this discovery only occasions further, deeper trauma. Fabiola's body, already dead a year, is discovered perfectly intact, and, as the play's action hurls in subsequent acts and scenes through the New Year's Eve four years later when Castro's troops enter Havana, through the events in the spring of 1961 surrounding the failed Bay of Pigs invasion, and finally to the moment in 1967 when what remains of the Marquez clan in Havana exiles itself to Miami, Fabiola's body remains unchanged. Unchanged, that is, until, in the final scene, we hear the report from Pedro that he has had it taken out of the mausoleum, exposed to light and wind, into which it disintegrates. Fabiola's odd disappearances and reappearances in this earlier version of the play thus occupy the opposed poles of absence/presence around which characters, actions, and themes orbit and collide like so many electrons in a crowded semiotic force field. Her impossible intactness immediately calls up associations not only with magical realism but also with older, even ritual and ecclesiastical, forms of performing supernaturalism. When the rediscovery of her body is announced, for example, the following conversation ensues:

PEDRO: There must have been some decay.

OCTAVIO: No, it must be the marble . . . no moisture gets into it, or worms. She looked perfect: beautiful, perfect and intact.

CUSA: Like she was dreaming?

OCTAVIO: Yes, and happy at last.

OSVALDO: But intact. They used to make people saints who stayed intact.

MIRIAM: Or they called them vampires; depends on how much money you gave the priest.[6]

The rush of historical events that propels the action in most of the earlier *Fabiola* is thus strategically framed by the stillness of Fabiola's stubborn refusal to mark "natural" time through what scenes like this report of her body's failure to undergo the "natural" process of decomposition.

"Fabiola" thus simultaneously names at least two contradictory narrative operations in the body of the text it also names: "Fabiola" names both the trauma that refuses naming and any other definitive symbolic capture at the same time that it names the paradoxical *necessity* of that naming; "Fabiola" in turn recounts the failure of any "syuzhet" to do real justice to a "fabula" the incommensurable "reality" of whose events defy all conventional (especially dramatic or historical) narration. At the same time it demands precisely such narration as perhaps the key instrument in its navigation toward what Geoffrey Hartman has termed a "traumatic knowledge" of such events.[7] In this (as in the later) version of *Fabiola,* Machado's political concerns are never upstaged, however, by the irresistible allegorical force of the story he recounts. As important as the haunting Fabiola's body performs on the Marquez family's collective psyche are the complex processes of political affiliation and disaffiliation enjoined on various members of the family. In the first act of version 1, we learn that the Marquez patriarch, Alfredo, secretly and actively supports Castro's guerrilla campaign, but his wife, Cusa, remains primarily caught in religious belief structures, both Catholic and Santeria. By Scene 2 in 1959, Cusa, whose name is an odd diminution of "Concepsion," has become an avid supporter of the revolution, spending her New Year's Eve not with her family dancing to Nat King Cole records in the ballroom but in the kitchen with the radio, following reports of Castro's advance toward Havana. By Act 2, however, everything changes: the Marquezes have already lost a farm to the revolution's nationalization of agriculture and stand eventually to lose their mansion in the Guanabacoa suburb of Havana; their sense of political betrayal at Castro's hands compels them to support the counterrevolutionary movements outside Cuba, to the point of participating actively in the 1961 U.S.-based conspiracy to invade the island at Playa Girón and, with the failure of that plot, to mark time as politically evacuated, ghosted subjects in a Cuba now radically foreign to them until their departure into exile in 1967.

When Machado revised *Fabiola* for the Taper production in 1994, much of what I have recounted from the earlier version remained in the second, but in highly compressed form; on at least one level, the later *Fabiola* thus represents a unique case of the flexibility of a narrative's "syuzhet" to tell differently a putatively identical "fabula." On another, it poses the question of what exactly we take to be either the defining "fabula" and the "syuzhet" of so historically explicit a narrative. Here perhaps I need to clarify further what I take to be *Fabiola* and the rest of *Floating Islands*'s times and countertimes; and how the plays' temporal, chronological, and historical locations and dislocations reverberate back into its more synchronically relevant mimetic operations. The temptations to read either version of *Fabiola* allegorically are great and perhaps not entirely worth resisting; especially if we keep in mind that *Fabiola* was first conceived and composed for production in the United States in the late 1980s; the competing temporalities at work in the earlier version especially correspond too neatly to the competing temporalities of revolution and exile not to take specific note of them. Because Machado himself belongs to that impossibly dislocated generation of Cubans who were too young at the time of immigration to understand fully, in the moment, the history so directly transforming their lives, I would argue that his retrospective, "postmemorial" appreciation of that history,[8] although powerfully mediated by his parents' renditions of it, left some remnant still to be remembered, still to be accounted for with the aid of some alternative historical and psychological paradigms still to be theorized or at least imagined.[9]

*Fabiola*s one and two, and the differences between them, represent

one significant attempt to imagine, and to dramatize, such an alternative paradigm. On the one hand, Fabiola in the earlier version embodies in her unnatural intactness something of the suspended *durée* of
exile, of a collectively imagined suspension of historical time in the
preservation of an impossibly unchanging object held in a memory
that, in its refusal to acknowledge time in its meaningful passing, operates more accurately as countermemory, or perhaps even as a retrospective desire. On the other, Fabiola in the later version remains
exclusively lost; she is never relocated, and thus her haunting of especially her husband Pedro, who in both versions is equally lost to, and
trapped by, his bewildering confluence of pathologies, takes on an
even more forceful and potent (and more conventionally *melancholic*)
abstraction. In both cases Fabiola's potency as lost object lends itself
readily to an allegorical correspondence to the "lost" Cuba haunting
the collective imaginary of the exile community for and against whom
Machado may be said to write; the changes he imposes, the interventions he makes into his own text in these revisions, counter this allegorical reading of both *Fabiola* and exile memory's resistances to time
and history.

    Beyond even the dramatically strategic motivation to compress the
action in *Fabiola*'s narrative to fit better into the more ambitious for-
mat of the Taper production, which attempted, as it had with Tony
Kushner's *Angels in America,* to make *Floating Islands* available in its
entirety to an audience in the course of an eight-hour day-long performance, Machado's revisions to *Fabiola* also mark the historical
changes occurring, or significantly failing to occur, in the years just
preceding the 1994 Taper production. As I have already observed at
other points in this study, the end of the Cold War and the fall of communism in the Soviet Union and most of its satellite nations promised
in turn similar changes in Cuba, changes the Cuban-exile community
anticipated would follow as the immediate and inevitable consequence of these events in the first years of the 1990s. Castro himself famously termed the moment following the end of the Cold War Cuba's
"Special Period," marking in his own way an acknowledgment that
perhaps unprecedented, radically transformative historical turns
could take on names other than "revolution." But just as everything

changed after the revolution in Cuba, the failure of "everything" to change with the equally revolutionary turn of events in the early 1990s seems to have exacted as severe a trauma on the exile community's collective psyche, a traumatic wound whose contours can be traced if not explicated, and certainly not healed, in precisely the revisionary violence Machado does to the body of his play.[10]

Fabiola shrinks as it compresses in its later embodiment; now the action takes place in two more dramatically focused acts, both set after the revolution (always already then in "Castro's Cuba"), the first in 1960, the second in 1961. The fluidity of the action in the earlier version surrenders to a greater rigidity or tightness of narrative structure and momentum, especially in the form of a more simplified set of political positionings and exchanges among characters, perhaps most significantly on the part of Cusa, the matriarch, who in the later *Fabiola* remains loyal to the revolution even as the men in her family side with the counterrevolutionaries plotting the Bay of Pigs invasion. Her stubborn refusal to change her affiliations guarantees in this later *Fabiola* a more intense rigor mortis; Cusa's political recalcitrance substitutes for the physical recalcitrance of Fabiola's corpse in the earlier version. There will be no resolution, even in disintegration, for the textual or other "bodies" of *Fabiola*/Fabiola in the later version; instead, everything will end in stalemate and suicide: Cusa will remain in Cuba even as most of her family flees, refusing to do any more to compromise her allegiance to Castro than to hide some of her relatives from the militia until they can escape to the United States. Pedro, her son, will commit a more violent and precipitous suicide than he did in the earlier version; rather than have him slit his wrists in 1967 after a prolonged psychosis, in the later *Fabiola* Machado has Pedro shoot himself in 1961, giving up the ghost of all possible redemptions much earlier and surrendering himself no longer to the hysterical but seductive pathology of "sensations" (to which he claims allegiance in both versions), but to the acutely historical but no less seductive logic of stalemate, impasse, and aporia.

The later *Fabiola* ends, evocatively, with an explosive, reflexive apostrophe: "Fabiola," Pedro invokes at play's end, as he commands himself to shoot himself in the heart, "Cubans are killing each other again. That's all. Cubans are killing each other again. Do it now! No one can move." The complex performatives in this brief speech, from the invocatory, apostrophic "Fabiola" to the repeated, helpless descriptives of historical documentary reportage ("Cubans are killing each other again.") to the immediate and effective imperative ("Do it now!") to the paralysis in suicide which that imperative effects ("No one can move.") all point to the complex interrelations of time and performance that the texts of *Fabiola,* and more generally of *Floating Islands,* manifest and embody. Indeed, Pedro's suicides at the ends of both *Fabiola*s mark dramatically, and grammatically, the interminable reflexivity of the general Cuban situation since the revolution: "Cubans," indeed, continue to "kill Cubans"; reflexively, then, we kill each other and in the process ourselves, and if a Cuban national body should survive this ongoing and self-generating suicidal pact, then that body only lives on, survives, in the impossible "times" marked by the variously imagined afterlives of *Fabiola.* If exile superficially seems to mark the time of counterrevolution, as staged in what can only emphatically be termed, for all its provocations of Cuban-exile political orthodoxy, a play of exile, *Fabiola* also demonstrates how exile operates as revolution's countertime; that is, rather than merely oppose one another, revolution and exile also and paradoxically *necessitate* one another as well. Machado's fastidious attention to dates and times and places, and his equally fastidious attention to the rhythms of dialogue punctuated and interrupted by strong aphoristic declaratives (in the second *Fabiola,* he has Cusa spout every clichéd quotation out of the *Communist Manifesto*)[11] thus perform quite explicitly the various and contradictory times not only of revolution and exile but of family and nation, and of history and drama. These corresponding contrapuntal dynamics will take up much of the discussion in the following two sections of this chapter.

Familial Countervalues[12]

The complex trauma of national division and destruction performed in and by *Fabiola* marks both exile and revolutionary players in this struggle as familially, and for that reason even more tragically, linked;

Fabiola thus marks the fall of a house and the fall of a nation as more than analogous, but as identificatory, without sentimentalizing either nation or home. The tagline advertising the 1994 Taper production read, "Politics begins in the family," and, according to Machado, it probably "ends" there as well.[13] To Machado's credit, both *Fabiola*s reflect his understanding that history's stages are everywhere, including and in this case foregrounding the spheres of domesticity;[14] literal historical events remain quite literally, and explicitly, offstage and therefore obscene in relation to the dramatic action his work recounts directly, and for this reason such historical events share that space of obscenity with the body of Fabiola itself, which is only ever manifested to the audience as the subject (or better put grammatically, the "object") of reports and rumors.

One significant difference between the earlier and later *Fabiola*s is the inclusion in the earlier of the drama of the Márquez family's final expulsion from their home in 1967. As two impatient government-assigned *milicianos* look on, Cusa and Alfredo inventory which few of their possessions they can take with them and, more importantly, which they must leave behind. The scene reads as follows:

MILICIANO 2: Four pairs of pants . . . shirts . . . an envelope.
MILICIANO 1: What's in it?
CUSA: Photos. Photos of my old farm, photos of my car, photos of my old house.
MILICIANO 2: Photos. Should we let them take the photos?
MILICIANO 1: It's against the rules.
CUSA: Take them. I don't need photos to remember.[15]

What poignancy there might be to Cusa's defiance of the police is certainly undercut by the consistency with which she reports that the photos she's willing to leave behind are of possessions, not people; but at least two of those possessions, the farm and the house, combine in themselves simultaneous references to domesticity, family, and property. By 1967 most of the Márquez family is in exile anyway, so it could be argued that what Cusa most needs to remember are the spaces where that family regenerated itself for almost a century. The photos presumably remain behind, but in their stead Cusa takes memories that, in the speech with which she exits, aggregate into a spectralized history of reminders, remainders, and remains:

> CUSA: In 1945 Pedro and Osvaldo had asthma attacks. The doctor said we needed to be near the beach. The first house I bought was haunted; we saw furniture move around. Two children had died in that house of scarlet fever in 1886. Their fever got so high they started to burn up and they screamed all night long before they died in 1886. . . . It was their ghosts we heard every night. I got my children out of that house. This house was built by an ambassador from Spain. He assured me that no one had died here; the gypsy said it was true. . . . I bought this place in 1945 for cash, my father's money. Only one person died here. Fabiola, June 11, 1954. The house was free of ghosts till 1954.[16]

Longish monologues like this one operate dramatically as set pieces in Machado's work; they are tableaux, or rather tables, on which a rather varied menu of leftovers may be displayed. In this case, the photos that remain, remain invisible, enveloped in the interdiction against their transportation, and they give way instead to the recital of a history, of a complex set of disappearances or, in Derridean coinage, *disparitions*. If the references to "ghosts" haunting the house from the nineteenth-century didn't sufficiently suggest that the hauntings of both domestic and national spaces in this scene are linked to colonial history, certainly the reference to the Spanish ambassador does. And if colonial and postcolonial, as well as revolutionary and exile, histories in Cuba all appear to Machado as perversions of Cuban domestic politics, they also and in the same gesture pervert Cuban domesticity and domestic familial relations and affiliations as such. Cusa's monologue results in nothing more than her expulsion from her home ("Lady?" one *miliciano* asks as she concludes, and when she responds "Yes?" he responds in turn, simply, "Get out."[17]), and nothing certainly would seem as perverse to the conventional Cuban patriarchal mentality than this expulsion of a woman, a mother no less, from her home, that most sacrosanct of spaces.

I want to suggest in the course of this discussion that if for Machado politics are not dissociable from family, they are also therefore not dissociable from domesticity and gender. All the "living" women in Machado's play, from Cusa to her daughter Miriam and daughter-in-law Sonia, to her maids, Sara and Conchita, eventually take political sides with respect to the revolution and its countermovements. Indeed, the only "living" character who doesn't is Pedro, who in both versions disintegrates psychologically as his wife Fabiola's body refuses to physically. In the complex gender play of both *Fabiola*s, Pedro stands as the perfect embodiment of hysteria; as everyone else is increasingly caught up in the force of historical and public events, Pedro's stage of operation focuses increasingly (and, eventually, exclusively) on the private and the bodily. His obsession with the state of his wife's body parallels his two other obsessions, one with alcohol and the other with his brother, Osvaldo; Osvaldo, in turn, requites his brother's desire but refuses to abandon himself so completely to it. As Pedro lives what is left of his life in the exclusive service of "sensations," a vocation that increasingly isolates him from the action of the play, Osvaldo is kept from falling into the same trap by his relationship with his own wife and son, the family he takes into exile and away from his brother in the second act. Osvaldo's fate does not, however, reflect any judgment of moral or other superiority in his favor; he meets his own perverse destiny in exile, a destiny recounted in *Broken Eggs,* the fourth of the plays, and one no less compromised by "sensations."

One of Machado's favorite methods of perverting the institution of the Cuban family is to emphasize its always already perverse relationship to the oedipal family romance as institutionalized in and since Freud. In both versions of *Fabiola,* Machado has the character Sonia berate others for not going to see therapists, and in general one of the more amusing asides one can cull from *Fabiola* is that Cubans to their chagrin have historically listened too seriously to Marx (and probably Hegel) and not seriously enough to Freud. It certainly does no justice to *Fabiola*'s deep subversiveness and its even deeper perversities, however, to dismiss its explicit representations of, say, the narcissistic homoeroticism of Pedro's love for Osvaldo along conventionally

Freudian or Lacanian lines of triangulated desire. The spectacle of Pedro's frustrated mourning of Fabiola does not at all mask or compensate for his scandalous love for his brother; it does not merely or predictably rehearse the hom(m)osocially conventional absenting of female figures in favor of stronger, and patriarchally enjoined, male–male bonds.[18] Osvaldo at one point in version 1 declares his ambivalence toward his older brother: "I love him. And yet I hate him." To which his wife responds, "No. Jealousy," and when he asks why he "should be jealous" of Pedro, she simply replies, "Oedipus."[19] Sonia's invocation of tragic drama's and psychoanalytic theory's paradigmatic text thus functions in this case as both the most, and the least, adequate of answers to Osvaldo's question.

According to Machado himself, *Fabiola* has historically been the most controversial of the *Floating Island* plays, especially with exile audiences, precisely, but not exclusively, because of its "homosexual content."[20] Exile audiences tend not to identify Pedro's hysteria as their own, but perhaps in this respect that is a "successful" response, the one the playwright desires to the extent that it alienates his audience from an easy identification with actions that are indeed central to their own conventional sense of identity; it is, after all, only in *Fabiola* that Machado comes even close to dramatizing the expulsion leading to exile and to its attendantly addictive, impossible mourning, but dramatizes it, indeed, behind a screen of homoerotic and incestuous spectacle just as impossible for its audience to ignore. Of course, the narcissistic and reflexive dynamics conventionally associated with both homosexuality and incest may be exactly what Machado wants his exile audience to identify with, rather than against. To this extent, what I have just called a screen dividing the audience and the piece may well operate as a mirror but one this specific audience would refuse to recognize as such.[21] And, indeed, there is much, especially in the revised *Fabiola,* to distract and even lure the audience's attention away from Pedro and his family's sexual excesses. Besides the failure of Fabiola's body to reappear at all, Machado's other major revision in the later text is, as I have already noted, Cusa's deeper and more consistent adherence to the revolution. What repulsion an exile audience might feel at the sight of two brothers (and, in one particularly provocative scene, the brothers *and* their sister Miriam) locked in highly sexual embraces or of the fully nude Pedro desperately trying to seduce a communist uncle before committing suicide in the last scene could only be surpassed and exceeded perhaps by their repulsion to Cusa's (and the play's) fervent, explicit, and frequent invocations of Marx and Castro.

If Pedro's intense mourning of his wife seems incongruous in the face of his equally intense desire for his brother, Machado gives us to understand that for Pedro both attachments grew out of the selfsame complicated libidinal and even moral architecture, one in which Fabiola herself found comfortable accommodation. Pedro confesses to Osvaldo while dancing with him in the darkened ballroom that Fabiola always knew of the brothers' relationship:

> PEDRO: She knew, Fabiola . . . Yes, you and me, . . . my little brother,..there was a time when I didn't know the difference between the two of us. There was a day when I looked at your face and thought it was me.
> OSVALDO: Is Fabiola watching us?
> PEDRO: Probably . . . she thought it was erotic.
> OSVALDO: She knew?
> PEDRO: Yes, I told her. . . . She was my friend. She wanted to know every detail. I told her. . . . How many times . . . who did what . . . what your lips were like. That's how we spent our honeymoon.[22]

At this point, their sister, Miriam, who had been spying on them, intrudes and, rather than panic, the brothers invite her to join in their intensely erotic dance, prompting Osvaldo to remark, "This is good. Evil, but good," which in turn prompts this response from Pedro, "All good things are evil." In this, one of the merely explicitly "queer" moments in a play that implicitly and emphatically "queers" moments, times, and histories, Machado seems to suggest that if Cubans to their detriment privileged Marx and/or Hegel over Freud, they also in this respect unfortunately ignored Nietzsche, from whom they might just as well have learned a queer lesson or two about history, about morality, and about desire.

Indeed, the direct connection of desire to history seems to be Machado's direct object of illustration in *Fabiola* and the other *Floating Island* plays, which thus challenges us to think in more complex and ambiguous ways as well about the deep perversity of both the political and the ethical. As the dance scene involving the three siblings suggests, the vectors of libidinal and social transgression in *Fabiola* respect no conventional set of prohibitions and taboos; there is no obvious fraternal rivalry between Pedro and Osvaldo for the love of their mother, Cusa, and their libidinal ties to both their wives and to their sister Miriam occasion some rather impressively perverse, because impressively positive, combinations of noncompetitive erotic exchange. Even the normally prudish Sonia finds herself caught in this network: when at one point she reports, for example, that she felt Fabiola's spirit enter her, Pedro asks, "She touched you?" in response to which Sonia confesses, "Yes, it was like a caress over my entire body. It was soothing," to which Pedro responds, in a swoon, and an echo: "Soothing?"[23] Explicitly eroticized desire (and its discharges) thus circulates among characters in Machado's play with no consistent regard for gender, kinship, vitality, or any of the other conventional and institutional categories governing official, normative sexual exchange in conventionally oedipalized societies. And if one certain instance of a paternal Logos appears to be dismantled here, others follow suit; Machado manages in scenes like the two just discussed to maintain the erotic, political, and even economic dimensions governing familial arrangements in most societies while at the same time skewing significantly all the conventions normally determining those arrangements.

This thoroughgoing subversion of the familial and social authority usually vested in these categories also characterizes Machado's treatment of fathers in his plays. Fathers in both *Fabiola*s are curiously, almost categorically, dismissed at least as dramatically important or even interesting characters. Even as harbingers of most of the political action in the two plays, neither Alfredo Márquez nor Oscar Hernandez bears any of the psychological complexity of their children. Indeed, the only fascinating patriarch in *Fabiola* one or two is Fidel Castro, who, given the historical setting of the plays, functions as much as the upstart rebellious son to Batista's father as he himself does as a father to anyone. Castro also functions as Fabiola's counter to the extent that his is the only other name repeatedly invoked through the course of the play without a body materializing to support it. In Act 1, Scene 2 of the earlier *Fabiola,* set on the eve of Castro's entry into Havana, the Márquez women discuss, not Castro's politics, but his body. "I think Fidel is sexy," Miriam confesses, to which Sara the maid responds, "I think Fidel should take a shower and shave," which prompts in turn from Sonia the observation that "He doesn't have time. He's a revolutionary."[24] Revolutionaries, like the dead, may be said to have "no time" (or perhaps to occupy some position outside of time, certainly outside of history) even, perhaps especially, for reasons of hygiene, of any regimen, that is (aesthetic, erotic, etc.), that distracts them from the heroic/historic effort of establishing more just regimes (politically, economically). This, at least, seems to be Sonia's greater point in the scene:

> "He's up in the hills fighting. . . . To get into power. . . . After he overthrows Batista, by force, revolution, he's going to have elections and he'll run for prime minister, and then he's going to stop prostitution."[25]

Of course, the "history" Sonia tells here turns to fantasy when, within the crucial terms "force, revolution" that history becomes prospective. Democracy, "free" elections, is of course the protocol, the "hygienic" instrument Castro failed to make available to a Cuban national body in dire need of it. His own charismatic sexiness notwithstanding, Castro's seduction of Cuba proved, at least for the class that Sonia and her family represent, a tragic reversal by betrayal as well as the occasion of their own being "cleansed" out of the national body through their own perceived expulsion off the island and into exile.

The aftermath of that paternal betrayal, as recounted in both *Fabiola*s, therefore primarily takes the form of the disappearance of bodies from the stage, especially as more and more members of the Márquez and Hernández families make their way into exile. In the later *Fabiola,* the two bodies that most significantly remain/persist in the play's simultaneous national, domestic, and dramatic stages are Cusa's and Pedro's, a mother and her son, but a deeply compromised oedipal pair to be sure. Pedro's body, given his insistence on making his disintegration explicit, is more fully, literally "embodied"; he insists in both *Fabiola*s on making his family the audience for that disintegration: "I want to have you watch me while I burn," he says, in one of the rare speeches from the first version that Machado keeps in the second, "while my brain dissolves in front of your eyes. I want you all to watch the destruction."[26] Pedro's line here echoes in part of course the "burning" child in Freud's famous case study who, although dead, appears to his father in a dream that wakes the father to the child's literally burning body. Pedro's "burning," however, occasions no significant awakening and little in the way of significant, productive effect. Indeed, his fall into alcoholism and psychosis barely impresses his family; they are usually too consumed with their own political misfortunes to give much attention, let alone credence, to Pedro's rants. This "burning" culminates, therefore, in the sterile nonact of Pedro's suicide, the ultimate manifestation of a performative but ineffectual, paralytic reflexivity, one performed in this case naked, and in isolation, as the act that marks the end of the play, and the play of the end, not only for Pedro but for *Fabiola* the play, and for the ghosted and suicidal "nation" it allegorically conjures.

Theatrical Counterframes

Having taken some considerable portion of the first two sections of this discussion doing the expository work of reporting mostly the narrative "facts" of *Fabiola* and of its familial and national histories, I now want to turn to an analysis of the play's most salient theatrical operations. Although on some level, and as I have just argued, Machado insists on overliteralizing the story of Cuba's internal national struggles as an extreme case of family romance leading to family tragedy, such hyperbolic literalization does nothing to simplify or resolve what I would call, following Geoffrey Hartman, his work's "literary knowledge" of the traumas, national, familial, and personal, to which it testifies. So having just discussed some of these more compelling topical concerns of the plays, now I'd like to devote some space here to certain questions of form, of the various legacies of especially theater, drama, and the strategic deployments of performance more generally, which I have begun to suggest in the preceding sections are as central to Machado's practice as its historical thematics. The analysis in this section also prepares in part an argument I make in the concluding section about all the plays', but especially *Fabiola*'s, relationship, through both theatricality and spectrality, to spirit (in both political—that is, nationalist—and religious senses of the term), especially as it might help us read at least one memorable (if already half-forgotten) spectral return to the Cuban American historical scene, that of Cuban Catholicism, as embodied in Pope John Paul II's highly theatrical visit to Cuba in January 1998.

Perhaps the most accurate term to characterize Machado's compulsive solicitations of Western theatrical traditions in the *Floating Island Plays* is to call them promiscuous. Reading through them one is reminded of forms as various as Sophoclean tragedy, medieval mystery plays, Golden Age Spanish honor plays, sex comedies ranging from Wycherley to Wilde, social reform drama from Ibsen, Shaw, and Brecht, to absurdist theater from Pirandello, Artaud, and Beckett, to modernist and postmodernist resuscitations of epic form from O'Neill to Kushner. Formally speaking, Machado is in bed with everyone. This promiscuity extends even further afield if one includes in the larger definition of theatrical performance as varied an array of public rituals; each of the plays may be said to center on some occasion of ritualized public action across various degrees of formality, from Oscar's courtship of Manuela in *Modern Ladies,* to a family lunch in *Hurricane* (which might as well serve as a Last Supper for the Cuban bourgeoisie) to the various attempts at mourning in *Fabiola,* to the wedding that disorganizes the dramatic inaction of *Broken Eggs.*

I want to term this disorientation toward the traditions of both theater and ritual "promiscuity" to work against the potentially serious and canonizing effect that such gestures as I am describing here on the part of the playwright might otherwise have. Machado signals his own concern for the manner in which such solicitations should be read in passages like this one between the Ripoll matriarch Maria Josefa and her granddaughter Sonia from *In the Eye of the Hurricane*:

> MARIA JOSEFA: We'd sit with whole tablecloths, big ones, and embroider, my mother and me. . . . Whole tablecloths we'd embroider for tables bigger than this one. People had bigger families back then, common to see a table that sat thirty. Easily.
> SONIA: I wish . . . that we still had one of those tablecloths so I could study it, maybe copy it. Maybe you could remember the stitch.
> MARIA JOSEFA: Too late. . . . I don't remember the stitches, the pattern, just remember that it was beautiful and people envied us. . . . We got too busy for those things. . . . Then one forgets.
> SONIA: I've learned how to at school, but small things, towels, handkerchiefs—
> MARIA JOSEFA: Your work, it's lovely.
> SONIA: Nothing as monumental as a tablecloth, but—[27]

So ambitious an undertaking as the composition of a four-play cycle covering a century's worth of one nation and three families' histories will inescapably have about it the appearance of a potentially hubristic ambition, an ambition one could legitimately term "monumentalizing" if not successfully monumental. Both nations and families may have passed the point in their histories when anything like monumentalizing cultural work (whether in, say, the embroidery of a tablecloth or in the composition of an unreconstructed dramatic epic) can be adequate to the more deeply compromised functions those institutions now play on either public or private stages. For these reasons I choose to read Machado's plays as ruins rather than as monuments; they certainly testify to certain forms of ruination, none so more than that of the Cuban ruiNation itself, as much as they engage in a certain ruinous, and ruinously critical, engagement of a tradition in theater that few relevant critics still treat as simply canonical or monumental.

This "ruinous" engagement with their own theatrical and ritual pasts may be precisely the chief activity that Machado's plays may be said to perform, and to perform both theatrically and critically. To this extent, Machado's plays, although they undoubtedly play well as "theater," manage to perform otherwise when they are read as "performance"; this neat but crucial conceptual distinction I borrow from the critical and scholarly movement that we now identify as Performance Studies, represented here by the work of Diana Taylor, who argues in her introduction to the collection *Negotiating Performance* that when we "replace the word theatre with *performance*," we can then not only "include all sorts of spectacle that 'theatre' leaves out," but can also "look at theatre itself from a more critical perspective."[28] The productive consequence of skewing, according to Taylor's prescription, the critical perspective we take toward Machado's plays is that such a reorientation of our own critical procedures will allow us to retain a set of terms and concepts central to, say, the canonical traditions of dramatic writing and its criticism, terms, and concepts indispensable to any comprehensive reading of the plays, without reactivating as we do so the usual political and cultural consequences of deploying this particular set of readerly protocols. This is crucial, regardless of whether we choose to favor either formal or topical elements in the plays; indeed, as Taylor suggests, these dimensions are really inextricably linked across practices of composition, production, and critical reception. There is no way, therefore, to read the complex play of gender in all of *Floating Islands* without some attention to the equally and commensurably complex play of genre. "The broad concept of performance," Taylor argues, not only "allow[s] us to explore numerous manifestations of 'dramatic' behavior in the public sphere which tend to drop out of more traditional approaches to theatre" but also allows us "to reexamine theatre itself as one of the various systems of representation in patriarchies which push women and popular audiences to the margins"; thus, she concludes, "Performance, seen as a deconstructive strategy in much feminist theory, enable[s] us to look at theatre in a way that critique[s] its own staging."[29] The leap here from deconstructive to ruinous is certainly short, and certainly ratified, by both Derrida and Taylor, to say nothing of Machado.

In both versions of *Fabiola*, Machado retains the vocabulary of both epic and tragedy to test the possibilities for certain forms of evaluation that might be applicable to the actions of his characters. In the later version, for example, one character's risky attempt to rescue a relative from the regime prompts the following dialogue:

> CLARA: They told me that [my husband, Fernando] had driven through a gate to get Oscar into safety. Unfortunately, there was no way for him to leave the embassy and not get arrested once he drove in. . . . I drove to the embassy, and I saw the car riddled with bullets. And I thought, "Your husband is a hero." And I told the children, "Your father is a hero. Now we must all escape." So I sent them all ahead because that is the moral thing to do. I will not let my children be raised without Jesus and the Virgin Mary.
> MIRIAM: We are lucky Fernando and Oscar didn't get shot.
> CLARA: No wounds, but still a hero.
> MIRIAM: Does one heroic act make a hero?
> CLARA: Yes.
> CUSA: Or a fool.[30]

In the earlier version, Sonia, Osvaldo's wife and Pedro's sister-in-law, comments that, in losing Fabiola, Pedro's "been in touch with real tragedy. Something devastating really happened to him."[31] But that "tragedy" is not the action of either of the plays that we call *Fabiola*; indeed, for all its complex choreography of characters' histrionics, *Fabiola* is more about movement(s) than about action and ultimately is about the impossibility of certain forms of productive action in Pedro's final paralysis and suicide. As Sonia goes on to generalize from Pedro's mourning to everyone else's (significantly, in a scene predating the revolution), we hear the play mark itself as primarily a play of aftermath, of a general and indeterminate consequence of loss. "What's [Fabiola's death] the beginning of?" Sonia asks her husband. "Before Fabiola died nothing bad happened to me, nothing unkind even. . . . But she's gone; she was our age. She's dead. Lost. We can't even find her body. There's nothing left of her."[32] The statement "she was our age" clearly resonates with a double meaning: Fabiola is both of Sonia's generation and the embodiment of a dead, or at least dying, historical epoch in (and out of) Cuba.

One can also raise here the related issues of, first, Machado's relationship to another form of epic theater, the Brechtian, and second, the consequences of this particular dramatic solicitation for an audience that might find any allusion to a Marxist aesthetic itself deeply alienating. Especially in the portrayal of Cusa's character in the later version, the aggressively explicit foregrounding of Marxist ideology in her speeches would presumably have a very mixed effect on a Cuban-exile audience; Brechtian alienation is significantly less likely to lead directly to raising either class or national consciousness in such a case.[33] The heightened attention Machado pays to Cusa's politics through her many exclamatory citations of Marx in the later *Fabiola* suggests that he both wants to present a more balanced picture of the Cuban ideological divide as well as perhaps transforming in the same gesture something of the piece's dramatic and generic functions.

In this respect Machado's dramaturgical moves recall Walter Benjamin's analysis of Brechtian epic theater in his famous essay on the topic. In his analysis of what he termed the "quotable gesture," Benjamin draws a structural connection between interruption and quotation: "Interruption," he argues, "is one of the fundamental devices of all structuring. It goes far beyond the spheres of art . . . [and] is the basis of quotation. To quote a text involves the interruption of its context."[34] Benjamin's formulation of this decidedly strategic use of interruption goes, he says, to the heart of the epic theater's operation since, "being based on interruption, [it] is, in a specific sense, quotable." Hence Machado's quoting of Marx through Cusa in a sense strategically interrupts the realistic flow of his own narrative enough to render it correspondingly interrupted and quotable, perhaps then memorable to an audience who, in spite of itself, might find such quotations at once alienating and compelling. The later *Fabiola* thus plays more like epic theater in the Brechtian sense than, say, a mourning play in the Benjaminian, if only because of the very exact narrative correspondences that I earlier stated compelled it be read as political allegory rather than as personal, or even collective, testimony (which is not the same as arguing that the plays do not serve a testimonial function). These correspondences can also be said to make certain important corrective gestures, to discourage the play's being read too classically, that is, within too ossified a set of traditional generic classifications.

At times, however, such traditional generic elements do engage each other in complex, paradoxical play in order to maintain the tension preventing any easy, conventional classification. In the later *Fabiola*, for example, Cusa's conversion to the revolution's vision for Cuba has already taken place, but she retells that story of conversion not as one of radical discontinuity (Fabiola's death does not figure the revolution as cataclysm) but of the most incongruous of progressions. Contrasted with Pedro's unlimited libidinal economy of "sensational" abundance, his mother declares herself from the beginning an embodiment of libidinal scarcity and even cruel self-denial. Before her conversion, Cusa dabbled in Santeria practices to curse her philandering husband Alfredo and to appease Fabiola's spirit: "I stopped eating," she declares to her children, "As an offering to Changó, I became a vessel for my soul, not my sensations. And now the gods have repaid me my sacrifice by bringing me the revolution. The fire that will cleanse us all."[35] This "cleansing," of course, bears its own peculiar and troubling semantic weight on stages other than the theatrical; on some level, the direct cause-and-effect link Cusa draws from her own ritualized self-denial to its consequence in the revolution figured as purification ritual invites in its recounting of her personal and Cuba's national history some haunting on the part of the political. If cleansing and purification here invoke the ghost of classical catharsis, one can only wonder if Machado has Cusa speak against herself here; although she would never consider the revolution tragic, her declaration nevertheless marks the necessary outcome of the revolution in a "cleansing," a purging from the national body of an entire enemy class (those presumably comprising some part of Machado's audience) who understand their expulsion from nation and home precisely as tragic and traumatic.[36]

Mother Cusa's fanatical devotion to the revolution is, however, no more the object of Machado's critique than her bourgeois children's devotions to their various pleasures, perversities, and pathologies. The second *Fabiola* opens with her children, all grown and either married or widowed, dancing and drunk in their mansion's ball-room. Any talk of politics, usually provoked by the women, is silenced by the men: "Mambo and forget," commands the third son, Fernando, and his brother Osvaldo chimes in, "I don't care about history, I just want to dance. I want to move to music and drown the world out."[37] This decadent generation and class, the object expelled in Cuba's political self-cleansing, clearly an anxious generation and class, leave more than one Cuba, to be sure. On some level, the "Cuba" they leave cannot be typified by their literal mother, Cusa, who is perhaps *too* engaged a political subject to tolerate any easy symbolic or allegorical objectification; instead, the Cuba they leave, the one they preserve and uphold as authentic in their collective memory, is the Cuba that "died" with Fabiola, the other mother, who died in a childbirth in which the child was also lost and whose body, either as impossibly intact or utterly lost, belies the exile fantasies, either of eventual return or of their immunity to moral and other forms of decadence.

What action(s), therefore, *Fabiola* may be said to stage play generally like a dance, an endless round of events that lead, and go, nowhere in particular and that just as dramatically problematize genre as they do time and space. Occasionally characters make what are only apparently casual remarks about the absence or failure of time in its passing. In the later version, Sonia reports one appearance of Fabiola's ghost, motivating an interrogation from Cusa that prompts in turn a dialogue covering most of the allegorical bases I've been covering:

cusa: Did you ask her what's happened to her body?
sonia: No, no time. . . . She was crying. And repeating the same thing over and over again.
cusa: I thought you said there was no time.
sonia: She just said, "Everyone is leaving me, everyone is leaving me."[38]

Although this touching scene seems to encourage a dangerously sentimentalized reading of Fabiola's generation's eventual departure into exile as the painful abandonment of at least a national spirit, if not a national body, in distress, Machado is careful in subsequent scenes to establish that such a departure may be read in as many ways, through as many historical and theatrical lenses as there are readers to read it, and that not all such readings bear well the weight of such sentimentality; this may in turn prove to be Machado's chief guard against the conventional effects of at least melodrama, another genre with which the plays flirt without full commitment.

This strong resistance to all sentimentalizing reactions to his plays may in the end be strategically necessary, given the primarily personal, domestic, and familial relations on which Machado focuses. In the later *Fabiola,* for example, Pedro's suicide is significantly preceded by a duet he performs with his mother, Cusa, whose aesthetically self-denying relation to her own body can be figured as antithetical to Pedro's indulgences of his. In a tableau reminiscent of a *Pietà,* Cusa cradles the hysterical Pedro and, although he demands rather hopelessly that she sing him a lullaby that he loved as a boy, she instead recounts Cuba's history to him, a history by turns permanently fulfilled, transformed, and fractured (I daresay *deconstructed*) by the revolution. But in addition to the obvious tension generated by the difference between personal and public narratives recounted here, Machado the playwright also dramatizes the further tension generated by genre itself in the performance-specific dimensions of their recounting.

The most effective way to play this scene would be as a duet rather than as a dialogue; Pedro and Cusa's lines here act out the contrapuntal relations of tempos and temporalities, of rhythms and rhetorics, which I've been arguing are *Fabiola*'s most symptomatic structurings. Were one to read this scene aloud, say, on a conference panel, no single voice and body could do justice to the scene as it should be played out. In performance, these lines, read simultaneously, mutually obscure each other's constative functions, deeply compromising the referential work they otherwise, at least on the page, so compellingly do. But this scene here, discussed and printed on the following pages, is not *Fabiola*'s; this time is not its time. This reading, even as mere reading, operates in the radically different time and scene of a critical analysis, which, in the following citation, can only hopelessly misrepresent what it hopes to explicate:

PEDRO: I want to remember nice times. Sing me to sleep. (He lies down on the ground)

CUSA: If things were fair, our class wouldn't be blamed for all the ugly things! For the whims of corrupt men.

PEDRO: Men's whims. I want to remember nice times. The one about the little boat.

CUSA: You're too old for songs.

PEDRO: There was once a tiny little boat, there was once a tiny little boat, there was once a tiny little boat, that just couldn't, that just couldn't, that just couldn't sail away . . .

CUSA: I used to tell you stories about Cuba. Remember them, Pedro? How we were discovered by Christopher Columbus and he said: "This is the most beautiful land that human eyes have seen."

PEDRO: He tried for one two three four five six seven weeks. He tried for one two three four five six seven weeks. He tried for one two three four five six seven weeks . . .

CUSA: And how the Spaniards and the Africans came. And how people, after they'd been here for a couple of generations, started calling themselves Cubans . . .

PEDRO: . . . but the little boat just couldn't, just couldn't sail away. And if the story doesn't seem long enough, and if the story doesn't seem long enough, and if the story doesn't seem long enough . . .

CUSA: . . . natives of a new land. So they fought to be Cubans, to have an identity. But how could you believe me? How could even a little boy believe in something that never really existed? It exists now, Pedro. Fidel has given us a country. Defend it, Pedro. It's worth it! Defend it for me!

PEDRO: We will repeat it, we will repeat it, we will repeat it once again. There was once a little boat . . .

CUSA: We deserve a country. We've lived through one dictator after another. (Pause.) When all you really wanted to do was to pick

up a gun and kill everyone that oppressed you. Shoot it now!
(Pause.) Defend your country. Do it now, Pedro.

PEDRO: Mother, I can't move.

CUSA: Cubans are killing each other again. Pedro, no one can move.[39]

The complex, simultaneous divergence and convergence of the
child's tale passing as national history and the lullaby free of any pre-
tension except to the interminable, lulling repetition of repetition
most eloquently punctuate and choreograph (to return here to Diana
Taylor's point) *Fabiola*'s play and dance, *as performance* with time
and history. Pedro the addict desires the narcotic whose fundamental
attraction is the fulfillment of the desire it itself generates ad infinitum, *ad absurdum;* Cusa the converted dialectical materialist now
sees the possibility for the first time of a genuine Cuban nation born
out of a revolution whose eventuality, not to say its inevitability, is
precisely what the history preceding it could never have predicted,
but whose logic it necessarily compelled. Between the an-aesthetic
narcosis of the lullaby's interminable refrain and the antiaesthetic,
pragmatic force of Cusa's imperative calls to political and historical
action ("Shoot it now! Defend your country. Do it now, Pedro!"), the
"force" devolving from these conflicting centripetal and centrifugal
movements seems itself to devolve into mere paralysis and, as this
scene prefigures the play's last, suicide.

Religious Counterpractices

In the Spring/Summer 1998 issue of its newsletter, *Cuban Affairs,* the
Washington- and Miami-based progressive and pro-dialogue Cuban
Committee for Democracy (CCD) devoted several major pieces to
Pope John Paul II's visit to Cuba the previous January. A minority voice
in Cuban-exile politics in the United States, the CCD very explicitly declared in these pieces its hope for constructive exchange with Cuba's
revolutionary government as a result of its good faith effort to restore
Catholicism as a sanctioned form of public worship in Cuba, an effort
capped by Fidel Castro's personal invitation to John Paul to make the
visit in the first place. Although the visit, for all its historic importance,

failed to effect any visible change in the U.S.–Cuban situation, it did provide commentators on that situation with an opportunity to think more fully through the relationship between the revolution and religion, a relationship Eduardo Machado foregrounds through all of *Floating Islands,* but especially in *Fabiola,* as one of the most fertile and most vexed of both theoretical and practical associations. Beyond the associations already covered between, say, the revolution and Cusa's conversions from Catholicism to Santeria to Marxism, and the Márquezes' failed attempts to mourn Fabiola as specifically a failure of spirit (and spirituality) in the face of a material fatality (or a fatal materialism), there may be ways left to read the theatricality of the pope's visit alongside the historicities rendered theatrically in Machado's plays to mark perhaps the paradigmatic (il)logic of Cuban "time," of a paradigmatic Cuban moment, and therefore of a "history" for which the pope's visit might stand as both an endpoint and an endgame, a point of punctual closure as well as a play of perpetual and indefinite (some might say interminable) reopening.[40]

My own paratextual compulsions have at times taken me away from "my" text, at least the one I signal in the title of this piece to be my chief object of analysis or the work of dramatic expression to which I address my interpretive and analytical commentary, and here I need to step outside of *Fabiola* one more time, back (or forward) to *In the Eye of the Hurricane,* Machado's counter-*Tempest,* his own retelling of the revolution in events that occur to the Hernándezes simultaneously with those that in *Fabiola* occur to the Márquezes. To the extent that Machado in his plays mimes something of the ecclesiastical, one may find that citation most explicitly in references to a temporality once marked theatrically by medieval mystery plays as both liturgical and allegorical. In a curious dialogue from *Hurricane,* Machado has Maria Josefa spy a lily blooming before its time and provoke the following exchange with her daughter Manuela:

MARIA JOSEFA: One of the lilies of the valley has come out to look at me.

MANUELA: It's too early for lilies to bloom.

MARIA JOSEFA: No, Look over there.

MANUELA: It's early, it's an early riser, that one.

MARIA JOSEFA: Flowers don't know about time.

MANUELA: Well, maybe not about time, but cycles, seasons.

MARIA JOSEFA: No, I don't think so. I think they just are. Once a whole field of lilies of the valley bloomed for me. . . . It's when we lived in a much more rural part of town. Guanabacoa was much more rural then, than now. More open fields, and we lived next to a huge field. It was the night before my first communion, I had been fasting all day, so I could be clean when the Sacred Sacrament entered my body.

Maria Josefa lights a cigarette. Pause.

MANUELA: And?

MARIA JOSEFA: What . . . ?

MANUELA: Did you fall asleep?

MARIA JOSEFA: The day before my first communion?

MANUELA: No, just now.

MARIA JOSEFA: And it bloomed, a field full of lilies, and I knew the Holy Sacrament wanted me. (She laughs) Wanted me, that was the last moment I ever had in my life that was simple. And today "He" only shows me one.[41]

Maria Josefa's pastoral reverie, we are told earlier, is very likely the hallucinogenic effect of a serious imbalance in her blood sugar (a bad sugar economy, to be sure) brought on by her degenerative diabetes; but her monologue quite effectively evokes the force of times other than the historical on the collective imagination of her class. If the force of dialectical, material history can still be argued to work mostly against the Cuban bourgeoisie, then one choice left to them is to revert to a belief in liturgical calendrical time; a cyclical time patterned after regular shifts in seasonal warmth, and marked, punctuated regularly by performance of both religious plays and rituals. This is a time that promises return *without* revolution; time "turns" but presumably always (re)turns back, giving (back) what it always inevitably takes: youth, innocence, a faith in life everlasting for the individual, the family, and all other life-giving forms of community, from the congregation to the nation.

But if Machado's motivation in composing these plays is decidedly not therapeutic, it is also decidedly not pastoral; it is, if anything, deeply vigilant and in part testimonial, and if it insists on witnessing the failed vigil of his own exile community for a failed return, it cannot help but witness as well, at least implicitly, some of the more perverse ways to think a Cuban future, one way at least which "returned" dramatically, in 1998, in the "promise" some witnesses have read into Catholicism's return visitation to Cuba in the spirited guise of the pope. It may, indeed, say something of Machado's own shift in perspective from the time of *Fabiola*'s publication in 1991 to its Taper showing in 1994 that the earlier version begins in supplicating prayer and the later version does not. The later version may in all ways be read for its greater secular orientation; the absenting of Fabiola's body entirely in the later version may be said in turn to absent the whole question of her beatification or anyone else's. But Machado certainly had the parallel legacies of medieval and even earlier Christian ritual and theatrical practices in mind, even in the earlier version of the play. As Sonia, Miriam, and the family maids wrap New Year's grapes on the very eve of the revolution, for example, they engage in the following suggestive discussion:

MIRIAM: Wrapping grapes every New Year's Eve. Eat a grape at midnight and you'll be lucky. Well, I'm living proof that it's a lie . . .
CLARA: It's a custom. We have to do it.
MIRIAM: Why? Why do we have to do anything?
SONIA: Because it's normal.
MIRIAM: It's superstition . . .
CLARA: Superstition is the truth.
MIRIAM: The truth. Little black balls around our necks. Saints with apples at their feet and glasses of water. Bodies that won't disappear . . . All these offerings . . . So Saint Barbara will do what Mama commands. Relics, icons; it's the Dark Ages[42]

All hope of beatitude or idyll seems even more cursorily dismissed, however, in the later version; the play of piety there gives way even more directly to the play of heresy, the play of the sacred gives way to the play of the profane, the play of spirit and specter gives way to the play of matter, especially as progressive or even revolutionary (and decidedly not providential) historical force.

Which is not to say there isn't some play of spirit in this greater attention to matter; something still haunts the mostly material dialectic in the later *Fabiola,* a spirit that some claimed to have witnessed returning some years after the play's revision with the pope's "historic" visit. Hear, for example, how, in the spirit of dialogic exchange, both Fidel and John Paul verged on heretical violations of their own respective orthodoxies: Castro was generally cited to have argued that "between Religion and Revolution there was no contradiction"; he also stressed the "great concurrence between Christianity's objectives and those we seek as communists," citing a speech he gave in Chile in 1971 where he observed the affinities "between the Christian teachings of humility, austerity, selflessness, and loving thy neighbor and what we might call the content of a revolutionary's life and behavior."[43] The pope, for his part, sounded, if not like a dialectical materialist, a least like a neoliberal political economist clearing the way for the greater circulation of global capital, if with a slightly more attuned sensitivity to a just distribution of goods: "The pope," the *New York Times* reported, "first stressed the pastoral side of his visit, . . . [then] also urged the faithful to take their fate into their own hands, words rarely heard in a Communist state where the individual must cede to the collective. 'You are, [he told the Cubans], and must be the principal agents of your own personal and national history.' "[44] Later he promised that, as "all things will be made new" through a resurgent devotion to Christ, that Cuba would be poised to "offer to everyone a climate of freedom, mutual trust, social justice, and lasting peace." Clearly the term absented here between the dialectical play of revolution and religion, but one fully present in the global audience, here embodied by the *New York Times* and for whom these performances were at least implicitly staged, is global capital itself, emanating primarily from the postindustrial West and "present" at least in the form of an information system installed beforehand to capture and disseminate this historic meeting to the rest of the world.

That John Paul was importing a peculiar brand of pope modernism for all the world to see was not lost on Castro. The same *Times* article reported that Castro justified the pope's visit to his fellow Cubans precisely through its value as spectacle: "Billions of people around the world are going to be watching images of Cuba these days and reading news about Cuba," Castro argued, concluding, "Nobody can change what is seen."[45] What may have been less obvious to Castro, and to Cubans, was the way the pope's visit functioned as well as speculation, especially as a way of testing Cuba's then-still-imaginable future profitability in an expanding world market. If, as John Paul declared, his intention was in part to encourage the United States to "Change! Change!" its standing policy of uncompromising economic embargo against Cuba, then one can only assume that he at least cautiously welcomed the possibility of an influx of capital into Cuba's economy, not only in the form of resources to improve the material quality of life there but also to reactivate a set of exploitative speculations into the profitability of Cuba's possible futures. Thus in the spectacle of the pope's celebration of mass in Revolution Square, and to the extent that it was served up as simultaneously political theater and consumable, commodifiable image for a speculating "global" audience, one at that point could have imagined witnessing the economic and historical transformation of Cuba into a potent, and potentially volatile, "futures" market.[46]

Machado's active revisions of the discourses of religion from one version of *Fabiola* to another at least suggest the impossibility of extricating them from any attempt to understand fully the vexed relation between religious and historical "spirit" in the Cuban context, before, since, and certainly even "after" the revolution. Machado may indeed employ Cusa in the later version to embody this coinstantiation of the devotee and the ideologue, as evidenced in speeches like this: "You see all the forces, everything, nature, ideology. The political gods and the mythic gods. The Earth itself is telling us to change. To give in . . . we all must disappear in a ball of fire and be redefined again";[47] but the jump from "political" to "mythic" gods may be shorter here than conventionally understood, and one need not deviate too far from Marx himself to be convinced on this point.

Indeed, this is where Jacques Derrida finds the most productive entry to his own reintroduction of the spiritual and the spectral in Marx. "Religion," Derrida argues, "was never one ideology among

others for Marx," and in fact it enjoyed "an absolute privilege" because Marx often equated "ideology as religion, mysticism or theology."[48] And as religion haunts the conceptualization of ideology, so
does the specter in general haunt the constructions of the twin circu-
latory lubricants of capitalism, money and the commodity. "Marx,"
Derrida argues, "always described money . . . in the figure of appearance or simulacrum, more exactly of the ghost," and similarly "[t]he
commodity" as the site of an appearance of value, as a link in a chain
of "the values of value, secret, mystique, enigma, fetish and the ideological" never fails to link back up with elements of the religious.[49] So
perhaps the pope's visit helped "redefine" in a "burning" transformation not far from sublimation not only the "contradiction" between
"revolution" and "religion" but between the mystifying and alienating
operations of capital and a not-so-incompatible "mystique" at the
heart of even communism's most material promise: "The religious,"
Derrida tells us, "gives to the production of the ghost or of the ideological phantasm its originary form or its paradigm of reference, its
'first' analogy" *in Marx,* which thus leads him to conclude that religion must also, and paradoxically, "inform, along with the messianic
and the eschatalogical, . . . [the] 'spirit' of emancipatory Marxism."
In a move against most of the conceptual orthodoxies at work in our
world, Derrida thus takes from Marx the cues he needs to make this
last, conclusively heretical statement, that, in Marxist terms especially, the "messianic is revolutionary, it has to be."[50]

There is, of course, more than one promise, more than one "messianic" and emancipatory arrival still awaited by Cubans on the island and across the diaspora. As Derrida makes explicit in the
epigraph with which this chapter begins, there is no way to extricate,
in any historical thinking after Marx, the advent of a pure democracy
from a commensurable communism. The ideological wish propping
the neoliberal discourse of democracy's so-called return to Cuba with
capital may in the end, or at least before any significant change, have
to be the ghost that those still holding on to some wish of return to
and recuperation/reparation of some past Cuba will have to surrender, abandon, or dispel. What freedom is likely to return to Cuba with
capital is no more than the restricted, difficult "freedom" that a certain set of neoliberal practices (which to be sure are nothing new, for

all that they may signal a modernity missing in Cuba for these forty
years and that are at once economic, political, cultural, and therefore,
certainly, spiritual) makes possible. What precise relation such freedoms actually have with anything like the ultimate justice that both
democracy and communism promise may be what remains still,
and, perhaps, always to be seen. And before any significant speculative capital moving from the United States to Cuba accompanies significant movements in policy on the part of either polity, Cubans
everywhere would do well to shatter the mirror on whose reflective
surface they've so violently and reflexively misrecognized each other,
and themselves, at least since January 1959, and learn anew at least a
practice, if not a politics, of mutually respectful recognition and
address.

Cuban exiles have traditionally excoriated the revolution's official
atheism as at least a sign if not a source of other various forms of
spiritlessness and immorality; for this reason, exiles, who already figured one chief audience for Machado's late– and post–Cold War
work, were also a chief addressee of the theatrical display passing as
John Paul's procession through Cuba already as long ago as January
1998. Similarly, revolutionaries have attacked exiles as decadent, ma-
terialistic bourgeois exploiters whose moral and political failures
earned them no better than the status of worms in revolutionary discourse; exiles continue, however, to pour significant dollar values
into the Cuban economy, primarily through gifts and contributions
of hard currency to family members on the island.[51] If (as mourning
play) Machado's *Fabiola* helps any of its possible audiences to see beyond consolation to some other way to "know" and remember even a
unthinkably traumatic past, and if (as morality play) it helps these
same audiences to see beyond good and evil to some other possible
stagings for not only the familial and the erotic but also the political
and the ethical, then perhaps in these ongoing gestures of a spirited
generosity and respect among all Cubans, gestures that have for a very
long time crossed all relevant national and ideological lines, we might
be able to think our way beyond the ungenerous acts of refusal (embargo, stalemate, impasse) that continue to outweigh that eminently
possible generosity and toward some future whose "hither side" (to
quote Homi Bhabha) we might still, together and at once, touch.

PART III

SOME CUBAN AMERICAN FUTURES

Chapter 7

Careers of Surplus Value in the Novels of Cristina García

*Most days Cuba is kind of dead to me. But every once in
a while a wave of longing will hit me and it's all I can do
not to hijack a plane to Havana or something. I resent
the hell out of the politicians and the generals who force
events on us that structure our lives, that dictate the
memories we'll have when we're old. Every day Cuba
fades a little more inside me, my grandmother fades
a little more inside me. And there's only my
imagination where our history should be.*

—Cristina García, *Dreaming in Cuban*[1]

Time is the ultimate factory for these novels.

—Cristina García[2]

What follows here is a series of close readings, in the chronological
order of their publication, of Cuban American novelist Cristina
García's first three novels. The discussion is meant in part to trace the
contours of what we can loosely term the "political unconscious"
working in and evolving through those three texts. Of course I mean
for the phrase "political unconscious" to invoke the work of Fredric
Jameson, especially as it demonstrates the manner in which the
(re)production of especially novelistic narrative form (rather than

content) contributes in complexly structural ways to the elaboration (critical and complicit) of ideologies responsive to the prevailing modes of production of a given historical epoch, whether that of a text's actual production or of its ongoing critical and even recreational consumption. On one level, I look at García's texts for the ways they directly address conditions (political, social, cultural, and economic) prevailing in the mostly post–Cold War "Cuban" America of which and from which she writes; but on another, I also extend those readings to include observations regarding the larger political and cultural economies shaping the transnational and global scene to which the novelist also clearly hopes to establish a significant relevance for her work. For this reason, the discussion draws less from Jameson's work in the previously mentioned volume from the early 1980s and more from his subsequent work on the "late" phase of finance capital collected in the late-1990s volume entitled *The Cultural Turn;* it also draws from critical work contemporary with that latter volume, work that is either involved in the same critical project as Jameson's or is directly influenced by it in some significant way.[3] This will include, for example, aspects of Arjun Appadurai's 1996 study *Modernity at Large: Cultural Dimensions of Globalization,* the introduction to Jean and John L. Comaroff's 2001 collection *Millennial Capitalism and the Culture of Neoliberalism,* as well as George Yúdice's 2003 study *The Expediency of Culture: Uses of Culture in the Global Era.* It is certainly not lost on me, nor would it be lost on García, that it is, ironically, a certain tradition in post-Marxist cultural and critical reflection that so effectively illuminates what might otherwise remain an imbedded and perhaps repressed structural narrative pattern common to three otherwise quite discrete and heterogeneous texts.

In *The Cultural Turn,* Jameson (following Giovanni Arrighi) traces the complex process by which a formerly unquestionably "material" dialectic has in the course of the further elaboration of "late" capitalism become not just increasingly but pervasively *im*material, driven less by processes of substantial production and their eventual manifestations in market-driven profit and more by purely abstracted forms of symbolic value (speculative, financial, deterritorialized, virtual). As I suggest in the following section, Marx himself certainly understood in his own time that capital's core operations hinged on certain highly symbolized (but given that no less exploitative) abstractions of "surplus" value. But Jameson has argued, in ways I find deeply convincing and useful, that this core process has in the intervening time metastasized into not only capital's defining but its general operation. With "the closing of its productive moment," Jameson argues, "Capital itself becomes free-floating. It separates from the 'concrete context' of its productive geography [and] . . . begins to live its life in a new context . . . on the floor of the stock market [and] . . . in the form of speculation itself (specters of value, as Derrida might put it, vying against each other in a vast worldwide disembodied phantasmagoria"); this "form of speculation," he concludes, characterizes "the moment of finance capital as such"(141–42). These new conditions characterizing the prevailing modes of an increasingly abstracted production pose a daunting set of challenges to both critical and cultural work that aspires in any way to be responsive to them. In ways that will bear direct relevance to my later discussion of García's novels, Jameson observes that especially "the new postmodern informational or global cities . . . result very specifically from the ultimate deterritorialization, that of territory as such—the becoming abstract of land and earth, the transformation of the very background or context of commodity exchange into a commodity in its own right," and such profound transformations in the basic ontological registers of what we can take (anymore) to be (materially) real obligates intellectual and cultural workers alike "to theorize" anew the equally profound "modification in the very nature of cultural tokens, and the systems they operate in" (153–54).

To the extent that her novels qualify as such "cultural tokens," my discussion of García and her work explores primarily how her first three novels have functioned both as participants in and comments on "the systems they [must] operate in" in order to be published, and purchased, and seriously, critically, productively read. I chiefly want to look at the way García's deceptively conventionally "mimetic" engagements of something like a Cuban American historical referent actually resist being read as being in any way so naïve or even disingenuous; instead I want to read into her undeniably directly legible "historical" representations a more complex, often ambivalent, but productive and strategic set of economimetic operations. These operations, I argue, allow García to respond not only to the specific issues relevant to Cuban America and its vexed historical legacy but also to the larger conditions of both political and cultural economy directly shaping those conditions. Finance capital, Jameson argues, requires a political economy based on a "play of [purely] monetary entities which . . . like cyberspace, can live on its own internal metabolism and circulate without any reference to an older type of content"; correspondingly, he concludes, "the narrativized image-fragments of a stereotypical post-modern language . . . suggest . . . [in turn] a new cultural realm or dimension which is independent of the former real world . . . because the real world has already been suffused with it and colonized by it, so that it has no outside in terms of which it might be found lacking" (161). What follows will therefore take Jameson's cues in attending to postmodernism's claim to having either caused, or at the very least witnessed, a radically reconfigured relation of sign to referent as the corollary by-product of value's radically reconfigured relation to matter. At the same time, I resist the apocalypticism of Jameson's conclusions regarding the colonizing saturation of the real by the sign, especially in the way I characterize García's attempts to extract some critical surplus from the symbolic economies that her texts set into motion, and put to work, as well as in her own conscious resistance to precisely what Jameson sees as most paralytically "stereotypical" in "post-modern language."

Cubana, Inc.: Motherhood, Authorship, and the Wages of Economimesis

In the course of his prolonged discussion of the generation of surplus value in volume 1 of *Capital*, Karl Marx has occasion to turn to some curiously unscientific terms to describe the nature of this almost "magical" production of something out of nothing; indeed, he begins the passage by calling this conversion of "money . . . into capital" a "trick." To quote Marx at some length:

This metamorphosis, this conversion of money into capital, takes place both within the sphere of circulation and also out-

side it; within the circulation, because conditioned by the pur-
chase of the labor-power in the market; outside the circulation,
because what is done within it is only a stepping stone to the
production of surplus-value, a process which is entirely confined to the sphere of production. . . . By turning money into
commodities that serve as the material elements of a new product, and as factors in the labor-process, by incorporating living
labor with their dead substance, the capitalist at the same time
converts value, *i.e.*, the past, materialized, and dead labor into
capital, into value big with value, a live monster that is fruitful
and multiplies.[4]

Marx's verbal play here can in part be attributed to an obvious sar-
casm on his part; throughout this section of *Capital*, Marx intends to
expose the lie behind the "trick" of capitalist profit by demonstrating
labor's role in the generation of the value whose "surplus" supplementation to the more immediately quantifiable "values" of use and exchange allows the capitalist the opportunity to perform the sleight at
capital's heart, the illusion that profit is solely the purview of capital itself as it realizes its nature in market exchange, that is, in consumption, and therefore outside and beyond the purview of labor in
production. As curious (and, perhaps, as unfortunate) as his use of the
terminology of magic and the supernatural in this context is, of
course, Marx's use of the terminology of pregnancy; the "surplus" of
the value generated by labor in production metamorphoses through
Marx's own rhetorical sleights into a "value big with value," an image
of "monstrous" fecundity that "is fruitful and multiplies," not as prog-
eny claimed by and for labor but as capital's bastard offspring, profit.

Something of Marx's discussion here of the perverse genetics from
which profit (and, therefore, capital itself) springs helps me frame
what I call, following Jacques Derrida, the economimetic operations
of all three of Cuban American writer Cristina García's novels, *Dreaming in Cuban* (1992), *The Agüero Sisters* (1997), and *Monkey Hunting*
(2003).[5] In doing so, I hope to situate García's texts as sites of specific
forms of production, production, that is, of both novelistic form and
the several "values" that might attach to it, from the commercial to
the symbolic (the latter of which subsumes corollary values that I still

insist on naming "cultural," "literary," and "aesthetic"), but also the political and the ethical, and these last through precisely the novelist's own insistence on exploring what we can safely call the logic of political economy organizing the complex social, commercial, and cultural environments within which García herself labors and into which she has launched these her first three novels. Because of the powerful similarities running through them, which I explore in great detail in what follows, I refer to them as a trilogy, if also in part for the sake of the convenience of the shorthand phrase; by referring to them as a trilogy I do not mean to suggest, however, that a single discernible narrative line threads its way through them. Indeed, García's fictions resist any defining adherence to either narrative or historical linearity, for reasons that will become apparent as I discuss the novels in turn. Indeed, I only take them on in the chronological order in which they were published because my argument does not require any alternative analytical or rhetorical procedure, although to the extent that it matters I do mean to situate them in the same post–Cold War historical context described in chapter 6 on Eduardo Machado's *Floating Island Plays.*[6]

García herself suggests in all aspects of her work her own considerable interest in the operations of capital and the perverse qualities of its specifically generative and productive capacities; significant Cuban(-exile) characters, in each of the novels comprising the trilogy, prove themselves successful entrepreneurs once they settle in their adopted homelands (the first two once they're exiled to the United States from Cuba after the 1959 revolution, the third after emigrating from China, then escaping slavery in Cuba and finding his way to Havana in the late 1850s). The two Cuban-exile characters who settle in the United States after the 1959 revolution are both also, significantly, women and mothers, and both, significantly, raise daughters who take on critical artistic vocations in part to rebel against their mothers' material ambitions and the personal, political, and cultural values that attach to and support those ambitions. In repeating this "rough" pattern (which, as we see, shifts somewhat in both gender, period, and even structure in the third novel) from novel to novel, García invites a reading that is in part structuralist, in part allegorizing, in order to understand the novelist's acute sense of ambivalence toward her own status as an ambitious Cuban American woman writer enjoying both significant critical and even some commercial success.

Ballantine, García's paperback publisher, perhaps sensing García's work's likely interest to academic study and teaching, includes interviews with the author as features appended to their editions of all three of her novels.[7] In the interview accompanying *The Agüero Sisters*, García answers a series of fairly predictable questions about the process of fiction writing; her answers, however, are not always so predictable. García confesses, for example, that *The Agüero Sisters* is actually her third novel and that she aborted the second when she realized after some frustration that "the book wasn't viable," primarily because she felt "depleted" after writing *Dreaming in Cuban*, which "had been percolating inside me since the 1980's," and that her "depletion . . . was compounded by having a child" around the time of the first novel's publication.

The coincidence of her having her first child around the time of the appearance of her first novel proved to have a direct impact on García's relationship to her own authorship: on the one hand, she "never realized how successful [her] first book was" because she was "rather preoccupied" with her pregnancy and her daughter's birth at the time; on the other, once she began her second project, she felt enough "pressure to follow up with a strong second novel" that her "efforts in that direction became a struggle." These competing and complementary preoccupations, motherhood and authorship, seem to have transferred themselves directly into García's early narratives, although in highly complex forms that, rather than serving to essentialize, mystify, or sentimentalize either status, consistently critique those more conventional tendencies or treatments. García accomplishes this primarily by casting these primary mother–daughter relationships as occasions for a more rigorous exploration of the analogous, and commensurably ambivalent, relations of commerce and art embodied in her characters (again, in the third novel, this pattern extends to parent–child relationships more generally because the focus there is primarily on male characters and by extension on roughly analogous father–son relationships). Without ever sidestep-ping issues directly relevant to gender and its constitutive histories and politics, García insists on casting gender in the specific contexts of economics and culture that for her provide especially her women characters with their more compellingly determinative genealogies (a statement that certainly holds for *Monkey Hunting* as well, in spite of its differing focus).

It perhaps bears noting here how directly these genealogies derive from García's own personal experiences, a life narrative García has certainly been willing to make public and to assume as part of the larger symbolic and practical contexts by which her texts should be framed. Certainly her fiction is in part fired by her preoccupation with her Cubanness and her relation to Cuba's ongoing national stalemate; in the same interview appended to *The Agüero Sisters,* García reports that, after several transformative return trips to Cuba in her twenties, she realized the "Cuban aspect of [her] identity has . . . become [her] wellspring . . . an indelible, strong and very visceral part of [her] identity." Even her sense of the quality of life in Cuba for the Cubans there suggests something of her characteristic conflation of the economic and the cultural. "When I visited Cuba," she reports, "I was dismayed at the utilitarian nature of many relationships. It's almost as if leaps of faith, true romance, even basic optimism are in short supply there." For García clearly one of the shortcomings of the revolution has been precisely its failure to maintain the qualities of life that are the specific purview of culture and perhaps specifically of art in radically secular and practical societies; ironically, for García the revolution seems to have failed the people by favoring the practi-cal so exclusively as to sacrifice the cultural (and, in its most general sense, the spiritual) altogether.[8] This may perhaps begin to explain García's symptomatic "early" literary practices most directly; García as a writer is as devoted to the production of a certain kind of "liter-ary" pleasure as she is to any critical intervention into the more sys-tematically exploitative, oppressive workings of practical, material culture. To her, indeed, the two practices are inextricable; inextrica-ble, perhaps, as the psychic and other bonds, oftentimes difficult to the point of impossibility, that unite especially her mothers and daughters, her entrepreneurs and artists. If readerly pleasure is the "surplus value," the experiential "profit" her novels produce, it is also the result of a practice that is as devoted to justice as it is to beauty. García may at times oppose her entrepreneurs and her artists, but she does so always with the understanding that artistry is as much a part of her (undeniably commercial) enterprise as profit is for her business(wo)men and is not incommensurable with a political, and certainly feminist, enterprise, one she must share in part with her (usually, but not always) female entrepreneurs.[9]

It bears noting here, too, that Cuban exiles, and especially Cuban-exile women, have had a significant and unique history as entrepreneurs after immigrating to the United States. Alejandro Portes and Rubén Rumbaut report in their well-known sociological study, *Immigrant America* (1996), that "Cuban-owned firms [in the United States] increased from 919 in 1967 to 8,000 in 1976 and approximately 28,000 in 1990. Most are small, averaging 8.1 employees at the latest count, but they also include factories employing hundreds of workers." The bare statistical data provided by Portes and Rumbaut has been augmented by other analysts who include in their work more specific accounts of the factors of history, class, education, race, and gender, all of which have helped produce this remarkable growth.

In his study *Latinos: A Biography of the People* (1992; discussed in my preface), Earl Shorris argues, rather problematically, that, as opposed to other U.S. Latino groups, "Cubans identify with the conquerors, not the conquered, the subject, not the object. As exiles rather than immigrants or sojourners," Shorris goes on, Cubans "think of the United States as a useful place, more like a rental than a home." On the basis of this observation, Shorris goes on to make the more troubling charge that Cuban exiles, with the help of significant assistance from the U.S. federal government, "set out to reproduce a Cuba-without-the-lower-classes (white Cuba) in Dade County," even though the ensuing "Cuban economic miracle" seems to have been fairly modest in scope for any given entrepreneur: "After nearly twenty years of exile," these conqueror-identified *gusano* businesses averaged "only a few employees," leading Shorris to admit in concluding that this *gusano reconquista* of South Florida actually amounted to "a mom-and-pop economy for the most part."[10]

For a more balanced, and less inconsistent, treatment of the same phenomenon, one can turn to historian María Cristina García's *Havana U.S.A.: Cuban Exiles and Cuban Americans in South Florida* (1996; also cited in an earlier section of this book). García the historian rounds out the characterization of this phenomenon with some specific attention to the contributions of Cuban American women to this "economic miracle": "Cuban women," García reports, "had a high rate of participation in the labor force; as early as 1970, they constituted the largest proportionate group of working women in the United States," although, García cautions, they "expanded their roles to include wage-earning not as a response to the feminist movement or the social currents of the 1960's but to ensure the economic survival of their families." When they turned to entrepreneurship, García observes, Cuban American women often chose to open businesses that catered to other working women's needs: these "entrepreneurial women," she tells us, "created businesses catering to the needs of women who entered the workplace: day-care centers, housekeeping and delivery services, laundries and dry cleaners, home ateliers and dress shops, beauty parlors, and even driving schools. Cubans discovered that any business that made life easier for the working woman had a good chance of flourishing." The novelist García's representations of her entrepreneurs both reflect and depart from these models of economic activity in ways that suggest something of her own deep ambivalence toward her own complex enterprise.

If this ambivalence takes on a markedly symptomatic form in the repeated narrative structure of the mother–daughter relationships central to the first two novels, the equally strong modifications of entrepreneurial, artistic, and filially related characters in the third novel reflect something of García's own incorporation of the broader globalist, diasporic, and postcolonial theoretical understandings of especially political and cultural economies prevailing in the post–post–Cold War early twenty-first century moment. Although ironically extending the narrative of 2003's *Monkey Hunting* further back into the historical past (its story begins around 1850 in Amoy, China) than she does either of the stories of her first two novels, García manages to reflect in her tracing of four geographically and generationally scattered members of her protagonist's family a more profound insight regarding a much more complex combination of sociohistorical conditions shaping and being shaped by a transnational Cuban experience that has certainly been better articulated in critical scholarship appearing after the more conventionally nation-centric 1990s-era historical accounts represented here by Earl Shorris and María Cristina García.

It reflects, for example, the work of historian Louie A. Pérez Jr., whose landmark historical study *On Becoming Cuban: Identity, Nationality and Culture* appeared in 1999 and redefined in important ways the conventional historical understanding of the conditions shaping the formation of Cuban national identity from especially the mid-nineteenth century on. In that study Pérez makes an especially strong case for two significant factors operating in that process: one is exile or (in Spanish) *destierro,* which for Pérez "was decisive to the ways Cubans arrived at nationality and identity," especially since it significantly "implied uprooting . . . to expose, to make vulnerable" while it also "suggested adaptation as a means of survival, of borrowing as a means of becoming"(37–38); the other is race, given that (as Pérez reports), "On the eve of abolition, people of color, both slave and free, constituted one-third of the total [Cuban] population" and that, therefore, "The abolition of slavery raised new questions about the character of national community and the means and implications of incorporating people of color into nationality" (90). Not only is *Monkey Hunting* therefore significant for turning the conventional Cuban national narrative of exile inside out (her protagonist Chen Pan is Chinese born, exiled to and not from Cuba), but it also features an almost exclusively nonwhite cast of mostly mixed-race major characters.

Even more striking than García's ability to sound such a resonantly contemporary chord with her most historically distanced story is her ability to make it so resonant to the increasingly transnational, diasporic quality of post–Cold War Cuban life (both on and off the island) by keeping her narrative so completely off the well-beaten path to post-1959 Miami. New York City provides the only (and very briefly used) U.S. setting in *Monkey Hunting*'s literally global narrative; at the same time, that globalist perspective certainly does not exclude or deny any realization that the globalist phenomenon has in any way sidestepped or avoided a significant and unique kind of manifestation in post-1990s Miami. Indeed, this post-1990s Miami appears in rather striking and provocative form in George Yúdice's *The Expediency of Culture: The Uses of Culture in the Global Era* (2003), where it prompts Yúdice's declaration that "it [now] becomes possible to speak of a post-Cuban and even a post-Caribbean Miami" typified by "a new economy that cannot be separated from culture . . . a cultural economy, on the model of a political economy"(197, 199) by virtue of its having served as a prime stage for what he calls the larger "globalization of Latin America." In the last section of this chapter, I trace in more specific detail the parallels between Yúdice's post-Cuban Miami and García's equally striking reimagining of a nonwhite Havana in the novel she published the same year that Yúdice's work appeared. There I pursue further what I see as García's own evolving sense of her participation, not to say complicity, in a cultural enterprise with decidedly political, commercial, and otherwise practical consequences. For now, it bears noting briefly that across her three novels García consciously and strategically situates herself and her work in contexts that suggest her at once critical and ambivalent awareness of her relationship to those contexts. And if with her first novel, published in 1992, the prevailing context had as much to do with the legacies of post-1959 Cuban-exile ideology on her generation of more fully if uncomfortably "Americanized" off-island Cubans as with the context of the "culture wars"-era embrace of multicultural, mostly immigrant American literary and cultural expression like hers, by the time she publishes her third novel a decade-plus later, she has clearly learned to re-situate that work, both as labor and as product, in contexts that far exceed the restrictive dualisms of either the (late) Cold War or the (short-lived) culture "wars" of the decade(s) before.

The Alternative Sugar Economy: Lourdes Puente's Yankee Doodle Bakery

Both of Garcia's chief female entrepreneur-protagonists only partially fulfill the stereotype of the profit-mad captains of industry that

Cuban-exile businesspeople are made out to be by writers like Earl Shorris. Lourdes Puente, the pivotal "exile-generation" character in 1992's *Dreaming in Cuban,* owns a bakery in a Brooklyn neighborhood, selling pastries and breads to her ethnically mixed population of customers; her practical ambitions are modest, but they're upheld by some fairly profound ideological investments. "Nobody works like an owner," Lourdes likes to think (67), and for this reason she rarely trusts her employees enough to keep them on for very long; this mistrust keeps her business, which she calls the Yankee Doodle Bakery, small if profitable enough. Profitable enough, indeed, both to support her family and send her daughter Pilar to art school. Pilar, who is approximately García's age and bears the name that García gave her own daughter, is the closest thing to a mouthpiece that García allows herself in any of her first three novels. As such, Pilar stands not only as the artist-in-proxy, as the occasion for García's displaced meditation on her own artistic vocation; she is also, and just as significantly, the chief critic of her mother's particular brand of entrepreneurship.

But if Pilar and her mother embody antithetical terms in a dialectic that can be read allegorically to exemplify something of the dialectic still haunting the U.S.–Cuban postexile scene in general, García's greater affinity with Pilar's sensibilities, both political and aesthetic, does not result in an unfair stacking of cards against Lourdes. At times, Pilar's take on her mother and García's narrator's take on her sound almost indistinguishable: this is because in part (but not entirely) the chapters foregrounding Pilar's experiences are written in the first person, whereas those describing Lourdes' experiences are cast in the more distancing third. When Pilar describes her mother's ambitious plans for a second bakery, her tone closely echoes the tone that García's narrator takes in her own description of Lourdes's larger econo-mythology: "this bicentennial crap is driving me crazy," Pilar complains at one point. "Mom has talked about nothing else for months. She bought a second bakery and plans to sell tricolor cupcakes and Uncle Sam marzipan. Apple pies, too. She's convinced she can fight communism from behind her bakery counter" (136). Compare this with García's third-person narrative account of the same decision:

It was her father who advised Lourdes to open up a second pastry shop. . . . Lourdes ordered custom-made signs for her bakeries in red, white and blue with her name printed at the bottom right-hand corner: *Lourdes Puente, PROPRIETOR*. She particularly liked the way the r's rolled in her mouth, the explosion of p's. Lourdes felt a spiritual link to American moguls, to the immortality of men like Irenée du Pont. . . . She envisioned a chain of Yankee Doodle Bakeries stretched across America. (170–71)

But for all that García seems to be laughing with Pilar at Lourdes in passages like these, she also at crucial, strategic points in her narrative of their relationship undercuts the validity of Pilar's (and, presumably, even her own, affectionate) disdain for the more pragmatically minded Lourdes, precisely by reminding herself, and us, that art (and, perhaps just as importantly, art informed by ideologically driven critique) never fully enjoys the kind of immunity from the contamination of the practical, and the material, that it oftentimes convinces itself it can enjoy.[11]

This immunity is in part a wish the young Pilar makes for her art, but not one García indulges for her own. "My paintings have been getting more and more abstract lately, violent-looking with clotted swirls of red" (29), Pilar offers at one point, and she defends this artistic move toward abstraction to her therapist by arguing that "Painting is its own language. . . . Translations just confuse it, dilute it like words going from Spanish to English" (59). The logic of Pilar's statement bears noting; "translation" here refers to the very mimetic operations of realism, and thus Pilar's refusal to paint realistically suggests something of the profound, structural foreignness of "real" things to even their most loyal visual and verbal representations, but in a scene of therapy, they also suggest something of a repression in the artistic act itself that would take us back to that "reality" Pilar most strongly wishes to keep out of her art, namely all the material practices her mother represents and embodies. The failure of translation here is countered by the inexorable successes of transference and transaction; nothing returns with quite the same vengeance as the maternal repressed, and in García's novel it speaks its truth in un-equivocally memorable terms. When Lourdes commissions Pilar to paint "a mural for her second Yankee Doodle Bakery," specifying, "I want a big painting like the Mexicans do, but pro-American" (138), Pilar refuses, to which Lourdes rebuts, "This bakery paid for your painting classes!" As Lourdes reminds her daughter of certain material conditions without which her art might not exist, so (I would argue) does García remind herself, and her audience, that her own art's critical interventions into the larger set of Cuban-exile and Cuban American material practices, cultural as well as commercial, do not in turn "free" that art from an implication (even perhaps a complicity) in, or a significant debt to, those practices.

Little changes when García poses these questions later in her narrative in a more directly Cuban revolutionary context; when Lourdes and Pilar find themselves in Cuba some years later, García makes sure that it's Pilar, the more potentially dangerous ideologue of the two *because* she's an artist, who learns certain object lessons about art's relation to its most salient political contexts. It's Pilar who observes, as she and her mother drive through Havana, "billboards advertising the Revolution as if it were a new brand of cigarettes" (215), and it's Pilar who reports the following conversation with her grandmother Celia, who had remained in Cuba and fiercely loyal to the revolution all of Pilar's life: "I ask Abuela Celia if I can paint anything I want in Cuba and she says yes, as long as I don't attack the State. Cuba is still developing, she tells me, and can't afford the luxury of dissent. . . . I wonder," Pilar concludes, "what El Líder would think of my painting. Art, I'd tell him, is the ultimate revolution" (235). Somewhere between the comparison of public revolutionary promotion to commercial advertising and the idea of dissent as political luxury, we might locate García's actual position on the question of political and other material contexts informing and enabling her art. Dissenting or not, what exercise there is of a creative and critical "freedom" in García's work situates her in the light, one might say the aura, of a function of the aesthetic that, try as one might, can never effectively be divorced from a certain praxis, a certain utility, a certain purposeful purposiveness. There's little irony in the fact that, if García's art can be called dissenting,

its critique is leveled more at the constraints she encounters in the political orthodoxy of the U.S.-based Cuban-exile community; at the
same time, she can not help but acknowledge that the same community may indeed provide her with what resources her chosen vocation
requires. She therefore works, and labors, as an "organic" intellectual
in the conventional Gramscian sense, but one with no easy claim to either a class, a community, and certainly not a nation, which she might
simply, or even safely, call home.[12]

But the "luxury" of dissent is not the only excess with which García
might justifiably be charged. She does not shy away from a certain
practice productive of a certain (surplus) value in her writing, a value
whose supplementary relation to the restricted mimetic economies
of, say, the regimes of literary realism or naturalism one could do
worse than to call "aesthetic." García takes the epigraph to *Dreaming
in Cuban* from Wallace Stevens, suggesting that her own "casual exfoliations of language" lie somewhere in what Stevens termed "the tropics of resemblances"; although most of the passages I have had
occasion to quote here have primarily served the rather functional
purpose of directly supporting my analytical points, one should not
come away from this discussion thinking Cristina García isn't serious
when she compares her fiction to the work of her admittedly naïve
abstract painter Pilar. When Pilar first rejects her mother's request to
do the mural, she explains to the reader, "I think about Jacoba Van
Heemskerck, a Dutch expressionist painter I've become interested in
lately. Her paintings feel organic to me, like breathing abstractions of
color. She refused to title her paintings (much less do patriotic mu-
rals for her mother's bakery) and numbered her works instead. I
mean, who needs words when colors and lines conjure up their own
language? That's what I want to do with my paintings, find a unique
language, obliterate the clichés" (138–39).[13] It is difficult, especially
with the resonance of Stevens's words behind Pilar's, not to hear in
this passage something of the traditional romantic wish for transcendence through the sublime, even into abstraction; but as a novelist
with a certain audience in mind, García also knows that radical abstraction in a verbal art has little chance in this cultural moment of
convincing anyone of its deeply political engagements, of its desire to

be "the ultimate revolution" by refusing all the available representational regimes and their symptomatic "clichés." It's also really hard (although not impossible) to tell a story that way, and García certainly has her stories to tell. So, rather than invest heavily in the risky stock of ambitious (and ambitiously postmodern) artistic innovation, García chooses instead to flirt with it, to diversify her portfolio with a strategically selected variety of representational (and occasionally nonrepresentational) practices.

La Raza Cosmética: Constancia Agüero's "Cuerpo de Cuba" Line of Beauty Products[14]

This flirtation, apparent but controlled through much of the first novel, all but overtakes the language(s) (dis)coursing through the second. García invents in *The Agüero Sisters* a more elaborate critical allegory of female entrepreneurship and female artistry than she does in *Dreaming in Cuban*. Constancia Agüero's successful line of beauty products makes Lourdes Puente's meek little bakery seem all but pathetic; at the same time, Constancia meets little resistance from her own artist-daughter Isabel, who spends at least the early part of the novel out of sight and voiceless. But the ascendancy of the second novel's entrepreneur over the first's, and over the figure of the artist-daughter, is countered in part in the second novel by what I dare here to call the greater critical and dialogical audacity of the novelist's language. At least in part, García seems to have learned a Bakhtinian lesson at some point between the writing of the first and second novels. *The Agüero Sisters*, which like its predecessor refuses to conform to any conventional narrative logic (or line) and to the basic exigencies of representational realism, is more a body of elaborately arranged discourses, speech genres even, ranging across various professions and disciplines, from the taxonomic ornithology and topography practiced by the sister protagonists' father, through the amateur chemistry Constancia uses to concoct her beautifying lotions, to her sister Reina's mastery of the electrician's art, to the most elaborately detailed (and described) of Santeria's esoteric rituals.

Even the ad-speak Constancia deploys to sell her beauty products to her customers suggests not only a critical, and satirical, familiarity on the writer's part with the logic of advertising but also a critical awareness of the material, historical logic enabling the success of both the cosmetic line and the aesthetic process through which it is imagined. In an alchemical scene whose simultaneities are multiple, García describes Constancia's early attempts to produce her lotions at home: "A vat of Constancia's new face emollient," she tells us, "simmers on the kitchen stove. She adds a cup of ground papaya stones, folds in the petals of a dozen yellow roses. . . . Constancia waits for an hour for the emollient to cool before pouring it through the minute funnels into her royal-blue bottles. The cream is sharply fragrant, like a season distilled. Constancia sweats in the heat and daze of its strange amplifications, in the long-ago summers in Cuba it conjures up" (129–30). The language here is well within the purview of the "casual exfoliations" that Stevens knew to be the true operations of what he termed the "tropics of resemblances"; phrases like "a season distilled" and "strange amplifications," perversely tropic, turn both toward and away from the world they mean to describe, both within and outside the registers of literary, and especially novelistic, realism.

But these perversely aesthetic gestures, these attempts on García's part to effect a "grace beyond the reach of art" in her work, never simply reject the more practical contexts within which that work must be situated. Practically speaking, Constancia's customers are also, and significantly, García's customers: "Each item in [Constancia's] *Cuerpo de Cuba* line," we are told, "will embody the exalted image Cuban women have of themselves: as passionate, self-sacrificing, and deserving of every luxury. . . . Her ads (glossy, soft-focus affairs with antique mirrors and tropical foliage) appeal to her clients' memories, to the remembered splendors of their Cuban youth. Her motto—*Time may be indifferent, but you needn't be*—appeals to their anxious vanity. . . . Politics may have betrayed Constancia's customers, geography overlooked them, but *Cuerpo de Cuba* products still manage to touch the pink roots of their sadness" (131–32). One can only surmise how García herself imagines she will "touch" the same "roots" with this passage, with this prose, and with the story it couches. These Cuban-exile women's supposed anxiety over a beauty that marks at once their relation to their lost youth and to their present affluence counters the anxiety García displaces onto Constancia over the manner in which one might profit from this community's experiences of dislocation, alienation, and loss. And although García in no way caters so indulgently to this audience, she knows her work cannot help but find itself enlisted in the larger cultural task of testifying to the very "sadness" Constancia's products are actually meant to soothe. García, however, seems bent on having it both ways; never shying away from the burden, the responsibility of her work's direct address to the difficult community it also represents, she also embraces the opportunity her vocation provides her to fashion a practice that in its very exercise aspires to produce effects at once critical, practical, and pleasurable.

In any case, *Cuerpo de Cuba,* as García's invention, allows her to reconstruct allegorically and satirically a certain (and certainly imaginary) anatomy for the Cubana-exile cultural and social body, one that is preserved artificially in an impossible suspension of time by means of a historical promise of redemptive return to the land of its (lost) youth, and (lost) beauty. It is this promise that García has Constancia commodify and peddle to her countrywomen, who are thereby and in the same gesture rendered subjects and objects of a consumption driven by an impossible fetishization of a body that can only be recuperated as simulacrum in specific libidinal and commercial markets. García has been publicly chastised by members of the politically conservative exile community in Miami for what they take to be a primarily unsympathetic portrayal of that community in her novels; but I take her portrayal of Constancia, which could (too) easily be read as a satirical jab at Cuban-exile entrepreneurship and at its willingness to exploit its own historical dislocations for profit, to allegorize García's own anxiety about her own success as a literary and commercial artist, one who herself chiefly traffics in representations of women that, for all her attempts to demystify them, often read like highly elaborate, literary embellishments of "real" life. To this extent Constancia's enterprise is a powerful if complex analogue to García's own, and it very specifically transforms García's art into the object of the kind of *critical* popular consumption she very likely wants it to be.[15]

Much more could and should be said concerning the other characters and subplots of *The Agüero Sisters;* here it must suffice to mention two additional and relevant elements of the novel. One concerns
Constancia's artist-daughter Isabel, who spends much of the narrative's time semiexiled to Hawaii, where she reports in letters on the
positive evolution of her artwork and on the negative evolution of
her marriage. In the middle of her own pregnancy with the child of
her increasingly estranged husband, Isabel reports to her mother that
she's "stopped her pottery" and has instead "been experimenting with
more conceptual pieces, involving traditional handicrafts" (182); of
these pieces Isabel sends her own increasingly estranged parents a
sample, as "a gift for their thirty-second anniversary: a collection of
dead wrens in jars of formaldehyde, dressed in woolen booties and
shawls, . . . pastel outfits" that Isabel claims to have "knitted . . . herself" (182). These *"Anniversary Birds,"* as Isabel entitles them, clearly
reinforce much of what I've been describing as García's profoundly
anxious, and often simultaneous, treatment of the themes of motherhood, artistry, and material (re)production. They operate, on one
level, to blur the conventional distinction between manual and conceptual production in the way that they require both physical and
mental labor; in addition, they clearly represent a strategic perversion
of the conventional ideology of pregnancy. Regardless of the kitsch
touch of dressing them in "woolen booties and shawls," these are *dead*
wrens, embalmed in formaldehyde, and not live fetuses immersed in
a life-giving amniotic fluid.

As pieces of artwork, they certainly overwhelm the comparatively
tame discussion of aesthetics presented through Pilar in *Dreaming in
Cuban;* here the question of what drives (or may be derived from) the
artwork under consideration exceeds the neat and limited binary between abstract and representational expression that mostly worried
Pilar Puente the painter. Isabel Cruz would have to collect if she does
not actively kill the birds she stuffs in her uterine jars, and thus her use
of once-living bodies to communicate, through what remains of their
symbolic life, her marking of her parents' perhaps already posthumous marriage certainly raises a battery of questions about how, in
García's eyes, the artistic production of meaning or nonmeaning can

or should intervene into (and even exploit) the more conventional operations of material, and biological, production and reproduction. One can only suppose here what if any "aesthetic" effect such pieces as the *Anniversary Birds* might have on an actual audience for Isabel's work; García only goes so far as to suggest that the birds provoke some concern on Constancia's part over her daughter's mental health.

The other point to raise here briefly is that, unlike *Dreaming in Cuban* or *Monkey Hunting*, *The Agüero Sisters* carries this anxiety about its own literary and commercial status more directly into a literal treatment of novelistic discourse itself, through its depiction, in a number of flashbacks, of the original Agüero patriarch's work as a *lector* (or reader) in a cigar factory in (the western-most Cuban province of) Pinar del Río during the early twentieth century.[16] Although the pivotal Cuban character in the cross-generational familial narrative that makes up *The Agüero Sisters* is arguably the sisters' father, Ignacio, whom García depicts as a world-famous ornithologist and whose murder of his wife Blanca serves as the defining act of violence from which all the family's consequent pathologies emanate, García allows Ignacio to retell (in first person) the narrative of his own father's arrival and settlement in Cuba and into the position of *lector*. It matters, therefore, that García names the patriarch "Reinaldo," knowing perhaps that in the context of late twentieth-century Cuban American fiction writing that name would immediately evoke associations with the novelist Reinaldo Arenas, arguably the most widely celebrated Cuban-descended novelist of his (and, roughly, García's) time. In addition, although Ignacio reports that his father, "a refined misfit among coarser men" (60), arrived in Cuba from Galicia with only a volume of "the Romantic poets" under his arm, the first volume he reads when he settles into his work in the factory is Cervantes's *Don Quixote*, followed soon after that by Dickens's *A Tale of Two Cities* (60, 64) and somewhat later by Zola's *La Bête Humaine* (88); one can certainly trace across this trio of titles an increasing focus on the practical, political obligations of novelistic art. The jump from Cervantes's profoundly ironic treatment of feudal idealism to Zola's deeply pessimistic social naturalism is significant but not without its cultural and historical logic, and certainly the reference to *A Tale of Two Cities* reinforces that logic and attests as well to *The Agüero Sisters*'s unique status, among the texts making up García's trilogy, as the only one to take on the conventional postrevolutionary "tale" of Cuba's "two (capital) cities," Havana and Miami. Finally, what expanding and deepening political consciousness might be traced across the titles of these three works leads finally to Reinaldo's active political engagement with, and on behalf of, the manual laborers to whom he reads and with whom he works.

In some respects, the dexterity and precision required in the necessarily manual labor of cigar rolling belies the distinction that only Ignacio notes between his "refined [if] misfit" father and the latter's "coarser" coworkers; in fact, Reinaldo's growing feeling of solidarity with his increasingly exploited comrades inspires him, his son reports, to become "involved in union policy" and to write "editorials for . . . the cigar workers' union newspaper, extolling the glories of revolutionary Russia," provoking in turn arguments between father and son, García has Ignacio tell us, "over what we considered each other's misguided politics" (113–14). These arguments continue for the rest of the elder Reinaldo's life, and clearly García means for us to hear their echoes in arguments that would split the larger Cuban national family in two; in addition, García also means to situate culture, and perhaps especially but not exclusively literary culture, in the midst of what might otherwise appear to be a set of exclusively political or economic clashes. Not only does she identify the character most closely associated here with literature with the most potentially controversial of political positions (especially in the post-1959 Cuban-exile context), but she reinforces that association by reporting later Reinaldo's continuing suspicion of "the vile cigar-rolling machines, those clanking monstrosities from America that were ruining the cigar-workers' way of life" (149–50). García's treatment of Ignacio's profound suspicion of the growing imperial reach of American economic (and, by extension, political) influence in Cuba thus challenges especially her late twentieth-century Cuban-exile audience to entertain the possibility of that imperial ambition's role in not only negatively affecting a treasured aspect of early twentieth-century Cuba's cultural life, but also of having to hear in the generalized language of the "clanking monstrosities from

America" some even larger naming of the apparently (to them) irresistible, and noisy, commercial and cultural force still dominating, and determining everything about, their own political and personal lives.

Orientalism en Español: Antiquities and Modernity in Chen Pan's Lucky Find

Although the readings of García's novels in this chapter have so far concentrated primarily on gender and its relation to the writer's representations of commercial and cultural enterprise, it bears noting here that nowhere in her work does García ever suggest that she's unaware of the vital role race also plays either in the formations and de-formations of Cuban national, Cuban-exile, and Cuban American identity across historical periods and geographic locations or as a central factor in all periods of the economic life of the nation and all its diasporic extensions. But in García's third novel, 2003's *Monkey Hunting*, we find an interesting intensification of focus on how the race/gender crucible has actually oriented and disoriented cultural and commercial life in Cuba; whereas *The Agüero Sisters* had already initiated the process in García's work of expanding her range of complex characterizations to include (white) male characters like Ignacio and (mixed-race) female characters like Reina (she and Constancia share a biological mother, but Reina is the product of Blanca's adulterous affair with a black man), *Monkey Hunting* represents a significant departure for García in that her chief protagonist in this case in neither female nor white. He is, in fact, male and Chinese, and imported to mid-nineteenth-century Cuba supposedly to work as an indentured servant. Chen Pan realizes, in the course of a variation on the narrative of the middle passage, that he will instead be sold into slavery upon arrival in Havana; his fears are realized, and the early part of the novel describes his brief time working as a slave on a sugar plantation, his escape and year-long *marronage* in the Cuban wilderness, his eventual arrival in Havana, and his subsequent life establishing himself as one of the leading businesspeople in late nineteenth-century Havana's burgeoning Chinatown.

These departures from the chronological, geographical, and gendered foci of García's previous work do not, however, signal a radical break from her established thematic and historical concerns. The conditions compelling Chen Pan's exile (he never returns to China) are certainly more violent and extreme, but in many ways he stands in strikingly direct correspondence to his sister-protagonist-entrepreneurs in the earlier novels, both in the way that García can spin thematic gold out of her depiction of his commercial activities but also in the way that she can link them up with issues of cultural as well as biological reproduction in her depictions of Chen Pan's relation to both his Chinese ancestry and his Cuban(-exile) destiny. Chen Pan's maleness certainly does not preclude his having developed as exquisite a sensibility for most things as either Lourdes del Pino Puente had for her pastries or Constancia Agüero Cruz had for her lotions and creams; if anything, Chen Pan seems more universally sensitive to all manner of sensuality, but it certainly includes an aestheticized appreciation for the antiques he collects to sell in his shop, *The Lucky Find*. Again, García fully indulges in lovingly detailed descriptions of her protagonist' wares, in this case supplying a perhaps more explicitly commercial source for the linguistic liveliness of her own verbal inventories. "Wherever he went," García's narrator tells us,

> Chen Pan priced everything. Sooner or later, he knew it would end up in his shop . . . [where] he sold all manner of heirlooms and oddities: ancient braziers, powdered wigs from long-dead judges, French porcelains, coats-of-arms, plaster saints with withering expressions, patriarchal busts (frequently noseless), hand-carved cornices, and a variety of costumes and accoutrements (63).

Clearly García means to stock Chen Pan's shop with a symbolically different set of wares than those crowding the displays of the Yankee Doodle Bakery or the vanity tables of Cuerpo de Cuba's clients; in *The Lucky Find* we encounter nothing so ersatz as the immediate pleasure of pastry or so personal as the consolations of either recovered youth or deferred mortality, but instead the detritus of empire, pure and simple, and on all its salient levels of operation, from the military, to the juridical, to the ecclesiastical, to the more generally but ubiquitously because domestically cultural.[17]

It is clear from many other elements in the novel that García means to mark, and measure, some more complex and extensive scope of historical time in her third novel than she did in the previous two. Although Chen Pan establishes the business in the 1860s, and so well before Cuba's long-deferred emergence out from under its colonial dependence to either Spain or the United States, García signals from the novel's earliest passages that she means to trace through her protagonist's life that larger emergence into an uneasy modernity. The "man in the Western suit" who first lures Chen Pan onto the slave ship for Cuba admonishes him to "spit the country dirt from your mouth!" and to trust in the legend that "one foreign year elapses twice as fast as a Chinese one" (5). Later, after recounting his experiences of enslavement, escape, and arrival in Havana, García has Chen Pan reflect on what she's already established as his past but also what she's established as his conception of "the past," and of history, more generally: "Chen Pan," she tells us, "wasn't the least bit nostalgic. He was grateful to Cuba for this: to be freed, at long last, from the harsh cycles of the land. He'd carried both books and a hoe in his youth. He preferred the books" (81). This passage, like everything else García writes, can of course be read many ways at once. For the purposes of the present argument, it suffices perhaps to show that through Chen Pan she means to track if not necessarily praise this emancipation from "the harsh cycles of the land" as at once an emancipation from feudalism, slavery, and traditional forms of land-based production and labor to a system that is decidedly more urban, mercantile, and modern; without pinning anything too strictly to the more definite movement in her main character's life from slavery to emancipation or to the historical movement of his adopted country from colony to sovereign nation, she does generally track here a movement one could do worse than to call deterritorializing, and in ways that might in part appeal to a community of readers who identify themselves as at once exiled, modern, democratic, bourgeois, and passionately pro-capital. By this point in the narrative, García's reader knows that Chen Pan's unhappy father was a poet and the "books" Chen Pan prefers to the hoe refer to the literature that his father taught him to enjoy; but in the passage in question, García allows the indefinite reference to "books" to connote simultaneously literary and financial "books," an ambiguity certainly reinforced in Spanish, where the verb *contar* refers simultaneously to both counting and recounting (the latter as in narrating), and where the term "story" in the literary sense translates not into *historia* but into *cuento*.

But in every respect García's depiction of Chen Pan, although generally more positive and less satiric than her portrayals of Lourdes and Constancia, nevertheless sends a decidedly mixed message to her Cuban-exile readership. One sees this in references to, for example, Chen Pan's rejection of nostalgia, an attitude García later refers to as his faith in the productivity of "Hard work that would leave no time for mourning" (86). She complicates this skeptical attitude toward the past further by adding to the store of Chen Pan's potential sources of nostalgia; if like Lourdes in *Dreaming in Cuban* Chen Pan feels any sense of vindication in his own success, he feels it toward the system of slavery that (like "communism" for Lourdes) so violently abused and exploited him. By the early decades of the twentieth century, the aging Chen Pan can take pleasure in noticing that "Now Chinese owned hotels and restaurants in several [Cuban] cities, laundries and chains of bakeries stretching from one end of the island to the other. Last year," the passage concludes, "three *chinos* had bought a sugar mill in Matanzas and quickly doubled its output. To Chen Pan, news of the mill in Chinese hands was more gratifying than any other success" (236). But this mixture of ethnic pride and political resentment spins quite differently as Chen Pan's historical wisdom deepens, and as he himself nears death; like Reinaldo Agüero in García's second novel, this immigrant to Cuba hears in the 1910s "the foreign news [of] a revolution in Russia and a war between Germany and the rest of the world" and understands precisely how such "foreign" news hits most directly and intimately home: "In Cuba," Chen Pan surmises, "the war meant the price of sugar was soaring. In times of misery, there were always profits to be made. Chen Pan knew this better than most. With every disaster, his secondhand shop flourished" (246).[18]

At its most skeptical, even cynical, García's message here can be read as follows: that regardless of their protestations to the contrary, what the hypernostalgic "boom" Cubans of the post-1959 exile generation have exemplified through their authentic suffering *and* their authentic success is that perhaps the only memories ultimately worth preserving aren't the ones that guarantee redemption but those that spur (re)production and, by extension, profit. This lesson, although certainly extractable from the narrative of *Monkey Hunting*, isn't for all that necessarily or finally applicable to the character who learns it: García allows Chen Pan, in his final wisdom, to abandon all need to carry the past with him into death. Although, as she tells us, Chen Pan "used to think forgetting was the enemy," he begins to realize in his last years that "oblivion seemed to him the highest truth" (234), and it was therefore better to "Forget everything," especially because "That island he knew no longer existed" (250). And if the Cuba promised to him in China had indeed never existed, and if indeed the Cuba in which he both suffered and prospered across half a century had by 1920 also ceased to exist, how does any Cuba, like any other homeland, remembered or imagined, survive any transformative historical moment, let alone remain, and remain long enough to welcome any exile's long-hoped-for, and always-impossible, return?

As with *The Agüero Sisters, Monkey Hunting* features at least two subplots that deserve some brief mention here for the ways they both reinforce and complicate what I have been loosely calling the economimetic operations of so much of García's fiction. The first subplot is actually more of a recurring submotif in the narrative of Chen Pan's material ascendancy in Havana's commercial world, and it has to do with García's more pointed observations regarding the speculative and highly chancy nature of entrepreneurial capitalism as practiced by her main character. As his shop's name suggests, Chen Pan assigns some measure of his success to chance, to accident, and to his own gambler's temperamental disposition to countenance at least financial risk; "Chen Pan," García tells us at one point, so "distrusted all forms of certainty" that he made a point of avoiding "the Protestant missionaries [who] besieged him constantly with the decrees of their god, Jesus Christ" (69). This is a pointed and in many ways resonant refusal on García's part of any mystifying and especially moralizing ideological rationalization for the basic motives of capitalists; she extends this critique in a subsequent passage, where she depicts Chen Pan as "perplexed by the names Cubans gave their shops. *La Rectitud. La Buena*

Fé. Todos Me Elogian. How could anyone guess what was sold inside? Once he'd walked into a shop called *La Mano Poderosa,* only to find huge wheels of Portuguese cheese for sale" (72). All the shop names that García invents here resound with both strong Catholic/Christian overtones and with experiential familiarity for anyone who's been to retail districts in either Latin American or U.S. Latino communities; the last of these, however, also connotes the both "invisible" and "mighty" hand that the most radically evangelical arm of classical bourgeois economics still invokes in all articulations of its faith in the inherently self-rectifying and self-justifying operations of a fully un-encumbered market-driven economy. Clearly García wants her readers to resist full adherence to this faith; the *Mano Poderosa* in this case only obscures via religious signification its own utility in functionally denoting the "huge wheels of Portuguese cheese" the shop sells, and it perhaps as well connotes the even more powerful "wheel of fortune" that a competing but not entirely incompatible mythology might want to assign to the fortune-producing market system as a just-as-viable rationalizing model for it.

Indeed, Chen Pan's personal philosophy regarding financial matters seems on the surface to combine a sensible practicality with a healthy respect for the unpredictable and highly variable twists in the life and the (il-)logic of political economy. In addition to running *The Lucky Find,* García tells us, Chen Pan regularly "issued loans to other *chinos* for a nominal fee" because he "believed that if you spread a bit of money around, blessings grew. To hoard it was to invite disaster" (69). This spreading of speculative "seed" money in his own community extends at one point to literal gambling because Chen Pan develops a taste for cockfights, but even there "he was blessed with good fortune. . . . His coins turned reliably to pesos, his pesos to silver, his silver to gold" (171).[19] But mostly García seems to position Chen Pan between the optimism of these passages, reinforced by a general idealization of Cuba as an abundantly productive and nur-turing tropical Eden ("in Cuba," the myth goes, "it was impossible to starve" [86]), and a skepticism that bears testimony especially to the time Chen Pan and his fellow Chinese spend enslaved on Cuba's plantations: Chen Pan's friend, the barber Arturo Fu Fon (who is gen-

erally fond of platitudes), intones at one point that "People will de-
vour each other when there's nothing else to eat" (80), and more than
once Chen Pan finds himself considering "the mountain of corpses
that had made these [Cuba's sugarcane] fields possible" (190). Through
Chen Pan, therefore, García offers her most trenchant as well as her
most sympathetic assessment of entrepreneurial capitalism's legacy
in the larger history of Cuban(-exile) political economy; she insists
more pointedly in *Monkey Hunting* than in her other two novels that
no assessment of either a productive or even redemptive materialism
in the Cuban(-exile) cultural disposition can occur without an honest and thorough acknowledgment of that disposition's historical ties
to slavery in the neofeudal, protocapitalist form it took in colonial
Cuba right up to both the end of the nineteenth century and the
point of (national) emancipation.

   This critical insistence manifests itself primarily in *Monkey
Hunting*'s other significant subplot, which involves Chen Pan's own
beloved, Lucrecia, herself a *mulata* whom Chen Pan purchases from a
sadistic criollo master, who we eventually learn is also her father, and
who in turn sells her to Chen Pan along with the child conceived
when he rapes her. Despite Lucrecia's strong resemblance to a line of
mixed-race fictional Cubanas who can be made to stand allegorically
for the racial and gendered alchemy informing Cuban cultural and
national *mestizaje* from at least the early nineteenth century on,
García's decision to marry her to Chen Pan does more than complicate the conventional black-white Cuban racial dyad by adding to it
her protagonist's Asianness.[20] It also matters here that the union of
Chen Pan and Lucrecia renarrates Cuba's social history as a direct
function of the emergence of its nonwhite communities into both
political and economic freedom if not full enfranchisement, an emergence not merely from one degree of empowered agency to another
but from a state of exploited objectification (as material requisite to
the operation of the then-prevailing mode of production) to the status of authentically productive, if decidedly limited, agency and self-
determination. Although Chen Pan first acquires his freedom through
escape and later secures it through the protection of a powerful and
wealthy benefactor in Havana, García has Lucrecia buy hers from her

new "master" through her own commercial efforts, a transformation in her status that therefore more directly traces her almost ontological transsubstantiation from abjected matter to mistress of her own flourishing enterprise.

Early in her character's time with Chen Pan, García has Lucrecia exhibit a deep sympathy with the artifacts in *The Lucky Find*; anxious regarding her master's acquisition of one wealthy widow's estate, Lucrecia, we learn, "could discern the history of an object by closely listening to it," a capacity that had allowed her to conclude, "Violence and unhappiness . . . seeped into things more tenaciously than the gentler emotions" (124). Therefore, instead of helping Chen Pan peddle wares whose histories were clearly steeped in such misery, Lucrecia instead takes up a craft she'd learned from the nuns who'd taken her in during her first pregnancy: she made custom-scented candles and sold them "all over Havana" (77). Lucrecia's products thus bear a closer relationship to Lourdes and Constancia's before her than they do to Chen Pan's; unlike the latter's antiques, her candles are more literally consumed, used up in being used at all, rather than merely kept, possessed, made to "bear" value by merely sitting there and looking the part, and hence not by virtue of any active capacity they might have to *do* anything. Here the allegorical correspondence to García's own mode of expressive production also reaches its full complexity because novels, of course, do both: as books, they're objects, commodities, things to be held, shelved, displayed, even fetishized; as texts, they're consumable, dynamic, actively participatory in acts of their own consumption and use, acts that leave them certainly changed (if not literally diminished or depleted), transformed at least in their capacity to produce such effects as pleasure, meaning, and value as the cumulative effect(s) of all possible readerly engagements (both critical and productive) with them.

Understandably, then, García invests Lucrecia's candles with a potency beyond their usefulness in emitting light. Not long into her new enterprise, Lucrecia begins "selling votives scented with crushed orange blossoms and calling them *velas de amor*. Word spread among the city's savviest women of the candles' stimulating effects in the *boudoir*. Every Thursday when Lucrecia offered a fresh batch of her love candles for sale, women came from everywhere to secure their week's supply" (77–78). Like Constancia Agüero, Lucrecia too acknowledges to herself the complex, ambivalent relationship she has with her mostly female clientèle; but whereas Constancia's product line mostly intervenes in the fantasies her customers indulge regarding their present lives' connection to the past, Lucrecia's products exploit her customers' either very immediate (or perhaps even more distantly future-oriented) hopes. This set of associations is reinforced by the much more direct relationship García draws between Lucrecia's candles and a more explicitly sexual eroticism, as well as among the candles, their production, and her own (re)productive history: "Lucrecia," we learn, not only "loved everything about making candles. The scent of the hot wax in the cauldrons. How it cooled so pure and smooth on the wicks. The way the candles burned in church, shrinking swiftly and painlessly, as she imagined a good life would" (130), but she developed this appreciation while "her baby grew and fattened inside her" and as she "dipped hundreds of candles in . . . bubbling vats, [l]ong white tapers for Sunday masses and society weddings" (135). It is, finally, from the revenues of her own candle sales that Lucrecia seizes what every other institutional structure in her world had kept from her since before her own birth: her freedom and her capacity for self-determination, by virtue of which she can finally choose to love Chen Pan and have children with him.

Lucrecia's decision to stay with Chen Pan after buying her freedom from him thus synthesizes rather effectively García's vision of the coinstantiated dimensions of Cuban national, racial, cultural, gendered, and economic life. Not only does she have Lucrecia secret her money away in one of Havana's Chinese banks, but she articulates Lucrecia's sense of her absorption into Chen Pan's world as correspondingly an absorption of his Chineseness into herself. As she faces her death after some decades of marriage to Chen Pan, Lucrecia finally insists on being buried in Havana's Chinese cemetery, knowing that her husband would eventually be buried beside her but also embracing the deeper cultural wisdom of her own experience of having become "Chinese" herself "in her liver . . . in her heart" (138), not only nowhere near China but emphatically on *Cuban* ground. Thus it is significant that Lucrecia's death and burial, figured at least implicitly as a "return" to a China she's never literally visited, also prefigure Chen Pan's own later passing as a "return" to a symbolically deviated (deterritorialized, diasporized) "home"-land embodied not by any literal China (to which he never manages to return), but by the "China" he reimagined and made real, with his *mulata* beloved, and on the same Cuban ground to which they both (in dying) "return." And although this diasporic complexity has institutional origins that certainly predate and exceed even the nineteenth-century Cuban setting of Chen Pan's sentimental (and sentimentally narrated) liaison with Lucrecia, it also has its extensions into the twentieth and certainly the twenty-first centuries. García makes these extensions into the twentieth century fairly explicit by devoting two additional narrative lines in *Monkey Hunting* to a granddaughter and a greatgrandson of Chen Pan's, the former ending in one of Mao Tse-Tung's political prisons, the latter on the streets of Saigon, and each in the late 1960s.

But the final episodes narrated in *Monkey Hunting* follow Chen Pan to the end of his life in 1920s Havana; there García has her protagonist reflect both backward into, and forward past, his extraordinary life. In one resonant consideration of his and Lucrecia's oldest son Lorenzo, who grows up to become an ambitious and well-known doctor, Chen Pan realizes that Lorenzo had returned from a trip to China "a stranger," prompting Chen Pan to ask himself in turn, "Now where could he call home? Lorenzo's skin, Chen Pan supposed, was a home of sorts, with its accommodations to three continents. Or perhaps home was in the blood of his grandson [Pipo] as it traveled through their flesh" (191–92). It would be tempting to read into this passage something like a version of the promise of at least a racially if not a culturally or politically redemptive *mestizaje* that we could trace in the Latin American context at least as far back as José Vasconcelos's 1920 pamphlet *La Raza Cósmica,* but García strikes me as too much a writer of her time to lend herself so readily to such an idealizing and in many ways disingenuous utopianism. Her postnational allegory works differently from those romances written to consolidate national identities in the nineteenth century precisely because she realizes that viable syntheses of otherwise conflictive and even combative differences in race, gender, and even class are, however desirable and even indispensable, no longer adequate in themselves to the task of forging the needed social, cultural, and political bonds in an era where the nation-state especially no longer enjoys the same relation to cultural coherence as it used to be able to pretend it did. This is perhaps why she allows *Monkey Hunting* to conclude roughly with this series of meditations on Chen Pan's part regarding the complexity and fluidity of human genealogies as resistant to all official attempts at cataloguing them. These meditations are the last, but not, however, the latest, things to happen in the narrative; we read them only after learning of the later fates of Chen Pan's descendants, who will go on, respectively, to die (as the much older Pipo will) under the tracks of a New York City subway train, or of cancer (as his granddaughter Chen Fang will) in a political prison during the cultural revolution in Mao's China, or to disappear (as his great-grandson Domingo Chen will) from the streets of 1970 Saigon, leaving behind a young Vietnamese prostitute, "pregnant" not only with the Afro-Sino-Cuban American child of a disaffected U.S. serviceman, but with the (still!) unwritten story of the world struggling to be born at roughly the same moment.

Back to the Future(s), or Gambling on the (Cultural) Enterprises That Remain

In their introduction to *Millennial Capitalism and the Culture of Neoliberalism,* Jean and John Comaroff observe a convergence of factors that for them characterizes the dramatically mixed, contradictory operations of the latest capitalism. Among these they number "the explosion of popular gambling, its legitimate incorporation into the fiscal heart of the nation-state, the global expansion of highly speculative market 'investment,' and changes in the moral vector of the wager," but instead of describing any outcome from this explosive mix of ingredients they first only pose the rhetorical question, "and what has happened?" Their not-so-rhetorical answer they find in an observation by a figure who is certainly of no small relevance to the discussion under way in this chapter. As they tell us, "'The world,' [according to] a reflective Fidel Castro, 'has become a huge casino.' Because the value of stock markets has lost all grounding in materiality, he says . . . their workings have finally realized the dream of medieval alchemy: 'Paper has been turned into gold.'"[21] Castro made these comments, the Comaroffs tell us, in Johannesberg, South Africa, in 1998, the same year Pope John Paul II visited Cuba and some years before Castro's visit to a profoundly transformed China that I briefly noted in chapter 6. One can only speculate here on what exactly this last of the old cold warriors makes of global capital's remarkable reascendance in the first years of the new millennium, even in places as far afield, but as significantly connected by historic and ideological ties as Cuba (and its Miamian and other U.S.-diasporic extensions), China and Vietnam. But clearly for him the reference to gambling and to the world as casino must invoke at least in part the legacy of his country's own ancien régime bourgeois, which had notoriously transformed Havana and the rest of the nation into just such a place (as well as into some of even more ill repute) in the decade(s) leading to his revolution. That regime, the story goes, exported such decadent practices and values with it when it went into exile, and it reestablished them in perhaps more palatable ways in the city to which most of its parties retreated. That enterprising, ambitious, and unforgiving tribe has already made a number of appearances in this chapter, but let me now in closing invoke it one more time, if only to connect certain lines of both narrative and analysis that will complete more fully the picture I have tried to compose in this discussion with Cristina García's help.

In addition to its appearance in work already cited by Earl Shorris, María Cristina García, and others, entrepreneurial Cuban Miami also makes splashy appearances in the works already cited by Louie A. Pérez, Arlene Dávila, and George Yúdice, and in each case it does so in part to either complete or confirm some analysis of its importance in the larger dynamic of global capital's transnational flows, especially although not exclusively in a Western Hemispheric context. Pérez mostly refers to it as the logical endpoint of the historical narrative of the U.S.–Cuban cultural dialectic stretching back into the nineteenth century that he tells in *On Becoming Cuban*.[22] For Dávila, the U.S. Hispanic marketing industry owes its very existence, not to mention its phenomenal success, to a cadre of "Cuban executives who had previously been involved in advertising and marketing in Cuba" and were subsequently "behind the development of the first and largest advertising agencies that targeted populations of Latin American background"; these "sons of '*pequeños comerciantes*' of Spanish background who had been steeped in the ideology of business ownership," Dávila concludes, owed their "entrepreneurial success . . . [to] their shared class background . . . and [to] the establishment of an ethnic economy where ethnic ties were central in dispensing credits, employment, and economic opportunities" (29–30).[23] George Yúdice extends Dávila's argument here, both chronologically and analytically, suggesting that in the twenty-first century it "becomes possible to speak of a post-Cuban and even a post-Caribbean Miami," even if the most recalcitrant of "Cuban-exile leaders clearly do not see that Miami is changing and that they no longer occupy the leading role in the next stage of the region's development" (197–98); and what Dávila terms in her work an "ethnic economy" on perhaps the more modest scale on which it might operate for newly immigrated if comparatively privileged groups expands in Yúdice's into a full-blown "cultural economy, on the model of a political economy," one whose success is no longer so restrictively tied to anything as local as a community or indeed to anything conventional construed as "locality."

"Post-Cuban Miami," therefore, operates in Yúdice's work as that which no longer names a place, whether a neighborhood, a city, or even a region but a much more abstracted, deterritorialized, and generalized space of production and consumption, one where especially what he goes on to call the "Latin culture industries in the United States" have set up shop to produce what he recognizes to be a considerable amount of decidedly *symbolic* value.[24] "On the one hand," Yúdice explains, these "culture industries . . . have a growing *market* value in Latin America, the United States, and elsewhere; on the other, they gain an extra *political* value as they are embraced by US discourses of diversity and multiculturalism" (211). Although the "doubling" of *symbolic* market and political values produced by the twenty-first century's increasingly globalized "cultural economy" may bear only a passing resemblance, and certainly not a structural relation, to the operations of *surplus* "value big with value" in the conventional Marxist sense, it does matter here that these two conceptualizations of value should be brought into productive contact. Whether or not Cristina García consciously composes her novels to cater to the cultural milieu that continues to be shaped in part by what Yúdice calls "US discourses of diversity and multiculturalism," those novels are indeed quite directly marketed to that milieu, and as a result of that marketing they derive part of their considerable cultural currency. That milieu is not, however, in any way identical to the U.S.–Cuban "milieu" to and about which she may be said in part to write, regardless of any significant overlap between them; in addition, her attempts to both represent and critique the entrepreneurial practices and legacies of that community bear no simple or straightforward relation of correspondence to the actual history of that community as told in much of the scholarly work I cite in this discussion. It may have to suffice here to observe, in closing, that García at least addresses that legacy quite directly, if perhaps ambivalently, but always with the hope that her active engagement of it can be read as less complicit than critical and even (perhaps) critically productive.

Chapter 8

Sounding the Body Politic: Sono-Grammatics in Rafael Campo's Sonnet Corpus

*Politics ... remains, at its core, conservative insofar as it
works to affirm a structure, to authenticate social order,
which it then intends to transmit to the future in the
form of its inner Child. That Child remains the
perpetual horizon of every acknowledged politics, the
fantasmatic beneficiary of every political situation.*

—Lee Edelman, *No Future:
Queer Theory and the Death Drive*[1]

*To reproduce the pattern is a noose
Whose knot I fatten with the hands I got
From ancestors who reproduced ...
The rope the generations weave
Is breaking yet is holding fast ...*

—Rafael Campo, "The Cycle Begins Anew"[2]

A Country for Old Men and Little Boys

In the last chapter of 2002's *Cuba Confidential* entitled "The Old Man
and the Little Boy," Ann Louise Bardach describes what she calls "the
largest march in Cuban history," which occurred on July 26, 2000,

both to commemorate one of the most important anniversaries in the revolution's calendar but also to celebrate the safe return (in June of the same year) of Elián González into the custody of his father and of his country of birth. The march, Bardach observes, proceeded down Havana's legendary Malecón and "past the new statue of José Martí clutching a young boy," a statue that had been "hastily erected during the Elián crisis," and although the "sculpted boy" clutched by Martí was, Bardach tells us, "officially designated as Martí's son, . . . [his] visage has an undeniable resemblance to Elián Gonzalez."[3] Bardach finds at least two things striking about the statue beyond its clear function as a marker of revolutionary Cuba's self-perceived "victory" in the Elián matter, mostly over its sworn enemies in exile Miami: one is the overt gesture that Martí's sculpted figure makes with his "free arm," in "pointing accusingly straight at the U.S. Interests Section," and the other is that at its base the statue bears "anti-American epigrams from Simón Bolívar and Martí," but not from Fidel Castro.

Indeed, as Bardach goes on to tell us, Castro kept a relatively low profile in the weeks just after Elián's return to Cuba that June, knowing full well that the best way to counter much of the negative fallout of the media spectacle that Elián's situation had spawned in the United States (what Bardach herself calls at one point the "ghoulish peep show in Miami") was to downplay its force, in his own country, precisely as spectacle. This strategy worked in part, as Bardach's report suggests, because Castro knew well to substitute for himself, in what pageantry he did allow to mark Elián's return to Cuba that summer, the only other official, and certainly more powerfully iconic, figure of Cuba's national patrimony, José Martí.[4] Not only is it Martí's hand that the sculpted pseudo-Elián holds, but it is Martí's words that literally underwrite what Elián's rescue back into his nation's familial embrace is allowed to mean. But putting this uncharacteristic media shyness on Castro's part aside, Bardach makes it clear that the "Old Man" she designates in the title of her chapter is indeed Fidel Castro, and that what became evident as the months following Elián's return passed was exactly how deeply cathected to young Elián the much, much older Castro had become. "It was clear to insiders,"

Bardach reports, "that Castro was dazzled by the boy's intelligence, charm and outrageous destiny," so much so that even a witness as odd as former California governor Jerry Brown remarked, during a visit to the island that summer, that "Fidel's obsessed with Elián . . . [and that] it almost feels to him [to Castro] like Elián was providential. I think," Brown concludes, "he's grooming him to be his successor."[5]

On one level, of course, Castro's fascination with Elián makes perfect psychological and political sense. Whether or not Elián ever takes on a political vocation, the fact that by the end of 2000 he was "almost as famous as Castro" in Cuba meant that he could figure quite effectively in any number of ideologically crafted fantasy scenarios for thinking a Cuban future, as many Cubans both on and off the island had certainly already begun doing, "beyond Fidel."[6] As Bardach herself observes, this renewed interest among Cubans in what might happen next may continue for some time to confront the stubborn fact of Castro's stubborn survival, and thus that the "next generation" for whom any kind of national reconciliation might be possible remains always whatever "next generation" follows the one that will die with Castro; but Bardach also suggests that such a transition will inevitably be influenced by deep psychological and emotional currents, given that the vast majority of Cuban families equate their historical experience of the larger national schism with much more intimate and immediate (because familial) experiences of "searingly tragic . . . separation and loss."[7]

One other striking aspect of Fidel Castro's intuitive sense of the potential efficacy of the Elián saga for his own purposes in determining his country's fate beyond his own passing is just how much it resembles the uses to which the same story had been put while Elián was still in the United States. In a 2003 *American Quarterly* article entitled "Elián González and 'The Purpose of America,'" Sarah Banet-Weiser shows quite convincingly how during his American sojourn "the transcendent, mediated image that situate[d] Elián as both a religiously blessed child and a national child" provided a "symbolic link between discourses of the nation, those of the family, and those of exile communities living in the US."[8] A journalist like Bardach might keep these connections more implicit in her reportorial narrative, but for a media scholar like Banet-Weiser, it is exactly these connections that drive her analysis. Elián may stand out as a uniquely spectacular case in Cuba, but in the United States he fits a larger pattern (the other example Banet-Weiser lists is JonBenét Ramsey) of an ongoing media-spurred national obsession with what she calls the "figure of the 'innocent' child," one that carries "enormous symbolic value in America's cultural, political and economic history, and is often used to invoke and fuel political battles over the 'fate of America's future.'"[9] Banet-Weiser argues that although this more generalized national fascination with the child accounts for the "currency" of the Elián story in national and even global media markets well beyond South Florida, the matter triggered a fascination of unprecedented intensity in that region precisely because Elián arrived on its shores at a moment of intense anxiety over what we might call "the fate of *Cuban* America's future." As Banet-Weiser tells us, the "history of the Cuban exile remains as a partial narrative in the Elián González case . . . [and] partial because the ambivalence surrounding the Cuban American exile community is felt more strongly given the collapse of the Soviet Union and the subsequent absence of [especially the Cold War] context that symbolized the Cuban exile."[10]

It matters here too that (as Banet-Weiser puts it) Elián washed up alone, "a motherless and a nationless child" and was therefore even more powerfully situated to provoke all the various, and variously hysterical, attempts to replace his lost mother with such a odd array of substitute (and always—to say the least—inadequate) parents of both genders and almost all possible ideological bents. Of these, and even before Elián ever returns to Cuba in his real father's custody, Banet-Weiser argues that Castro himself was, perhaps most surprisingly, "cast as a particular kind of state parent in this nationalist family saga, a new variation on the 'dead-beat dad' who provided such a dismal and oppressive homeland that Elián and his mother were forced to run away."[11] This demonizing rendering of Castro, of course, backfired to the extent that the entire matter resulted not only in Elián's return to his one surviving birth parent but also in the reinforcement, once he was back in Cuba, of the logic, as well as the fantasy, of a patriarchal succession as that which will govern all likely

Cuban futures. Elián González, to the extent that he continues indefinitely in his youth to embody the promise inherent in any construction of that future, will function thus without any reference to what actual care he may be enjoying from his actual stepmother but exclusively as a function of his ongoing continued patronization by Fidel Castro, a relationship of ideologically "blessed" patrimony presided over at one remove (and thanks of course to Castro himself) by the spirit of the iconic "father" of the Cuban nation, José Martí.

What I hope this protracted discussion of Bardach's journalistic and Banet-Weiser's scholarly accounts of the Elián González matter (as it unfolded on both sides of the Florida Straits) will allow me to do is to underscore, in ways that should be clear by now, the operations of what I have been calling political and cultural erotics in the ongoing elaboration of a diasporic Cuban American subjectivity, one that cannot be reduced exclusively to the ideological and identitarian terms established by the first generation of Miami-based Cuban exiles, and one that certainly cannot rely on those terms as it turns from the past to the future and begins to imagine what exactly of its *cubanidad* will survive into a future that will only render it, and at once, more diasporic and more American. What strikes me as much as anything else about both Bardach's and Banet-Weiser's accounts is the attention each devotes (without ever doing so explicitly) to what I would call the political and cultural *homo*-erotics of the whole affair. The death of Elián's mother in the passage to Florida clearly allows (in everything that followed) an intense competition on the part of a number of highly visible male candidates to assist in the fathering of the boy and certainly well beyond the efforts of his own father to claim that exclusive right. Situations like this clearly underscore the accuracy of one of queer theory's founding claims regarding the hom(m)o-social dynamic governing all prevailing forms of sociopolitical bonding in patriarchal society. In societies as intensely patriarchal as Cuba's and Cuban America's, it's not surprising then that the manner in which that patriarchy's heteropresumptive ideology needs to manage its equally necessary but clearly threatening dependency on its functionally hom(m)o-social glue will produce some very odd and surprising filial and familial arrangements, especially in the larger sociosymbolic spaces where fantasy and ideology very often, and simultaneously, collude and collide.

Indeed, some years before Elián washed ashore alone north of Miami, at least one U.S.-based literary critic uniquely versed in both the deconstructive procedures of queer theory and the defining gendered and ideological tendencies in Latin American culture had published a brief but powerfully suggestive piece on that very sexual dialectic as it already presented itself more than a century earlier in the work of José Martí himself. In 1996's "His America, Our America: José Martí Reads Whitman," Sylvia Molloy begins by invoking generally the "obsessive meditation on male progeniture and filiation [that] runs through the pages of José Martí," in order to situate strategically, and in an explicitly queered context, Martí's famed essay on the poet Walt Whitman. Molloy begins by observing how, even before he turns his admiring attention to Whitman's work and persona, Martí had already, especially in written work (like his *Ismaelillo*) dedicated to or inspired by his own son, effected what she calls the "very fertile conjunction of fathers, sons and just causes," an imaginative and discursive "family romance" from which "women are [explicitly] excluded."[12] This family romance certainly extends beyond the immediate scope of Martí's own family, and it is generalized to the point of shaping not only Martí's vision of the just-emerging Cuban national romance but also (and with Whitman's help) of a larger hemispheric force, one that could thereby embody not only the epochal spirit of an emerging "American" democracy but also the absolute register of all "American" democratic politics to come.

What begins, therefore, in the respective poetical imaginations of either Whitman or Martí as "the polymorphous, unhierarchical exchange of all-male feeling" takes on "indubitable political significance" for Martí even before he encounters Whitman; but from the point of that encounter on, Molloy continues, "Whitman's communal masculinity," especially as celebrated in the *Calamus* poems, becomes for Martí the touchstone for "his own all-male affiliative model, the revolutionary family of sons and fathers confounded in a continuum of natural, unhierarchical masculine emotion." What Martí will finally recognize in that model, Molloy concludes, is its "political, specifically American, potential," a potential Molloy finds most significantly evident in the celebration of a "naturally" virile (and decidedly gynophobic) Americanism in what is perhaps the most iconic articulation of Martí's mature political vision, the "Our America" essay of 1891. Small wonder, then, that the ideological and cultural patrimony born of this encounter (whether born of Whitman by Martí, or vice versa) should find itself very much alive and newly rebegotten, both in what the exile patriarchs in Miami hoped to make of Elián had those in Washington allowed him to stay "in America," but also in what Fidel Castro and his supporters made (and presumably still make) of Elián upon his actual return to Cuba (beginning, of course, with their "handing him off, or back," to Martí, at least in sculptural form). In Cuban America, however, and from one of its many non-Miamian, diasporic outposts, a radically alternative, and strategically queer, deconstruction of this hypersymptomatic patrimonial dialectic was already (by the time Molloy published her essay and well before the uncannily millennial Year of Elián) under way, and in the work of another U.S.-based poet, like Martí, of Cuban descent. That poet is Rafael Campo, and in what remains of this chapter, I both describe and comment on his attempts in aspects of his own larger poetic project to intervene into the business as usual of the paradoxically heteropresumptive but exclusively patrimonial process of cultural reproduction in Cuban America, a process at least as old as its inaugural moment in Martí's loving encounter with Whitman.

"My Awful Hybrid Muse": Rafael Campo's Song(s) of Him- (and Her-) Selves

In a January 2004 interview, the Cuban American poet Rafael Campo half joked to his interviewer that he was born in the "northern part of Cuba known as Elizabeth, New Jersey," and that although he had never literally been to Cuba himself, he had devoted a good deal of energy in both his verse and prose work to imagining such a visit, given that for him "the language— . . . the imaginative capacity for language—is a kind of medium for return, even if I can't be there physically."[13] Campo's seemingly straightforward remarks are striking for many reasons. They resonate with a decidedly diasporic quality to the extent that they highlight the ability of a successfully diasporic community to begin the process of reproducing itself imaginatively with the very first generation born away from the homeland, and to do so in a way that clearly mixes elements of collective fantasy into its necessarily practical attempts to survive, and outlive, its very real displacement(s). Campo's complex identification with his family's Cuban origins and his own negotiation of the legacy of that past in his own life take up much of the remaining work of this chapter. For the moment it suffices to notice here two aspects of the remarks just quoted: first, the insistence of characterizing the Elizabeth, New Jersey, where he was born as almost exclusively Cuban (a little later in the interview he'll add that it was "a very comfortable community, a community of Cubans and [presumably other] working-class immigrant folks"); second, that although he's never been to Cuba, he imagines any visit to the island as a *return*.

Campo's public accounts of his life, in his poetry, his prose work, and in published interviews, all favor the Cuban part of his heritage and not only over the obviously "American" facts of his birth and his upbringing but also over his mother's Italian American heritage, which appears so rarely in those accounts that even the January 2004 interview states incorrectly that he was born "to Cuban exile parents." The mistake is understandable, given the considerable amount of space Campo devotes to the historical, political, cultural, and personal aspects of his *cubanidad* across all four of the verse collections that he'd published by the time of the interview, as well as in his prose memoir *The Poetry of Healing*, which came out in 1997, after the publication of his first two verse collections and before the publication of the second two. It matters, therefore, to the larger issue of the literary and cultural reflection on the Cuban-diasporic experience that concerns this study, that Campo is not only U.S. born, but literally only "half" Cuban, and although the ethnic and cultural alchemy comprising his identity might compel us to formulate quite awkwardly that he is either Cuban Italian, or Cuban American or Cuban Italian American, much of the hybridizing fluidity of his various possible guises can certainly be attributed to factors in his history that render him especially both diasporic and American. It also bears noting here that Campo, of all the major figures who have received significant attention in this study, is the only one who is U.S. born; in addition, he is actually more Miami identified in some ways than any of those other writers, if only because he spent considerable time in Miami visiting his Cuban grandparents there while they were still alive.

It also matters here that, along with the cultural and national aspects of his identity, Campo has devoted even more attention in his published work to his experiences as a gay man, and in particular a gay man who found himself attending medical school during the first full decade of the AIDS epidemic and who decided as a result of that experience to dedicate himself, through a specialization in internal medicine, to treating people with HIV and AIDS (many of them indigent, gay, and nonwhite) in his adopted home city of Boston. Although his homosexuality may in part explain his more intense embrace of the lineage he can trace through his male progenitors back to Cuba, how that sexual disposition does and does not allow him to situate himself beyond his own generation to that identical bloodline is a chief point of interrogation in what follows here. Clearly, however, Campo's strategically avowed queerness also positions him in quite another genealogy, and a decidedly rich and varied one at that, including certainly a major progenitor in Reinaldo Arenas and an impressive gathering of sibling near-contemporaries in the likes of Achy Obejas, Albita Rodriguez, and Eduardo Machado. Because my concern with Campo's work requires that I address it mostly on its own terms, I do not make any connective, comparative references to any of these other writers beyond what I do here to observe the remarkable coincidence of the emergence of this generation of queer Cuban-diasporic literary and cultural voices in roughly the same decade, a decade inaugurated by Arenas's tragic death and the more ambiguously consequential "passing" of the Cold War era.

Like Achy Obejas in the passage from *Days of Awe* where she has her protagonist Ale collaborate with her parents on imagining a Cuban-diasporic-American future where even her (Ale's and Achy's) queer intervention into the business as usual of cultural and even biological reproduction might have a meaningfully productive hand, Rafael Campo has across all his published work imagined and performed an even more elaborate and complicated scenario for his own vision of a queered practice of Cuban-diasporic reproduction. Although that scenario certainly exceeds the verse pieces and prose passages I discuss here, its primary elaboration can be traced across an extended cycle of sonnetlike, sixteen-line lyrics, a cycle that débuts in the first collection (*The Other Man Was Me*, 1993) in a section entitled "Familia" and consisting of four sixteen-piece "Songs," dedicated, sequentially, to the poet's grandfather, father, lover, and son. Of these, the only figure who is completely imagined is the last, the "son" who projects the loose family narrative traced through preceding and present generations into a future that is at once merely fantasized and strategically ambiguated. In his second published collection (*What the Body Told*, 1996) Campo extends the life of the family romance to include four additional sixteen-lyric "Songs," two of which (dedicated together in Spanish to "la Vida") are addressed to "Las Mujeres" (that is, to women) and to "Our Daughter"; the other two (dedicated together to "la Muerte") include a "Song Before Dying" and an "Immortal Song." Although this already-ambitious eight-song cycle arguably concludes (by refusing to concede to absolute conclusions) with that "Immortal Song," the poet's ruminations on its compelling themes did not end there, and thus further extensions can be found in his 1997 prose memoir and in the two verse collections that followed *The Poetry of Healing: Diva* (1999) and *Landscape with Human Figure* (2001).[14]

The argument that follows also proceeds fairly directly from the discussion of Campo with which chapter 3 in this study on Retamar's *Caliban* concluded. The sonnet "In the Form," that I analyzed there appears just before Campo launches his "Song" cycle and in many ways announces many of the significant themes that concern that cycle. These themes have as much to do with the complex political erotics of what begins as a series of sonnetlike lyrics by a male poet and addressed to other men to whom he's related by various forms of (af)filiation, as with the imbedded question of literary form per se, concerning both the poet's deployment of (and departure from) the whole erotic history of the sonnet itself, as well as the sonnet's pliancy in the service of the larger narrative demands of the cycle and its eventual extensions in subsequent volumes. For Campo, clearly form and content are inextricably linked, and often in his work he articulates that synthesis through the language of corporeality (in order, one might say, to demonstrate most articulately the corporeality of language). Witness, for example, the following long passage from *The Poetry of Healing,* where he describes an early phase in his evolving sense of his dual vocation:

> what grew inside me throughout medical school . . . was a strange and unsatisfying relationship to language I did not expect. The healthy impulse to look inside was for a time corrupted by insiderliness. I began to wonder whether the stirrings I felt inside myself might not be the viable fetus of my desires given flesh at all, but rather represented some unborn potential in me doomed always to lurk, defying expression and impossible to articulate, an unintelligible language to which I would never give voice with the rhythmic contractions of birth. There it was, . . . the horrible monster of my early poetry, the only thing I could possibly parent, the frightening product of some misguided experiment where the sperm of a poet fertilized the egg of a scientist: yet I yearned to feed my awful hybrid muse, and resolved always to keep it chained up very close to me.[15]

The recourse here to images of physical pregnancy and childbirth may initially appear both conventional and heavy handed, but they're certainly not incidental to the larger symbolic economy of Campo's written work. The conventionality of this passage is in fact always effectively countered by the writer's willingness to invert, and indeed to pervert, that conventionality. Campo here does not simply feminize his position in the creative situation by taking on primarily a maternal rather than paternal parental role; he also makes sure to implode the conventional logic of sexual opposition altogether by staging the inseminating "fertilization" of his scientist-self by his poet-self, and by invoking the figure of his "awful hybrid muse," who is identified with neither of these conjugating selves, and who is also strategically not gendered, remaining rather perversely an "it" whom the poet nevertheless insists on keeping "chained up very close to" himself.

Frequently in the course of the memoir, Campo returns to this question of the dual vocation compelled on him by this "hybrid" muse, and frequently discussions of that theme will represent his poems' complex embodiments as equally renderings of the body as vital (erotic, productive) and mortal (diseased, dying). "I have always been in love with the muscularity of formal verse," he confesses in a later passage; but beyond the immediate attractions of its "muscularity," formal verse because of its structural and citational impersonations of existing work in the same or similar form offers him "a way to sew myself into the body of traditions from which I might sometimes feel excluded, as if I were an amputated clubfoot yearning to have its blood supply restored."[16] The reference to the clubfoot here is also not incidental; clearly Campo has Lord Byron's experiments in long-form (and sexy) verse narratives as much in mind as he has Shakespeare's or anyone else's accomplishments in the sonnet form itself. Unlike Shakespeare or Byron, however, Campo realizes that he can never claim to occupy the same relation to the erotic (either to its conventional protocols or its conventional consequences) as they could presume to occupy without explicit claim. This does not, however, preclude him in the end from using his chosen variants on "formal verse" to explore his own creative potency in ways more suited to his own erotic dispositions. He declares near the end of the memoir, in fact, and in characteristically ambivalent form, that (on the one hand), "My poems have an unfortunate tendency to wallow in the misery of their own creation, besides being obsessed with my patriarchal past" while (on the other), "I look like the hybrid that I am. Like most hybrids I will never reproduce. I am toxic to my own aspirations and dreams; in my veins run both the promise of a better life and its incessant denial."[17] My argument in what follows insists that these mostly dour pronouncements are actually ironic declarations of a kind of perverse fertility, one comprised in equal parts of virility and vitality. His poems' obsession with their maker's "patriarchal past" especially requires further exploration here because that past is itself multiple and involves not only his closest literal male progenitors but also more indirect progenitors of his national and cultural (especially literary) "pasts." In addition, his eventual identification with his de-sexualized "hybrid" muse requires further exploration as well, especially for the ways it helps to explain those instances where he produces elaborate fantasies about procreation in the "Songs" dedicated to his imaginary "Son" and "Daughter."

It is striking that Campo devotes so much more attention to the influence of his father's family and culture on his life and work than his mother's, and that distinction is nowhere clearly accounted for in his published work. It very directly contributes to the sense he generally gives his readers that *all* he has is a "patriarchal" past, as though he'd himself been born of some magical, and magically male-exclusive, reproductive process. This also, as I observed earlier, produces the effect that Campo was more powerfully Cubanized than anything else by this acculturating process. This is evident in the following rare passage devoted to his Cuban (hence paternal) grand-mother:

> Music and magic, and particularly their expression and ab-sorption in the physical body, were primary modes of healing recoverable in the bits and shreds of Cuban culture that I en-countered as a child. . . . I would hear [my grandmother] pray-ing or singing quietly in Spanish, believing perhaps that she was restoring health to an infirm relative back in Cuba whom she would never see again. . . . In her songs, my mind transported all the way from sickly Elizabeth, New Jersey, and its bleak re-fineries and landfills, to the verdant, lush Cuban countryside I imagined was her real home. Healing had a voice, and seemed rooted in a most potent physical longing.[18]

"Longing" here is primarily a political longing, figured in his grand-mother's suggested longing to return to Cuba, and it is also an em-bodied longing in its simultaneous desire for the curative healing of disease; it is not, however, explicitly eroticized. In a parallel but much later passage, Campo describes another associative connection to Cuba, this one involving his paternal grandfather:

> I remember how I felt when I touched my grandfather's scars, those deep imprints left by Cuba: I was a blind child reading the past in Braille, understanding for the first time the vast plantation, the raging river, the cattle, the dark jail, and the soldiers' clubs. . . . Pain must be too personal, held too deeply, to be known without actually experiencing it. Though my grandfather's smile emphasized a certain scar on his forehead, and therefore could feel like a blow to the head, so bitter and full of loss, I never felt the pain he must have known. I can only imagine it.[19]

Clearly both grandparents embodied Cuba for the writer, and therefore both powerfully conditioned what he felt of his own *cubanidad;* but although his grandmother's healing prayer seems to presage something of Campo's own eventual vocation as a healer, that connection remains more distanced and abstract than the very tangible, even tactile connection he feels upon touching, and thereby reading, his grandfather's scars. In both cases, he's also left merely to "imagine" for himself experiences that were once directly available to them, but whereas his grandmother only calls up for him a generalized (and again rather conventional) picture of Cuba's "lush" countryside, his grandfather's legible scars open for him volumes of detail about his family's actual past, a past whose poetic reimagination has been a central feature of Campo's ongoing literary endeavor, an endeavor already significantly under way by the time he publishes the memoir containing these passages.

Indeed, as early as the 1993 publication of *The Other Man Was Me,* his poems' obsession with especially his Cuban "patriarchal past" was already in full view, as were the rather perverse particulars of that obsession, not only as it related to his feelings toward both his grandfather and father but also as it related toward what these figures who embodied his past could determine about his expectations for his own future. The "Song" for his grandfather, comprised of sixteen 16-line lyrics, inaugurates the longer cycle in the elegiac mode because his grandfather is mostly described in the process of dying and being mourned. This is, of course, true to the spirit of the Cuban-exile experience as undergone by the grandfather's generation; everything begins with mourning, in the moment of awakening to a loss impossible to recover precisely because of the impossible temporal and spatial logics of exile itself, the loss having occurred before the beginning and somewhere beyond any accessible elsewhere. Campo thus begins with a piece entitled "Guantánamo," suggesting this is the part of Cuba where his family lived but also invoking the unofficial Cuban national anthem, "Guantanamera," whose lyrics are partly taken from a famous poem by José Martí, who looms here as a different but equally significant embodiment of Campo's "patriarchal past." Guantánamo is for this reason, according to the poet, "the town/My oldest country will forever mourn," but also the town where everything begins for him, since there, he claims, "I was born when he was born."

What's "born" here, too, is the series of lyric meditations on precisely how the poet will not only rescue through his work the specific memory of his grandfather but will also bear and breed himself the legacy of his grandfather's (hence his own) *cubanidad*, past even the point of the older man's final passing. The fourth piece in the "Song," entitled "Grandfather's Will," describes quite literally the nature of this transmission, and in the grandfather's voice: "I give you the plantation. I give you/A seed inside your penis"; and while this gift has some relation to a literal piece of real estate in Cuba, it clearly operates more ambiguously here, where "plantation" can denote both an object and an act, in this latter case the (im)plantation of the grandfather's "seed" in the grandson's "penis." What exactly might issue forth from that seed as the result of the grandson's active cultivation of it also remains quite open to question. The thirteenth entry in the "Song," entitled "The Funeral," transforms that seed into a rather different kind of remainder, "His corpse," the "residue," which, according to the poet, is all that "the blood and bitterness" of his grandfather's life "have left." The subsequent piece, however, quickly refuses to surrender to the finality of death, and although it's entitled "The Things I Don't Remember," it also does not surrender to the inevitability of forgetting. Significantly, what the poet claims to have remembered from his grandfather is a lesson regarding the "proper use of the future-perfect tense./(He taught me that.)" This reference to the grammatical rules governing the "proper use of the future-perfect tense" in Spanish suggests, finally, that the genealogical line traced in these lyrics, and opening them up to the trajectory of a compelling but open-ended narrative, may lead both the poet and his readers toward something like a "future" but one that bears no necessary, conventional relation, temporal, logical, or spiritual, to anything that precedes it, hence one that can only be conceived, or imagined, in the extended, projected provisionality of a complex (and foreign) verbal "tense."

We take a step closer toward that future in the "Song" that the poet dedicates to his father. If the poet's grandfather was so fully Cubanized as to resist all aspects of Americanization beyond the grudging concession to the fact of exile, the poet's father more directly embodies the immigrant experience of cultural accommodation and synthesis; the third of the pieces in "Song for My Father," entitled "Planning a Family," strikes quite a different genetic chord than the one heard before in "Guantánamo": "I wished to make a boy from her," the poet has his father declare, "a son/Of numerous abilities, a true/American, the way I could salute/The country that had rescued me." This projective "planning" for a "future son [who] would learn the language well" does not preclude some reference to the cultural past, but here that past is rendered (in the sixth piece, entitled "Advice for the New World") more in the language of division than of continuation: "I populate with you, my son, this place./My feet found clefts in the cliff dividing you from Cuba." Nevertheless, the striking homoerotic dynamic of this process of generational transmission *does* continue; clearly there is more than one way to "populate" a space "with" someone else, even one's own son, and by this point in the telling of his family narrative, the poet is certainly willing to give up a confessional point or two, as he does (in his own voice) in "Honest," the piece following "Advice": "He's/My homonym: he gave to me his name./I guess I'm being honest," the poet claims, "when I say/I was in love with him when I was young." "Honest" concludes with the further confession that the poet sees his vocation to write "My pretty verse/So fearful, shameful—honest, yet perverse" as an offering, a "gift" to his father, perhaps in part as a way of marking the fulfillment of his father's immigrant wish that his son "learn the language well," even though that fulfillment comes for the father, perversely enough, at the cost of his son's honesty about his own queerness and about how that queerness itself issues directly from their own intense affiliations.

Campo connects in the course of the lyrics dedicated to his father the issues of his sexual, cultural, and professional identities and the threats they all posed together to the intense filial bond he and his father shared. In "My Father's View of Poetry" (number eight in the series), the poet outlines this conflict, and again in his father's voice: "You can't tell stories—poems fight/A narrative. You surely can't cure night's/Forgetfulness with it, or say with it/Important histories and truths." By the eighth installment in the second of a cycle of four impressive series of lyrics, of course, the reader already has a sense for not only what the poet thinks about, but also what he can do in response to, this argument; it matters, though, that he identifies these as his father's clearly thoughtful objections to poetry, to how it distracts us from the real and more valuable work of language in deploying narrative especially to "cure . . . Forgetfulness" by telling "with it/Important histories and truths." The poet's father only hints at the possibility that poetry may not be manly enough, but that suggestion more than lurks behind his later and more emphatic claim that poetry is inadequate to the task of witnessing a history whose dominant mode of operation is violence: "When you die—/I've seen a revolution, so I know—/You're never counting syllables. You know/The murderers will drain your throat of sighs." "Sighs," then, the products primarily of pleasure and emotion, cannot (his father urges) withstand the force of a violence the knowledge of which it is the task of the historically engaged writer to document. It is, however, precisely the strategic, critical modulation of these "sighs," and especially of their origins in both pain *and* pleasure, that Campo takes on as his primary task in writing his poetry, and in doing so to demonstrate, against his father's stated objections, how and what indeed "poems" can and do "fight."

In *The Poetry of Healing,* Campo devotes an entire chapter ("The Fairiest College") to the episode of his meeting, befriending, and

courting Jorge Arroyo, the man who would become his lifelong partner, during their first year together as undergraduates at Amherst
College. Jorge, as he usually appears in Campo's accounts of him, is of
Puerto Rican and before that Argentine descent, and like Campo he
too attended Harvard Medical School after college. They settled eventually into a domestic life together, and into different medical practices, in the greater Boston area in the mid-1990s. The "Song for My
Lover" that follows the "Songs" to his grandfather and father in *The
Other Man Was Me* both sustains and disrupts the narrative tracing
of Campo's genealogical line already under way, and already under
discussion here, and it primarily does so by intensifying further the
dialectical stress between all the conventions of succession, transmission, and reproduction already active in the cycle and the various
anticonventional modes of queerness activated to resist and exceed
them. Although, as we have seen, the "Songs" for his grandfather and
father roughly followed the sequential logic leading from "exile" to
"immigrant" phases in the post-1959 Cuban American experience,
Campo's description of his encounter with and commitment to his
fellow U.S.-bred Latino lover does not so much take on the elements
of a more fully Americanized degree of ethnic establishment, but it
instead favors a different discursive tack, one far more resistant to the
undeniable pull of the narrative of ethnic success available to him
here. The discovery of Jorge's Puerto Rican past instead pulls Campo
imaginatively to the same place(s) that he'd already explored in his
writing about his grandfather and father, although in Jorge he also
finds an opportunity to replace some of the burdens of loss and nostalgia with qualities one might better describe as hopeful and even
liberating.

"Jorge's past," Campo confesses in the memoir, "had transpired on
an island not too distant from the one lost to me, and I imagined the
view from the sailboat"—during a month-long sail that they took together through the Caribbean—"affording me a glimpse of what
might have been my own world."[20] That vision takes the following
quite telling form, one that mostly reinforces the treatments of Cuba,
already published in the earlier verse collections, which render it a
"mythical place I could never visit, where my father had killed sharks

and herded cattle, where my grandmother had prayed when hurricanes ran their hands roughly under her dress, where Spanish was spoken boastfully and freely, where the indomitable sun beat dark colors into the skin of all people. Could such a paradise truly exist?"[21] The short (and the long) answer to that final semi-rhetorical question is, of course, no: not in Cuba, nor in the United States, before 1959 or after, regardless of anyone's either nostalgic or otherwise fantasized need to assert that it had or could. But in this passage and others like it, Campo manages to frame his narrative of gay love and marriage in such a way that it both issues directly from the family history he's already set about retelling and becomes the governing factor in determining whatever direction the story will take from this point on.

In the memoir Campo insists on tracing his and Jorge's conjugal journey as only ever in process, often but not always in progress, and therefore never arriving anywhere with any finality but always at least tending toward some powerfully imagined, if always necessarily deferred, destinations:

> We created our own country of origin, crossed oceans to our own undiscovered continent, wrote anthems for our own America the Fabulous. We planned to create a new life together in blissful harmony in Cuba some day—the choice of that most impossible and unimaginable of all locations was not exactly accidental—reclaiming my grandfather's lost plantation as our own, liberating it from the centuries of both capitalist and communist oppression. We would invent our own utopian political system, we would make idealistic lyrics like Martí's the law of the land. We who belonged neither to Spain nor to the United States, but to one another.[22]

One of course has to wonder how much license to allow the poet when it comes to squaring his assertion of property rights to his "grandfather's lost plantation" with his rejection of those "centuries of both capitalist and communist oppression," but clearly Campo's only purpose here is to queer, and to pervert, not only the conventional fantasy of exile return and restitution but any merely political

fantasy regarding Cuba's possible futures, and especially as functions
of any of the prevailing (and often conflicting) official versions of its
past. Thus the "Poem in Jorge's Voice" (number fourteen in the "Song
for My Lover") anticipates the passage just quoted from the memoir
in declaring, for both of them, that "We've always known together
was the place,/The only place, from which we'd walk on earth/Alive.
We have no other homelands . . . ," and that last reproach applies not
only to the decidedly unfabulous "America" that manages with every
electoral cycle to invent new ways to restrict the rights of its queer citizens but also to the other national cultures of origin they might
more fully want to embrace. Because the poem concludes, "It is," after
all, "a Latin custom to disown/The only things you love, the people
who/Remind you of the places you can't go,/The children whom you
never really owned," then the only recourse left to such queer and exiled children (sons in this case) is to embrace one another more fully
and together declare, "We are each other's father now," as well as (one
might add) each other's fatherlands.

Campo's "Song for My Lover" activates two additional features relevant to the larger cycle of which it is the arguable pivot if not center;
one is a more explicit and intense recourse to descriptions of gay sex
and the other is a definitive turn toward the temporal mode of the
"future-perfect tense," especially as it concludes by invoking the figure
of the imagined "Son" to whom the "Song" to follow will be dedicated.
Campo makes the explicit connection between having queer sex and
building queer pseudo nations in another set of parallel passages from
both the memoir and the verse collection. In the former, Campo concludes the threaded narrative of his own evolving acceptance of queer
sexuality on both the personal and political levels as a coming to terms
with the basic fact that queer *sex* remains the irreducible sine qua non
of all attempts, friendly or hostile, to make anything more than sexual
(that is, anything political or cultural) out of queerness per se:

I realized that our sexual acts are among the few scraps of identity that we do own, that we must own. The kiss that locates us
on the map of the known world, the interlocking legs that are
the sextant pointing the way home, the renewing embrace that

does not transmit HIV—even if they do not make up our identities entirely, we must give them to ourselves freely and without remorse or encumbrances.[23]

The poet does not, of course, arrive at this striking conclusion regarding the relationship between what we do and what we are on his own, but with the help, and as the result, of many forms of interaction (and intercourse) with other people. These certainly include patients with HIV and AIDS whom Campo has treated and come to know over the years, but at least in the context of the "Song" cycle under scrutiny here, his chief interlocutor in this process of realization has been his lover. It should be clear at this point that Campo is an accomplished ventriloquist, having cast so many of the lyrics already under discussion in the voices of the people to whom they're dedicated and often addressed; that dynamic too intensifies in the poems dedicated to Jorge. Witness the sixth and seventh entries in the "Song for My Lover," entitled, respectively, "Our Country of Origin" and "He Interprets the Dream," where in the former the poet confesses to his lover that he's "dreaming geographically these days," having recently in one such dream "found our island home./My finger traced a slick, gigantic globe/Atilt in its mahogany while days/Flashed by because I spun the world so fast." This prompts in the lover the following interpretation:

The globe that you're exploring represents
My body. I'm the island—look at me,
How much I'm like your island . . .
              . . . it's clear
You want the earth to fuck you everywhere,
The way I do, to raise you from yourself,
Transport you there—I'm here, you mustn't be
Afraid. I'm resting like an island, home
Upon this sea of sheets . . .

This erotic geography lesson thus confirms the logic of the argument that Campo makes in the memoir regarding queer acts and queer states; it's what we do as bodies and with (other) bodies that situates us, practically and symbolically, on all available maps and thereby gives us what currency we might have to circulate, with or without restriction, through all available worlds.

This lesson, in addition, bears both a spatial and a temporal logic; it opens out not only in terms of the localizing dynamics of "here," and of "home," and of the various possible forms of transport, displacement, and expulsion from them, but also in terms of the temporalizing dynamics of "now," especially in a world (or on a "globe") "spun . . . so fast" that "days/Flash . . . by" and propel us both further away from a past we bear irresistibly with us and toward a future into which we're always (and only ever) waiting to be born. Or, in Campo's case, fantasizing an access into that future through two very elaborately imagined scenarios of child rearing, one immediately following the "Song for My Lover" in the form of a "Song for Our Son," which itself concludes with a piece entitled "The Daughter of Our Imagination," which in turn opens onto an additional "Song," this time for "Our Daughter," this last of which does not appear until the publication of the poet's second verse collection, *What the Body Told*, three years later in 1996. These last two "Songs" both complete and complicate beyond all resolution the narrative line begun back in "Guantánamo," the first lyric in the poet's "Song for My Grandfather"; that line necessarily and strategically breaks with the "Song for My Lover," both because what follows it cannot simply, logically continue on the path from past historical fact, not as it launches into an only ever imaginable future, and also because, as Campo himself declares in the memoir, "I look like the hybrid that I am. Like most hybrids I will never reproduce. I am toxic to my own dreams and aspirations; in my veins run both the promise of a better life and its incessant denial."[24] In what remains of this critical, exegetical engagement of Campo's queer genealogical song cycle, I hope to demonstrate how the poet does more (and other) than indulge conventional sentimentality in invoking the figures of these imagined children (always, in America, the figurative and necessary embodiment of every other clichéd expectation summoned up by the "promise of a better life"), especially as he challenges himself, and his readers, to imagine any possible queer, and Cuban, future, and in an America that, after the turn of the twentieth into the twenty-first century, appears bent on legislating the former out of all existence and appears increasingly to have forgotten that the latter exists at all.

Campo's "Song for My Lover" concludes with a poem entitled "Sonnet for Our Son," thus preparing the reader for the "Song" to follow and its ambivalently futurized temporal orientation, with some odd temporal play of its own. It anticipates a pointed interrogation of the couple's motives for having had or adopted children with a series of possible explanations: "Perhaps/We wanted . . . to ensure/That someone loved us at the end. Perhaps/We wanted children simply to defend/Whichever arguments/They'd make to shock the world." It concludes, however, by shifting out of the mixed temporal mode of the twice-enjambed "Perhaps/We wanted" phrase in favor of the starkly present, and frank, concession (on the poet's part) that "I can't explain the edge/Of people's understanding, why it stops/Where we begin." This admitted incapacity to explain what frankly has no explanation does not, however, prohibit the poet from embarking nevertheless on the project of imagining as fully as he can the lives of the only children he might ever bear. In the "Song for Our Son," many of the pieces pose familiar if abstract arguments regarding gay parenting and gay adoption: the second (entitled "Adoption"), for example, declares that "It means, especially for us, the state/Decides if we deserve what we're denied"; and in the sixth ("My Brother's Opinion") the couple hear from a supposedly otherwise sympathetic (straight) source, "the bottom line is that you guys/Are different. No matter how hard you try— . . . —you can't/Be us." In others the poet imagines fairly predictable changes in the couple's life, like falling out of the social circles of other gay men (in the tenth piece, "Gay Parents Are Neither") and taking their son to a "Gay Freedom Parade" (the twelfth piece), where the chief lesson learned is that "the innocence in all things gay/Belongs to every people. Even us."

And if gays are a "people" to whom the son will learn (or not) to belong (whether or not he turns out to be gay himself) because of his upbringing, so too Cubans in America are a people to whom that same son will only learn (or not) to belong, presumably because of the same upbringing. So even before imagining the trip to the "Gay Freedom Parade," the poet also imagines, in "I Take Our Son to Cuba" (the eleventh piece), a voyage that both continues and transforms the complex meditation on his "patriarchal past" that this discussion has been tracing. This imagined voyage does not, in fact, dramatize anything to do with what the poet's son might discover there because the only son who really matters in the piece is the poet himself. "My island," the poet tells the boy, "I inherited/From men who gave me all I need but confidence/In who I am." This admission effectively aborts the project of carrying past this point any further cultivation of the boy's *cubanidad*, given the queer poet's acknowledgment of his own incomplete and therefore ineffective inheritance of a patriarchal legacy that both worships his masculinity and condemns his homosexuality: "And so it is," he goes on, "the dance/We do for those we love, for them, for them/We'll never know. I want to know the tree/That's poisonous . . . the one where sons/Discover who their fathers are, and speak." These lines explain most directly why the "son" to whom they're dedicated barely manages to appear in any fully embodied form in any of the poems that make up this "Song"; the poet 's overwhelming identification with that son, with his logical function as substitute and foil for himself (and even as he himself functions as placeholder in an ongoing patriarchal line the knowledge of which turns out to be "poisonous"), depletes the poet of any remaining imaginative resources for completing the family picture he'd set out to paint.

He drops the whole endeavor of imagining a life for his son even before the "Song" to him is over, declaring in the fourteenth piece (entitled "The Sonnet After This Must Wait") that "This fantasy is ending here: a ledge/One page away from where my heart begins," and that although "These sonnets hold/The world for me, the world I want to sing/Like lullabies to him," those actual songs will have to wait for some actual child to inspire them. Perhaps because a son, one who might someday "issue forth from me, and fill the void/I'm leaving in this world" will also necessarily continue the masculine and patriarchal line sustained through the present and through the poet himself, all he can do in refusing to imagine that child further is make the assertion, for better or worse, that "with this" *not* imagined "boy—/The future hurts—another promise comes." And because that "promise" will only ever be fulfilled (if at all) in reality, it remains beyond imagination, and beyond representation, for any purpose to which the poet might want to put it. Campo does not, however, drop his reproductive project completely at this point; instead, he opts for a different fantasy, one that allows him some greater space of disidentifying opportunity to imagine an alternative child, one who allows him to resist better the pull of gendered succession because she is *not* a boy.

It will, in fact, be "Elise," the "Daughter of My Imagination" first named in the penultimate poem ("Afterthought") of the "Song for Our Son," who will not only rise from the ashes of what turned out to be the poet's burning rejection of both his "patriarchal past" and any likely patriarchal future (because any such future "hurts") but who will outlive the fantasy of that "Song" entirely, to reappear quite dramatically in a "Song" all her own in the poet's subsequent volume. As with the "Song for Our Son," this new "Song for Our Daughter" also devotes its attention to a variety of issues regarding especially the politics of parenting, but here they're less trained on sexual than on cultural politics. This daughter, for example, inherits what traces remain of her father's *cubanidad* through a rather attenuated relationship to some of the culture's more domestic (and traditionally feminine) characteristics. A poem (tenth) in the sequence entitled "Rice and Beans" observes that preparing the Cuban national side dish is not only not "women's work to her," it's also "not/A culture anymore" because "she hasn't got/A grandmother" as the poet had "whose Cuban appetite/To serve her husband rice and beans each night, . . . was more like starving." Beyond that, the daughter (in being herself adopted and hence not sharing any "inborn" racial or cultural traits with her parents) will have other cultural minefields to navigate in an increasingly post-identitarian America; here, the poet, tells us, "Identity,/Disguised as fortress—worse, immunity—/Is what both parents and their children kill/Each other to possess." But in his daughter the poet spots embodied if not articulated a more-than-viable answer to the question, "Who are we?" when, in looking to her, he notices first that she is "woman, black,/Pure African (we cannot give her back)/American," but then, and much more importantly given all the domestic arrangements that matter in this intimate scene, that "she's left her door ajar." That open door is really all the poet can offer to indicate here some better, alternative version of the future that in "Song for Our Son" devolved into the "promise" posed by the son, whose advent could only entail the foreboding observation that "the future hurts." As he concludes this quite literally epic cycle of poems to his family and its now-perverted, no longer quite so patriarchal, line, the poet reveals that what there has been of a (pro-)creative and (re-)productive "cycle" in that sequence has actually been the product of his intimate collaboration with a feminine version of himself, at once his daughter and his muse. The last poem in the last "Song" of this six-"Song," ninety-six-poem opus is entitled (passively) "The Choice Was Never Made" and is again an imperfect sixteen-line "sonnet." The poem appears here almost in its entirety and serves as the conclusion to this part of my discussion of Campo:

> She tells me what to write, and how to say
> I want a son, although a daughter is
> The part of me my parents didn't want.
> I want a son the way my father can't
> Pretend he never wanted me: because
> We want to love my grandfather, because
> My grandfather was unattainable.
> Because my father's unavailable,
> My daughter must exist in me. She does
> Her cartwheels inside my heart for guys
> She thinks are cute. She writes her poetry
> Inside my ears. She wears like fantasy
> My wedding dress. She's happy, and I'm gay.

The Birth of the (Poet-)Clinician

In addition to the explorations of the paterfamilial dimension of the Cuban-diasporic experience that mostly take up the argument of this chapter, Campo has also (as I briefly mentioned earlier) explored in equal depth and seriousness his experience as an out gay doctor (a specialist in internal medicine) committed to treating people with AIDS. I want to explore that aspect of his work briefly here, if only to contextualize more fully the poet's meditations on queer cultural and biological reproduction by reading them alongside his meditations on the interplay of life and death, of vitality and morbidity, in his medical work (both in practice and in writing). I begin this part of my discussion by putting the theorist Michel Foucault in direct dialogue with another poet, Percy Bysshe Shelley, because particular gestures in the work of both Foucault and Campo point back to certain important cultural and intellectual traditions for which Shelley's opening argument to his famous essay in "defense" of poetry can arguably serve as touchstone. There Shelley argues as follows:

According to one mode of regarding those two classes of mental action, which are called reason and imagination, the former may be considered as mind contemplating the relations borne by one thought to another, however produced; and the latter, as mind acting upon those thoughts so as to colour them with its own light, and composing from them, as from elements, other thoughts, each containing within itself the principle of its own integrity. The one is the *to poiein*, or the principle of synthesis, and has for its objects those forms which are common to universal nature and existence itself; the other is the *to logizein*, or the principle of analysis, and its actions regard the relations of things, simply as relations; considering thoughts, not in their integral unity, but as the algebraical representations which conduct to certain general results. Reason is the enumeration of quantities already known; imagination is the perception of the value of those quantities, both separately and as a whole. Reason respects the differences, and imagination the similitudes of things. Reason is to Imagination as the instrument to the agent, as the body to the spirit, as the shadow to the substance.[25]

Foucault, for his part, modifies the intellectual dialectic that Shelley organizes here between Enlightenment analysis and Romantic

synthesis to accommodate an account of a specifically medical knowledge, and wisdom. "Medicine," he tell us,

> offers man the obstinate, yet reassuring face of his finitude; in it,
> death is endlessly repeated, but it is also exorcized; and although
> it ceaselessly reminds man of the limit that he bears within him,
> it also speaks to him of that technical world that is the armed,
> positive, full form of his finitude . . . in this culture, medical
> thought is firmly engaged in the philosophical status of man.[26]

Both Foucault and Campo, I would argue, arrive from vastly different
directions at the same conclusion, that considerations of language are
indispensable to any intellectual and/or artistic engagement with the
more conventionally scientifically construed phenomenon of disease.
Although Foucault could not at the time of writing *The Birth of the
Clinic* have known how his analysis of the general operations of language would condition the specific discursive formations generated
in response to the historical phenomenon of AIDS, Campo's strategically poetic interventions into this discursive field offer at least one
valuable example of certain possibilities for reforming our understanding of medical knowledge and the experience of disease one
finds already half analyzed, and half imagined, in Foucault's work.

What Foucault effectively does in the conclusion to *The Birth of the
Clinic,* and what Campo professes he hopes to perform in his poetry,
is to put the lie to the paradigmatic romantic opposition of reason to
imagination so famously laid out in Shelley's essay. In some ways,
Shelley could have cooperated more in this regard if, instead of opposing poetic to logical thinking as irreconcilable modes of human
mental action, he'd opposed *poesis* and *tekhne* as the more conventionally and frequently polarized nodes of active human making; he
at least nods toward this latter dichotomy in the analogy he draws between reason as instrument and imagination as agent, an especially
helpful (and logical, I might add) relation if one is to explore further
the intricacies of the relation between what agency one might want to
ascribe to poetic imagination and its reliance on not only some blunt
instrument but on some generally available instrumentality enabled

by reason, a general "technicity" as ascribable not merely to reason but to language in ways that are as legitimately the purview of poetry as of technical medical knowledge.

Foucault signals, and Campo performs, the deconstruction of this symptomatically romantic discursive opposition in his continuation of the argument already cited. In a discussion occasioned by a mention of Hölderlin that could as readily have been made with Shelley, Foucault asserts,

> In what at first might seem a very strange way, the movement that sustained lyricism in the nineteenth century was one and the same as that by which man obtained positive knowledge of himself; but is it surprising that the figures of knowledge and those of language should obey the same profound law, and that the irruption of finitude should dominate, in the same way, this relation of man to death, which, in the first case, authorizes scientific discourse in rational form, and, in the second, opens up the source of a language that unfolds endlessly into the void left by the absence of the gods?[27]

Foucault's question here is hardly or exclusively rhetorical; he answers it himself in the last paragraph of the book when he observes the deep paradox at the heart of all post-Enlightenment discourse: "When one carries out a vertical investigation of this positivism," he concludes, "one sees the emergence of a whole series of figures—hidden by it, but also indispensable to its birth—that will be released later, and, paradoxically used against it";[28] prominent among these antipositivist "figures" for Foucault is all post-Kantian phenomenology, a movement certainly fueled in the literary realm by the kind of romantic idealism, the proto-theological spiritualism embodied in the figures of, and in a figure like, Percy Shelley. And although Shelley may not loom as the most technophobic of the tradition thus constituted, he certainly had, especially through the legacy of his essay, as much as anyone else to do with establishing and maintaining the bias against mere rational positivism as long as it continued to embrace solely the empirical solidity, and attendant mortality, of the body as opposed to the possibilities of the indefinite if not infinite spiritual vitality onto whose promise secular-humanist postromantic poetry so stubbornly held (and holds).

One need only look around today to find something of this proto-romantic personalism still at work in even the vast majority of AIDS poetry; a study still needs to be done of the manner in which technology and technique both play into the formation of a discourse one might call the body of poetic responses to AIDS, especially as those elements are generally presumed to obstruct the urgent human need to make AIDS poetry work as either an immediate (and unmediated) cry of pain, a call to action, or both. No one, certainly not I, would in their right minds fault the legitimacy and necessity of such a response; no one, certainly not I, would in their right minds discount the effect of poetic practice as either personal therapy or political intervention. But the fact is that neither of these ends requires that the means toward their realization be poetry. For this reason it can be troubling that what oftentimes is easily dismissed, often even made suspect, in studies of AIDS poetry is precisely poetic technique and just as often any mention of the discourse of AIDS emanating from the clinical, impersonal practices of medical technology. Most AIDS poetry explores the experience from the perspective of the mourner or the person living with AIDS; Campo's work, in contrast, offers us the unique opportunity to imagine the experience from the perspective of the technician, the medical doctor trained to intervene into and to lessen the suffering of his patients by virtue of both his compassion and his technical knowledge, and to have the experience rendered in the technical language of a literary form that (more often than not in the past two centuries) has held that technicity in deep suspicion if not contempt. Far, by the way, from being an apologist for a profession whose failures in responding to AIDS as a medical crisis still outnumber its successes, Campo exploits his medical training to refine into admirable precision the language in which he casts both his observations about his own medical work and his pointed criticisms of the professional culture in which he performs it.

Unlike noted poets like Mark Doty, Paul Monette, and Essex Hemphill, who choose freer lyrical forms, Campo aligns himself more closely with Thom Gunn in his adherence to the more technical demands of verse; but in more meaningful ways Campo's literary investments extend, as we have already seen, well beyond the immediate context of contemporary AIDS poetry to include especially traditional practitioners of the sonnet and other short verse forms, including Shelley himself. Campo's many sonnet-based short-form variations bear within them the mark of a poet who understands that traditional lyrical forms can still today offer readers some access to the body, especially as source and origin of the material "sonority" from which these forms derive their names. The sonnet, traditionally the most efficient of the major poetic forms designed to explore emotional and other complex forms of experience in compressed verbal space and structure, can in its performative operations be said to "sound" those experiences in ways analogous to what the ultrasound examination can today produce as the sonogram, the sound image or sound writing of the body's internal contours, its regular and pathologically irregular properties and functions. One can say, indeed, that the sonnet has through its techniques for centuries performed an exploration and writing of subjective interiority that is only recently commensurably emulated in the sonogrammatic articulation of the objective body's interior.

To this extent, the ultrasound even more than the X-ray, makes literal a radical reorientation between seeing and sounding, between the gaze and its verbal articulation, than the transformation in the production of medical knowledge that Foucault ascribes to a certain revolution in the procedures of medical examination in the late eighteenth century; then, Foucault argues, "the relation between the visible and the invisible . . . changed its structure, revealing through the gaze and language what had previously been below and beyond their domain. A new alliance was forged," concludes Foucault, "between words and things, enabling one to see and to say."[29] One can already sense here the approach of a more productive (and deconstructive) synesthesia than any the romantic poetic mind could have imagined; we now can "hear" our way to a visual image and can at the same time more deeply problematize the conventional opposition (which these two formerly opposed senses used to authorize) between interior and exterior. We now can, in other words, through a "sounding," literally *see* physical interiority in ways that previously only promised a communication of psychic interiority, and that latter chiefly through discursive and specifically literary techniques that belied their own exterior materiality in promising figurative access to the "inside" of the spirit, mind, or heart of the subject offered to us as lyrical, confessional poet/speaker.

It bears noting at least in passing here that even the most familiar use to which ultrasounds are nowadays put, the discovery of a fetus's anatomical sex, puts into even further relief just how far this technology goes to dismantle traditional conceptions of not only seeing and hearing, inside and outside, but also how access to one interiority only exposes another exteriority, allowing us to "gender" bodies well before birth by exposing them to the general cultural regimes of sexed difference well before they're even exposed to light.[30] It comes as no surprise, then, that an individual as concerned about the exploration of interior states that are at once physical and psychoemotional should, as Campo has done, not only chosen poetry and medicine as complementary professions but should at the same time find himself committed to maintaining their mutual and reciprocal intercontamination; even among medical subfields, Campo's choice of general internal medicine over diagnostic radiology suggests that he would always have found some way to maintain his fascination with the vexed border between our insides and our outsides. Campo's fascination with that border and the unique capacity poetry has to occupy it informs much of what Campo has to say about his twin professions in *The Poetry of Healing*. In a chapter specifically on "AIDS and the Poetry of Healing," Campo presents his own version of a "defense" of poetry, especially of formal poetry, as a vital instrument in his own coming to terms with his complex relationships to both language and the body, both his doctor's language and his poet's language, both his queer, seronegative body and the symptomatic bodies of his seropositive patients, not all queer, but all mortal and ailing.

In that essay Campo presents what can be termed as simultaneously a politics, a poetics, and a technology of the related practices he professes. "I wrote a sonnet not long ago," he reports, "that I devised to be a sort of contraption, a spring-locked box . . . a condom made of words";[31] never specifying which sonnet he means, Campo leaves open the possibility that this description may apply to any one of a number of sonnets devoted to the topic of AIDS or, indeed, to the even larger number of sonnet-style poems of varying length that populate his work. One in the first collection, a thirteen-line lyric entitled "Technology and Medicine,"[32] describes the doctor's metamorphosis into the instruments of his practice as concurrent with the poet's transformation into the instruments of his; in each case, the transference of identification from subject to object enables in turn a transference of identification from one subject to another, from doctor to patient and from poet to reader. The truncated sonnet reports this unquestionably "imaginative" alchemy in intimate first person, speaking therefore at once from the "position" of the sonnet and of the various and analogous tools of the doctor's trade: "My eyes," it reads, "Are microscopes and cathode X-ray tubes/In one, so I can see bacteria,/Your underwear, and even through to bones./My hands are hypodermic needles, touch/Turned into blood: I need to know your salts/And chemistries, a kind of intimacy/That won't bear pondering. It's more than love." This excess of love might be compared to a kind of Keatsian negative capability, a paradoxical capacity to be, indeed, capacious, to open in oneself a space into which the other might be allowed in, a space perhaps traditionally identified as sympathy's, perhaps even desire's, home, and one that counters the conventional reading of such instruments of medical perception, diagnosis, and treatment as those named by the poem as primarily invasive and threatening. Certainly the eroticization of these exploratory procedures contributes to this counterreading and contributes to the reading the poem invites us to make of it; namely, that by naming the poem "Technology and Medicine," it encourages us to look at poetry as in its own way fulfilling the functions of technology *and* medicine.

But "Technology and Medicine" performs perhaps too interpenetrative a poetic act to be said to qualify as the verbal prophylaxis Campo describes in his essay. He may instead refer to any one of a trio of sonnets that thread their way through the second collection and punctuate a narrative of gay desire, risk, and trust imbedded in the text of that collection. The sonnets bear the titles "Before Safe Sex," "Safe Sex," and "After Safe Sex," and they bear as well a testimony to the poet's simultaneous discoveries of desire, poetry, and death.[33] "Before Safe Sex" relates the poet's discovery of Sappho's works and with that discovery the related one of his own sexuality: "I found an unknown fragment," the poet tells us, "really,/Stripped from inside a mummy's thigh. 'Kiss me,'/It began, and that was all. I began/To write, to kiss a man so my copy/Would be right . . . But something stopped me—/ . . . when I say his hips,/My cock—Sappho my strength!—my tongue is tied/In an excruciating knot." "Safe Sex" compensates for the prophy-lactic interruption of coitus in the "knotting" of the tongue by bring-ing contact to fulfillment and, paradoxically, by confessing to the failure of prophylaxis. In the second poem, the beloved has also been transformed from a distant, inaccessible third person to the more inti-mate, available, and proximate second: "Protected in your arms, I dreamed while death/Passed overhead," it opens, and it continues with a report of deepening, but ever riskier love:

We fell in love
When love was not protection in itself;
Misled by poetry, I'd always felt
The pleasures of the tongue were very safe.
Before your urgent, pleading face I knelt
To say your love had come to represent
In me a willingness to die. You came
Inside my mouth, and eagerly death bent
Its ear to listen to my heart. The same
Astonishment without restraint sang out—
Protected in your arms, I died of doubt.

Medicine actually makes a sinister appearance here alongside poetry; if "the pleasures of the tongue" denote both oral sex and oral song, then the "death ben[ding] its ear to listen to [the poet's] heart" as a re-sult of his having, in swallowing his lover's cum, given himself too readily to "the pleasures of the tongue" does so much like an attentive physician. "Safe Sex Revisited" closes the narrative by making explicit what has only been introduced figuratively in the second poem. The poet writes "in retrospect" about the moment of his risky brush with love and death, asking with a newfound wisdom, "What is love without the risk of some/Catastrophe to be someday relived?" and from that wisdom turning to an active, even activist prophylaxis, one that both finally explicitly names AIDS as the chief cause of his mortal risk and implicitly begins to perform the simultaneously poetical, political, and medical interventions against it: "I've learned/A power," he tells us, "to protect myself from AIDS./I call it "Poetry of the Absurd."/ . . . The virus tries/To penetrate, but I write poetry/And so it finds no place to multiply—/My blood cells are replaced by words for 'bleed,'/ My penis is a pen with which I write/These contradictions."

Although the "Safe Sex" triptych contains less of the technical language of medicine than one finds in other poems (like "Prescription" or "Antidote") collected in *What the Body Told,* it certainly presents itself as the most evocative example of the conflation of Campo's many professions. It allows for the most explanatory and decisive reading of the simultaneous erotic, aesthetic, and effective operations of a poetry too thoroughly involved in the specific life world from which it emanates to be dismissed as having isolated itself from that world through the vagaries or rarefactions of form. Technique in this case is emphatically not Campo's prophylactic, his artistic guard against worldly contagion, but his therapeutic instrument and his weapon in the struggle for change. "Formal poetry," he tells us in the memoir, "holds the most appeal for me because in it are present the fundamental beating contents of the body at peace . . . The poem is a physical process, is bodily exercise: rhymes become the mental resting places in the ascending rhythmic stairway of memory," and as such formal poetry ultimately reembodies the body itself, perverting if not violating its own deepest orthodoxy by confusing the vital and constitutive distinction between the figurative and the literal: "If poetry is made of breath, or the beating heart," Campo explains, "then surely it is not unreasonable to think it might reach those places in the bodies of its audience, however rarefied."[34] So poetry, more than an instrument, becomes at once a space and a body of erotic, aesthetic, and therapeutic contact that, in enabling this complex set of possibilities, renders each and every one of the subjects it addresses, solicits, and seduces into its readers, its lovers, and its patients.

AIDS, as it happens, is thus not an opportunity Campo poetically exploits so much as a critical, urgent challenge, one to whose occasion he rises as both doctor and poet. "In ravaging our collective immunity," he concludes, "in literally wearing its victims down to the bones, AIDS by its very existence makes the naked body that much more clearly delineated . . . [and thus] The spoken word becomes that much more urgent and honest, the poem that much more purely language."[35] And at the same time that he acknowledges "that most of the interventions Western medicine makes available to AIDS patients have their basis in scientific principles," Campo also insists that he "can compare the feeling of placing an endotracheal tube in a patient in respiratory distress only to the feeling of writing about the experience afterward."[36] As we turn now to the concluding section of this larger examination of Campo's work, I want to underscore the way in which Campo's simultaneous explorations of the birth cycles of his queered Cuban American genealogical line and of the mounting tally of deaths from AIDS in the United States mutually inform one another. The two, of course, are not mutually exclusive; Reinaldo Arenas and the AIDS activist Pedro Zamora, for example, represent two of the many queer Cubans in America to have been afflicted and to have died because of AIDS. To the extent that Campo's work synthesizes, rather than alternates between, the nostalgic, elegiac, and actively (and activist) erotic modes of poetic lyricism, it fulfills the promise and the threat of the "hybridity" that he ultimately claims (and which I have already observed) at the conclusion of the memoir, an always paradoxical, constitutively ironic, and ironizing hybridity, one that compels him to declare, "I am toxic to my own aspirations and dreams; in my veins run both the promise of a better life and its incessant denial." It would be Campo's position, I think, that his queerness runs "in [his] veins" as much as his *cubanidad* does, and in addition that one is inextricable from the other and together they do not reinforce or stabilize but instead productively complicate and problematize whatever always-interested claims to "simple" identity anyone might want to make for him and for his work.

The (No) Future Hurts

The penultimate entry in Campo's "Song for My Lover," discussed at length earlier in this chapter, is a lyric entitled "Political Poem," and it reads in part as follows:

> . . . When
> Your lover dies, a victim of their hate,
> You must extend your hand, pretend
> To be like them. You must believe. You must
> Forget. You must. To write political poems,
> You must, you *can* create a world which seems
> Both unattainable and not unjust.

I open my closing section here with it to touch on the argument with which the entire chapter actually began, in the epigraph from Lee Edelman's *No Future: Queer Theory and the Death Drive* on the relationship between the discursive constitution of the political field as such, the presumption in almost any conceivable political vision of what Edelman calls "reproductive futurism," and the compelling task before queer theory, and before what there must (still, and ever) be of a queer politics, as we pass beyond the middle of the first full decade of the twenty-first century. Edelman's bracing polemic on the necessity for queer theory of resisting and in fact rejecting the prevailing cultural presumption ensuring the centrality of the abstracted figure of the Child as embodiment of all imaginable and therefore possible versions of a society's future strikes me as essential to any discussion (like the one I have been conducting here) of how even cultures as marginal and compromised as Cuban (or gay) America's nevertheless manage to invoke such powerful, and powerfully abstracted, figures of fully potentialized childhood in managing their own likely survivals within a larger body politic to which they remain primarily (and dangerously) expendable. This clearly helps explain the variously obsessive responses to such images as those I've traced here on the part of José Martí (for his own son) and of both Fidel Castro and his exile enemies (for Elián González). Certainly both Sylvia Molloy's and Sarah Banet-Weiser's theoretically informed analyses of these respective obsessions connect quite productively with the more developed (and more explicitly queered) analysis offered by Edelman.

Edelman accepts in *No Future* the risk of appearing to be antichild, but this is not to him the same as being anti-Child. The latter, what he calls "the image of the Child as we know it," is an exclusively discursive, symbolic element, one so central and familiar to any group, society, or culture that it immediately produces the effect of a naturalness that just as immediately obscures its status as image, as figure, as artifice. As such, however, this image stands "as the very figure of politics, because [it is] also . . . the embodiment of futurity collapsing undecidably into the past."[37] This abstracted image of the Child, precisely because of its constitutive abstraction, enables a group in any present moment to convince itself that the image not only consolidates whatever versions of its own past (that is, of its history) it wants to use to condition, and to project onto, whatever version of its future it wants to use to justify how it conducts itself, politically, in that *present* moment, which is all it actually ever occupies, knows, or has. "Historically constructed," Edelman tells us, "to serve as the repository of variously sentimentalized cultural identifications, the Child has come to embody for us the *telos* of the social order and come to be seen as the one for whom that order is held in perpetual trust."[38]

It is of course this powerful teleological function that compelled Martí to fantasize from his own paternal, patrimonial vision a bracing, and bracingly eroticized, democratic order fulfilling not only Cuba's but the entire hemisphere's democratic promise; this is also the function that allowed the most profoundly interpellated of all Cuban-exile subjects to see in Elián González the embodiment of their own political and historical redemption while at the same time he could figure for Fidel Castro the inevitability of his own revolution's indefinite (if not infinite) continuation. So long, therefore, as (in Edelman's words) this "figural Child alone embodies the citizen as an ideal, entitled to claim full rights to its future share in the nation's good," then queer citizens and certainly anyone else who refuses not only to identify with, but also to participate in, this "collective" and primarily but not exclusively symbolic "reproduction of the Child," will have to run the risk of being blamed for having succumbed to the "fatal lure of sterile narcissistic enjoyments understood as inherently destructive of meaning and therefore as responsible for the undoing of social organization, collective reality, and inevitable, life itself."[39] To embrace one's queerness as the condition that fundamentally exempts one from the mandates of this order of "reproductive futurism," Edelman concludes, requires a "determined opposition to this underlying structure of the political . . . to the governing fantasy of achieving symbolic closure through the marriage of identity to futurity in order to realize the social subject," and, as a further result, "the queer must insist on disturbing, on queering, social organization as such—on disturbing, therefore, and on queering, *ourselves* and our investment in such organization. For queerness," he goes on to insist, "can never define an identity; it can only ever disturb one."[40]

Although it's not at all clear that Rafael Campo fully activates to the degree to which Edelman would require the profoundly negative political operation of his own queerness, I would suggest that in the critical operations of the Song cycle discussed earlier he does at least attempt to reject, to the extent that he can and still remain within the conventional registers of especially literary legibility, the interpellative call of reproductive futurism in the way that he finally refuses to indulge in either a sentimentalized or idealized construction of the fantasy children he claims to imagine raising. The "Political Poem" quoted in the opening to the present discussion, especially because it immediately precedes the "Sonnet for Our Son" discussed earlier, does in part anticipate some aspects of the argument Edelman makes regarding the theoretical and practical stakes of a queer politics. Written in a second-person address to the reader, the poem makes no clear claim for where or how the poet might situate himself with regard to what it states; whether this is a formula for political engagement that the poet actually endorses or one he merely mimes in order to rehearse for the reader remains open for the latter's determination. How exactly the widowed partner, whose "lover dies, a victim of their hate," should then "extend your hand, negotiate/With those who say they understand, pretend/To be like them" remains unclarified, as does the relationship of that imperative statement to the ones that follow, the string of *you must*'s whose varied imperative offerings obey no effective logic ("You must believe. You must/Forget. You must.") except to the extent that they lead to the strategically open final proposition, which concludes little in its ambivalent arrival at the idea that all such "political poems" *can* do is "create a world which seems/Both unattainable and not unjust."

This is certainly no propitious conclusion with which to leave us, especially just as the poet is about to embark on so elaborate a fantasy of potentially redemptive reproduction. But it does, I think, provide us with the proper frame in terms of which to read that fantasy, not as an obsequious attempt to show reproductive heterosexuality how much the poet and his lover want to "pretend/To be like them" but exactly how much they don't want, or plan, to do so. In this refusal, I would argue, Campo demonstrates his appreciation of what Edelman calls "the efficacy of queerness, its real strategic value," which for him "lies in its resistance to a symbolic reality that only ever invests us as subjects insofar as we invest ourselves in it, clinging to its governing fictions, its persistent sublimations, as reality itself."[41] To this extent, Campo's realization in the memoir that "our [queer] sexual acts are among the few scraps of identity that we do own, that we must own," seems to square with his sense of the limited and risky efficacy of our ever "clinging" too fully to the "governing fictions" of any society organized primarily against (or without reference to) queer existence; this is also why, to the extent that what he considers "a brave, heartfelt" poem can articulate a queer politics at all, it does so only by virtue of its ability to constitute a "private space where the rhythms of ecstatic lovemaking can be felt without barriers . . . [a] place where anything can be said, where nothing like it has ever before been imagined."[42]

I hear in the negative construction of all that's potentially sayable in poetry (the "anything" that turns a phrase later into a "nothing like it") an echo of Campo's queerly skeptical attitude toward a future (poem, statement, act), which in "Political Poem" had already been articulated as the "world" he can only describe as both "unattainable and not unjust." This oddly nihilistic vision on the part of a poet who is so often accused of being merely sentimental leads me to conclude that Campo has both the capacity and the willingness to appreciate the potential in queerness, to "insist," as Edelman puts it, "on the negativity that pierces the fantasy screen of futurity, shattering narrative temporality with irony's always explosive force."[43] This logic does not apply merely to what we might want to isolate as a U.S.-based queer politics, although in Edelman's work there is no clear indication of how completely his analysis might be transported beyond a fairly Anglo American (and gay male) cultural sphere. It certainly has, however, some direct efficacy for the Cuban American diasporic cultural scene, especially as so many of its politicized queer cultural and literary producers have taken on the task of at least imagining, if not actively participating in, the conception or constitution of any viable Cuban American future. Campo's "Political Poem," then, may be said to have been strategically situated, in the context of the longer Song cycle, in order to rupture the narrative inevitability of any imagined Cuban American future that anyone might have wanted to read into the Songs for either his (merely) imagined "Son" or "Daughter." That conventional readerly expectation must give way, I want to argue in concluding here myself, to the queerly "explosive force" of the ironic double negative that allows the poet to posit for the children he does not have (and for all the "people" who might issue forth from them) a future world that can only ever "seem . . . both unattainable and not unjust."

Conclusion

On Our American Ground

[At] Guantánamo Bay, Cuba . . . contemporary empire building in the Middle East meets the history of imperialism in the Americas, pointing to an ominous transnational future. If homeland names a place that doesn't exist on a map, Guantánamo is a place for which there are no adequate names. Where is Guantánamo? In America, yes; in the United States, yes and no; in Cuba, well, sort of.

—Amy Kaplan[1]

Literary criticism is today unsatisfactory in its traditional forms and objects, and it can no longer claim the position it once held as arbiter of national culture. . . . Cultural Studies is apparently the new tool for hegemonic articulation. Literary criticism is powerless and cannot develop viable counterhegemonic strategies, and theory is in a similar situation. The problem of succession to the old is open, and it involves and interpellates us all.

—Alberto Moreiras[2]

My frequent half-joking response to the question, "What do you think will happen with Cuba once Fidel Castro dies?" was for a long time, "Nothing . . . compared to what's likely to happen when Celia

270

Cruz dies." Then, of course, she did die, in the summer of 2003, and for all the understandable grief with which Cubans, other Latinos, and salsa lovers everywhere very publicly mourned her, nothing (at least nothing political) came of her passing after a long and valiant battle against cancer. The half-serious side of my remark, of course, had to do with the fact that Celia embodied perhaps better than any other public figure the intensely contradictory conditions that the post-1959 diasporic experience had visited upon all Cubans who either chose or were chosen to undergo it. And, therefore, my thinking went, no other death would embody more poignantly the utter futility of the exile construction of post-1959 off-island Cuban existence; along with their very stagy farewell to Celia, wouldn't more of her fellow-exile Cubans, especially those with any power or influence over U.S. policy toward Cuba, want to bid farewell to those policies and to the exile fantasies that sustained them, given their utter failure in restoring their quasi-official cultural patroness to her homeland before her demise? Three years into the post-Celia moment in Cuban-diasporic history, the answer to that question remains a resounding and depressing "no."

This intransigency seems to me sadly disrespectful in part to Celia's own vision, if not in political then certainly in cultural terms, of a world where reified, naturalized categories of nation, race, and even gender gave way to the irresistible force of a cultural movement, or set of movements, that scarcely acknowledged let alone tolerated the conserving, paralytic demands based on the authority of these categories. I would take as my prime example of Celia's bracing transcultural optimism her appearance on Haitian-American hip-hop impresario Wyclef Jean's 1997 CD, *Carnival,* where she introduces listeners to a track entitled "Guantanamera." That title, of course, would immediately provoke an association with Celia's signature song, often performed and often recorded, the unofficial (post-)national anthem of all Cubans everywhere, whose lyrics, first written by José Martí in the late nineteenth century, were only decades later set to music and embellished with the chorus' invocations of a peasant woman, or *guajira,* from the eastern Cuban city of Guantánamo. Celia's own sung invocations of this *guajira Guantanamera* might be said to short-circuit the heteroerotics of the patriarchal nationalist desire, instituted (of course) by Martí, for a female, and darkly earthy, embodiment of the motherland; instead, she might be said to offer a kind of filial identification with, rather than an erotic longing for, the figure of a *guajira*, who (in Celia's rendering) might also be said to better exhibit her mixed-race status and thereby better symbolize Cuba in her embodied joining of all that nation's races and ethnicities.

Celia does not, however, appear among Wyclef's band of "Refugee All-Stars" merely to reproduce a performance that she's already recorded numerous times; instead, she only appears to ratify, and underwrite, the authenticity or legitimacy of a performance, also entitled "Guantanamera, " that will belong entirely to Wyclef. Celia introduces herself, declares her enthusiasm in joining the celebration of Wyclef's *carnaval,* sings the opening lines of the song as originally penned by Martí, yells her trademark ¡*Azucar*! then fades, gracefully and seamlessly, into and in favor of Wyclef's rap, which goes, and reads, in part as follows:

> Hey yo I'm standing at the bar, with a Cuban cigar
> Hey yo I think she's eyeing me from afar
> Yo, I wrote this in Haiti, overlooking Cuba
> I asked her what's her name, she said, "Guantanamera"
> Remind me of an old latin song, my uncle used to play
> On his old forty-five when he used to be alive . . .

Like most of his compositions, Wyclef's "Guantanamera" is busy and crowded, featuring an array of especially pop-cultural allusions (from Madonna to the Rose of Spanish Harlem) and concluding with a feminist rap by fellow-Fugee Lauryn Hill to complement his playfully salacious own. What Wyclef's track first stages as a sexual encounter between the male rapper and some female object of his desire telescopes pretty rapidly, however, into a meditation on, and critique of, the sexualization and fetishization of the woman of color in the American pop-cultural imaginary. Wyclef's disseminating appropriation of Martí's, and Celia's, and Cuba's, beloved Guantanamera, and his re-situation of that Guantanamera in a more explicitly

North American, trans-Caribbean, late twentieth-century context, does less, I would argue, to de-Cubanize her than to situate her diasporically in a manner that is perhaps more congruent with what I have tried to describe and analyze in these pages as the diasporic condition of some considerable part of especially the post–Cold War Cuban postnation.

I'm not exactly sure how any of the remaining members of the first and definitive Cuban-exile generation would respond to this appropriation by a black Haitian rapper with a political agenda that's decidedly different from their own, even with Celia's indelible stamp of approval. But that appropriation is anything but casual or expedient; couched in Wyclef's claim to have written his song "in Haiti, overlooking Cuba," the situation actually parallels Martí's own when, at the start of his final, fatal campaign to liberate Cuba from Spain in 1895, he spent time organizing that campaign in Haiti and keeping a diary that today stands as one of his most important, and importantly literary, compositions. In addition to the biographical parallel, I would want to suggest something of an ideological parallel as well. That is, if a statement as programmatic and still influential as Martí's famed 1891 essay "Our America" could be termed "the theory," then in some ways Wyclef Jean's transnational, polyvocal, and polymorphously critically perverse homage might be termed its most appropriate and appropriately congruent "practice." Wyclef's postnational "Guantanamera," according to this argument, no longer merely substitutes for Celia's, or anyone's, nationalist version of the same figure. She metamorphoses, instead, from Martí's "América," whose traditional allegorizing, fetishizing anthropomorphism he for the most part resists in that essay.

Indeed, if we follow the (free?) play of allusive associations from Wyclef's rap to Lauryn Hill's, we find an endless but not random and, ultimately, explicitly figural sequence of metamorphoses:

The lexicon of Lexington, parents came from Cuba
Part Mexican, pure sweet, dimes fell to her feet
She like Movado and move her hips like Delgado
And broke niggaz down from the Grounds to Apollo.

Thus in Wyclef and Hill's capable hands, "our" Guanatamera, like "our" America, finds herself as legitimately at home on the streets of Harlem as in the eastern provinces of Cuba. To this extent she might also be said to reappear two years later, in Wyclef Jean's much more commercially successful collaboration with Carlos Santana (on 1999's *Supernatural* CD), as the character in the song "Maria, Maria," who begins her career as the Puerto Rican heroine of *West Side Story* only to find herself forty years later surviving poverty and violence on the streets of East Los Angeles. Across at least these two songs, but really in all of his work, Wyclef Jean is clearly developing an extraordinary expressive practice out of his own diasporic experience, and it is a practice that pays significant homage to an American vision at least as old as Martí's essay and addresses an American challenge at least as current as the one formulated in Amy Kaplan's remarks, quoted in an epigraph to this conclusion, to the 2003 national meeting of the American Studies Association.

I have attempted in the course of this study to forge an idiom if not a program for the current and future elaboration of the national, the cultural, and the literary as increasingly vestigial, and increasingly ruinous, registers of experience, in part to address the challenge laid down by Alberto Moreiras in the other epigraph to this conclusion. Of these three, of course, "the cultural" may be the only one that promises anything like a viable afterlife that in any way resembles its past and traditional formations. Things don't look so rosy for a particular "modernist" formation of nationhood, and they look even less good for literature, even for the novel in its most unrecognizably postmodern and experimental of manifestations. This explains for the most part why I would never admit to have written a book "on Cuban-American literature," no matter how comforting all those terms can still be in their particular forms of cultural concretion. I've written instead (or at least I'll claim here) a study of "political and cultural erotics" as an expressive, strategic, and critical practice among a collection of writers, artists, and performers situated in an increasingly far-flung diaspora whose only defining feature is the retention of some relationship to a quality of *cubanidad* that has survived, culturally at least, from the heyday of the nation, of national cultures, national politics, and national conflict. And I have written it in part, I'll also claim, to demonstrate what some forward-looking derivative (or survivor) of an increasingly obsolete literary-cultural-critical practice might appear to do in the service of tracing at least the vestiges, and the ruins, of formerly national cultures, both in the current moment and in the moment(s), for better or worse, to come.

For Cubans, wherever they find themselves situated, I think the challenge certainly remains to think outside and beyond the parameters of the nation (and certainly of the nation-state) and of a unified national history and destiny, when considering what to do next about Cuba. Fidel Castro will die, and his Cuba will in part die with him; but that Cuba would die just as readily, if not more expeditiously, with the immediate, unilateral, and absolute lifting of the U.S. embargo, which has done nothing for almost fifty years except guarantee the stability of all Cubans, on and off the island, whose power is primarily if not exclusively the direct function of the maintenance of the national divide. But, as most people interested in the topic are beginning to realize, "change in Cuba" is far less likely to trigger an exodus of homesick exiles back to the island and instead will trigger a flood of immigrants from the island to the mainland, to join their relatively well-heeled relatives in South Florida and parts north and west. What we'll witness as a result of that eventuality isn't, therefore, some re-Cubanization of exiles, but an even more profound and complex Americanization, Latinoization, and diasporization of the culturally still-Cuban populace. At that point, even more than in the current moment, we'll certainly have to look elsewhere than Guantánamo for our most viable and compelling Guantanamera; she might still be found in Miami, but just as likely she'll be in Harlem, hanging in spirit with Celia, Wyclef, and Lauryn, or she might even be in East LA, not just with Wyclef and Carlos Santana, but with me, near where I grew up, and where I learned, and still love, to be Cuban, to be Latino, to be queer, and to be American.

Notes

Preface

1. Iyer sets his novel *Cuba and the Night* almost entirely in contemporary Havana. Iyer's protagonist, a U.S. photojournalist, observes that in Havana one may see history "in the unmaking"; there "history's on the pause button," making it "the only place . . . where everything's moving and nothing ever changes . . . like instant replay round the clock" (5). These observations lead him to the conclusion that, rather than hoping for social reconstruction after the Cold War, "Deconstruction seems to be more the Cuban way" (17). Iyer's strategic choice of terms here suggests he understands the larger historical analysis of the post–Cold War situation presented by Derrida in *Specters of Marx: The State of the Debt, the Work of Mourning, and the New International.* There Derrida articulates with some precision the quality of experience of this still dangerously undertheorized historical moment; this quality of experience, of being left behind, remaindered, spectralized, and even disappeared by a history purported to be finished, by the failure of an opposing set of historical and political promises, is one both Cubans on and off the island share. Certainly Fidel Castro's almost helpless naming of post–Cold War Cuba's "Special Period" begs to be read as a capitulation to historical aporia, but the equally hapless attempts of the United States to address either the "problem" of Cuban *balseros* in 1994 or the Elián Gonzalez fiasco in 2000 reveals its own incapacity to understand with any sympathy, let alone coherently theorize and produce policy regarding the larger historical and political "problem" of Cuba after the Cold War. See especially Derrida's discussion of interminably deferred historical promises (*Specters*, 65) and his later comment (which serves as an epigraph to this preface and will certainly haunt this entire book) that "Certain Soviet philosophers have told me in Moscow a few years ago: the best translation of *perestroika* was still 'deconstruction'" (*Specters*, 89).

2. And for this reason, according to the editors of an anthology entitled *Cuba, the Elusive Nation*, "the discourse on national identity, at least in the Cuban case, has been studied mostly from a literary perspective" (Fernández and Betancourt, 2).

3. Cabrera Infante, *Mea Cuba*, 248.

4. Cabrera Infante, *Tres Tristes Tigres*, 9. Available in an English translation "from the Cuban" as *Three Trapped Tigers*. Cabrera Infante's playful idiomatic *cubanidad* enlivens both his fiction and his nonfiction, almost all of which he has produced from his exile perch in Europe, first in Brussels and later in London.

5. An alternative, although I think complementary, attempt to characterize Caribbean writing generally can be found in the introductory chapter of Benítez-Rojo's *The Repeating Island: The Caribbean and the Postmodern Perspective*, 1–29. There Benítez-Rojo terms writing deriving from the Caribbean "as a *mestizo* text, but also as a stream of texts in flight, in intense differentiation among themselves and within whose complex coexistence there are vague regularities, usually paradoxical" (27). Although Benítez-Rojo speaks here of relations among literatures of the various nations and cultures of the region, his observation is just as apt when applied to the internal properties of any specific "national" literature. Certainly fine distinctions remain to be made between literature deriving directly from the island and that produced away from it, but in some cases (as we see with Reinaldo Arenas later), such a distinction will not account for what these supposedly disparate "Cuban" literatures might have in common or might have to say to each other in a common language.

6. Because my main concern in this book will be writers of Cuban descent who have lived for some significant period of time in the United States, I will not devote as much attention in this study to Cabrera Infante as I do to, say, Reinaldo Arenas. He will, however, contribute a number of the theoretical propositions that I hope to test in my own readings of Cuban American cultural figures. Two other writers similarly less emphasized in the present work but who will nevertheless bear mentioning are the poet Heberto Padilla, whose 1990 memoir, *Self-Portrait of the Other*, will explicitly inform my discussion of Cuban political imprisonment in chapter 2; Severo Sarduy, whose considerable contribution to the production of a Latin American literary and critical postmodernity will more generally inform my analyses throughout this book. Of Sarduy's work, see, for example, *Written on a Body* and *From Cuba with a Song*.

7. See Derrida's *Specters of Marx*, 65–75. In that long passage, Derrida provides a rich, provocative analytical frame with which to articulate with some precision the experience Cubans on and off the island have of being left behind, remaindered, spectralized, and even disappeared by, and with, a history purported to be finished by the failure of an opposing set of historical and political promises.

8. Bhabha, *The Location of Culture*. This book also owes an obvious, but mostly implicit, debt to Benedict Anderson's work in the revised edition of *Imagined Communities: Reflections on the Origin and Spread of Nationalism*.

9. Beyond its well-known relevance to the same Derridean deconstructive discourse with which this preface flirts, *aporia* as a rhetorical and logical concept describing either a practical or logical impasse both exceeds and predates that Derridean deployment and would in any case therefore offer itself as relevant to the ongoing discussion.

10. Bhabha, 140.

11. See Pérez-Firmat, *The Cuban Condition: Translation and Identity in Modern Cuban Literature,* 14.

12. In using this term I am taking my cues from both Susan Sontag, whose call for an erotics rather than a hermeneutics of art in *Against Interpretation* I attempt to answer in these readings, and Kutzinski, whose *Sugar's Secrets: Race and the Erotics of Cuban Nationalism* provides both historical and theoretical background for my own work here.

13. Benítez-Rojo, 23. Vera Kutzinski takes issue from a feminist standpoint with a number of readings of Caribbean and Cuban cultural texts by both Benítez-Rojo and Pérez-Firmat. See, for example, chapter 6 of *Sugar's Secrets,* "Sublime Masculinity," 163–98. By taking up the issue of erotics in the work of a number of women and queer artists in this book, I hope to extend somewhat further the conversation already under way among at least these three scholars.

14. Pérez-Firmat, *Life on the Hyphen: The Cuban-American Way,* especially the introduction and chapters 1 and 2. It would be incorrect to call Pérez-Firmat's work the point of departure for my own, although some of our areas of interest overlap. Beyond the fact that we come from different disciplinary perspectives, we also operate from differing generational and geographical perspectives. My primary goal in this book is to reach colleagues in English and American Studies Departments interested in expanding course offerings to include U.S. Latino/a literature and culture; I am also interested in demonstrating the manner in which Cuban American culture, certainly since 1980 but especially in the post–Cold War era, has freed itself of the geographical isolation of South Florida. Most of the writers I study here were never based in Miami, and thus they fight to attain a kind of visibility as writers from a minority culture without falling back on the kinds of stereotypes that would most easily lend them that visibility.

15. One helpful discussion of what does and does not bind Cubans in the United States to other Latino and ethnic-minority groups can be found throughout Portes and Stepick's *City on the Edge: The Transformation of Miami.* See especially chapter 6, "How the Enclave Was Built," which provides much of the sociological background for the cultural analyses I conduct here.

16. I offer here as supremely visual testament to this threat of cultural disappearance for non-Miami Cubans one of the innumerable pictorial, coffee-table-style books on the off-island Cuban experience; 2001's *CubanTime: A*

Celebration of Cuban Life in America features among its hundreds of snap-shots but a handful that are marked as non-Miamian.

17. Bhabha, 7.

18. The aporetic conjunction of the necessary and impossible here owes a substantial debt to Derrida's discussion of the performative dislocation of the Marxist injunction toward the realization of some future event (justice, democracy); this dislocation jives well with the air of interminable anticipa-tion among some, perhaps still most, exiled Cubans for the ever-imminent end of communist rule in Cuba. See chapter 2 of *Specters of Marx* (espe-cially 65–66).

19. Portes and Stepick, 33–34, 148–49.

20. Portes and Stepick, 103–4.

21. Shorris, *Latinos: A Biography of the People,* 68.

22. Shorris, 346–50.

23. Shorris, 386.

24. Rieff, *The Exile: Cuba in the Heart of Miami.* See also Rieff, *Going to Miami: Exiles, Tourists and Refugees in the New America,* and Didion, *Miami.*

25. Rieff, 30.

26. Rieff, 29–30.

Introduction

1. Braziel and Mannur, 3.

2. See Behar's essay, "The Erotics of Power and Cuba's Revolutionary Children," in *Cuba, the Elusive Nation,* 145.

3. See especially chapter 10, entitled "Diasporas," 244–77.

4. In *Cuba Confidential: Love and Vengeance in Miami and Havana.* Bardach's "Preface," which is quoted in the main text, was first published in 2003. Bardach is not, however, the first writer to field the "two Cubas" argument; see, for example, political scientist María de los Angeles Torres's important 1999 study, *In the Land of Mirrors: Cuban Exile Politics in the United States.* Torres's observation of what she calls "haunting symmetries in the ways both states [i.e., the Cuban and the American] dealt with Cuban exiles" leads her initially to conclude that "[t]his parallelism in the policies of the two feuding states" rendered them "mirror images" of one an-other(18). By the end of her introduction, however, Torres re-situates that mirror to force a confrontation and enable a reconciliation between on- and off-island Cuban populations. The mirror, Torres concludes, thus stands as "a metaphor for still another stage in [a] complicated and often painful process of discovery: not only must we find ourselves reflected in the other, we must also recognize our differences and our distinct ways of observing one another" (21).

5. The phrase recurs with some frequency throughout Alvarez-Borland's study, *Cuban-American Literature of Exile: From Person to Persona*. Alvarez-Borland's work figures prominently in the last section of this introduction.

6. Perhaps the most cogent discussion of the waves of post-1959 Cuban immigration to the United States, and of their political, social, and cultural consequences at least for South Florida, remains historian María Cristina García's *Havana USA: Cuban Exiles and Cuban Americans in South Florida, 1959–1994*.

7. In addition to the "Love" and "Vengeance" governing Castro, González, and even Bush family "ties" that, according to Bardach, have managed to choke all hope out of the Cuban/exile/American national political scene for nearly a half century, issues of sex, passion, and kinship have profoundly informed a whole recent outcropping of titles in Cuban/exile/American studies. Witness the following representative list: Bejel, *Gay Cuban Nation;* Fernández, *Cuba and the Politics of Passion;* Kutzinski, *Sugar's Secrets: Race and the Erotics of Cuban Nationalism;* and Behar, "The Erotics of Power and Cuba's Revolutionary Children" in *Cuba, the Elusive Nation,* 134–54.

8. In *Havana USA,* García makes brief but informative mention of the exile *municipios,* impressive in longevity, influence, and number, that began sprouting up in South Florida in 1962; García's study, already a decade old, was even in its own time quite limited by its focus on South Florida as generally representative of the larger post-1959 U.S.–Cuban experience. "Diaspora," not surprisingly, never comes up as a viable rubric within which to situate, let alone make sense of, that experience; her remarks about the *municipios* (see *Havana USA,* 2–3, 91–93) nevertheless have some contextual value for the purposes of the present discussion.

9. It says everything about the mentality of the exile-generation Güineros in both Miami and Los Angeles that every January they continue to hold banquets to celebrate both the feast day of San Julián de los Güines, the town's patron saint and symbolic figure of the "Güinero ausente," that is, the absent Güinero, whom they all identify as and with. Snapshots from these banquets usually command a good deal of space in the subsequent issues of both *La Villa* and *Ecos.*

10. See 31–35.

11. See García's *Havana USA* for another brief but useful description of the rise in "anti-Cuban sentiment" in 1980s Dade County, which led to the repeal that November of "the Bilingual-Bicultural Ordinance," originally passed in 1973; the repeal, García tells us, "made it unlawful to use county funds 'for the purposes of utilizing any language other than English, or promoting any culture other than that of the United States'" (see García, 74, 114).

12. Fernández, 153.

13. Albita's first three U.S.-produced discs were released and distributed by the Estefans' production team's parent company, Sony Music. Her less commercially driven and far more artistically interesting and adventurous discs, like 2000's *Son* and 2002's *Hecho a Mano* were both released by smaller independent labels.

14. Although she falls outside of the purview of this study for a variety of reasons, Cuban-born and Iowa-trained conceptual artist Ana Mendieta's extraordinary "body" work demands some mention here; Albita's moment of assertive corporal exposure stands, I would argue, in eloquent relief against the complex play of corporal dis- and reappearance in especially Mendieta's signature series of *Siluetas,* or Silhouettes, etched into varying natural surfaces. See the images and commentaries collected by Moure in *Ana Mendieta,* as well as Blocker's important 1999 study, *Where Is Ana Mendieta?* and the scattered allusions to Mendieta's work in Fusco's *The Bodies That Were Not Ours and Other Writings.* See also Viso, *Ana Mendieta Earth Body: Sculpture and Performance, 1972–1985.*

15. In my admittedly unprofessional English translation, the lyrical demand in "Tócame . . ." runs roughly as follows: "Give me one more kiss/One more kiss does no harm/Tomorrow's another day/Tomorrow's another year," and so on.

16. One can only imagine what more María de los Angeles Torres might have made of this image in 1999's *In the Land of Mirrors.* Torres, however, mentions Albita only once, as an example of an important transition in late-1990s Cuban Miami's cultural and political sensibilities. Albita's ability to become "a sensation" in and even beyond Miami so soon after arriving from the communist Cuba in which she grew up marks for Torres one among many positive consequences enabled by the moment when "the children of the revolution met the children of original exiles," who together, she tells us, undertook "an intense search for new ways of rethinking Cuban identity, art and politics" (161).

17. See *Havana USA,* 170.

18. García, 211–12; on the Prida affair, see García, 196–97.

19. The most constructive, and exhaustive, critical engagement of Pérez-Firmat's argument in *Life on the Hyphen* remains Max J. Castro's "The Trouble with Collusion: Paradoxes of the Cuban-American Way," which concludes the collection *Cuba, the Elusive Nation* edited by Fernández and Betancourt. Although the present book owes an undeniable if mostly implicit debt to Pérez-Firmat's groundbreaking study, here it will suffice to register my explicit agreement with Castro that "Pérez-Firmat's work is valuable" primarily "as an embodiment of Cuban-American ideology rather than as a critical analysis or deconstruction of it, and [that] as such it reflects some of its mystifications and denials" (304). With this in mind, I offer my present

work as one, and certainly not the only, or the definitive, contribution to an ongoing and necessarily unfinished project that Castro calls the telling of the story of "the multiple real and possible Cuban-American ways" (305).

1. Pleasure's Exile: Reinaldo Arenas's Last Writing

1. See Reinaldo Arenas, *Before Night Falls*, 288. See also the Spanish original, *Antes que Anochezca*, 7.

2. See the *New York Times Book Review* piece of October 24, 1993 by Roberto González Echevarría. In his review of Koch's English translation of *Antes que Anochezca*, Echevarría observes in Arenas's temperament a clinging to transcendent innocence, "a sense of liberation attached" especially to "lovemaking that seems pre-Freudian in its candor." In general what I term "excess" in Arenas translates into utopian idealism for Echevarría: "It is as if on some deep level Arenas had innocently believed in Castro's rhetoric . . . and could only measure imperfect human performance against absolute [and therefore impossible] standards of purity." Arenas is therefore for Echevarría "a true son of the revolution and of Castro," and his ultimate disillusionment with and alienation from the Law attached to the Name of this father translates into a more-than-familiar dramatic paradigm: *Before Night Falls* is for Echevarría "a narrative linking poignantly the personal and the political levels of [the] family romance, told from the point of view of the abandoned son."

3. This comparison to Swift is anything but incidental. It marks a curious genealogy in the work of political theorists, who, like Edward Said in *The World, the Text and the Critic* and Roberto Fernández Retamar in *Caliban* have observed in Swift's thoroughgoing political satires a paradigm for an ironic politics of impossibility. There are undeniable Swiftian elements in much of Arenas's apocalyptic political fiction; in addition to the references in *The Doorman* to *Gulliver's Travels*, one can find in the cannibalistic references in *The Assault* elements of the genocidal vision of a totalizing rationalism that Swift developed between Part Four of the *Travels* and "A Modest Proposal."

4. Arenas says of his friendship with Lázaro: "In exile Lázaro has been my only link to my past, the only witness to my past life in Cuba; with him I always had the feeling of being able to return to that irretrievable world" (*Before Night Falls*, 308).

5. This is precisely Arenas's take on New York as the exemplum of North American culture. In the chapter of the autobiography entitled "Eviction," Arenas discusses his disillusionment with New York at length. Although at first New York had seemed to him the fulfillment of Havana's promise of cultural and communal richness, that idea of social value is quickly replaced

by one bled of its spirituality. Because in the United States "everything re-volves around money," even its great cities are rendered soulless; "New York," Arenas argues, "has no tradition, no history. The city is in constant flux, con-stant construction . . . a huge, soulless factory with no place for the pedes-trian to rest, no place where one can simply be without dishing out dollars for a breath of air"(*Before Night Falls,* 293–94, 310).

6. Arenas, *The Doorman,* 3.

7. Ibid., 3–4.

8. Young's text is available even in the United States in both English and in a Spanish translation, which is what I use here. Young argues for the exis-tence of an emergent homosexual subculture in pre-Castro Havana, one which fed very directly and very profitably into the larger sexual economy of the pleasure industry for which the Cuban capital especially was justifi-ably famous. See Young, *Los Gays Bajo la Revolución Cubana,* 29–33. See also the more recent study, Marvin Leiner, *Sexual Politics in Cuba: Machismo, Homosexuality and AIDS.* Leiner, chiefly an education specialist with a deep regard for socialist Cuba's social policy successes, attempts to address the seemingly regressive treatment of people with HIV and AIDS in Cuba (espe-cially in the late 1980s and early 1990s) by supplying a cultural and political history of Cuban sexual attitudes. Leiner is far kinder to the Castro gov-ernment's treatment of homosexuals, especially in the crucial two decades preceding the publication of his study. It makes for curious reading along-side Arenas's personal testimony and Young's more distanced study of the same topic.

9. See *The Doorman,* 8, and all of chapter 14, which is devoted to the Oscars, whose names are derived from the Cuban Oscar's desire to obscure his ethnicity. Born Ramón García, the character renames himself after "what he considered to be the supreme icons of his new country: the Hollywood Oscar and *The New York Times*" (*The Doorman,* 69).

10. This distaste partly explains why the gay male community in 1980s New York gets precious little direct mention in any of Arenas's work. This latter "culture of desire," as Frank Browning named it in 1993, posed in a marked way for Arenas the equally problematic materialism of the liberal West, which he condemns with a vigor equal to that with which he condemns the bankrupt materialism of Marxist-Leninist-Stalinist Cuba. Although Browning's text includes a fairly conventional discussion of Cuban culture's attitudes toward homosexuality (see *The Culture of Desire,* 142–48), it serves the larger purpose of my own discussion in its analysis of the assimilationist tendencies characteristic of much of the mainstream commercializing of es-pecially gay male urban culture, tendencies that arguably not only persisted but strengthened into the first decade of the new century.

11. *The Doorman,* 71.

12. *Before Night Falls,* 290. For Arenas, the philistine attitude of bourgeois exiles toward writers was no more forgivable than their active repression at the hands of the communists in Cuba. No Cuban writer, Arenas finally admits, could escape "the tragic fate Cuban writers have suffered throughout our history; on our island we have been condemned to silence, to ostracism, censorship and prison; in exile, despised and forsaken by our fellow exiles" (291).

13. Ibid., 292.

14. Arenas's descriptions of his alienation from Miami's bourgeois Cuban culture often draws on the figure of the ghost or phantasm: "In exile," he writes, "one is nothing but a ghost, a shadow of someone who never achieves full reality" (*Before Night Falls,* 293). Like the exiled individual, the entire exile community, especially in Miami, seemed to Arenas little more than a pathetic, ghastly echo or remnant of an irrecoupably lost Cuba; Cuban Miami was for Arenas "like the ghost of our Island, a barren [*arenosa,* or sandy] and pestiferous peninsula, trying to become, for a million exiles, the dream of a tropical island: aerial, bathed by the ocean waters and the tropical breeze" (*Before Night Falls,* 292). It is worth noting how the language in this passage submerges in its semantic resources the whole psychological drama of Arenas's own life. It is the embodiment of the phallic wish to detach itself from a solid, but infected body (the infection here also identified with the barren sand [*arena*/Arenas] of the mainland), and to float/bathe once again in the fluid body of the ocean.

15. Echevarría, 32.

16. *The Doorman,* 188.

17. *Before Night Falls,* 296.

18. *AIDS and Its Metaphors,* 6–7.

19. Ibid., 62.

20. *Before Night Falls,* xvi–xvii.

21. *AIDS and Its Metaphors,* 76–77.

22. *Before Night Falls,* 93.

23. Ibid., xvii.

24. Ibid., 239.

25. Ibid., 292.

26. In scattered passages recounting his time in exile, Arenas makes dismissive mention of "this festive and fascist left," which, he observes, had no better understanding of the complexity of the political experience of Cubans both in and out of the homeland as the most rabidly anti-Castro Cuban rightists had. Both sides, in enlisting selectively what elements of his story could serve their respective political needs, reduced him to a curiosity, a free-floating symbolic presence, a promiscuous political fetish-object, invited to cast its aura at events and functions. "I was surrounded," Arenas tells us, "by gossip and difficulties, and by an endless succession of cocktail parties, soirées, and

invitations. It was like being on display, a strange creature that had to be invited before it lost its luster or until a new personality arrived to displace it" (*Before Night Falls*, 292).

27. See Kipnis, "Aesthetics and Foreign Policy" in *Ecstasy Unlimited: On Sex, Capital, Gender, and Aesthetics*, 207–18. The passage quoted in the main text of this article can be found on p. 215.

28. See Sontag, "Some Thoughts on the Right Way [for Us] to Love the Cuban Revolution," 6–19.

29. Kipnis, 216–17.

30. Ibid., 212.

31. See *The Dialectic of Enlightenment*.

32. *Otra Vez el Mar* is available in a fine English translation by Andrew Hurley (see *Farewell to the Sea: a Novel of Cuba*). The last page of the text is devoted to a record of its complex underground existence: "First version disappeared, Havana, 1969/Second version confiscated, Havana, 1971/The present version smuggled out of Havana, 1974/and published in Barcelona, 1982" (*Farewell to the Sea*, 413). Arenas also makes frequent reference to the history of this text in *Before Night Falls*.

33. See Žižek, *Enjoy Your Symptom!: Lacan in Hollywood and Out*, 131–36. This discussion practically applies to filmic discourse theories developed in Žižek's earlier work, *For They Know Not What They Do: Enjoyment as a Political Factor*, 2 and 236–41.

34. Žižek, *Enjoy Your Symptom!* 131–32.

35. Arenas's scream should also be heard, I think, as an echo of that Adamic, "barbaric yawp" of Walt Whitman's, the pure noise of an original, still-originating New World poetics; as such it also echoes the guttural "no" of Retamar's insurgent, antitraditional Caliban. Because it also marks Arenas as that most stereotyped of subversive homosexuals, the flaming, effeminate "screaming" queen, reading Arenas's work as Adamic certainly puts a subversively sexualized spin on both Retamar's and even Whitman's butch constructions of the "new" man. I turn to a more focused analysis of Retamar's influential 1971 essay "Caliban" in chapter 3.

36. I have already had occasion to cite Pérez-Firmat's *Life on the Hyphen: the Cuban-American Way* in the Introduction.

37. *Before Night Falls*, 311, and *Antes que Anochezca*, 335.

38. *Before Night Falls*, 317, and *Antes que Anochezca*, 343.

2. Docile Bodies, Volatile Texts: Cuban-Exile Prison Writing

1. See Guillermo Cabrera Infante, "Bites from the Bearded Crocodile," in *Mea Cuba*, 77. Cabrera Infante left Cuba permanently in the mid-1960s after

his own violent estrangement from Castro and the revolution; after that he was based in Brussels and in London, and together with the Paris-based Severo Sarduy, whom I discuss in a later section of this chapter, provide some measure of the truly diasporic reach of off-island Cuban resettlement after 1959.

2. Implicit in much of what I say here and in all the chapters of this book is the profound influence of some general theoretical works on the complexities of national and global cultural politics as they arose with the end of both colonialism and the Cold War and as they've persisted into the era of globalization and the new century more generally. The first I cite is the graphing of the term "DissemiNation," following Bhabha's work in chapter 8 ("DissemiNation: Time, Narrative and the Modern Nation") of *The Location of Culture,* 139–70.

3. Gutiérrez Alea's film, *Strawberry and Chocolate,* appeared in limited U.S. distribution in late 1994, after a series of very successful festival showings, beginning with the 1993 New Latin American Film Festival in Havana. Paz's novella, *El lobo, el bosque y el hombre nuevo,* appeared in 1990 in Cuba and in the rest of Latin America the following year. The English-language title is my literal translation. Two articles on the political context of the film's production and distribution appeared in the *Los Angeles Times* in the wake of the film's general opening there in January 1995. One is a sympathetic interview with Senel Paz by Eric Gutierrez (*Los Angeles Times Calendar,* January 22, 1995, 33); the other, "Artists and Homosexuals: 'Non-Persons' in Castro's Cuba," is a critical editorial piece by Kenneth Freed (*LA Times World Report,* January 24, 1995) on the revolution's history of cultural repression.

4. A brief discussion of *Improper Conduct* occurs in Marvin Leiner's *Sexual Politics in Cuba* (1994), 51–52. Leiner's sympathy for the Castro revolution's achievements in education reform and health care restrains his overall critique of the revolution's treatment of homosexuals and colors his analysis of the film. In addition to his incorrect identification of one of its makers, the Spanish cinematographer Nestor Almendros, as Cuban, Leiner in general faults the film for dwelling on the worst periods of homosexual persecution, the period of the UMAPs (Unidades Militares para la Ayuda de Producción) in the 1960s. He wonders why the filmmakers didn't also document the "improvements" in Cuba's policies since then, improvements that by the 1980s brought Cuba "down" to the more tolerable levels of homophobia in the rest of Latin America. *Improper Conduct,* produced in 1984 by Almendros and Orlando Jimenez-Leal, has been shown periodically on PBS in the United States since its making. Another view of Almendros can be found in Reinaldo Arenas's *Before Night Falls,* 300.

5. The rest of this chapter will continue to make considerable use of

Arenas's writings. The most informative cultural texts of Pedro Zamora's life are MTV's commemorative video of Zamora's life and death, which aired in November 1994, a month after his death, and his friend and *Real World* co-star Judd Winnick's 2000 graphic-memoir, *Pedro and Me.* As I note in the introduction to this book, Achy Obejas's first collection of short stories, *We Came All the Way from Cuba so You Could Dress Like This?*, appeared in 1994, and Albita's first U.S.-produced work, *No Se Parece a Nada,* appeared in the summer of 1995.

6. As viable constructions of nation evolve and proliferate, so do viable constructions of citizenship. As far back as the early 1990s, work like John Brenkman's essay "The Citizen Myth" had already begun the process of re-analyzing in a post–Cold War context the basic presumptions behind citizenship in Western liberal democracies. Brenkman's reading of the concept of civic republicanism in Benjamin R. Barber's *An Aristocracy of Everyone,* for example, demonstrates how even a strong reading of an actively participatory model for U.S. citizenship cannot resist the historical weight of its legacy of exclusions based on gender, race, class, culture, language, and sexual orientation. Brenkman poses his questions in the context of a then-still-emerging U.S. multiculturalism, and he concludes his interrogation by linking to the "histories and aspirations" of communities traditionally excluded from the polity a resurgent "cultural creativity" that will in turn produce "a new narration of the nation" (Brenkman, 144). "Pieces of that narration," Brenkman argues, "suggest that its voice will be more polyglot, more plural, more tragic, than the triumphant Citizen Myth. It will also, therefore, offer a stronger promise of justice and equality." It is my hope to add the voices I analyze here, in all their conflict, to the weave of narration that Brenkman describes.

7. Arenas's 1991 memoir, *Before Night Falls,* already received considerable attention in chapter 1. Armando Valladares's *Against All Hope,* chronicling his twenty-two years in Cuba's prisons, was translated by Andrew Hurley and published by Knopf in 1987. Heberto Padilla's *Self-Portrait of the Other,* translated by Alexander Coleman and published by Farrar, Strauss, Giroux in 1990, is discussed at length later in this chapter. It provides an informative context for my analysis of Arenas's work, in that Padilla's notoriety as a writer preceded Arenas's by almost two decades, making it more difficult (but certainly not impossible) for the revolution to persecute him openly. Padilla was also quite openly heterosexual and gave the revolution little in the way of an artificial (i.e., "moral") excuse to imprison him. Finally, Ana Rodríguez's *Diary of a Survivor: Nineteen Years in a Cuban Women's Prison* was cowritten and translated by Glenn Garvin and published by St. Martin's Press in 1995.

8. See Pau-Llosa, *Cuba,* 86.

9. Although it does not figure centrally in the constellation of prison memoirs I study here, Mandela's own autobiography, *Long Walk to Freedom* (New York: Little, Brown) appeared in 1994, and must certainly contribute to my discussion of texts with which it shares more than a common chronology of publication. See especially the informative references to his history with the South African Communist Party cited in his index, as well as the oddly brief references to Castro and Cuba cited there as well. For a brief but helpful analysis of exile Cubans' unfortunately negative views of Mandela, see, for example, García's *Havana USA* and Alejandro Portes and Alex Stepick's *City on the Edge: The Transformation of Miami*, 140–43.

10. Pau-Llosa, *Cuba*, 87.

11. Cinnamon, 77–78.

12. Ibid.

13. Ibid., 38.

14. Ibid., 169.

15. Ibid., 48, 56–58.

16. Ibid., 102.

17. Ibid., 142.

18. Ibid., 143.

19. Ibid., 146.

20. Cabrera Infante, 74–75.

21. Ibid., 78.

22. Ibid., 79.

23. Arenas, *Before Night Falls*, 179.

24. Ibid; emphasis added.

25. Ibid., 180–81.

26. Foster, 67–71.

27. Ibid., 68.

28. Arenas, *Before Night Falls*, 185.

29. Foucault, *Discipline and Punish*, 194.

30. Arenas, Old *Rosa: A Novel in Two Stories*, 71.

31. Foucault, 138.

32. Ibid., 187.

33. Padilla, 245.

34. Foucault, 101.

35. Ibid.

36. Cabrera Infante, 70–71.

37. Padilla, 48.

38. Foucault, 102.

39. Ibid., 30.

40. Arenas, *Before Night Falls*, 180.

41. Foucault, 106.

42. Sarduy, *Written on a Body*, 6–9. Sarduy's three remarkable sections on Sade are suggestively entitled "Fixity," "Theatre," and "Passion/Repetition."
43. Sarduy, 6.
44. Ibid., 7.
45. Ibid.
46. Ibid., 8.
47. Ibid.
48. Padilla, 236–37, 245.
49. Sarduy, 8–9.
50. Ibid., 9.

3. Revolution's Other Histories: Legacies of Roberto Fernández Retamar's "Caliban"

This chapter owes a significant debt to groups of people too numerous to mention here individually, all of whom have generously responded to it on the several occasions I have had to present it publicly. These include a workshop group at the 1997 American Comparative Literature Association Conference, a Humanities Seminar on the Futures of American Studies conducted at Dartmouth College during the summer of 1997, the Harvard Center for Literary and Cultural Studies (special thanks to William Handley), and the Dartmouth College Humanities Forum. A version of this chapter also appeared in a volume of *Social Text* in 1999 and was the co-winner of that year's Crompton-Noll Award for best article in Lesbian and Gay Studies. My thanks go to the selection committee of the Lesbian and Gay Caucus of the Modern Language Association for that honor.

1. Epps, "Proper Conduct: Reinaldo Arenas, Fidel Castro and the Politics of Homosexuality," 231–83. See especially the discussion on pages 255–58, out of which all the passages I cite in the main text are taken.
2. In addition to texts cited in this essay by Heberto Padilla, Guillermo Cabrera Infante, José Quiroga, and others, see the studies by Marvin Leiner, Ian Lumsden, and Allen Young cited in the preceding chapters of this book. I want to stress here that the revolutionary abuses of queer and dissident writers documented in these texts are rarely merely proffered to anger and outrage; Leiner, Lumsden, and Young all situate these practices in contexts that can explain without necessarily exonerating them. Certainly there were compelling historical reasons to link especially male bourgeois homosexual tourism to some of the more decadent and exploitative practices of Cuba's former colonizers; but in the revolution's hands this link became a full and uncompromising identification, one that excused any sort of suppression of criticism of the regime as both ideologically and libidinally collusive with those colonizers.

3. Retamar, *Caliban and Other Essays,* 42–43. See also generally the Spanish text of Retamar's essay, "Caliban: Apuntes sobre la cultura en nuestra América."

4. Padilla's detailed account of his experiences and the international controversy they inspired appears in his *Self-Portrait of the Other,* 128–89.

5. Padilla, 134, 165.

6. See Cabrera Infante, *Mea Cuba,* 74–78.

7. Retamar, 52–53.

8. Ibid., 3, 30.

9. The list here is necessarily incomplete, but direct and indirect echoes of Retamar's work may be detected in, for example, Hortense Spillers's introduction, "Who Cuts the Border?: Some Readings on 'America,'" to *Comparative American Identities: Race, Sex, and Nationality in the Modern Text,* 1–25, in Gayatri Spivak's "Three Women's Texts and a Critique of Imperialism" in *"Race," Writing and Difference,* 262–80, and in Coco Fusco's "El diario de Miranda/Miranda's Diary," in *English Is Broken Here: Notes on Cultural Fusion in the Americas,* 3–20. Perhaps not surprisingly, these three critics raise at least obliquely the question of gender politics in any invocation of Caliban, but mostly apologetically; see Spillers's forced identification of Caliban with his mother, Sycorax, in her attempt to feminize his symbolic function in postcolonial discourse (Spillers, 6–8), and Fusco's own benign attempt to recast Caliban as Miranda's "seducer" rather than rapist before taking on the role of Miranda herself (Fusco, 6) in order to report on late–Cold War cultural and political relations, mostly failed, between Cuba and the United States. This chapter will take up the work of at least three additional critics, José David Saldívar, Ramón Saldívar, and Edward Said, who also make strategic use of Retamar's "Caliban."

10. Epps, 234.

11. The gender complexity implicit in the Ariel/Caliban pairing is aptly summarized in Stephen Orgel's "Introduction" to the *World's Classics* edition of *The Tempest,* 27. "In contrast to Caliban's elemental sameness," Orgel argues, "Ariel is volatile and metamorphic. He is male, the asexual boy to Caliban's libidinous man, but (in keeping with his status as a boy actor) all the roles he plays at Prospero's command are female: sea nymph, harpy, Ceres."

12. See, for example, Carlos Fuentes's "Prologue" to Margaret Sayers Peden's translation of *Ariel,* 13–28, which apologizes almost embarrassingly for the author's interest in a text which so "irritating[ly]" embodies salient qualities of Latin American *modernismo,* a movement that, according to Fuentes, "sought a cosmopolitan atmosphere for Latin American poetry, cultivated art for art's sake, and affected an accompanying languor, elegantly settled into the semirecumbent position of turn-of-century ennui"(Fuentes, 13). Fuentes's thinly veiled associations of modernist aesthetic sensibility and a too-relaxed (presumably for men) semirecumbent sensuality buttress much

of his discussion of Rodó's legacy, especially among Latin American public orators, young men obviously so seduced by Rodó's rhetorical "excesses" that they were compelled to rehearse them in public performance. Even Fuentes has to confess that he "went to hear them out of some kind of educational yet sensual need: a warning to myself, with a dash of masochism. It was rare," he goes on, "for the tremulous orators of our youth not to quote Rodó in their speeches: the topics of the spiritual versus the utilitarian, blithe Latin American Ariel fighting off brutish North American Caliban, beauty confronting ugliness, followed by a whole parade of simplistic dualisms . . . were facile, tempting devices. . . . And Rodó had wrapped *Ariel* in such a glowing sycophancy of youth! Bathed in virtue, the young orator appeared to prolong the puzzling fame of José Enrique Rodó" (Fuentes, 14). Certainly the nature of Fuentes's intimately detailed, obviously fascinated account of such openly if rhetorically performed homoeroticism might strike a contemporary reader as equally "puzzling." What remains too depressingly predictable is Fuentes's equally obvious need to distance himself from such scenes. See also Oscar Montero's article "*Modernismo* and Homophobia: Darío and Rodó," in *Sex and Sexuality in Latin America*, 101–17.

13. Retamar, 15.

14. Retamar, 24–25.

15. I do not mean to suggest in anything I say across these three chapters that nothing has changed in Cuba since 1970 with regard to official policies or unofficial attitudes toward homosexuals. Both of the texts by Leiner and Lumsden referenced in note 2 here trace many of the advances made on both levels in Cuba in the past three decades. I also refer to these advances in my brief discussion in chapter 2 of Gutierrez-Alea's *Strawberry and Chocolate* and of the Senel Paz novella on which it is based. The "spirit of the times" in Cuba in 1970 were, of course, characterized by more than a repressive anxiety about alternate sexualities and their relation to alternate cultural practices; 1970, as a representative group of historians concurs, was as much of a political and economic watershed for Cuba and for the revolution as the Special Period itself was, a watershed occasioned primarily by a disastrous, and disastrously overprojected, sugar harvest, which led in turn to both political and cultural retrenchments on the part of the government. See, for example, Herbert Matthews's mostly sympathetic analysis of Cuba in the early 1970s in *Revolution in Cuba: An Essay in Understanding*, especially chapter 1, "The 1970 Watershed," and chapter 14, "The Cultural Revolution," and Marifeli Pérez-Stable's *The Cuban Revolution: Origins, Course and Legacy*.

16. Retamar, 28.

17. Ibid., 30–34.

18. Ibid., 36 (75 in the Spanish text cited in note 3).

19. Ibid., 44.

20. Quiroga, "Fleshing Out Virgilio Piñera from the Cuban Closet," in
¿Entiendes?: Queer Readings, Hispanic Writings, 168–80. A version of this article reappeared as chapter 4 of Quiroga's *Tropics of Desire: Interventions
from Queer Latino America,* 101–23. Quiroga's work is as exemplary as
Epps's in its intelligent critique of Cuban revolutionary culture's homophobic sensibilities and practices; see also his own fine reading of *Strawberry
and Chocolate* in both "Homosexualities in the Tropic of Revolution" (in
Balderston and Guy's *Sex and Sexuality in Latin America,* 133–51) and in
chapter 5 of *Tropics of Desire,* 124–44.

21. Epps, 249.

22. Ibid., 252.

23. Ibid., 256.

24. Saldívar, *The Dialectics of Our America: Genealogy, Cultural Critique,
and Literary History,* 139.

25. Ibid., 143–45.

26. This, I think, is the point missed by such otherwise comprehensive
analyses of the Calibanic call for a radical reconfiguration of postnational,
postcolonial cultural (and specifically "American") studies as Carolyn Porter's
"What We Know That We Don't Know: Remapping American Literary
Studies," 467–526. Porter praises what she calls the "critical synthesis" that
Saldívar's work "performs by bringing 'the school of Caliban' to the fore-
front of an American cultural studies that is . . . radically reconfigured as
a field" (504). But although Porter emphasizes what she calls the "historical location" of "the school of Caliban . . . as the latest version of an anti-
colonialist politics that achieved its first victory with the Haitian Revolution"
and can count among its subsequent moments the 1959 revolution in Cuba
(510–11), nowhere in her essay does Porter actually specifically "locate" the
essay by which Saldívar's is fired in its own specific (and, as I have tried to
argue, troublingly complex) historical moment.

27. Saldívar, *Dialectics,* xvi.

28. Ibid., 15, 10.

29. Piedra, "Nationalizing Sissies," in *¿Entiendes?: Queer Readings, Hispanic
Writings,* 372.

30. See, for example, Gilles Deleuze's analysis of the sadomasochistic con-
tract in his essay "Coldness and Cruelty" collected alongside Sacher-Masoch's
Venus in Furs in the volume *Masochism.*

31. Piedra, "Sissies," 387.

32. Ibid., 386.

33. Ibid.

34. See Butler's work in both *Excitable Speech: A Politics of the Performative,* especially the Introduction, "On Linguistic Vulnerability," 24–28, and
The Psychic Life of Power: Theories in Subjection.

35. Pérez-Firmat, *Life on the Hyphen,* 6.

36. Ibid., 23–45.

37. Padilla, 144–48.

38. Epps, 268.

39. It is also worth noting briefly here that even Martí has not been immune to a little "queering"; in a novella by Reinaldo Arenas called "Trip to Havana" and in two articles by Benigno Sánchez-Eppler and Sylvia Molloy, explorations of Martí's curious tendency to overcelebrate father–son filial love and of his anxious fascination with Walt Whitman's "Calamus" poems have already begun the work of queering Retamar's own revered paragon, the model of the Calibanic intellectual of Our America. See especially Sánchez-Eppler's article on Arenas's story, "Call My Son Ismael: Exiled Paternity and Father/Son Eroticism in Reinaldo Arenas and José Martí," and Molloy's elegant and erudite "His America, Our America: José Martí Reads Walt Whitman."

40. Gosse, *Where the Boys Are: Cuba, Cold War America and the New Left.*

41. Retamar, 12.

42. Ibid., 55.

43. Edward Said, *Culture and Imperialism,* 212–18.

44. Said, 213.

45. Ibid.

46. Ibid., 214.

47. Ibid. In her analysis of Retamar in "Who Cuts the Border?" (see note 10 here), Hortense Spillers has occasion to cite Fredric Jameson's Foreword to the English translation of "Caliban" published by the University of Minnesota Press. There, Spillers tells us, Jameson calls for a more vigilant "situation-specificity" in the work of locating cultural products in their historically specific moments—this, I think, is also what Said calls for in his discussion of Retamar and the uses, good and bad, to which his essay may be put.

48. See note 2.

49. Saldívar, *Chicano Narrative: the Dialectics of Difference,* 211.

50. Islas, *La Mollie and the King of Tears.*

51. Islas, 136–37.

52. Islas, 141–42.

53. Islas's criminally undervalued work certainly calls for further critical and scholarly engagement; in my own future work I hope to develop what I see as his simultaneous deployment of a Chicano dialect(ics), which keeps his work tethered to the historical "real" as Ramón Saldívar would have it, and a queer dialogics which engages in precisely the kind of open, comic Bakhtinian play which never loses sight of the traditionally subversive potential intrinsic to a "novelistic" discourse which Bakhtin might argue could include Shakespeare. Islas even comes close to the language of Rabelais in

Louie's brief observation that one of the more memorably named of the Mexican sweet breads was the *pedo de monja*, or nun's fart.

54. This chapter only covers the poems in "Learning the Language," the first section of *The Other Man Was Me*, 13–27.

55. At the same time, "Fernando" is the Spanish translation of Ferdinand, and thus might just as readily apply to the son Prospero hopes to acquire through Miranda.

4. Hemispheric Vertigo: Cuba, Québec, and Our (New) America

1. This quote comes from the concluding paragraph of an early draft of what became the last chapter of Harper's *Private Affairs: Critical Ventures in the Culture of Social Relations*, 150–51.

2. The "funny" chance encounter Harper recounts having in Toronto produces in him feelings he later describes in far more general but consistent terms as "the disorientation characterizing the transnational imaginary in the era of global capitalism"(130) and, later (quoting Gloria Anzaldúa), "the subjective discomfort that marks life in the borderlands"(131).

3. The unease I'll insist on maintaining across these remarks emanates in part from the numerous disciplinary dislocations I feel as I make them; what follows in my reading of a concert by Gloria Estefan that I attended in Montréal soon after arriving in New England certainly resonates with "queer" possibilities that I do not take up. A reading of this concert within the disciplinary contexts of queer and performance studies will remain to be done, I'm afraid, deferred in favor of the "transnational/translational" reading it more immediately compelled. I do not want, however, to pass up the opportunity here to acknowledge at least the promise of productively queer effects imbedded in such a reading, especially one that insists on my more evanescent "memory" of the concert in Montréal with its complex trilingual interplay than the more conventionally archived version recorded in Miami weeks later. For a valuable analysis of the relation queer critique must have to the ephemeral register of performance, see José Muñoz's essay, "Ephemera as Evidence: Introductory Notes to Queer Acts."

4. See Lewis and Wigen, *The Myth of Continents: A Critique of Metageography*, 181–82. In their provocative work of critical meta-geography, Lewis and Wigen go on to produce a number of practical, compelling conclusions from these historical observations about ongoing reconfigurations of the world map. Of these, the following has direct application to the argument I make throughout this chapter: "[T]he geography of social life in the late 20th century," they tell us, "has outgrown not only the particular contours of the postwar world map, but also the very conventions by which we represent

spatial patterns in image and text. The cultural territories once confidently mapped by anthropologists are increasingly being crosscut and redefined, by the convulsions of peacetime mobility as well as those of war. Historical border zones in particular have acquired unexpected prominence as sites of cultural innovation . . . [T]he accelerating diaspora of merchants, migrants, and refugees around the world has jostled peoples together, not only along traditional boundary zones, but deep within every major historical region as well . . . local conceptions of macro-level identity are mutating rapidly . . . [thus requiring] a new sociospatial lexicon capable of analyzing and representing such developments" (192).

5. Still the most useful critical account of Estefan and the Miami Sound Machine's work is Gustavo Pérez-Firmat's, in "A Salsa for All Seasons," chapter 4 of *Life on the Hyphen,* especially 125–33. Estefan performed the *Evolution* concert in Miami for "live" transmission on HBO just weeks after her appearance in Montréal; HBO, Sony, and Estefan Enterprises coproduced and distributed for sale a videotape with the same title (1996). Remarkable for many reasons, the taped performance begins with Estefan exclaiming her pleasure to be "home" in Miami ("There's no place like home!"), and needless to say, for the benefit of the U.S. TV audience watching "at home," she kept mostly to English in her banter with the audience at the Miami Arena.

6. Wilhelm, "The Miami Report," 8.

7. McKenna, "Canada's Southern Exposure," 26–29.

8. The English translation I use here is collected in Martí, *Reader: Writings on the Americas,* 111–20. On Martí, see also Hortense Spillers's essay "Who Cuts the Border?" (cited in an earlier chapter), and in the same collection, see the essay by Robert Schwarzwald, "Fear of Féderasty: Québec's Inverted Fictions," which bears a more-than-tangential relevance to the discussion I conduct here, especially in the first section, regarding the intricate relation of national to sexual subjectivity.

9. My admittedly cautious and modest disloyalty to Martí feels as anxious as it is necessary; Canada may only have come into being as a nation-state some decades before Martí penned "Our America," but the significance of its role in determining the contours of North America should not have been discounted then and must not be discounted now, especially by those of us practicing the disciplines of either "American" or "U.S. Latino" Studies. Merely to take up the dialectic between "Our" and "North" America as both imagined and instituted by Martí in that essay exercises the worst kind of countercritical disciplinary mimicry. I thus invoke here Robyn Weigman's concluding argument in *American Anatomies: Theorizing Race and Gender,* 201–2, concerning the "alchemical" productions of her own respectful, critical disloyalties to feminism in fashioning my own disloyalties to the orthodoxies of the disciplines I mostly implicitly claim here.

10. Pearlstein, "Clinton Declares Québec Better Off in Canada," 20. A year later Pearlstein also reported on the current debate in Canada about the nation's very future as a united confederation; according to Pearlstein, "perhaps no nation feels the effects" of globalization "more keenly, or is more threatened by them," than Canada (see Pearlstein, "O, Canada! A National Swan Song?" A22). To balance Pearlstein's account of the external forces compromising Canadian national identity, see Michael Ignatieff's account of Québecois nationalism's internally negative effects on the cohesion of the confederation in chapter 6, "Québec," of his *Blood and Belonging: Journeys into the New Nationalism,* especially 143–63.

5. *Café, Culpa, and Capital: Nostalgic Addictions of Cuban Exile*

1. Rieff, *The Exile: Cuba in the Heart of Miami,* 11–25.
2. The Judeo-Cuban analogue, which I first raised in the Introduction and develop here further, has had some very practical and even troubling applications in post–Cold War international politics. In the mid-1990s, for example, the founder of the conservative Cuban American National Foundation, Jorge Mas Canosa, was honored in Israel by the Tel Aviv Foundation. At their gala dinner, Mas Canosa praised Israeli Jews for their consistent support of U.S. (and U.S. Cubans') anti-Castro policies; he told his audience that Cubans "understand their passion for Israel" and "the Jewish experience has taught us a great many things . . . [a]bout dedication, discipline, sacrifice, and never compromising one's principles no matter how hostile the environment or enemy, and never, ever wavering in the pursuit of one's goals— goals that are right, goals that are just"("Remarks" at the Tel Aviv Foundation Gala Dinner, March 28, 1996, online posting, *Cuba Brief,* eWorld, May 2, 1996 [URL no longer accessible]). Mas Canosa pushes the analogue further, invoking the success with which Jews were able "to reconstruct and rebuild Israel after so long a separation . . . as a symbol of hope to us that no matter how dark, how endless, the night might seem, a new dawn is sure to come in our homeland. And we can begin the task—all Cubans, those in exile today and those still suffering under tyranny—of rebuilding a new Cuba, a Cuba respectful of human dignity, a Cuba that can once again take its rightful place among the family of free, democratic nations." I want to note here the lurking apocalypticism (the "dark . . . endless night") of Mas Canosa's otherwise redemptive-sounding message; this rhetoric will resonate later in this chapter (see the section "Capital" later in this chapter) when I discuss Derrida's deployment of a secular messianic promise, especially as a promise of redemptive justice through restitution and reappropriation in "conjuring Marxism," chapter 2 of *Specters of Marx: The State of the Debt, the Work of*

Mourning and the New International, 49–75. If Mas Canosa's comments reflect something of the danger of an overdetermined archetypal thinking, certainly much that is valuable remains to be studied of a more anecdotal nature in the Cuban–Jewish experience. In addition to the discussion of Cubans as the "Jews of the Caribbean" in Achy Obejas's *Days of Awe*, see also anthropologist Ruth Behar, "Juban America," 151–70, Robert Levine, *Tropical Diaspora: The Jewish Experience in Cuba*, and Caroline Bettinger-López, *Cuban-Jewish Journeys: Searching for Identity, Home and History in Miami*.

    3. Rieff, *Exile*, 32–33.

    4. Ibid., 22.

    5. Ibid., 54–55.

    6. Mario Ripoll to his brothers in Machado's *The Modern Ladies of Guanabacoa*, in *The Floating Island Plays*, 19. Machado and his play first came to my attention in the fall of 1994 when the Mark Taper Forum in Los Angeles produced the whole *Floating Islands* cycle. The production resonated historically in that it was mounted immediately following the *balsero* crisis of August 1994; it also generated some controversy in Los Angeles over its handling by the mainstream press. The *Los Angeles Times* printed two excellent background pieces on Machado and the play by Jan Breslauer in October and November, but the review by Laurie Winer (October 25, 1994, F1–F3) struck a nerve with some readers, who found her response limited by her failure to appreciate the play's and the production's larger cultural and historical contexts. To Winer's complaint that "Machado's epic . . . doesn't so much evoke [the Cuban-American experience] as overexplain it," Migdia Chinea-Varela (*Los Angeles Times*, November 14, 1994, F3) counters that what might appear as a "leaden" or "scripted" didacticism (to quote Winer) in Machado's dramatizing of Cuban history might serve some legitimate aesthetic purpose. Machado's "epic on dislocation," Chinea-Varela argues, takes on the formidable task of articulating to an audience, whose knowledge the playwright does not take for granted, a "history so mired in contradiction that [even] four . . . plays could not explain the extent to which political events have shaped our mentality." Chinea-Varela surmises that "Machado . . . believed that it was incumbent upon him to explain our collective *raison d'être*—our tragedy as well as our comedy," thus countering Winer's comment that Machado's broad, often "hyperbolic" dramatics border on a "soap opera" style that even his "vast historical backdrop" cannot "dignify." Machado himself confesses to his penchant for melodrama bordering on farce; Breslauer observes in one of his articles that Machado's work occasionally "hovers near the purple emotions of *telenovela*" (*Los Angeles Times Calendar*, October 16, 1994, 57), to which Machado adds that "Laughter is an opiate in the theatre," a necessary ingredient for a writer

who, in confronting painful historical realities, must "be willing to be some-one that a lot of people" including perhaps unsympathetic drama critics, "don't like"(Breslauer, 88).

7. A fine recent analysis of Ortiz's work, which first appeared in Spanish in 1940, may be found in Benítez-Rojo's *The Repeating Island: The Caribbean and the Postmodern Perspective*, 150–76. Benítez-Rojo argues in "Fernando Ortiz: The Caribbean and Postmodernity" that *Cuban Counterpoint* resists tradition *and* modernity, especially of the European varieties, by remaining poised in the "counterpoint" between narrative and scientific forms of knowl-edge, a counterpoint defined by the allegorical cultural values assigned to to-bacco and sugar, and by the competing values of a text that performs simultaneously its allegorical and anthropological functions. I have occasion to return to Benítez-Rojo later in my discussion of Albita Rodríguez's work.

8. And Cubans mark themselves more according to capacities for pleas-ure than through any other criteria. In fact, the repeated (categorical?) im-perative phrase in much of Cuban music is "*¡goza cubano!*" which commands the explicitly Cuban audience precisely "to enjoy," or *gozar*.

9. Machado, 19–20.

10. Ortiz, 207.

11. Ibid., 206.

12. Ibid., 209.

13. Ibid., 208.

14. See especially Eagleton, *The Function of Criticism*.

15. Avital Ronell, *Crack Wars: Literature, Addiction, Mania,* 22–23. A number of Ronell's arguments in this volume have influenced my analysis in this chapter; see, for example, her later observation that even when "Detached from the strictly determined referent, addiction can also hanker after a mys-tified communion of community, a mythology of 'Volk' or even economy, which is why one is also susceptible to becoming intoxicated with any regime of reunification" (Ronell, 42). Certainly this intoxicating "regime of reunification" can describe one fantasy among others for a possible Cuban future.

16. Machado, 20.

17. Ibid., 20–21. Interestingly, Richard Klein tells an imperfectly analo-gous political history of tobacco in *Cigarettes Are Sublime*, 12. "The history of the struggle against tyrants," Klein argues, "has been frequently insepara-ble from that of the struggle on behalf of the freedom to smoke, and no time was this more the case than during the French and American revolutions." Indeed, Klein asserts "the earliest political history of this country, from the time of the first English settlers, who survived on the commerce of tobacco, to the revolutionary struggle against English taxes, was forged in the name of the right and freedom to grow and use tobacco—free from the impositions

of the state" (12). Like Ortiz and like Machado's character Oscar, Klein situates tobacco in the defining moment of *European* modernity, arguing later
in the same chapter that tobacco's "use is an index of whatever revolution in
consciousness may have occurred to transform the culture and the mores,
the ethics and principles of antiquity," primarily because its "introduction . . . into Europe corresponded with the Age of Anxiety, the beginning of
modern consciousness that accompanied the invention and universalization
of printed books, the discovery of the New World, the development of rational, scientific methods, and the concurrent loss of medieval theological
assurances"(27). Although tobacco in Klein's scenario fuels action externally, as opposed to the more direct, internal stimulation of thought and action by coffee, the analogous stimulations of political and organic bodies
works well here to affirm precisely the conventional, and still compelling,
analogy, supplied by the prevailing cultural concept of the body between
polity and organism. It is perhaps the historical weight of such an analogy
that informs Jacques Derrida's remark in "The Rhetoric of Drugs" that
"whole theses, even whole departments of literature . . . should perhaps be
devoted to the study of tobacco and coffee"(Derrida, 238).

18. Machado, 45–46.

19. Readers interested in pursuing the issue of racial semiotics further are
directed to Benítez-Rojo's chapter on Ortiz in *The Repeating Island,* as well
as to Vera Kutzinski's *Sugar's Secrets.* Kutzinski's analysis of the evolution of
the figure of the mixed-race mulatta woman as iconographic marker of
Cuban national identity tackles directly the many "tricky questions about
how race, gender and sexuality inflect the power relations that obtain in
colonial and postcolonial Cuba"(7), questions my own rather limited study
can only indirectly raise.

20. Machado, 171.

21. Ibid., 176, 216–17.

22. Ibid., 193, 215.

23. Ibid., 177, 200.

24. This observation is certainly not meant to be read as incidental.
Machado's juxtaposition of Miriam's desire for immersion not only in her
Valium's mediating effects but also in the medium of her community's common illusions with Sonia's individualistic refusal of both the drug and the
promise quite readily recalls Tennyson's juxtaposition of the collective
"choric" voices of the lotus eaters with the singular voice of Odysseus. The
narcotic effect of collective fantasy was also not lost on Reinaldo Arenas,
whose novel *The Doorman,* I argued in an earlier chapter, is cast in the
"choric" narrative voice of the million Cuban exiles. Indeed, any return to
the Homeric or even the Tennysonian precedent immediately calls up a
question haunting this entire study, the question of the possible efficacy of

a free and individuated will. The most cogent articulation of the problem that practices and discourses of addiction pose for the presumption of free will may be found in Eve Sedgwick's "Epidemics of the Will," in *Tendencies,* 130–42. There Sedgwick argues that, since "any substance, any behavior, even any affect may be pathologized as addictive," then "Addiction" (certainly as I treat it in this chapter), "resides only in a *structure* of a will that is somehow insufficiently free, a choice whose voluntarity is insufficiently pure" (132).

25. Machado, 202, 215.

26. Ibid., 218. It is worth noting that Machado does not leave *his* final statement to Sonia. Her declaration of newfound independence is not only juxtaposed to Miriam's willing capitulation to the pleasures of Valium, but it is also mitigated by her own passive voicing of her suggested expulsion from Cuba. Machado literally gives the last word in the play to Sonia's son, Oscar, who sings "a little tune my mother taught me," a traditional song called "Isla," which ends with the lines "isla mía/te dejé," or "my island/I left you"(Machado, 216–18) and therefore puts responsibility for the estrangement squarely on the one who left. David Rieff comments on this final scene in his note in the *Playbill* for the 1994 Taper production of *Floating Islands* (see Rieff, "Paradise Lost: A Perspective on *Floating Islands*"). Machado, Rieff argues, successfully casts "belonging and non-belonging" as the "principal subtext of the play," which is "as it should be" if only because "exile is the paradigmatic contemporary condition," making it "unavoidable" when traveling in postcolonial times "to move not so much between nations as between diasporas" (Rieff, "Paradise," 8).

27. Perhaps one way to theorize the operation of repetition in a text as compulsive as Machado's, especially to the extent to which it articulates an experience as complicated by compulsion as that of Cuban exile, is to turn to Antonio Benítez-Rojo's more general formulation of repetition in Caribbean culture (see his Introduction to *The Repeating Island,* 1–29). As Cubans in exile isolate themselves historically and politically in a repetition that approximates the islandized national life for which they yearn, so Benítez-Rojo explains the quality of this complex general repetition as a symptom of postmodern Caribbean experience: "in the discourse of Chaos," he argues, "every repetition is a practice that necessarily entails a difference and a step toward nothingness" (3). And indeed, Machado's text, in the history it retells before arriving back in an unresolved present, plays rather emphatically with the ongoing *fort-da* of this exile, repeating legacies, curses, and addictions across epochs, generations, and borders. Machado's "tropisms" of addiction, of which coffee is one among others, thus occur "in series; mov[ing] in approximate direction," like the "repeating" islands in Benítez-Rojo's Caribbean (4), toward what might be called a "tropic entropy"

(Derrida, *Specters*) made tolerable only by the narcotic effects of the "tropium" (Ronell, 27) they themselves produce.

28. See "Shipwreck with a Sunrise in the Background" in *Mea Cuba*, 4.

29. Like the Taper production of Machado's work, Albita's first U.S.-recorded CD, *No Se Parece a Nada*, generated a considerable amount of press coverage. See, for example, Susan Miller, "A Diva from Old Havana" (*Newsweek*, July 17, 1995, 61); Mike Clary, "A Singer Unlike Anything Else" (*Los Angeles Times*, July 28, 1995, F1, F21); Julie Reynolds, "Albita's Miami" (*El Andar: The Latino Magazine*, January 1996, 8–9); and Susan Orlean, "The Homesick Restaurant" (*New Yorker*, January 15, 1996, 36–41).

30. Clary, F1.

31. Enrique Lopetegui, "*No Se Parece* Shows Albita as a Refreshing Vocal Force" (*Los Angeles Times*, July 28, 1995, F21).

32. See Cruz-Malavé's "Towards an Art of Transvestism: Colonialism and Homosexuality in Puerto Rican Literature," in *¿Entiendes?: Queer Readings, Hispanic Writings*, 157.

33. This statement should by no means be taken to declare my own position on anything like the causes or origins of homosexuality. This merely describes the general orientation of Albita's lyrics, which typically cast constructed identity categories as aspects of "essential" being.

34. These translations, my own, are necessarily rough. Albita's lyrics are as poetically and philosophically ambitious as I suggest, and therefore too complex to facilitate easy domestication into congruent English.

35. Cuban national identity, like others, often finds itself under construction in that anxious place where ontology borders on metaphysics. Machado, too, jokes in his interview with Jan Breslauer about the difficulty of articulating that "anxious" state, that "unbearable lightness of being Cubano" (Breslauer, 88). This anxiety, as both Richard Klein (142–43) and Avital Ronell (43–44) have both observed, travels through Heideggerian discourse as well, where it poses the question of freedom for Heidegger's *Dasein*. According to Ronell, Heidegger distinguishes a "freedom" available to *Dasein* as an "openness to anxiety which addiction and drugs are seen to divert," a freedom, that is, driven by necessity but not by compulsion, by a categorical performative (if not imperative) informed by the "guilty" acknowledgment of (passive, "thrown") being as being-indebted, not being-on-drugs.

36. See, for example, the essays collected by Frances R. Aparicio, Cándida Jacquez, and María Elena Cepeda in *Musical Migrations: Transnationalism and Cultural Hybridity in Latin/o America* and by Celeste Delgado and José Muñoz in *EveryNight Life: Culture and Dance in Latin/o America*. See also Gustavo Pérez-Firmat's analysis of U.S.–Cuban traditional and popular musical forms, from the introduction of the mambo in the 1930s through

recent work by Gloria Estefan and the larger "Miami Sound" phenomenon in *Life on the Hyphen*, 113–33. See also Benítez-Rojo's chapter on Fernando Ortiz in *The Repeating Island* (150–76). There Benítez-Rojo develops most fully his notion of the operation of rhythm in Caribbean narrative, a narrative the author (following Lyotard, see 168–71) reads as traditional and counter to the scientific narrative of the modern West. It bears looking more closely at the vestiges of such an authenticating rhythm in, say, the very technically sophisticated recordings of an Albita or of Gloria Estefan in her *Mi Tierra* mode (see chapter 4), recordings that provoke a deeply emotional response in any audience looking for a "naturalizing" nationalist affirmation.

37. Pérez-Firmat, 108.

38. Ibid., 122.

39. I cannot let this opportunity pass without glancing briefly at Derrida's comment on nostalgia in "The Rhetoric of Drugs" (242). There Derrida excavates the etymological layers of experience as "the voyage that crosses the boundary . . . the passage, the odyssey with or without nostalgia," an excavation that leads him back to Adorno and Horkheimer's work on the *nostos*, the "wandering from which there is no return" typified for the Frankfurt theorists by Homer's lotus eaters (see Horkheimer and Adorno, "Odysseus, or Myth and Enlightenment," in *Dialectic of Enlightenment*, 63–64). In a note on this passage (note 7, 472) Derrida argues that for Horkheimer and Adorno the Lotus Eaters embodied an "unproductivity," a refusal to work imbedded in a failure of memory, of the historical orientation without which there is also no community, an oblivion and surrender to "non-work" as alarming to them as it was to Tennyson. The Cuban twist to this archetype, of course, is the exile community's paradoxical combination of material productivity with a narcotized ideological stupor; our addiction to nostalgia is an odd form of amnesia indeed.

40. Although I do not make the connection as literal or direct as I might in this discussion, it certainly should not be lost on the reader that addiction in the forms it does take in the present analysis of Albita's attachments to her various forms of identity always bears in it an insistent and profound erotics.

41. Pérez-Firmat, 11.

42. José Esteban Muñoz has articulated the peculiar qualities of this generational condition best. In "*No es fácil*: Notes on the Negotiation of Cubanidad and Exilic Memory in Carmelita Tropicana's Milk of Amnesia," a chapter of his very influential *Disidentifications: Queers of Color and the Performance of Politics*, Muñoz confesses that as "a Cuban American who grew up in the US but was nonetheless born on the island of Cuba," he has "lived in Cuba through the auspices of memory," that "exilic memory has

reproduced Cuba for [him . . . as] a collection of snapshots, disembodied voices over the phone line, and most vividly, exilic memories" (1).

43. See Julie Reynolds, "Albita's Miami" (*El Andar: The Latino Magazine,* January 1996, 9).

44. Rieff, 178.

45. Ibid., 179.

46. I certainly do not mean to abuse such national categories by burdening them with too much symbolic or practical weight. It seems just as disingenuous, however, not to acknowledge some specific forms of intellectual traffic here among specific nations and other cultural groupings. Certainly the knot formed by a certain German-Jewish philosophical thread (with some occasional French commentary) with its Cuban filiations bears some scrutiny here.

47. Padilla, *Self-Portrait of the Other,* 15.

48. Ibid., 16–17.

49. Perhaps the most entertainingly hyperbolic treatment of the kind of xenophobia that has riled so many of Didion's critics appears in James Ellroy's *American Tabloid,* which opens with the following description of a demented Howard Hughes watching television footage of Fidel Castro's encampment in the Sierra Maestra in 1958: "He always shot up by TV light. Some spics waved guns. The head spic plucked bugs from his beard and fomented. Black and white footage: CBS geeks in jungle fatigues. A newsman said, Cuba, bad juju—Fidel rebels vs. Fulgencio Batista's standing army. Howard Hughes found a vein and mainlined codeine" (5). Didion's and Ellroy's comprise but two of a varied constellation of texts that might be termed the "Cuba–bad juju" school of U.S. political and fictional analysis of the Cuban "situation." I would certainly include among these Ann Louise Bardach's *Cuba Confidential,* already cited, whose title echoes the title of one of Ellroy's other novels.

50. Didion, 20.

51. Ibid., 160.

52. Ibid.

53. Derrida, *Specters* 58. Although I turn in concluding here primarily to Derrida's work in *Specters of Marx,* the analysis in this passage also makes an implicit nod at another observation of Derrida's, again from "The Rhetoric of Drugs," that "A certain form of drug addiction . . . can also reflect this . . . phantasm of reappropriation. It can do so naively or with a great 'cultivation,' dreaming of an 'ego,' of a self, or of the self's own body, or even of a subject once and for all reclaimed from the forces of alienation, from oppression and repression, and from the law that speaks in religion, metaphysics, politics, the family, and so forth" (Derrida, "Rhetoric," 241–42).

54. Derrida, *Specters,* 59.

55. Ibid., 65.
56. Ibid.
57. Ibid.
58. Ibid., 66.

6. *Beyond All Cuban Counterpoints:* Eduardo Machado's Floating Island Plays

1. See Derrida, *Specters of Marx: The State of the Debt, the Work of Mourning, and the New International,* 42. In addition to this important meditation of the relationship between spectrality and history, two additional performances of Derrida's also inform this article; one is his reading of religion and history in *The Gift of Death,* and the other is his less well-known reading of *Romeo and Juliet* in "Aphorism/Countertime" (in *Acts of Literature*). Although I mostly call on Derrida's work here to help me explicate the uniquely deconstructive elements of Cuban American history, I also want to make a mostly implicit case for Derrida's salience in reading theater, ritual, drama, and performance as historical modes; since his very early work on Artaud in *Writing and Difference,* to his work on Genet the playwright in *Glas,* to the more recent work cited here, Derrida spent much of his career demonstrating that, just as deconstruction should continue to have a hand in the ongoing critical elaboration of theater, so theater has always had a hand in the ongoing critical elaboration of deconstruction.

2. Hartman, "On Traumatic Knowledge and Literary Studies," 548. My thanks to Brian Reilly for bringing this article to my attention. A brief elaboration of Hartman's argument occurs in note 36.

3. See Machado, *The Floating Island Plays.* This chapter also makes liberal use of a substantially revised script of *Fabiola* supplied by the playwright. For purposes of citation, references to the published version mostly appear as F1, and references to the unpublished revision appear as F2. Since the 1994 Taper production of *Floating Islands,* Machado has continued to explore the Cuban American experience in such plays as *Waiting for Havana* (2001), *The Cook* (2003), and *Kissing Fidel* (2005), all of which remain unpublished, although they enjoyed successful productions in New York City in the early years of the first decade of the new millennium.

4. Ortiz wrote most of *Cuban Counterpoint* in the 1930s; the standard English edition is *Cuban Counterpoint: Tobacco and Sugar,* translated by Harriet de Onís. Two other more recent works by Cuban intellectuals that implicitly but emphatically inform my understanding of more island-centered (and at the same time more diasporic) Cuban cultural and political dynamics are Benítez-Rojo's *The Repeating Island: The Caribbean and the Postmodern Perspective* and Rafael Rojas's as yet untranslated *La Política del Adiós.*

5. In "Aphorism/Countertime," Derrida goes on to argue that, precisely through the dramatization of this spatio-temporal disjunction, *Romeo and Juliet* does more than tell a truth theatrically; it also tells the "truth" of "theater": "Disjunction, dislocation, separation of places, deployment or spacing of a story because of aphorism . . . would there be any theatre without that? The survival of a theatrical work implies that, theatrically, it is saying something about theater itself, about its essential possibility. And that it does so, theatrically, then, the play of uniqueness and repetition, by giving rise every time to the chance of an absolutely singular event as it does to the untranslatable idiom of a proper name, to its fatality . . . to the fatality of a date and of a rendezvous" (Derrida, "Aphorism," 419). Derrida's formulation may thus also guide us past the fatal untranslatability of *Fabiola*'s name and namings. Certainly the play may be said in part to speak its own theatrical "truth" as a "truth" about a "theater" we usually name "history."

6. F1, 67.

7. Hartman, 537.

8. "Postmemory" is a term deployed quite productively by Marianne Hirsch in *Family Frames: Photography, Narrative, Post-Memory* to describe the persistence of historical trauma's effects on the children of immigrants. It "is distinguished from memory," Hirsch argues, "by generational distance and from history by deep personal connection," and it "characterizes the experience of those who grew up dominated by narratives that preceded their birth, whose own belated stories are evacuated by the stories of the previous generation shaped by traumatic events that can be neither understood nor recreated"(Hirsch, 22).

9. The best reading of the varying political and cultural sensibilities of Cuban-exile and Cuban-American immigrant generations remains Gustavo Pérez-Firmat's 1994 study *Life on the Hyphen: The Cuban-American Way* (cited in earlier chapters). In the decade-plus since its publication, Pérez-Firmat's founding contribution to U.S.–Cuban cultural studies has been usefully supplemented by book-length studies (all already mentioned in my Introduction) across various fields and methodologies, including political science (Maria de los Angeles Torres's *In the Land of the Mirrors*, 1999), sociology (María Cristina García's *Havana USA*, 1996), and literary studies (Isabel Alvarez-Borland's *Cuban-American Literature of Exile*, 1998).

10. It bears noting here that although the post–Cold War period has been frustrating to Cuban exiles and others off the island who hoped the fall of the Soviet empire would lead fairly precipitously to the fall of Castro's regime, that "Special Period" did usher in profound changes within Cuba. According to Damián Fernández, "the Special Period . . . was an austerity program" that "reduce[d] social programs dramatically" in Cuba (see Fernández, *Cuba and the Politics of Passion,* especially 59–60). He goes on in a later pas-

sage to specify that during the mid-1990s the Cuban government "closed factories, laid off workers, opened the economy to tourism and foreign investment and expanded the legal *space* for self-employment" (Fernández, 126). In perhaps more vivid language, Román de la Campa has called the "long" Special Period "Cuba's . . . current moment of indecision: a post-socialist void jumbled with pseudo-capitalist reforms" (see *Cuba on My Mind: Journeys to a Severed Nation,* 79–80). These measures, as both Fernández and de la Campa suggest, take on even greater resonance in light of the discussion of Cuba's post–Cold War negotiations with global capital, which I undertake in the last section of this discussion.

11. In the first act of version 2, Machado has Cusa read out of a selection of Marx's texts, from the "Theses on Feuerbach" to *The German Ideology* to *Capital;* all the quotations, immediately recognizable, simultaneously delay the momentum of the actual dialogue and distract the audience from a larger ideological and theatrical message to which they must attend. In Derrida's terms, Cusa's aphoristic ejaculations demonstrate why "each aphorism['s] temporal logic prevents it from sharing all its time . . . with the discourse of the other," and why, then, these aphorisms might be strategically out of place, or not at home, in a dramatic dialogue. Aphorism marks, for Derrida, the "[I]mpossible synchronization . . . of the discourse of time, of its marks, of its dates, of the course of time and of the essential digression which dislocates desire and carries the step of those who love one another off course"(Derrida, "Aphorism," 418).

12. This section of the chapter also owes an implicit debt to Marianne Hirsch, who further observes in *Family Frames* that "In the postmodern moment, the family occupies a powerful and powerfully threatened place: structurally a last vestige of protection against war, racism, exile and cultural displacement, it becomes particularly vulnerable to these violent ruptures, and so a measure of their devastation" (Hirsch, 13).

13. The Cuban American situation has, of course, traditionally played itself out in part as a very public, even scandalous, narrative of familial crisis, most memorably perhaps in the media circus surrounding the Elián González affair in late 1999 and early 2000 (see chapter 8 on Rafael Campo below). For an exhaustive treatment of that moment in the context of post-revolutionary and post–Cold War Cuban American history, see again journalist Ann Louise Bardach's *Cuba Confidential: Love and Vengeance in Miami and Havana.* In her preface to that volume, Bardach addresses her decision to "view this forty-four-year-old quagmire" through the "prism . . . of the broken family," explaining in part how this "trope of the shattered family has infused the Cuban conflict with an emotionality that is the stuff of Greek drama, with plotlines borrowed from Shakespeare and afternoon *telenovelas*" (Bardach, xvii).

14. This analysis owes something at least in spirit to Lora Romero, to whom this chapter is dedicated. In her trenchant, cautionary introduction to *Home Fronts: Domesticity and Its Critics in the Antebellum United States*, Romero makes a typically articulate case for analyzing the operations of power in radically local and localizable ways, for acknowledging, in other words, that power's stages are, because they are also history's, everywhere and ultimately not given to conceptual generalization or totalization.

15. F1, 106.

16. Ibid., 107.

17. Ibid.

18. See Melissa Zeiger's argument connecting gender, homosociality and mourning in *Beyond Consolation: Death, Sexuality and the Changing Shapes of Elegy;* for Zeiger, "the complex, often fraught interplay between male ho-moerotic desire and heterosexual cultural norms embodied in marriage is prefigured in the Orpheus story, as is the conflict between the erotically charged impulses of the living to remain connected to the dead or aggressively disconnect themselves from them" (Zeiger, 2). Zeiger's formulation of this tradition helps illustrate the congruence rather than the contradiction between Pedro's hysterical mourning of his wife and his equally compulsive desire for his brother. Indeed, the shift from an Oedipal to an Orphean model does some of the work of refiguring, and reconfiguring, the familial and gender paradigms at work in *Fabiola*, which can be argued generally to resituate familial relations outside prevailing and constitutive political and symbolic "frames," like the Oedipal model, in favor of (m)any others. This shift also exposes the tortured logic behind a kind of gendered division of labor determining who traditionally bears the burden for mourning in most patriarchal societies. Judith Butler in *Antigone's Claim: Kinship Between Life and Death* also suggests ways to extend the analysis here further in this direction.

19. F1, 61.

20. From various conversations with the playwright in the course of the late 1990s.

21. The conflation of Cuban and (mostly male) homosexual identities here could just as easily hold a mirror up to Cuban audiences on the island as well as off; by now we can point to the long complex history of both creative and critical commentary on the way that the politics of gender and sexuality have been implicated in Cuban cultural, national, and state politics. Reinaldo Arenas's life's work was arguably dedicated to the documentation of precisely this vexed node of political forces, and from that work and work like it has issued in turn a very rich critical legacy, especially in the United States by scholars in a variety of fields. See, for example, José Quiroga's chapters on Virgilio Piñera and the film *Strawberry and Chocolate* in *Tropics of*

Desire in the section entitled "Critical Cubanía" of José Muñoz's *Disidentifications* and in all of Emilio Bejel's *Gay Cuban Nation* (all cited in an earlier chapter).

22. F2, 36.

23. F1, 62.

24. Ibid., 72.

25. Ibid.

26. Ibid., 53.

27. Machado, *Hurricane*, 133. This play, which is set on two days in Havana in 1960, and *Fabiola* actually overlap chronologically; depending on the production, either play can be performed as the second or the third installment in the cycle, constituting, in their ambiguous, even dubious interchangeability yet another instance of theatrical countertime. Maria Josefa is the matriarch of the Ripoll clan; she is Sonia's maternal grandmother. Sonia is the same woman married to Osvaldo in *Fabiola,* and as such she is the character bridging the major generational and familial divides in the four plays. This dialogue occurs as the Ripoll women prepare a lunch for the family on the day the revolutionary government will come to claim title to the family's bus company for the state.

28. See the volume coedited by Taylor and Juan Villegas entitled *Negotiating Performance: Gender, Sexuality and Theatricality in Latin/o America* (especially 11–14 of Taylor's introduction). By no means do I intend to give sole credit to Taylor for inventing the theoretical distinction between theater and performance, although her work on this topic is the most useful to me here; in addition to Taylor, this argument owes a significant and profound debt to the work of other influential practitioners of performance studies. These include Joseph Roach, who in his *Cities of the Dead* argues, in ways that resonate through much of my reading of Machado, "Performance . . . stands in for an elusive entity that it is not but that it must vainly aspire both to embody and to replace. Hence flourish the abiding yet vexed affinities," Roach concludes, "between performance and memory, out of which blossom the most florid nostalgias for authenticity and origin" (*Cities of the Dead: Circum-Atlantic Performance*, especially 3–4).

29. Taylor, 13–14.

30. F2, 65.

31. F1, 60.

32. Ibid.

33. I take Machado's solicitation of Brecht, and especially of *Mother Courage and Her Children,* to mark his dramaturgy as profoundly as any other I may discuss here; Cusa in the later *Fabiola* witnesses the disappearance of each of her children, victims either to death or to exile, as distractedly as Courage does hers in Brecht's play, and, at the time of the composition of

Floating Islands, Machado could be said to be witnessing himself the fallout of a different kind of "thirty years' war" in chronicling the thirty-plus years' "cold" war waged between revolutionaries and exiles since 1959.

34. See Benjamin, *Illuminations: Essays and Reflections,* 151. Benjamin's own work can certainly be said to constitute its own theatrical history; in addition to the explicit discussion of both his and Brecht's theories of epic theater in this section, Benjamin's variously "theatrical" analyses of both seventeenth-century German mourning plays (in *The Origins of German Tragic Drama*) and of history as such in his own famous (and famously discontinuous and aphoristic) "Theses on the Philosophy of History" implicitly inform everything I say in this section. Benjamin's essay can also be read as a resonant precursor to Derrida's own "Aphorism/Countertime," discussed earlier.

35. F2, 15.

36. A considerable body of scholarship has in the last decade taken up the challenge of articulating the relation of literature and theater to trauma more explicitly and helpfully. In his essay "On Traumatic Knowledge and Literature," Geoffrey Hartman analyzes literature's negotiation of the pain or wound of trauma in a manner that reactivates both Freudian and Lacanian psychoanalytic terms in the service of a new ethics (rather than, say, a new therapeutics or even epistemology) of reading. To this end, Hartman reads "against" catharsis as a chief aim of literature that takes on the responsibility of testifying to historical trauma; as such, he also reads, in ways applicable to Machado, against sentimentalism and melodramatic "seriousness." See also in this respect Cathy Carruth's equally unflinching reading of theater's responsibility to a witnessing of the traumatic (with specific and, in relation to Machado, resonant reference to the dream of the burning child in Freud), in "Traumatic Awakenings" (89–107) and Elin Diamond's fascinating, antitherapeutic retheorization of catharsis in "The Shudder of Catharsis" (152–72), both of which appear in the collection *Performativity and Performance.*

37. F2, 5–7.

38. Ibid., 19–20.

39. Ibid., 86–87.

40. John Paul II's visit to Cuba faded quickly from at least U.S. public awareness and public memory because of two far more showy events; it coincided to the week with the disclosures in the U.S. press of former President Bill Clinton's affair with Monica Lewinsky, and it was upstaged again exactly two years later by the Elián González matter, which turned its own peculiar kind of trick in marking Cuban time.

41. Machado, *Hurricane,* 116–17.

42. F1, 70–71.

43. This was reported by the *New York Times* in an article dated January 22, 1998, A12.

44. *New York Times*, A12. This declaration was echoed by an equally astonishing one in John Paul's homily during the mass in Havana's Plaza de la Revolución, where he told Cubans that they should continue to struggle to be subjects rather than objects of history.

45. *New York Times*, A12.

46. Months after John Paul's visit, an article in *The Nation* describing the ongoing crisis afflicting both Cuba's revolutionary economy and culture left no doubt of the kind of speculation still presiding over both (see Baxter, "Cuba's Suspended Revolution"). Baxter's article describes how, "in the postcold war era, the social fabric of the revolution [was] unraveling," and how in turn Cuba had turned to policies like the following to "stave off a complete meltdown" of its economy. Castro's government, Baxter reported, had by that time "participated in more than 200 'joint ventures' with major foreign capitalists—with the Cuban state's 'investment' often no more than its supply of a cheap and disempowered work force. The US dollar," Baxter goes on, "has been legalized as a parallel currency and has, to no one's surprise, created a parallel speculative economy" (20–23). This process has, also to no one's surprise, both slowed down and gone underground since the ascension of the more conservative (and exile-friendly) Bush administration in 2000, but it has not halted completely; there remain congressional lawmakers in the United States from both major parties who see in Cuba the potential for further, if incremental, democratization through strategic economic engagement of the kind that has slowly relaxed some forms of state repression in nations like China and Vietnam. It bears noting that, in February 2003, as attention in most of the world remained fixed on the impending U.S. invasion of Iraq, Fidel Castro visited a China so transformed by liberal market reforms that it left him, according to one Associated Press report, "amazed" ("Castro Stunned By Changing China," http://www.CNN.com, February 27, 2003). The characteristically cagey Castro didn't let on whether the amazement was positive or negative; certainly nothing has changed so dramatically on the Cuban as it has on the Chinese scene. One can only wonder whether Castro left China having witnessed a version of a Cuban future that he might welcome or resist.

47. F2, 20.

48. Derrida, *Specters*, 42, 148.

49. Ibid.

50. Ibid., 168.

51. If Benítez-Rojo called Cuba *la isla que se repite* (the repeating island), I have grown fond of calling it *la isla a la cual se remite* (the island to which one [sends] remit[tance]s).

7. Careers of Surplus Value in the Novels of Cristina García

1. The speaker is Pilar Puente (137–38).

2. See the unpaginated interview with García featured in Ballantine's paperback edition of *The Agüero Sisters;* informative interviews with García also appear in the paperback editions of *Dreaming in Cuban, Monkey Hunting,* and in Heredia and Kevane's *Latina Self-Portraits.* I'm primarily but not exclusively interested in García's interviews as part of the commercial packaging of her work; they therefore serve to frame the readerly consumption of that work in ways that cannot be easily equated with the work of conventional literary criticism or commentary.

3. In any case, see both Jameson, *The Political Unconscious: Narrative as a Socially Symbolic Act* and *The Cultural Turn: Selected Writings on the Postmodern.*

4. Karl Marx, *Capital,* volume 1. This translation is excerpted in *The Marx-Engels Reader,* ed. Robert C. Tucker, 358–59.

5. See Derrida, "Economimesis," 3–25.

6. In a conversation I had with García in the summer of 2004, she told me that she views *Dreaming in Cuban, The Agüero Sisters,* and *Monkey Hunting* as forming a "rough trilogy" of Cuba-related work. She also claims that she made no conscious decision to have a significant character in each novel open and run a business.

7. This practice is a regular feature of a series of paperback publications by Ballantine, including as well Achy Obejas's *Days of Awe* (2001), discussed in detail earlier in this book.

8. Although such a negative estimation of the fate of culture in revolutionary Cuba seems to fly in the face of much of what we know of the revolution's very public sponsorship of the arts in Cuba and even abroad, this skepticism haunts a significant body of work regarding especially the politics of free artistic expression in Cuba since 1959. See, for example, Reinaldo Arenas's frequent asides on that subject in the course of *Before Night Falls* (discussed at length in preceding chapters of this book), in Coco Fusco's accounts (in the "Miranda's Diary" section of her *English Is Broken Here*) of her attempts to participate in and to keep open the channels of cultural flow between Cuba and the United States in the 1980s and early 1990s, and even in the highly critical representation of the artist Germán's troubles with the government in Tomás Gutierrez Alea's film *Strawberry and Chocolate.*

9. The balance that I see García trying to strike here between her aesthetic and her practical concerns constitutes in part her direct response to shifts in the larger social and cultural conditions in which she writes, conditions that have in turn transformed both the status and the function of cul-

tural artifacts in the decade-plus following the end of the Cold War; as George Yúdice argues in *The Expediency of Culture* (2003), this post–Cold War "understanding of culture is quite complex, located at the intersection of economic and social justice agendas"(17) because it is increasingly deployed "as a resource for both sociopolitical and economic amelioration"(9) and therefore "no longer valued, experienced or understood as transcendent" (12).

10. It might have been easier for Shorris to make these claims while he was researching Cuban Miami in the last days of the Cold War; clearly Portes and Rumbaut, García the historian, and other scholars researching Cuban Miami in the decade-plus following the end of the Cold War saw a more complex and fluid community working to accommodate itself to a decidedly different and in many ways more challenging set of political, economic, and even cultural conditions. See, for example, the chapter on Miami in Héctor Tobar's *Translation Nation* (2005). There Tobar describes the "rise of Cuban Miami" as the process by which "Cubanos became the most affluent and influential group in the multinational Latin American diaspora in the United States . . . fervent aficionados of that quintessential American pastime called making money." And although Tobar observes that "They came to Miami with engineering and medical degrees, with a merchant's nose for lucrative possibilities and untapped markets, and remade Miami into the capital of the Caribbean and South and Central American elites" (193), he does so in the contexts of both their waning political and cultural dominance in that city and their waning obsession with return to any other post-Castro Cuba than the one they invented and maintain in South Florida.

11. It's very helpful to read García's characterization of Pilar alongside Coco Fusco's account of the often rocky history of cultural exchange between Cuba and the United States in the decade or so preceding the publication of *Dreaming in Cuban;* although García has Pilar develop her aesthetic and political philosophies in the 1970s, her attitudes in part reflect García's own experiences traveling between Cuba and (Cuban) America in the 1980s. Fusco tells us, for example, that for Cuban artists working in the last decade of the Cold War "the celebration of cultural identity was experienced as official policy of the State, and . . . radicalism could be measured in terms of one's distance from [that] official policy," and therefore they would "tend to look upon the identity politics of the [U.S.-based] new New Left with skepticism if not disdain." And because this North American turn to an embrace of "Multiculturalism more often than not spell[ed] manipulation of art for political ends to them," these Cuba-based artists often had "difficulty acknowledging the grass-roots dimension of efforts toward cultural pluralism in the North and [did] not recognize the advantages of an alliance based on a shared interest in cultural democracy" (15). Fusco, of course, does not fail

to observe how gender also contributed to this already complex scene; "This is not to say," she cautions later in the same essay, "that all Cuban women dissent from official points of view on Cuba. However, given that the areas that kept Cubans bound *despite* politics are primarily those of family and culture, and that women have traditionally been ascribed the role of their keepers, it doesn't surprise me that women would take the lead in these areas or that they would cast a skeptical eye toward a political sphere that excluded them before the Revolution, as well as outside the island" (Fusco, 20).

12. In an interview with García published just after the appearance of *The Agüero Sisters* in 1997, Laura Shefler reports that García herself "never questioned *her* Cuban identity, until she moved to Miami in 1987 as a correspondent for *Time* magazine"; there, and "To her surprise, [that year] was one of the most difficult of her life," leaving her "alienated both by the pervasive nostalgia for pre-revolutionary Cuba and by what she calls the 'with us or against us' political intensity" of the place. See Laura Shefler, "Cristina García: When Are You Cuban Enough?" (http://sfl.com/issue_08_97/interview.html).

13. An almost directly corresponding passage describing the character of Isabel and her artwork appears in *The Agüero Sisters;* from a narrative perspective that's fairly directly aligned with her mother Constancia, we learn that in her pottery "Isabel has always been drawn to more free-form work, odd shards of clay and other materials combined to suggest something recycled, something tampered with or incomplete" (212). And if the issue of representationality would seem to be averted in the context of pottery, which is conventionally not made to "represent" anything other than, well, pottery, here the issue of what pottery as an art can mean seems correspondingly displaced onto the question of its utility. Garcia's passage on Isabel's work most fully suggests that her character sculpts increasingly abstract clay pieces as she moves from an orientation toward the practical to an orientation toward the conceptual.

14. This section of my discussion owes a profound debt to *Latinos, Inc,* Arlene Dávila's impressive 2001 study of the corporate cultures and mentalities of U.S.-based marketing agencies either run by or targeting members of U.S. Latino populations. Dávila's work directly informs the analysis I conduct here of Constancia Agüero's strategy for marketing her beauty products to her clientele. "Hispanic marketing," Dávila argues in that study, "[is] a self-identified arena of Latino self-representation which, dominated by corporate intellectuals of Latin American background in the United States and directly tied to structures of the US economy, serves as a fruitful entry point into an analysis of complex interests that are currently involved in the public representation of this emerging identity . . . [and engages] the premise that the reconstitution of individuals into consumers and populations into markets are central fields of cultural production that reverberate within public understanding of people's place, and hence their rights and entitle-

ments, in a society" (2). Dávila concludes from these observations that the "industry's political economy, history and composition," although U.S. based, are directly implicated in the global processes and transnational bases that sustain commonplace understandings of Latinos as a 'people' and a 'culture,'" which in turn participate as well in what she later calls "the global rendering of marketable identities" (3, 6).

15. See, for example, the passage late in the novel where García recounts the success of Constancia's commercial enterprise from the rather unimpressed (and even sarcastic) perspective of her sister Reina, herself recently arrived in Miami (231–32).

16. It bears noting here that *The Agüero Sisters* predates Nilo Cruz's Pulitzer Prize–winning play *Anna in the Tropics* (2003) by more than half a decade; although Cruz's play also prominently features a Cuban *lector* of novels and news reading to workers in a cigar factory, it is set in the Cuban colony already long established by 1929 in the Tampa, Florida, quarter known as Ybor City rather than in Cuba itself. There are, however, striking enough similarities between García's and Cruz's depictions of these *lectores* in their respective settings and texts to merit further comparative study.

17. There are striking parallels between this passage from García's novel and the analysis by Arjun Appadurai of an antiquating "patina" in a certain kind of commodity in the new global culture. See especially the passage in Appadurai's *Modernity at Large: Cultural Dimensions of Globalization* (75–76) that concludes his discussion of the function of what he (following Grant McCracken) calls the "problem of patina, . . . that property of goods by which their age becomes a key index of their high status" (75). Given that García chooses in her most historically distanced narrative to make her protagonist a purveyor of fine antiquities, Appadurai's analysis of the relation of temporality to consumption assists me directly in developing the most appropriate frame for a detailed critical elaboration of this particular text. Appadurai's work helps me consider most directly, for example, how the highly cultivated and strategically executed "gloss of age" in this novel reveals something new concerning García's own evolving critique of her Cuban-exile audience's consuming and consumptive dependency on imaginative work that indulgences its defining, nostalgic obsessions. "Objects with patina," like, perhaps, the texts that impersonate them, "are perpetual reminders," according to Appadurai, "of the passage of time as a double-edged sword, which credentials the 'right' people, just as it threatens the way they live. Whenever aristocratic lifestyles are threatened," he concludes (and in terms that arguable apply to other formerly privileged castes), "patina acquires a double meaning, indexing both the special status of its owner and the owner's special relationship to a way of life that is no longer available" (76).

18. Passages like this one suggest quite forcefully that García has more than intuited the same critique of nostalgia-driven cultural marketing in the

global age as that developed by Appadurai generally in *Modernity at Large*, but certainly specifically in the passage on patina already cited. Appadurai goes on there, for example, to observe that, as "patina . . . always indicates the fact that a way of living is now gone forever," it is also "a guarantee against the newly arrived, for they can acquire objects with patina, but never the subtly embodied anguish of those who can legitimately bemoan the loss of a way of life" (76). Even this mechanism of determining inclusion in and exclusion from a given romanticized, fallen elite has been superseded in the pervasively simulacral, posthistorical "age" of global commerce by a radical fusion of mass fantasy and nostalgia as wrought by advertising. "Rummaging through history," Appadurai tell us, "has become a standard technique of advertising," which includes in its repertoire "Catalogs that exploit the colonial experience for merchandising purposes" and is designed chiefly to produce an "inculcated sentiment," one "calculated to intensify the tempo of purchasing by toying with the merchandiser's version of the end of history, . . . [and is hence] the latest twist in the compact between nostalgia and fantasy in modern merchandising" (78).

19. Chen Pan's twin predilections toward both speculation and gambling mark him as both classically capitalistic in ways consistent with capital's operations in the time and the place where García sets his story, but they also resonate quite directly in the time and the place where García writes (and markets) hers; as Jean and John L. Comaroff observe in their introduction to *Millennial Capitalism and the Culture of Neoliberalism,* by the moment of the "turn" into the twenty-first century, "production appears to have been superseded, as *fons et origo* of wealth, by less tangible ways of generating value: by control over such things as the provision of services, the means of communication, and above all, the flow of finance capital. In short, by the market and by speculation," and in a directly related development, "gambling, in its marked form, has changed moral valence and invaded everyday life across the world" (5).

20. The scholarship on the histories of race and culture in Cuba is as vast as it is deep; in a 2000 volume entitled *Afro-Cuban Voices: On Race and Identity in Contemporary Cuba,* editors Pedro Pérez Sarduy and Jean Stubbs include an interview with Rogelio Martínez Furé, who in turn usefully summarizes anthropologist Fernando Ortiz's famed formulation of Cuban culture as "the synthesis . . . of European antecedents, principally Hispanic and French, with African antecedents, fused on what remained of Indo-Cuban cultures, and enriched by those brought by the Chinese and others" (156).

21. See the Comaroffs, *Millennial Capitalism* (7), and the note citing the context for Castro's statement (14, note 13).

22. The irony for Pérez is that Miami, which by the late twentieth century had been "transformed into a Cuba-in-exile, . . . began as an imitation of

Havana in the 1920's and 1930's, then was imitated by Havana during the 1940's and 1950's" so that by "the 1960's it was a copy of a copy that was copied"; notwithstanding the simulacral vertiginousness of these conditions, Pérez admits, exile "Cubans prospered [there] as bankers, industrialists, real estate developers, sugar planters, merchants and shop owners" (502–3).

23. See also Alex Stepick et al., *This Land Is Our Land: Immigrants and Power in Miami* (2003); in chapter 5 the authors argue that "Because of the relatively privileged background of the first Cuban arrivals and the assistance afforded them by the US government, Miami is the only US city where Latino immigrants have created a successful and self-sustained ethnic economy in which they have a high likelihood of being able to work with co-ethnics in enterprises owned by co-ethnics, shop in stores owned and operated by co-ethnics, and obtain professional services from co-ethnics" (139).

24. This analysis in Yúdice's work is based in part on a more general analysis of the operations of cultural economy in the age of globalization. "[C]ulture," Yúdice argues, "encompasses more than the entertainment and tourism industries" in these most recent contexts; "it is also," he concludes, "a medium in which new intellectual capital is reproduced and maintained in a range of experiences that cut across different classes and social and ethnic groups" (196).

8. Sounding the Body Politic: Sono-Grammatics in Rafael Campo's Sonnet Corpus

1. Edelman, 2–3. Edelman's provocative, polemical work in this volume implicitly informs every stage of the discussion I undertake here, but it only figures explicitly in its concluding section.

2. The "Song" cycle from which all the poems in this section are quoted begins with the "Familia" section of *The Other Man Was Me: A Voyage to the New World,* consisting of four sixteen-poem "Songs" (31–94); it concludes with two more sixteen-poem "Songs" (21–52), in *What the Body Told.* All poems quoted in the second section of this chapter appear in the pages of the editions cited here. *What the Body Told* features an additional pair of "Songs," but those depart from the project of recounting Campo's once and future family narrative to more abstracted meditations on life, mortality, and immortality.

3. Bardach, *Cuba Confidential,* 335–36.

4. Bardach also reports in that chapter that once Castro did visit Elián (two weeks following the boy's return to Cuba), he "bestowed" on the boy "a copy of José Martí's verse and a large box of chocolates" (336).

5. Bardach, 336–37.

6. Ibid., 342, 359.

7. Ibid., 358.

8. Banet-Weiser, "Elián González and 'The Purpose of America,'" 152.

9. Ibid., 153.

10. Ibid., 162.

11. Ibid., 163.

12. Sylvia Molloy. "His America, Our America: José Martí Reads Walt Whitman," 83, 84.

13. Robert Birnbaum, "Robert Birnbaum v. Rafael Campo," http://themorningnews.org, January 29, 2004.

14. All of Campo's poetry collections following *The Other Man Was Me* have been published by Duke University Press. *The Poetry of Healing* was first published in hardcover by W. W. Norton.

15. Campo, *The Poetry of Healing*, 111–12.

16. Ibid., 116–7.

17. Ibid., 268, 270.

18. Ibid., 15–16.

19. Ibid., 170.

20. Ibid., 88.

21. Ibid.

22. Ibid., 264.

23. Ibid., 193.

24. Ibid., 270.

25. Shelley's essay, written in 1821, appears in the second edition of David H. Richter's *The Critical Tradition: Classic Texts and Contemporary Trends* (Boston: Bedford Books, 1998), 339–56.

26. Foucault, *The Birth of the Clinic*, 198.

27. Ibid.

28. Ibid.

29. Ibid., xii.

30. Campo explicitly mentions the ultrasound at least once in the memoir; he anticipates that "medical school would soon allow me to ultrasound the body" and thereby assist him in his mission to "prevent the ailing human body from failing to keep time" (111).

31. Campo, *The Poetry of Healing*, 166.

32. Campo, *The Other Man Was Me*, 111.

33. Campo, *What the Body Told*, 10, 58, 121.

34. Campo, *The Poetry of Healing*, 166.

35. Ibid., 170.

36. Ibid., 167–68.

37. Edelman, *No Future*, 10–11.

38. Ibid., 11.

39. Ibid., 13.

40. Ibid., 13–16.
41. Ibid., 18.
42. Campo, *The Poetry of Healing*, 193, 195.
43. Edelman, *No Future*, 31.

Conclusion

1. Kaplan, "Violent Belongings and the Question of Empire Today," 14.
2. Moreiras, *The Exhaustion of Difference*, 3.

Bibliography

Adorno, Theodor, and Max Horkheimer. *The Dialectic of Enlightenment*. Trans. John Cumming. New York: Continuum, 1991.

Alvarez-Borland, Isabel. *Cuban-American Literature of Exile: From Person to Persona*. Charlottesville: University of Virginia Press, 1998.

Anderson, Benedict. *Imagined Communities: Reflections on the Origin and Spread of Nationalism*. Rev. ed. London and New York: Verso, 1991.

Aparicio, Frances R., Cándida Jacquez, and María Elena Cepeda, eds. *Musical Migrations: Transnationalism and Cultural Hybridity in Latin/o America*. New York: Palgrave-Macmillan, 2003.

Appadurai, Arjun. *Modernity at Large: Cultural Dimensions of Globalization*. Minneapolis: University of Minnesota Press, 1996.

Arenas, Reinaldo. *Antes que Anochezca*. Barcelona: Tusquets Editores, 1992.

———. *The Assault*. Trans. Andrew Hurley. New York: Viking Press, 1994.

———. *Before Night Falls*. Trans. Dolores Koch. New York: Viking, 1993.

———. *The Doorman*. Trans. Dolores M. Koch. New York: Grove Wiedenfeld, 1991.

———. *Farewell to the Sea: A Novel of Cuba*. Trans. Andrew Hurley. New York: Penguin Books, 1986.

———. *Old Rosa: A Novel in Two Stories*. Trans. Ann Tashi Slater and Andrew Hurley. New York: Grove Press, 1989.

Balderston, Daniel, and Donna J. Guy, eds. *Sex and Sexuality in Latin America*. New York: New York University Press, 1997.

Balido, Giselle, ed. *CubanTime: A Celebration of Cuban Life in America*. New York: Silver Lining Books, 2001.

Banet-Weiser, Sarah. "Elián González and 'The Purpose of America': Nation, Family, and the Child-Citizen." *American Quarterly* 55, no. 2 (June 2003): 149–78.

Baxter, Kevin. "Cuba's Suspended Revolution." *The Nation* 24/31 (August 1998): 20–23.

Bardach, Ann Louise. *Cuba Confidential: Love and Vengeance in Miami and Havana*. New York: Vintage Books, 2002.

Behar, Ruth. "Juban America." *Poetics Today* 16, no. 1 (Spring 1995): 151–70.

————, ed. *Bridges to Cuba/Puentes a Cuba*. Ann Arbor: University of Michigan Press, 1995.

Bejel, Emilio. *Gay Cuban Nation*. Chicago: University of Chicago Press, 2001.

Benítez-Rojo, Antonio. *The Repeating Island: The Caribbean and the Postmodern Perspective*. Trans. James Maraniss. Durham, N.C.: Duke University Press, 1992.

Benjamin, Walter. *Illuminations: Essays and Reflections*. Ed. Hannah Arendt. Trans. Harry Zohn. New York: Schocken Books, 1968.

————. *The Origins of German Tragic Drama*. Trans. John Osborne. London: NLB, 1977.

Bentley, Eric. *Brecht Commentaries*. New York: Grove Press, 1987.

Bergmann, Emilie L., and Paul Julian Smith, eds. *¿Entiendes?: Queer Readings, Hispanic Writings*. Durham, N.C.: Duke University Press, 1995.

Bettinger-López, Caroline. *Cuban-Jewish Journeys: Searching for Identity, Home and History in Miami*. Knoxville: University of Tennessee Press, 2002.

Bhabha, Homi K. *The Location of Culture*. New York and London: Routledge, 1994.

Birnbaum, Robert. "Robert Birnbaum v. Rafael Campo." Accessed from http://www.themorningnews.org, January 29, 2004.

Blanco, Richard. *City of a Hundred Fires*. Pittsburgh: University of Pittsburgh Press, 1998.

Blocker, Jane. *Where Is Ana Mendieta? Identity, Performativity and Exile*. Durham, N.C.: Duke University Press, 1999.

Braziel, Jana Evans, and Anita Mannur, eds. *Theorizing Diaspora: A Reader*. New York and London: Blackwell, 2003.

Brecht, Bertolt. *Mother Courage and Her Children: A Chronicle of the Thirty Years' War*. Trans. Eric Bentley. London: Methuen, 1962.

Brenkman, John. "The Citizen Myth." *Transition* 60 (1993): 138–44.

Browning, Frank. *The Culture of Desire: Paradox and Perversity in Gay Lives Today*. New York: Crown, 1993.

Butler, Judith. *Antigone's Claim: Kinship Between Life and Death*. New York: Columbia University Press, 2000.

————. *Excitable Speech: A Politics of the Performative*. New York: Routledge, 1997.

————. *The Psychic Life of Power: Theories in Subjection*. Stanford, Calif.: Stanford University Press, 1997.

Cabrera Infante, Guillermo. *Mea Cuba*. Trans. Kenneth Hall. New York: Farrar, Strauss, Giroux, 1994.

————. *Tres Tristes Tigres*. Barcelona: Editorial Seix Barral, 1983.

————. *Three Trapped Tigers*. Trans. Donald Gardner and Suzanne Jill Levine. London: Pan Books, 1980.

Campo, Rafael. *Diva*. Durham, N.C.: Duke University Press, 1999.

———. *Landscape with Human Figure*. Durham, N.C.: Duke University Press. 2002.

———. *The Other Man Was Me: A Voyage to the New World*. Houston: Arte Público Press, 1994.

———. *The Poetry of Healing: A Doctor's Education in Empathy, Identity and Desire*. New York: W.W. Norton, 1997.

———. *What the Body Told*. Durham, N.C.: Duke University Press, 1996.

Cinnamon, Deborah. "Close-Up: Ricardo Pau-Llosa." In *Poet's Market '93*, eds. Michael J. Bugeja and Christina Martin, 77–78. Cincinnati: Writer's Digest Books, 1993.

Clifford, James. *Routes: Travel and Translation in the Late Twentieth Century*. Cambridge, Mass.: Harvard University Press, 1997.

Comaroff, Jean, and John L. Comaroff, eds. *Millennial Capitalism and the Culture of Neoliberalism*. Durham, N.C.: Duke University Press, 2001.

Cortina, Rodolfo J., ed. *Cuban American Theatre*. Houston: Arte Público Press, 1991.

Croucher, Sheila L. *Imagining Miami: Ethnic Politics in a Post-Modern World*. Charlottesville: University of Virginia Press, 1997.

Cruz, Nilo. *Anna in the Tropics*. New York: Theatre Communications Group, 2003.

Cruz-Malavé, Arnaldo, and Martin F. Manalansan IV, eds. *Queer Globalizations: Citizenship and the Afterlife of Colonialism*. New York: New York University Press, 2002.

Dávila, Arlene. *Latinos, Inc: The Marketing and Making of a People*. Berkeley: University of California Press, 2001.

de la Campa, Ramón. *Cuba on My Mind: Journeys to a Severed Nation*. London and New York: Verso, 2000.

Deleuze, Gilles. *Masochism*. New York: Zone Books, 1991.

Delgado, Celeste, and José Muñoz. *EveryNight Life: Culture and Dance in Latin/o America*. Durham, N.C.: Duke University Press, 1997.

Derrida, Jacques. "Aphorism/Countertime." In *Acts of Literature,* ed. Derek Attridge, 414–33. Trans. Nicholas Royle. New York: Routledge, 1992.

———. "Economimesis." Trans. Richard Klein. *Diacritics* 11 (Summer 1981): 3–25.

———. *The Gift of Death*. Trans. David Wills. Chicago: University of Chicago Press, 1994.

———. *Points . . . : Interviews, 1974–1994*. Ed. Elisabeth Weber. Trans. Peggy Kamuf et al. Stanford, Calif.: Stanford University Press, 1995.

———. *Specters of Marx: The State of the Debt, the Work of Mourning, and the New International*. Trans. Peggy Kamuf. New York: Routledge, 1994.

Didion, Joan. *Miami*. New York: Simon & Schuster, 1987.

Eagleton, Terry. *The Function of Criticism*. London: Verso, 1983.

Edelman, Lee. *No Future: Queer Theory and the Death Drive*. Durham, N.C.: Duke University Press, 2004.

Ellroy, James. *American Tabloid*. New York: Alfred A. Knopf, 1995.

Epps, Brad. "Proper Conduct: Reinaldo Arenas, Fidel Castro and the Politics of Homosexuality." *Journal of the History of Sexuality* 6, no. 2 (October 1995): 231–83.

Estefan, Gloria. *Abriendo Puertas*. CD. Sony Music, 1995.

———. *Destiny*. CD. Sony Music, 1996.

———. *Gloria Estefan: Evolution Tour Live in Miami, 1996*. VHS/DVD. Sony/Columbia, 1996.

———. *Mi Tierra*. CD. Sony Music, 1993.

Fernández, Damián. *Cuba and the Politics of Passion*. Austin: University of Texas Press, 2000.

———, and Madeline Cámara Betancourt, eds. *Cuba, the Elusive Nation*. Gainesville: University of Florida Press, 2000.

Fernández, Roberto G. *Raining Backwards*. Houston: Arte Público Press, 1988.

Foster, David William. *Gay and Lesbian Themes in Latin American Writing*. Austin: University of Texas Press, 1991.

Foucault, Michel. *The Birth of the Clinic: An Archaeology of Medical Perception*. Trans. A. M. Sheridan Smith. New York: Vintage, 1994.

———. *Discipline and Punish: The Birth of the Prison*. Trans. Alan Sheridan. New York: Pantheon Books, 1977.

Fusco, Coco. *The Bodies That Were Not Ours and Other Writings*. New York: Routledge, 2001.

———. *English Is Broken Here: Notes on Cultural Fusion in the Americas*. New York: The New Press, 1995.

García, Cristina. *The Agüero Sisters*. New York: Alfred A. Knopf, 1997.

———. *Dreaming in Cuban*. New York: Alfred A. Knopf, 1992.

———. *Monkey Hunting*. New York: Alfred A. Knopf, 2003.

García, María Cristina. *Havana USA: Cuban Exiles and Cuban Americans in South Florida, 1959–1994*. Berkeley: University of California Press, 1996.

Gosse, Van. *Where the Boys Are: Cuba, Cold War America and the New Left*. London: Verso, 1993.

Gutierrez Alea, Tomás, and Juan Carlos Tabio, dirs. *Strawberry and Chocolate/Fresa y Chocolate*. Miramax Films, distributed 1993.

Harper, Phillip Brian. *Private Affairs: Critical Ventures in the Culture of Social Relations*. New York: New York University Press, 1999.

Hartman, Geoffrey. "On Traumatic Knowledge and Literary Studies." *New Literary History* 26, no. 3 (Summer 1995): 537–63.

Herrera, Andrea O'Reilly, ed. *ReMembering Cuba: Legacy of a Diaspora*. Austin: University of Texas Press, 2001.

Hijuelos, Oscar. *The Fourteen Sisters of Emilio Montez O'Brien.* New York: Farrar, Strauss, Giroux, 1993.

———. *The Mambo Kings Play Songs of Love.* New York: Farrar, Strauss, Giroux, 1989.

Hirsch, Marianne. *Family Frames: Photography, Narrative, Post-Memory.* Cambridge, Mass.: Harvard University Press, 1997.

Ignatieff, Michael. *Blood and Belonging: Journeys into the New Nationalism.* New York: Noonday Press, 1993.

Islas, Arturo. *La Mollie and the King of Tears.* Albuquerque: University of New Mexico Press, 1996.

Iyer, Pico. *Cuba and the Night.* New York: Alfred A. Knopf, 1995.

Jameson, Fredric. *The Cultural Turn: Selected Writings on the Postmodern, 1983–1998.* London: Verso, 1998.

———. *The Political Unconscious: Narrative as a Socially Symbolic Act.* Ithaca, N.Y.: Cornell University Press, 1981.

Kaplan, Amy. "Violent Belongings and the Question of Empire Today: Presidential Address to the American Studies Association, October 17, 2003." *American Quarterly* 56, no. 1 (March 2004): 1–18.

Kipnis, Laura. *Ecstasy Unlimited: On Sex, Capital, Gender, and Aesthetics.* Minneapolis: University of Minnesota Press, 1993.

Klein, Richard. *Cigarettes Are Sublime.* Durham, N.C.: Duke University Press, 1993.

Kutzinski, Vera. *Sugar's Secrets: Race and the Erotics of Cuban Nationalism.* Charlottesville: University of Virginia Press, 1993.

Leiner, Marvin. *Sexual Politics in Cuba: Machismo, Homosexuality and AIDS.* Boulder, Colo.: Westview Press, 1994.

Levine, Robert. *Tropical Diaspora: The Jewish Experience in Cuba.* Gainesville: University Press of Florida, 1993.

Lewis, Martin W., and Kären E. Wigen. *The Myth of Continents: A Critique of Metageography.* Berkeley: University of California Press, 1997.

Lumsden, Ian. *Machos, Maricones and Gays: Cuba and Homosexuality.* Philadelphia: Temple University Press, 1996.

Machado, Eduardo. *Fabiola.* Revised script, April 15, 1994. Provided to the author in November 1997.

———. *The Floating Island Plays.* New York: Theatre Communications Group, 1991.

Mark Taper Forum. *Playbook: Floating Islands.* Los Angeles: Mark Taper Forum, 1994.

Martí, José. *José Martí: Selected Writings.* Ed. Esther Allen. New York: Penguin Classics, 2002.

———. *Reader: Writings on the Americas.* Eds. Deborah Schnookal and Mirta Muñiz. Melbourne: Ocean Press, 1999.

Marx, Karl. *Capital*. In *The Marx-Engels Reader*, ed. Robert C. Tucker. New York: W. W. Norton, 1978.

Matthews, Herbert. *Revolution in Cuba: An Essay in Understanding*. New York: Scribner's, 1975.

Medina, Pablo. *Exiled Memories: A Cuban Childhood*. Austin: University of Texas Press, 1990.

McKenna, Peter. "Canada's Southern Exposure." *Hemisphere: A Magazine of the Americas* 8, no. 3 (Fall 1998): 26–29.

Molloy, Sylvia. "His America, Our America: José Martí Reads Walt Whitman." In *Breaking Bounds: Whitman and American Cultural Studies*, eds. Betsy Erkkila and Jay Grossman, 83–91. New York and Oxford: Oxford University Press, 1996.

———, and Robert McKee Irwin, eds. *Hispanisms and Homosexualities*. Durham, N.C.: Duke University Press, 1998

Moreiras, Alberto. *The Exhaustion of Difference: The Politics of Latin American Cultural Studies*. Durham, N.C., and London: Duke University Press, 2001.

Moure, Gloria. *Ana Mendieta*. Barcelona: Ediciones Polígrafa, 1996.

Muñoz, José E. *Disidentifications: Queers of Color and the Performance of Politics*. Minneapolis: University of Minnesota Press, 1999.

———. "Ephemera as Evidence: Introductory Notes to *Queer Acts*." *Women and Performance* 16, no. 8 (1996): 5–16.

Obejas, Achy. *We Came All the Way from Cuba So You Could Dress Like This?* Pittsburgh: Cleis Press, 1994.

———. *Memory Mambo*. Pittsburgh: Cleis Press, 1996.

———. *Days of Awe*. New York: Ballantine, 2001.

Ortiz, Fernando. *Cuban Counterpoint: Tobacco and Sugar*. Trans. Harriet de Onís. Durham, N.C.: Duke University Press, 1995.

Padilla, Heberto. *Self-Portrait of the Other: A Memoir*. Trans. Alexander Coleman. New York: Farrar, Strauss, Giroux, 1990.

Parker, Andrew, and Eve Kosofsky Sedgwick. *Performativity and Performance*. New York and London: Routledge, 1995.

Patton, Cindy, and Benigno Sánchez-Eppler, eds. *Queer Diasporas*. Durham, N.C.: Duke University Press, 2000.

Pau-Llosa, Ricardo. *Bread of the Imagined*. Tempe, Ariz.: Bilingual Press, 1991.

———. *Cuba*. Pittsburgh: Carnegie Mellon University Press, 1993.

Paz, Senel. *El lobo, el bosque y el hombre nuevo*. Mexico City: Ediciones Era, 1991.

Pearlstein, Steven. "Clinton Declares Québec Better Off in Canada." *Washington Post*, October 9, 1999, A15, 20.

———. "O, Canada! A National Swan Song?" *Washington Post*, September 5, 2000, A1, A22.

Pérez, Louie A., Jr. *On Becoming Cuban: Identity, Nationality, and Culture.* Chapel Hill, N.C.: University of North Carolina Press, 1999.

Pérez-Firmat, Gustavo. *The Cuban Condition: Translation and Identity in Modern Cuban Literature.* Cambridge: Cambridge University Press, 1990.

———. *Life on the Hyphen: The Cuban-American Way.* Austin: University of Texas Press, 1994.

———. *Tongue Ties: Logo-Eroticism in Anglo-Hispanic Literature.* New York: Palgrave-Macmillan, 2003.

Pérez-Stable, Marifeli. *The Cuban Revolution: Origins, Course and Legacy.* Oxford: Oxford University Press, 1993.

Poey, Delia, and Virgil Suarez, eds. *Iguana Dreams: New Latino Fiction.* New York: Harper Perennial, 1992.

Porter, Carolyn. "What We Know That We Don't Know: Remapping American Literary Studies." *American Literary History* 6, no. 3 (Fall 1994): 467–526.

Portes, Alejandro, and Alex Stepick. *City on the Edge: The Transformation of Miami.* Berkeley: University of California Press, 1993.

Quiroga, José. *Tropics of Desire: Interventions from Queer Latino America.* New York: New York University Press, 2000.

Retamar, Roberto Fernández. *Caliban and Other Essays.* Trans. Edward Baker. Minneapolis: University of Minnesota Press, 1989.

———. *Caliban: Apuntes sobre la cultura en nuestra América.* México: Editorial Diogenes, 1972.

Rieff, David. *The Exile: Cuba in the Heart of Miami.* New York: Simon & Schuster, 1993.

———. *Going to Miami: Exiles, Tourists and Refugees in the New America.* Boston: Little, Brown, 1987.

Roach, Joseph. *Cities of the Dead: Circum-Atlantic Performance.* New York: Columbia University Press, 1996.

Rodó, José Enrique. *Ariel.* Trans. Margaret Sayers Peden. Austin: University of Texas Press, 1988.

Rodríguez, Albita. *No Se Parece a Nada.* CD. Sony Music, 1995.

———. *Una Mujer Como Yo.* CD. Sony Music, 1997.

Rodríguez, Ana, and Glenn Garvin. *Diary of a Survivor: Nineteen Years in a Cuban Women's Prison.* Trans. Glenn Garvin. New York: St. Martin's Press, 1995.

Rojas, Rafael. *La Política del Adiós.* Miami: Ediciones Universal, 2003.

Romero, Lora. *Home Fronts: Domesticity and Its Critics in the Antebellum United States.* Durham, N.C.: Duke University Press, 1997.

Ronell, Avital. *Crack Wars: Literature, Addiction, Mania.* Lincoln: University of Nebraska Press, 1993.

Said, Edward. *Culture and Imperialism.* New York: Vintage, 1993.

————. *The World, the Text and the Critic*. Cambridge, Mass.: Harvard University Press, 1983.

Saldívar, José David. *The Dialectics of Our America: Genealogy, Cultural Critique, and Literary History*. Durham, N.C.: Duke University Press, 1991.

Saldívar, Ramón. *Chicano Narrative: The Dialectics of Difference*. Madison: University of Wisconsin Press, 1990.

Sánchez-Eppler, Benigno. "Call My Son Ismael: Exiled Paternity and Father/Son Eroticism in Reinaldo Arenas and José Martí." *differences: A Journal of Feminist Cultural Studies* 6, no. 1 (1994): 69–97.

Sarduy, Pedro Pérez, and Jean Stubbs, eds. *Afro-Cuban Voices: On Race and Identity in Contemporary Cuba*. Gainesville: University of Florida Press, 2000.

Sarduy, Severo. *From Cuba with a Song*. Trans. Suzanne Jill Levine. Los Angeles: Sun & Moon Press, 1994.

————. *Written on a Body*. Trans. Carol Maier. New York: Lumen Books, 1989.

Schnabel, Julian, dir. *Before Night Falls*. New Line Cinema, 2000.

Sedgwick, Eve Kosofsky. *Tendencies*. Durham, N.C.: Duke University Press, 1993.

Shakespeare, William. *The Tempest*. Ed. Stephen Orgel. Oxford: Oxford University Press, 1984.

Shefler, Laura. "Cristina García: When Are You Cuban Enough?" Retrieved from http://sfl.com/issue_08_97/interview.html.

Shelley, Percy. "A Defense of Poetry." *The Critical Tradition: Classic Texts and Contemporary Trends*. Ed. David H. Richter, 339–56. Boston: Bedford Books, 1998.

Shorris, Earl. *Latinos: A Biography of the People*. New York: W. W. Norton, 1992.

Smorkaloff, Pamela Maria. *Cuban Writers on and off the Island*. New York: Twayne Publishers, 1999.

Sommer, Doris. *Foundational Fictions: The National Romances of Latin America*. Berkeley: University of California Press, 1991.

Sontag, Susan. *Against Interpretation and Other Essays* New York: Farrar, Strauss, Giroux, 1966.

————. *AIDS and Its Metaphors*. New York: Farrar, Strauss, Giroux, 1989.

————. "Some Thoughts on the Right Way [for Us] to Love the Cuban Revolution." *Ramparts* (April 1969): 6–19.

Spillers, Hortense, ed. "Who Cuts the Border?: Some Readings on 'America.'" *Comparative American Identities: Race, Sex, and Nationality in the Modern Text*. New York: Routledge, 1991.

Spivak, Gayatri. "Three Women's Texts and a Critique of Imperialism." In *"Race," Writing and Difference*, ed. Henry Louis Gates Jr., 262–80. Chicago: University of Chicago Press, 1986.

Stepick, Alex, Guillermo Grenier, Max Castro, and Marvin Dunn. *This Land Is Our Land: Immigrants and Power in Miami*. Berkeley: University of California Press, 2003.

Taylor, Diana, and Juan Villegas, eds. *Negotiating Performance: Gender, Sexuality and Theatricality in Latin/o America*. Durham, N.C.: Duke University Press, 1994.

Tobar, Héctor. *Translation Nation: Defining a New American Identity in the Spanish-Speaking United States*. New York: Riverhead Books, 2005.

Torres, María de los Angeles. *In the Land of Mirrors: Cuban Exile Politics in the United States*. Ann Arbor: University of Michigan Press, 1999.

———, ed. *By Heart/De Memoria: Cuban Women's Journeys in and out of Exile*. Philadelphia: Temple University Press, 2003.

Troyano, Alina, with Ela Troyano and Uzi Parnes. *I, Carmelita Tropicana: Performing between Cultures*. Ed. Chon Noriega. Boston: Beacon Press, 2000.

Tucker, Robert C., ed. *The Marx-Engels Reader*. New York: W. W. Norton, 1978.

Valladares, Armando. *Against All Hope: The Prison Memoirs of Armando Valladares*. Trans. Andrew Hurley. New York: Alfred A. Knopf, 1986.

Viso, Olga, ed. *Ana Mendieta Earth Body: Sculpture and Performance, 1972–1985*. Washington, D.C.: The Smithsonian Institution and Hatje Cantz Publishers, 2004.

Waldinger, Roger, and Mehdi Bozorgmehr. *Ethnic Los Angeles*. New York: Russell Sage Foundation, 1996.

Wiegman, Robyn. *American Anatomies: Theorizing Race and Gender*. Durham, N.C.: Duke University Press, 1995.

Wilhelm, Silvia. "The Miami Report," *Cuban Affairs* 4, no. 3–4 (Fall–Winter 1998): 8.

Winick, Judd. *Pedro and Me: Friendship, Loss and What I Learned*. New York: Henry Holt, 2000.

Young, Allen. *Gays under the Cuban Revolution*. San Francisco: Grey Fox Press, 1981.

Yúdice, George. *The Expediency of Culture: Uses of Culture in the Global Era*. Durham: Duke University Press, 2003.

Zeiger, Melissa. *Beyond Consolation: Death, Sexuality and the Changing Shapes of Elegy*. Ithaca, N.Y.: Cornell University Press, 1997.

Žižek, Slavoj. *Enjoy Your Symptom! Lacan in Hollywood and Out*. New York: Routledge, 1991.

———. *For They Know Not What They Do: Enjoyment as a Political Factor*. London: Verso, 1991.

Index

Ricardo L. Ortíz is assistant professor of U.S. Latino studies in the Department of English at Georgetown University.